Uncle John's
BATHROOM
READER.
PLUNGES INTO
CANADA,eh

The Bathroom Readers' Institute
Ashland, Oregon, and San Diego, California

OUR "REGULAR" READERS RAVE

"Before the BRI came along, I had a small library of just books. After BRI, I now have a great library filled with incredible books."

—Green S.

"I just happened to see one of these sitting on the back of a friend's toilet one time 8 years ago. Instead of reading the shampoo bottle, I picked this up. I have been hooked every since."

—Angela D.

"Comment heard from friends, 'How do you know so much stuff about any topic?' I learned it all from my Uncle John."

—Shane A.

"My hubby was on a couple of game shows, and I know we can thank his love of the *Bathroom Reader* books for the winnings."

—Donna E.

"I have them all, and cherish every one! My 20th anniversary edition sadly fell into the (clean) toilet. I managed to dry it out sufficiently enough to continue reading."

—Butch H.

"My friend in school was reading *Bathroom Readers*, so then I bought a couple, and now my mom says I'm just threatening her with my intelligence."

—Chase O.

"I love these books! I read them on my commute bus in the morning, and during my lunch hour. They are definitely not just for the bathroom."

—Alison G.

UNCLE JOHN'S BATHROOM
PLUNGES INTO CANADA, EH!

For information, write...
The Bathroom Readers' Institute
P.O. Box 1117, Ashland, OR 97520
www.bathroomreader.com
e-mail: mail@bathroomreader.com

Beaver cover photo by Steve Hersey.

ISBN 13: 978-1-60710-100-0

Library of Congress Cataloging-in-Publication Data

Uncle John's bathroom reader plunges into Canada, eh.
 p. cm.
 ISBN 978-1-60710-100-0 (pbk.)
 1. Canada--Anecdotes. 2. Canada--Humor. 3. Curiosities and won-
ders--Canada. I. Bathroom Readers' Institute (Ashland, Or.)
 F1008.4.U53 2010
 971--dc22

 2009044177

Printed in the United States of America

10 11 12 13 14 5 4 3 2 1

THANK YOU!

The Bathroom Readers' Institute thanks the following people whose hard work, advice, and assistance made this book possible.

Gordon Javna
JoAnn Padgett
Melinda Allman
Jack Mingo
Erin Barrett
Derek Fairbridge
Sue Steiner
Brian Boone
J. Carroll
Stephanie Spadaccini
Michael Brunsfeld
Dan Mansfield
Jeff Altemus
Jay Newman
Thom Little
Amy Miller
Brian Bose
Barbara Brodnitz
Kathie Meyer
Rick Robinson
Jayne Hitchcock
David Larkins
Kevin McKinney
Linda Lombardi
Sharon Ufberg
Aaron Coder
Angela Sanders
Brian Hudson
Karen Simmons
Mary Lee Shalvoy
Nancy Bennett

Dave Smith
Julia Cianci
Farley Walker
Becky Holland
Julie Clark Robinson
Corinna Underwood
Lavina Galbraith Anderson
Chrissy Winsor Kennedy
William Penrose
Kerri Mckenzie
Eric Eales
Bill Cassel
Tamara Moffett
Allan MacD.
John Counsell
Daphne O'Neal
Gordon Gross
Peter Anthony Holder
Paddy, Sandy, Pete, Jamie, Big John, and all the fabulous folks at Raincoast
Amy, Monica, and Lisa
Jennifer Frederick
Ginger Winters
Sydney Stanley
David Cully
R. R. Donnelley
Donna Gibbings
Team Canada
Sophie and JJ
Porter the Wonder Dog

Disclaimer: No Canadians were harmed during the making of this book.

CONTENTS

Because the BRI understands your reading needs, we've divided the contents by length as well as subject.

Short—a quick read

Medium—2 to 3 pages

Long—for those extended visits, when something a little more involved is required.

* * *

#1 IN CANADA

Despite Canadian Content regulations (which require radio stations to play a Canadian artist every fifth song at the very least), Canada's music world is still dominated by American and British musicians. Of the thousands of songs that have charted in the country since 1969, only 86 by Canadian singers or bands have made it to number-one. The longest-running hits are...

• Ryan Malcolm, "Something More" (11 weeks)

• Bryan Adams, "Please Forgive Me" (10 weeks)

• Bryan Adams, "(Everything I Do) I Do It For You" (9 weeks)

• Eva Avila, "Meant to Fly" (9 weeks)

• Alanis Morissette, "Head Over Feet" (8 weeks)

• Sarah McLachlan, "Building a Mystery" (8 weeks)

• Kalan Porter, "Awake in a Dream" (8 weeks)

• Melissa O'Neil, "Alive" (7 weeks)

(Malcolm, Avila, Porter, and O'Neil are all *Canadian Idol* winners.)

HELLO UP THERE!

One day last year, Melinda, a BRI editor, came to my desk and plopped down yet another letter from a Canadian reader asking why we'd never dedicated an entire book to "the greatest country on Earth." After all, she reminded me, Canadians have always been among the BRI's most loyal fans. So here it is—the Bathroom Reader you've been waiting for:

Uncle John's Bathroom Reader Plunges Into Canada, Eh

We dug deep into our tank of knowledge to find overlooked nuggets of all things Canadian: history, pop culture, obscure facts, friendly provincial rivalries, and (this being a *Bathroom Reader*, after all) some really strange stories. Along the way, we realized that most people south of the world's longest unmilitarized border (and maybe north of it, too) know too little about Canada. Sure, it's North America's giant beer cooler, the colossus of icy roads, and the homeland of William Shatner, but did you know that it's also the birthplace of instant mashed potatoes? Probably not. What else awaits you on the pages ahead? Check out...

• The Canadians who pirated music...way back in 1897.

• Why Santa is a Canadian, and Rudolph is a red-nosed caribou.

• Famous Canadian rock bands and how they got their names.

• How to make your own cold-weather thermometer with mercury, coal oil, 150-proof Jamaica ginger, and patent medicine.

• The saints who accidentally killed off most of the people they ministered to (before their parishioners returned the favor).

• The Canadian city accused of killing a U.S. president.

• The Irish army from Boston—led by a one-armed general—that tried to capture Montreal.

• Canadians who climbed Mount Everest, swam Lake Ontario, and went over Niagara Falls in a barrel (some of whom actually survived).

• The true stories of Johnny Canuck, Gander the Dog, and the bishop who ate his shoes.

• What your Postal Code says about you.

In the end, there was so much more to learn about Canada than any of us here at the Bathroom Readers' Institute ever knew…and maybe more than even *you* knew. So if you enjoy this edition, and you keep writing us such nice letters, perhaps we'll do a second one in the future.

One last thing before you start out: a big "CHEERS!" and extra rations of beer and poutine to Jack and Erin, who've been part of the Bathroom Reader family for decades, and without whom this book would not be possible. But for now, hop into our canoe and lets paddle down a river of weird and interesting stories about the best darn neighbors we at the BRI could ever hope to have!

And as always…

Go with the flow, eh?

—Uncle John, the BRI Staff,
and Porter the Wonderdog

GEESE IS THE WORD

Look up! Graceful birds, displaying black heads and white "chinstraps,"
flying in an elegant "V"…and accompanied by that honking.

NAME GAME: It's not Canadian goose. It's *Canada* goose.

BIG BIRDS: Canada geese usually look the same to an untrained
eye, but scientists say there are seven different subspecies. The
smallest: the Aleutian Canada goose, which weighs just 1.8 kilo-
grams (4 pounds) and was once among the most endangered birds
in the world. The largest? The giant Canada goose, spreading its
wings 2 meters (6.5 feet) and weighing 8 kilograms (17.6 pounds).

AIR CANADA: During migration, Canada geese fly 3,000 to
5,000 kilometers (1,800 to 3,100 miles) each way, but it doesn't
work the same in both directions. Going south, they move fast,
as far as 1,000 kilometers (620 miles) per day. When they head
north in spring, the geese take their time, generally spending a
few weeks on the trek and making frequent stops along the way.

HONK! The geese are highly vocal. They don't even wait until
they're hatched—goslings can be heard "talking" from inside the
egg. Scientists have picked out at least 13 separate goose calls,
each representing something different: for example, a call can
mean "Hello," "Danger," "Come over and join us here," or even
"Hey baby, looking for a good mate?"

LOVE BIRDS: Most birds seem to have trouble with long-term
relationships, but Canada geese mate for life. If one of the partners
dies, though, the survivor often finds a new mate before the next
mating season.

WATER BIRTH: Goslings are led to water almost immediately
after they hatch. This is why Canada geese often nest near shore-
lines, municipal parks, and golf course water hazards. In a pinch,
even a city fountain or a backyard swimming pool will do.

BOMBS AWAY: One Canada goose can produce 57 kilograms
(125 pounds) of poop annually…meaning a flock of 50 geese
hanging around a football field can bless it with more than three
tons every year.

YOU KNOW YOU'RE CANADIAN IF...

- You can eat more than one maple sugar candy without getting sick.
- You cried when you thought Gus had died on *Road to Avonlea*.
- You can recite the entire Molson's "I Am Canadian" rant.
- You eat buns and chocolate bars.
- You aren't embarrassed by the phrase "Tickle Trunk."
- You think Elvis Stojko looked better with hockey hair.
- You don't understand what all the fuss is about Cuba.
- You've ordered poutine at McDonald's.
- You use hockey tape to fix...everything.
- You wear a toque.
- You consider beers under 6 percent to be for children and the elderly.
- You've never ridden on a moose, built an igloo, or said "sore-y."
- You know what a sweeper does in curling.
- You know that "This Hour Has 22 Minutes."
- You've ever told a Newfie joke...like this one:

A Newfie was having a hard time attracting women at the beach, so he asked a friend for advice. "It's dem big baggy swimming trunks," said the friend. "Dey're years outta style. Yer best bet is to grab yeself a pair of Speedos and drop a fist-sized potato down inside 'em. Ye'll have all de babes ye wants!"

The next day, the Newfie sauntered onto the beach with his new Speedos and his potato. Everybody he walked past immediately started pointing at him and laughing. So the Newfie went back to his friend and said, "I did what ye said, but it's still not working."

"Lard-Tunderin' Jeezus b'y!" said the friend. "The potato goes in the front!"

Look up, *way* up: the Friendly Giant was only 5'11".

WORLD CAPITALS

Have you ever wanted to visit the world's blueberry, kissing, or root cellar capital? Well, you don't have to travel overseas for that because many of them are right here in Canada.

Houseboat Capital of the World: Sicamous, BC

Blueberry Capital of the World: Oxford, NS

Norseman Capital of the World: Red Lake, ON

Polar Bear Capital of the World: Churchill, MB

Scallop Capital of the World: Digby, NS

Balsam Fir Christmas Tree Capital of the World: Lunenburg, County, NS

Kissing Capital of the World: Sarnia, ON

Lily Capital of the World: Neepawa, MB

Potash Capital of the World: Saskatoon, SK

Moose Capital of the World: Hudson Bay, SK

Chicken Capital of the World: Wynyard, SK

Maple Capital of the World: Plessisville, QC

Tuna Capital of the World: North Lake, PEI

Nickel Capital of the World: Sudbury, ON

Waterfall Capital of the World: Hamilton, ON

Iceberg Capital of the World: Qikiqtarjuaq, NU

Dinosaur Capital of the World: Drumheller, AB

Root Cellar Capital of the World: Elliston, NL

Bathtub Racing Capital of the World: Nanaimo, BC

Chainsaw Carving Capital of the World: Hope, BC

Fruit Stand Capital of the World: Keremeos, BC

Swan Capital of the World: Fraser Lake, BC

The collective term for Canada's national animal: a *malocclusion* of beavers.

THE NIAGARA COW

The Great Blondin is famous for walking across the Niagara River on a tightrope in 1859, but how many people remember Bossy the cow?

THE BRINK OF DOOM

If you run across a copy of the *Niagara Falls Guide Book*, published in 1901, you'll see a curious photo that's so unbelievable you may think it was faked. It shows a cow standing in the Niagara River about 10 meters (33 feet) upriver from American Falls, a spot that came to be known as the "Brink of Doom."

The cow (named Bossy) belonged to George Simms, a local farmer on the New York side of the river. She wandered freely, as many family milk cows did in those days, grazing as she went. Bossy discovered she liked the water in the Niagara River, and she often waded in, drinking, keeping cool, and chewing her cud. At least once (some say many times), Bossy walked all the way over to Goat Island.

ONE HECK OF A TOURIST ATTRACTION

Bossy seemed to have no fear of the falls. In that 1901 photo, she's described as "nonchalant," standing there in the water, her strong, thin legs providing little resistance to the river rushing around them. She amazed and amused tourists to both the Canadian and American sides of Niagara Falls. And Simms, who was also the operator of the Prospect Point Incline Railway (which carried travelers to the top of the gorge), decided that increased tourist traffic around his railway more than made up for the risk of losing a cow.

Eventually, though, other attraction operators complained that Bossy walking across the lip of the falls made a mockery of their stories of the river's power, majesty, and danger. So Simms decided to confine the cow, and her jaunts into the Niagara River stopped… but her legacy lived on.

* * *

"Never kick a cow chip on a hot day." **—Proverb**

The maple leaf on the flag has 11 "points." Actual maple leaves have 32.

WHO YOU GONNA CALL?

If you need stuff hauled away, ring up 1-800-GOT-JUNK?

THE RUBBISH BOYS

In 1989, Brian Scudamore was 18 years old with no money to finish college. He found the answer to his financial troubles at a McDonald's drive-through, in the form of a truck with "Mark's Hauling" painted on its side. The neat freak in Scudamore was inspired. He always kept his own living spaces clean and uncluttered; maybe he could get paid to help others do the same.

He spent $753 of his savings on a used pick-up truck and nearly all the rest on business cards and flyers. He called his business the "Rubbish Boys" and came up with a catchy slogan: "We'll stash your trash in a flash."

THEY'VE GOT YOUR NUMBER

Scudamore was a born entrepreneur. Growing up in Vancouver, he'd made money with his own car-washing business, and while attending boarding school, he ran a candy and school supplies store out of his dorm room until administrators shut it down. But no one was going to put the Rubbish Boys out of business. From the beginning, Scudmore's customers appreciated the emphasis on efficiency and service. The business did so well that Scudamore quit the University of British Columbia to (as his unhappy father put it) "become a junkman."

By 1997, the Rubbish Boys had eight trucks and had expanded from Vancouver into Victoria. A year later, sitting on his parents' deck, Scudamore mapped out an ambitious plan to expand across Canada and over the border, too. Inspired by the "Got Milk?" ad campaign, he decided on a new business name: 1-800-GOT-JUNK?

When he called the number, Scudamore found out that it was already taken by an air-traffic control office in Idaho. Undaunted, he called again...and again, until he convinced the Idaho Department of Transportation to give him the number, which they did, free of charge.

Anne of Green Gables was rejected by 4 publishers before being accepted for publication.

JUNK ALL OVER THE PLACE

Business came in immediately. In 1999, Scudamore began selling franchises, and today, more than 300 of them are operating in North America and Australia. The company recycles whenever possible, and is a member of the VetFran program, which helps veterans start their own franchise businesses.

As CEO of the world's first billion-dollar junk-hauling company, Scudamore is proud of what he's accomplished. And he's become a leading expert on junk: "It's difficult for people to get rid of junk. They get attached to things and let them define who they are. If there's one thing I've learned in this business, it's that you are what you can't let go of."

*　　*　　*

BURIED TREASURE

Did pirate captain William Kidd bury an undiscovered treasure trove somewhere in Canada? Maybe. Canada has two sites where X might mark the spot.

• **Oak Island, Nova Scotia:** The presence of a mysterious pit has led to speculation that excavation might reveal Kidd's hidden treasure. (Other speculation says the pit really contains Blackbeard's treasure, Marie-Antoinette's jewels, or the Holy Grail.) On the other hand, some spoilsports note that the sinkholes located elsewhere on the island come from underground limestone giving way, and that this "money pit" is just another one of those. Nothing's been uncovered there...yet.

• **Grand Manan Island, Bay of Fundy, New Brunswick:** Local legend, dating back 200 years, claims that Kidd buried his treasure in "Money Cove" on the west side of the island. The main problem with this theory is that it hinges on a widow's dream that "a headless Negro" told her Kidd had killed him to force his truncated spirit to guard the treasure for eternity. No treasure has been found on Grand Manan yet, either.

These are just two of many Captain Kidd treasure stories the thrive around the world. Everywhere from Massachusetts to Madagascar has been named as a treasure spot, even though nobody's ever proven that Kidd actually buried any undiscovered treasure anywhere. (But hey, why ruin a good story?)

WELCOME TO PARKS CANADA

Canada offers a wealth of national parks. Can you match the sites below with the features that make them famous? (Answers on page 451.)

1. Glacier (British Columbia)
2. Wapusk (Manitoba)
3. Cape Breton Highlands (Nova Scotia)
4. Pukaskwa (Ontario)
5. Grasslands (Saskatchewan)
6. Mount Revelstoke (British Columbia)
7. Torgat Mountains (Newfoundland and Labrador)
8. Kluane (Yukon)
9. Point Pelee (Ontario)
10. Aulavik (Northwest Territories)

a. Includes a third of the scenic and world-famous Cabot Trail
b. The world's largest known polar bear maternity den
c. The place to which Sitting Bull escaped after the Battle of the Little Big Horn in 1876
d. Called a polar desert (a region that gets no more than 250 millimeters (9.8 inches) of precipitation every year.
e. Home to Mount Logan, Canada's highest peak
f. The only wilderness national park in Ontario
g. Rogers Pass through the Selkirk Mountains
h. Protects an old-growth rain forest that contains ancient western red cedars
i. Canada's newest national park
j. Includes the southernmost point of the Canadian mainland

Closest North American city to Europe: St. John's, NL.

REAL OR RUMOR? PART I

Misinformation runs rampant through the countryside and on the Internet.
Uncle John considers it his duty to chase it down and club it with a stick.

Rumor: The 11 points on the flag's maple leaf symbolize the 10 provinces and Canada.
True? No.
The story: They also don't stand for the country's 11 national holidays, 11 regional phone companies, 11 Ikea stores, the 11 million people residing in its southernmost fifth…or the fact that its total population equals 11 percent of the United States'. The leaf on the flag started out with 13 points (no symbolic meaning), and two were lopped off at the last minute because the design looked too "busy."

Rumor: Santa Claus has his own Canadian postal code.
True? Yes.
The story: Although the North Pole isn't technically in Canada, Santa drops by sometimes to pick up his mail and cash money orders. The best part? His easy-to-remember postal code. It's H0H 0H0.

Rumor: The Hudson's Bay Company's original royal charter, still in effect, requires it to send an annual shipment of beaver pelts to the queen of England.
True? No.
The story: This rumor may have started because, during the last century, company officials presented furs and decorative mounted animal heads to King George VI and Queen Elizabeth II when they visited Canada. On the queen's second visit in 1970, she received live animals, which she donated to Winnipeg's Assiniboine Park Zoo.

Rumor: Tim Hortons adds nicotine to its products to make them addictive.
True? No.

The story: Almost every mainstream brand gets this sort of rumor attached to it at some point, but this one seems completely unnecessary. The caffeine in coffee and the fat in fast food are already sufficiently addictive.

Rumor: During a performance at the North Dakota state fair in July 2006, country star Keith Urban asked Canadians in the audience to stand up. When they did, he ordered them to leave because their country didn't support America's foreign policy.
True? No.
The story: Here's what he really said: "I hear we have a lot of Canadians in the audience tonight." Then he asked them to shout or stand. When they did, he told them, "It's good to see you." (And anyway, Urban is Australian.)

Rumor: A tragic Canadian car accident led to the invention of those "Baby on Board" signs.
True? No.
The story: The yellow-and-black signs seen everywhere in the 1980s were first created by an unmarried and childless American named Michael Lerner. After a friend brought back a similar sign from Europe, which was simply meant to remind people to drive carefully, Lerner bought the rights to it and created his own sign. Safety 1st, the company he started to market the signs, branched out into an extensive line of products before being bought out by a Canadian competitor, Dorel Industries, in 2000. (Dorel is the only Canadian link in the whole story.)

More "Real or Rumor?" on page 111.

* * *

DON'T FIGHT THE LAW
In 1859, the offenses punishable by death in Upper and Lower Canada were as follows: "Murder, rape, treason, administering poison or wounding with intent to commit murder, unlawfully abusing a girl under ten, buggery with man or beast, robbery with wounding, burglary with assault, arson, casting away a ship, and exhibiting a false signal endangering a ship."

...It refers to the cat's bright eyes.

THESE BOOTS WERE MADE FOR NOSHING

How hungry would you have to be to eat your shoes?

WHERE AM I?

The boots that Charlie Chaplin ate in the classic silent movie *The Gold Rush* were made of licorice. But that scene was based on a real incident…and a real guy who ate the real thing. In 1909, Isaac Stringer, bishop of the Yukon diocese, spent a few months filling in for a bishop in the Northwest Territories' Mackenzie River area. In September 1909, when the placement was over, Stringer headed back to the Yukon. The fact that there were 800 kilometers (500 miles) of mountains, brush, and snow between the two dioceses was just one of those Canadian problems that needed to be overcome.

Stringer and a companion named Charles Johnson set off early in the month, hoping to beat the winter. No such luck. Hit by storms and carrying little food and only two blankets, the two soon discovered that they couldn't even depend on their compass. Because they were so close to the north magnetic pole, it was giving them all kinds of incorrect readings. Pretty soon, they were lost.

At first, they managed to scrounge berries and kill some small birds and a squirrel, but by early October, things were desperate. Finally, the bishop made a decision: it was time to boil their boots, which were made of sealskin and had soles of walrus skin. The skins hadn't been tanned, so technically, they were edible. (The chemicals in tanned leather can be poisonous.)

FILET OF SOLE

Stringer and Johnson cut the boots into pieces and boiled them for hours. That hydrated the flesh, sort of like reconstituting jerky. But the results weren't very appetizing, so they roasted the pieces over a fire. In his journal, Stringer wrote that the dinner was "palatable."

The men ate the walrus soles first, and the rest of the boots did not last long. On October 20, the day they polished off the boots, Stringer noted: "Breakfast from top of boots. Not so good as sole."

At this point you're probably wondering the same thing we were: These men were in the wilderness, in the snow, in the middle of winter, and they were eating their shoes. What were they wearing on their feet? Fortunately, they were handy enough to make two pairs of snowshoes out of tree branches and leather scraps.

SOMEBODY UP THERE LIKES THEM

The very same day that they finished eating their boots, Stringer and Johnson discovered sled tracks and freshly cut trees; eventually they staggered into a campsite. They had lost 50 pounds each during the 51 days they were lost. The men at the campsite were aware that Stringer and Johnson were missing and quickly realized who their weather-beaten visitors were. One of the men, Andrew Cloh, lived nearby; he took the pair to his house and revived them with real food: fish and rabbit.

Stringer and Johnson traveled the next 160 kilometers (100 miles) back to Dawson City in a dogsled—Stringer called that ride "perfect happiness." But the experience in the wilderness so traumatized him that he didn't speak publicly about it for a long time. (Once he recovered, though, he did so in a big way, in a series of speaking tours, giving vivid accounts of his days in the wild.)

SPEAKING OF THE FROZEN NORTH

On a trip in 1911, Stringer heard about a four-man patrol of the Royal Northwest Mounted Police that hadn't been as lucky: they'd frozen to death in the same area where he'd been lost two years earlier. The Mounties had eaten their dogs, one by one, to stave off starvation, but they had been done in by average temperatures of $-46°C$ ($-51°F$) and brutal headwinds that generated a wind chill of $-80°C$ ($-112°F$). Stringer was badly shaken by the news and wrote in his journal, "It is a sad day with many unwritten and unspoken chapters. No one will ever know the full story of the struggle."

GONE BUT NOT FORGOTTEN

Stringer lived until 1934 and continued his work in the church, but his boot-eating story followed him wherever he went. For example, when he was in England in 1914 attending to church business, he got a summons from King George V, who specifically wanted to meet "the Canadian bishop who ate his boots."

The iconic "stubby" beer bottle was first introduced in Canada in 1961.

H-E-DOUBLE
HOCKEY STICKS!

American hockey players tend to shoot right-handed.
Canadians, left-handed. We wondered why.

AMERICANS THINK THEY'RE SOOO RIGHTY
In February 2010, the *New York Times* took note of a
strange anomaly: hockey stick manufacturers send mostly
left-handed sticks to Canada, and mostly right-handed ones to the
United States. A check of professional teams discovered that,
indeed, most Canadians play lefty—with their right hand at the
top of the stick and their left hand lower, controlling it—and most
Americans play righty. (The exceptions are players from British
Columbia, who play like Americans.)

It doesn't stop there, though. According to the Professional
Golfers Association, left-handed golfers are more common in
Canada than in any other country. But the reason isn't because
the Great White North has more left-handers. By percentage,
Canada has about the same number of left-handed residents as
the United States. So what's the story?

WHY AMERICANS MIGHT BE DIFFERENT

Many Canadians take the approach that right-handed people
should logically put their right hand on the top of the stick; it
works better for them to have the stronger, more dexterous hand
there. The lower hand, they say, mostly just acts as a fulcrum for
the top hand's strength and dexterity.

So why don't Americans do that too? One theory is that it's the
fault of American parents and store clerks who don't know any
better. A kid goes in to buy a hockey stick and the clerk asks,
"Are you right-handed or left?" Then the clerk gives the kid the
hockey stick that matches the answer. Another theory is simply
that new players do what they see their friends, coaches, and
teammates do—but that only explains why the practice contin-
ues…not how it got started.

The most likely reason is this: people tend to imprint on what-

CBC ice hockey commentator Don Cherry played in only one NHL game.

ever sports equipment they first start playing with. In the United States, that's almost universally a baseball bat. After getting used to the bat's hand position, reversing it feels unnatural. As a result, righties on the ball field usually stay righties on the ice.

This would also help explain the disproportionate number of left-handed golfers in Canada: starting out with a hockey stick makes self-taught golfers more comfortable slap-shooting the ball off the tee as lefties.

* * *

LUCKY 13

Is there something to numerology? We're not sure, but even beyond the provinces and territories, the number 13 shows up a lot when talking about Canada.

• Of the 19 polar bear populations in the world, Canada is home to 13 of them.

• 13 percent of Canadians are older than 65.

• In Europe, there are 13 battlefield memorials to Canada's contributions to World War I. (Nine are in France, the rest in Belgium.)

• Under Canada's surface, you can find 13 percent of the world's oil reserves.

• According to the Conference Board of Canada, compared to countries in Western Europe, the United States, Australia, and Japan, Canada ranks 13th out of 17 in child poverty.

• Canada is 13 times bigger than Turkey.

• The average Canadian buys 13 presents during the holidays.

• 13 percent of Canadians report having had sex before the age of 13.

• Canada's average daily fiber consumption is 13 grams, about half what Health Canada recommends.

• There are 13 international airports in Canada.

• Of the three daily meals, breakfast is the one that 13 percent of Canadians say they eat outside the home most often.

VICTUAL VISIONARIES

Food is often (sadly) overlooked when talking about inventions and discoveries. Yet, we all have to eat every day. Here, we raise our glasses to the Canadian accomplishments in gustatory science.

PABLUM

Still used today as a baby food, Pablum was the first pre-cooked and dried infant cereal to hit the market, and it's 100 percent Canadian. In 1931, three doctors at the Hospital for Sick Children in Toronto developed a cereal made of easily digested grains and fortified with necessary vitamins and minerals. They called it Pablum after the Latin *pabulum*, meaning "food." The Mead Johnson Company marketed it, and the doctors insisted that for the first 25 years after the sale, the Toronto Pediatric Foundation get a royalty for every package sold.

POUTINE

There are several claims to the origins of this dish, but most likely *poutine* (meaning "mess" in French) was invented in Warwick, Quebec, in 1957. Rushing to fill a trucker's order for fries and cheese, restaurant worker Fernand Lachance quickly threw together a bag of French fries and cheese curds...dumping them all in the same bag. As the trucker left, Lachance warned, "It's going to make a damn mess." (For good measure, diners eventually added gravy.) The tricker liked it, and more than 50 years later, that "mess" is still one of Canada's most popular fast foods.

INSTANT MASHED POTATOES

Canada's largest vegetable crop was transformed in 1962 when Edward Asselbergs, a Canadian Ministry of Agriculture employee, turned the familiar potato into instant mashed potato flakes. Asselbergs developed the dehydrated flakes to provide an easy-to-carry food for military rations and for campers.

CANOLA OIL

In the 1970s, Canadian doctor Richard Keith Downey and University of Manitoba researcher Baldur R. Stefansson created

an edible version of the rapeseed plant—a toxic member of the mustard family. Because the new crossbred variety was cheaper to grow than other oil crops, it was soon in high demand. In 1978, scientists at the Rapeseed Association of Canada changed the name from the fairly unpalatable "rapeseed oil," or "rape oil," to "canola"...a blend of "Canada" and "oil."

BLOODY CAESAR

The Bloody Caesar cocktail was invented in 1969 at an Italian restaurant inside the Calgary Inn (now the Westin Hotel). Bartender Walter Chell was asked to invent a cocktail to commemorate the restaurant's opening. Taking cues from the classic Italian dish linguini in clam sauce and riffing off the Bloody Mary, he mixed clam juice, tomato juice, and oregano with vodka and called it the "Caesar." When a British man sitting at the bar declared, "That's a bloody good Caesar," the drink's name was born. Today, the Bloody Caesar is Canada's national cocktail.

GINGER ALE

Back around the turn of the 20th century, Toronto pharmacist John J. McLaughlin was busy making fruit-and-herb-flavored soda water that he sold to local drugstores for their soda fountains. In 1904, he developed a ginger-flavored soda he later called Canada Dry Pale Ginger Ale. Although some people argue that ginger ale had been invented 50 years earlier in Ireland, McLaughlin's distinctively dry recipe—combined with an innovative bottling technique that pumped out large numbers of sealed bottles ready for sale—put the drink on the map.

* * *

APRIL FOOLS, NEWFIE!

Newfoundland—the last holdout to confederation—was scheduled to join Canada on April 1, 1949. As the date approached, though, somebody realized that April 1 was April Fools Day. Since many citizens of the province-to-be were unhappy about losing their independence, the "joke's on us" symbolism of joining on April Fools seemed like a bad idea. Supposedly, that's why the signing was moved to take place "immediately before the expiration of March 31, 1949."

I ♥ MANITOBA

Snakes, polar bears, Slurpees, coins, Bachman-Turner Overdrive, and more! Here are 12 reasons to love Manitoba.

1. FLIN FLON'S FICTIONAL FLIMFLAM. Flin Flon is probably the only Canadian municipality named after a science-fiction character. In 1914, prospector Tom Creighton read a copy of a pulp novel called *The Sunless City* that somebody had discarded along a wooded path. In the book, professor Josiah Flintabbatey Flonatin, the genius hero whom everybody calls "Flin Flon," pilots his super submarine through a lake in the Rockies and discovers a mysterious underground world. Spoiler alert: After various adventures in the subterranean culture where women have enslaved the men, the good professor escapes through an inactive volcano.

Creighton was impressed by the story, and the next year, while digging for gold, he made a joke that they'd discovered Flin Flon's escape hatch. The name stuck to the area and was adopted by the town that grew up around the site.

2. SNAKES ON THE PLAINS. After a long winter, you can see more sex-crazed snakes than you'd ever want to at the Snake Dens in the Narcisse Wildlife Management Area. Thousands of male red-sided garter snakes looking for mates writhe and roll into a balls around females as they emerge from the cracks and holes where they hibernate.

3. PARTS OF THE PROVINCE HAVE GENUINELY SCARY HALLOWEENS. Halloween safety is a concern everywhere, but even the toughest neighborhood has little to match the dangers in Churchill, Manitoba. This "Polar Bear Capital of the World" warns its kids not to wear furry white costumes and to take cover if they hear the sound of "firecrackers" (a.k.a., gunshots), because Halloween takes place during the season that polar bears are hunting day and night in anticipation of winter. Conservation officers and Mounties ring the town and take to the air, keeping their eyes out for foraging bears. Traps are set with seal meat, and officers are armed with bright lights, tranquilizer guns, and shotguns loaded with "cracker shells" that go 200 feet and explode.

4. IT'S GOT THE CARB CAPITAL, PORTAGE LA PRAIRIE. When you eat fast-food French fries, the odds are good that they came from a potato processing plant in Portage la Prairie. Simplot and McCain Foods both produce standardized fries and other potato products for McDonald's, Wendy's, and other food chains there. (Meanwhile, the Can-Oat Milling plant across town is one of the largest oat mills in the world.)

5. THE SYNERGY OF COLD WINTER AND ROMANCE NOVELS. When temperatures get down below freezing and stay there for months on end, romantic fantasies are one thing that can warm the body and soul…which may explain why romance juggernaut Harlequin Enterprises got its start in Winnipeg.

6. CARTOON CREATORS. First you've got the character of Flinty, a city statue designed by *Li'l Abner* cartoonist Al Capp in 1962, supposedly a representation of the fictional founder of Flin Flon, Josiah Flintabbattey Flonatin. Then you have *For Better or for Worse*, the comic strip created by Lynn Johnston when she lived in Lynn Lake. And going back a ways, you've got Winnipeg native Charles Thorson, who designed Bugs Bunny, Elmer Fudd, and hundreds of other cartoon characters for Warner Bros.

7. ROCK 'N' ROLL. Manitoba has given us three or four rock 'n' roll legends. The core of the bands the Guess Who and Bachman-Turner Overdrive (musicians Randy Bachman and Burton Cummings) were both from Winnipeg; Neil Young appeared in several Winnipeg bands before going American; and in the 1990s, Winnipeg's own Crash Test Dummies had a few international hits, most memorably "Mmm Mmm Mmm Mmm."

8. A GREAT PLACE TO BEG FOR SPARE CHANGE. Since 1976, all of Canada's loonies, toonies, quarters, dimes, nickels, pennies—all of its coins—have been produced in Manitoba at the Royal Canadian Mint in southeastern Winnipeg. The mint also coins the jingling currency for dozens of other countries.

9. 911. Winnipeg set up the first emergency phone system in North America in 1959. Back then, you had to dial "999" for help (Canada converted to "911" in 1972) and would get only a female operator. Why? Women were paid less than men (about $200 a

The bird in the popular French-Canadian children's song "Alouette" is a lark.

month, instead of $345), and the city's budget was too small to hire male operators.

10. MOST SLURPEES SOLD. According to official 7-Eleven sales figures, Winnipeg is the Slurpee capital of the world, consuming an estimated 400,000 oversized cups of brightly colored slush per month. As a province, Manitoba beats all other provinces, even those with substantially higher populations.

11. POLAR BEAR MATERNITY DENS. Wapusk National Park, established in 1996 as Canada's 37th national park, is a favorite spot for polar bear moms to settle in, give birth, and nurture their cubs. (*Wapusk*, by the way, is the Cree word for "white bear.")

12. SUNSHINE. Manitoba averages more sunny days per year than any other Canadian province. Sure it's cold, but it's a *sunny* cold.

* * *

IN 499, HUI SHEN SAILED THE OCEAN FINE?

Maybe the Chinese beat everybody to Canada. In AD 499, a Buddhist missionary named Hui Shen described traveling to a wonderful country he called "Fusang," about 8,700 kilometers (5,400 miles) to the east. Some historians speculate that Hui Shen was talking about the New World. In fact, the distance between China and British Columbia is about 8,600 kilometers, well within early navigation's margin of error. And a free-floating boat leaving China could easily be pulled into the Pacific Ocean's currents, which flow northeast past Japan and on to British Columbia.

You decide: Does this sound like British Columbia? According to Hui Shen, the land of Fusang was rich in copper, gold, and silver, but had no iron. Its civilized natives produced paper, cloth and houses from red mulberry trees; raised deer for meat, milk, and cheese; drove carts and sleds pulled by horses, buffalos, or deer; and maintained two penal areas, one north and one south, with the worst criminals exiled to the north for their entire lives. They also had no religion and so welcomed the message of Buddhist non-attachment to material things.

First patent filed in Canada: 1824 (for a washing machine).

WHO'S THAT BAND?

*The stories behind the names of some of
Canada's most beloved musical groups.*

THE GUESS WHO: This 1960s rock band from Winnipeg was named Chad Allan & the Reflections when they recorded their first single. Trying to add some mystique (and maybe fool customers into thinking it was a more famous band traveling incognito), the band's record company printed "Guess Who?" on its promotional record labels. Even after the record company revealed the group's real name, radio DJs continued to call them "Guess Who?" forcing the band to adopt that as their real name on subsequent hits like "American Woman."

BARENAKED LADIES: Ed Robertson and Steven Page were bored at a Bob Dylan concert in 1988, so they started to make up improbable band names. When the two had to put together an impromptu set at the last minute for a charity event, one of the organizers asked Robertson the name of his band. To Page's embarrassment, all Robertston could remember was one of the names from the Dylan concert: Barenaked Ladies.

MOXY FRÜVOUS: This satirical and sometimes political band from Thornhill, Ontario, often gave frivolous answers about its name, which comes complete with heavy metal umlaut (possibly borrowed from Mötley Crüe?). A member eventually admitted that—contrary to the normal criterion for a band name—they purposely chose "a name that wasn't easy to remember and doesn't mean anything."

BUFFALO SPRINGFIELD: Neil Young met Stephen Stills when they were performing with other bands at a folk club in Thunder Bay, Ontario. After recruiting Canadian bass player Bruce Palmer, they named the group after a nameplate they saw while briefly detained by road work being done with an old steamroller from the now-defunct Buffalo Springfield Roller Company.

More bands on page 116.

The shores of B.C. are home to the Pacific octopus, the world's largest.

DAMMING EVIDENCE

North American beavers are Canada's official emblem and the third-largest rodent in the world. They mate for life, their teeth never stop growing, and they can live for 20 years. But that's just the beginning; here are even more beaver facts.

• North American beavers are smaller than only the South American capybara, which looks sort of like a big guinea pig, and the European/Eurasian beaver. Typically, North American beavers weigh between 16 and 30 kilograms (35 and 66 pounds), but the largest-ever caught weighed 45 kilograms (99 pounds).

• Scientists say that in prehistoric times, beavers were the size of modern black bears.

• There are two to four "kits" in a typical beaver litter, and they can swim within 24 hours of being born. "Teenage" beavers—kits born the previous year—help babysit the new brood, although they'd probably rather be hanging out by the dam with their friends.

• Beavers chew wood to wear down their ever-growing front teeth.

• Beavers can cut down a tree with a 15-centimeter (6-inch) diameter in 20 minutes, gnawing around and around its base. They've been known to fell trees as large as 1.15 meters (5 feet) in diameter.

• Beaver dams are so well built that dynamite is often the best way to remove them.

• The longest known beaver dam is more than 800 meters (0.5 mile) long. It's in northern Alberta.

• Two hundred years ago, North America was home to about 60 to 80 beavers per mile of stream. Because of their pelts, though, the animals were hunted to near extinction by the end of the 19th century. Nowadays, they're protected enough to have come back with a vengeance in most of North America, including parts of New York City.

• During the Middle Ages, beavers were categorized as fish, which allowed Catholics to eat them during Lent. Why? They live in the water and have scaly tails...like fish.

• According to one Native American horoscope, people born under the sign of the Beaver (April 20–May 20) are methodical, smart, inventive, and headstrong.

• *Castoreum*, a yellow liquid secreted from beavers' scent glands, is used in some perfumes. Castoreum and the glands themselves have been used as pain relievers for many ailments, including headaches. What makes it work? Salicylic acid, which beavers accumulate from chomping on willow bark. It's also the active ingredient in aspirin.

• According to a 12th-century book called the *Aberdeen Bestiary*, "[W]hen [a beaver] knows that a hunter is pursuing it, it bites off its testicles and throws them in the hunter's face and, taking flight, escapes." This is, of course, a very unlikely story, and a very old one, first written down by the Roman writer Claudius Aelianus in the second century. (It wasn't true then, and it isn't true now.)

• Beavers that live in ponds and lakes don't generally build dams; only stream- and river-dwellers do. Why? Scientists believe that the sound of running water spurs them to action. A quiet, deep-water environment is safer and more hospitable for the beavers: they can hear predators coming, can escape danger easily in deep water (they're great swimmers, but slow on land), and can hunt the fish that collect nearby. One researcher even did a study in which he set up speakers in a pond. The speakers emitted the sound of water rushing over rocks. When he came back the next day, the pond's resident beavers had buried the speakers under mud and sticks.

*　*　*

RANDOM CANADIAN RECORDS

• Highest-grossing movie: *My Big Fat Greek Wedding*
• Most-recorded pop song About Canada: "Four Strong Winds," by Ian Tyson
• Most-successful Broadway show: *The Drowsy Chaperone*

...The "J" was chosen as a tribute to Oscar-winning actor Michael J. Pollard.

HIGH FIVE

*If you yell "Strike!" when your first ball knocks down five pins, and
you cheer when you make it into the 450 club, then you're definitely
in Canada. Why? Because obviously, you're five-pin bowling.*

LET'S DO LUNCH

Ten-pin bowling is one of the oldest sports in the world.
Some archaeological evidence points to a version of the
game being played 5,000 years ago in Egypt. The ancient Finns
played it too, and Germans were bowling by about AD 300. In
fact, the sport is so old that no one really knows how it began.
However, there are fewer doubts about the origins of five-pin
bowling, which was officially born in 1909. And the first place it
was played was at the Toronto Bowling Club.

Five-pin bowling was invented by Thomas F. Ryan of Guelph,
Ontario. Ryan was a talented baseball player who gave up the
game to go into business for himself. In 1905, he decided that
Toronto executives might like to bowl on their lunch hours. So
Ryan found a spot in the downtown Boisseau Building and
opened the Toronto Bowling Club, the first ten-pin bowling
alley in the city.

Ryan's bowling club was for "gentlemen only," no women
allowed. The exclusive establishment sported potted palms for
decor, a lunch counter, and even had a string orchestra and a
piano player to provide background music. The club soon also had
a clientele of successful businessmen who often came to bowl on
their lunch breaks. But the popularity of lunchtime games led to
problems: Some of the sedentary executives complained that toss-
ing the 16-pound bowling ball tired them out for the rest of the
afternoon. And sometimes the games went on too long. The
bowlers often asked the pin boys to set up only half the pins so
they could finish up and get back to their daily grind.

A GENTLEMAN'S GAME

Inspired by the complaints, Ryan began working on a new game
for his club members. With the help of his father, who shaved
down the maplewood pins on a lathe, Ryan experimented with a

Score a goal, an assist, and fight in one hockey game and you've got a "Gordie Howe hat trick."

game that used five pins that were three-quarters the size of the old ones. The pins were set up in the shape of a V, and players bowled them down with a smooth, cantaloupe-sized wooden ball that had no need for finger holes. When the new ball hit the lighter pins, though, they scattered and flew, making a lot of noise and mess. So to improve the pin action and lessen their clatter, Ryan put wide rubber bands around the pins' lower halves.

To make the game more complex, Ryan also invented a new scoring system. Unlike ten-pin bowling where all the pins are worth one point, in the new game, the center (or head) pin was worth five points. Those on either side were worth three, and the corner pins counted for two points each. Ryan also made a rule that the left corner pin (called a counterpin) had to be over-turned for a bowler to score any points in a frame. This form of scoring forced bowlers, who knew it was difficult to knock over every pin, to strategize and try to hit the more valuable pins for more points.

By 1909, the kinks had been worked out, and some of Canada's most powerful men of the day—including Toronto mayor Sam McBride—were playing five-pin bowling at Ryan's club. That same year, an entrepreneur named Charles R. Gibson opened several five-pin bowling alleys across Canada, and they were a huge success.

100 STRIKING YEARS

More than a century later, Canadians are still playing five-pin bowling. Of course, there have been rule changes and modernizations. For example, a player can now score without knocking out the counterpin. And modern five-pin bowling alleys use automatic pinsetters and automatic scorers. Even the pins and balls that used to be made of maplewood are now made entirely of hard plastic.

For the most part, though, Ryan's game is still played in much the same way as when he first invented it. A bowler gets three balls per frame to knock down five lightweight, rubber-banded pins. There are 10 frames per game. The pins, in total, are still worth 15 points, and the game still encourages players to strategize.

THE 450 CLUB

Part of the fun of five-pin bowling is that the combination of the

lightweight ball and the spaces between the small pins require the bowler to aim correctly and control the ball's speed so that the pins actually knock each other over. In fact, many bowlers find that five-pin requires more skill than regular bowling because five-pin games often lead to splits that allow the ball to pass without touching any of the remaining pins. Even for experienced five-pin bowlers, it's common to hit nothing but air.

A perfect game in five-pin bowling gives a score of 450 (that's a strike on every one of the game's 10 frames), but perhaps as a testament to the need for skill, perfect games are more rare in five-pin than in ten-pin. A good bowler can go a lifetime without making it into that 450 club. In fact, in 2009, the Ontario 5 Pin Bowling Association listed only one perfect game. And during the past five years, the group has listed no more than five perfect games occurring in any one year, making that 450 club one of the most prestigious in Canada.

* * *

HOW PROVINCIAL

Eleven of Canada's 13 provinces and territories have their own mottoes. (The exceptions are the Northwest Territories and the Yukon.) Here's the list.

Alberta: "Freedom to Create, Spirit to Achieve"

New Brunswick: "Hope was Restored"

Newfoundland and Labrador: "Seek Ye First the Kingdom of God"

Manitoba: "Glorious and Free"

Quebec: "I Remember"

Prince Edward Island: "The Small Under the Protection of the Great"

Nunavut: "Our Land, Our Strength"

Saskatchewan: "From Many Peoples, Strength"

Nova Scotia: "One Defends and the Other Conquers"

Ontario: "Loyal She Began and Loyal She Remains"

British Columbia: "Splendour without Diminishment"

PINGOS & PLÉES

Don't know brandies from blow me downs? To help you, here's a short, only-in-Canada list of unusual geographic terms.

Blow me down: A downdraft of wind and you're suddenly falling into the water; it happens all too often on Labrador's steep, windy bluffs. What better name for such a cliff than "blow me down"? There are at least 15 places in Labrador with that name attached.

Brandies: Irish settlers in Newfoundland thought some clusters of partially submerged rocks looked like a *brandise*, a sort of cooking tripod from the old country. The last letters got transposed in translation.

Échouerie: A term used mostly in Quebec for a ledge extending into the ocean where herds of seals and walruses hang out.

Esker: Eskers are long, snakelike ridges that can stretch for hundreds of kilometers. Although they look man-made—like a curvy railroad embankment—they're actually formed by glaciers.

Mal bay: This New Brunswick term is for a saltwater lagoon that's mostly separated from the sea by a sand bar. No one knows for sure, but it probably comes from the Irish word *meall-bhaigh*, which means "treacherous coast."

Oxbow: A U-shaped loop or former loop of a meandering river that resembles the U-shaped frame holding an ox's yoke in place.

Pingo: A cone-shaped mound with a core of ice that occurs in permafrost areas. The word comes from the Inuit language.

Plée: A treeless area. The term may be a mutation of *pelé*, a French word that means "bare."

Roche moutonnée: A teardrop-shaped rock formation with parallel grooves caused by glaciers that ripped strips of land off the surface. They are named for their similarity to 18th-century French wigs that were smoothed with mutton fat. (The formation is also known as a "sheepback.")

Cheech and Chong formed their comedy act in Vancouver.

THEY LOVE US...

They really love us!

"When I'm in Canada, I feel this is what the world should be like."
—**Jane Fonda**

"Canada is a place of infinite promise. We like the people, and if one ever had to emigrate, this would be the destination...The hills, lakes, and forests make it a place of peace and repose of the mind, such as one never finds in the U.S.A."
—**John Maynard Keynes, British economist**

"You Canadians have given us such hope to carry on. We admire your bravery. You are the neighbor of such a rich, powerful country, and yet you don't mind clashing with them. Well, that gives us more confidence."
—**Pedro Gutiérrez, Cuban novelist**

"I love Canadians because I don't see very much racism in Canada."
—**Patti LaBelle**

"Canada is a good country to be from. It has a gentler slower pace—it lends perspective."
—**Paul Anka**

"I had no idea Canada could be so much fun."
—**Bruce Willis**

"I love America...whilst performing in Canada."
—**Charlotte Church, British singer**

"I am much more receptive to Canada than to the United States. There is more balance, a calm rhythm of life...Canada has created harmony and co-operation among ethnic groups, and it must take this experience to the world."
—**Valentyn Moroz, historian**

"Canada is a very nice place. And we intend to keep it that way."
—**J. P. Morgan, American financier**

CBC Radio discovered news anchor Peter Mansbridge while...

APPLE, McINTOSH

Before the Apple Macintosh, there was the McIntosh apple.
The popular fruit came from Ontario with absolutely no
microchips or Internet capability, just juicy goodness.

THE MAN KNEW HIS APPLES

Back in the 1800s, in the virgin wilds of Dundas County, Ontario, John McIntosh was clearing land for spring planting when he came across a small cluster of apple tree saplings. He'd started a farm in Canada in 1811, but had been born and raised in New York's apple country, so he knew that apple trees weren't native to North America. These had to have come from somewhere else, probably—indirectly—from a neighboring farm, perhaps sprouted from undigested seeds excreted by an animal or bird, or from an apple core discarded by a hunter. And the first apple trees to grow in McIntosh's neighborhood may have come from New York, just like McIntosh himself. (Parts of the area had been settled years earlier by a few hundred German-American soldiers from New York who fought with the British in the American colonial revolt and had subsequently been left stranded in Canada when their side lost.)

TAMING THE WILD APPLE

Whatever the story, McIntosh didn't want a stand of apple trees in the middle of the ground he intended to plow. He thought about yanking out the saplings, but then the thought of having a supply of fresh, canned, and baked apples took root in his mind. He dug up the tiny trees and replanted them closer to his farmhouse. By midsummer, only one of them had survived, and it wasn't exactly thriving. But the dream of apples had taken root in his wife Hannah's imagination as well, so the two showered the surviving sapling with attention—watering it, fertilizing it, and fencing it off from herbivores and human feet.

HOW DO YOU LIKE THEM APPLES?

Eventually, all that attention paid off. The sapling became a tree and, after a few years, began bearing fruit. And what fruit it was:

...he was working as a flight announcer at a Churchill, MB, airport.

firm, colorful, tart, with tender white flesh, perfect for baking, cooking, or eating straight off the tree. This was an especially lucky find in those days—before hybridization produced the enormous variety of color, flavor, size, and texture available today. The McIntoshs' tree reliably provided apples, but nobody seemed to know what kind of tree it was. (Nowadays, people think it was a cross between a fameuse, a.k.a. a snow apple, and another variety.)

For years, the family was content to enjoy the fruits of their labors. One of the 11 McIntosh children, Allan, seemed to be the first to realize the significance of what they had: a one-in-a-million accident that loved the Canadian soil and weather and produced superior apples. Young Allan tried to convince his father to start an orchard, but John—illiterate and getting older—was uninterested in starting a new business. He left that to his son.

THE BIRDS AND THE BEES, APPLE-STYLE

Allan started by planting some of the apple seeds, but the few trees that grew to maturity didn't live up to their parent's promise. None of the apples were as good as the fruit from the original tree. What Allan didn't know was that apple trees can't pollinate themselves. They need to cross-pollinate with at least one other variety of apple to generate fruit, using bees as their pollen carriers. This cross-pollination doesn't affect the type of fruit—a red delicious tree will grow a red delicious apple no matter what it cross-pollinates with. But the trees won't produce very much (or very tasty) fruit if the mate isn't another apple tree.

In 1835, though, Allan learned about grafting. By cutting a branch off the original tree and attaching it to the roots and stem of a new one, he could create genetically identical clones that produced exactly the same type of apples as the first. *That* was doable. Before his father died in 1846, Allan McIntosh had himself a small orchard, with all the trees producing the new variety of apples. In fact, to this day, every McIntosh apple tree is an exact genetic copy of the sapling John McIntosh found in the forest.

McINTOSH: THE NEXT GENERATION

Allan's son Harvey took on the job of trying to sell the trees to other farmers, even though the apple still didn't have a name. "Gem apples" and "granny apples" (in honor of Harvey's grand-

mother Hannah) were considered, but neither stuck. It wasn't until 1870 that the newly named "red McIntosh" apple started to gain a foothold locally. Another six years passed before its new name appeared in print, and at least another 30 years before the variety was widely distributed—largely due to the efforts of William Macoun, chief horticulturist for the Central Experimental Farm in Ottawa. Macoun was a fan of the McIntosh apple, and made it his goal to convince skeptical farmers that "it is one of the finest appearing and best dessert apples grown." Furthermore, he noted, the red McIntosh tree was well suited to Canada's mild climate.

BAKED APPLES

Due to a series of tragedies, neither Allan nor the original tree lived to see the McIntosh's mass acceptance. In 1895, the family's farmhouse burned down. Not only was it destroyed—the fire singed the old tree pretty badly. Allan tried to nurse it back to health, but the tree was never the same. It died in 1910, just a few years short of its centennial, but by then, its "children" had already spread across Canada and into the United States. These days, the clones of that one apple tree account for about half the apples grown in Canada. In the United States, the McIntosh is the third most widely grown variety of apples, after red and golden delicious.

LOCAL HERO

The townships of South Dundas and Dundela have commemorated the McIntosh's remarkable story by putting up three historic plaques. The first, placed there in 1912, gets the date wrong by 15 years. It says, "The original McIntosh red apple tree stood 20 rods north of this spot. It was one of a number of seedlings taken from the border of the clearings and transplanted by John McIntosh in the year 1796." The other two plaques—one placed by the Ontario Heritage Foundation in 1962 and the second by the Historic Sites and Monuments Board of Canada in 2001—are more accurate. Observes the 1962 plaque:

> (T)his new species…was widely acclaimed in Ontario and the northern United States, and was introduced into British Columbia about 1910. Its popularity in North America and propagation in many lands attest to the initiative and industry of John McIntosh and his descendants.

First nonEuropean to win a downhill skiing World Cup: Toronto's Steve Podborski, 1982.

IT'S ALL POLITICS

Canadians do the darndest things.

APPLE OR CHERRY?
In January 2010, Gail Shea (the government's minster of fisheries and oceans) got an unexpected greeting from a member of PETA. During a conference in Ontario, a man walked up to the podium where Shea was speaking and threw a pie in her face. The incident prompted Liberal MP Gerry Byrne to call for the government to reclassify PETA as a terrorist organization that was out to intimidate public officials. PETA was undeterred. According to the organization's president, "Mr. Byrne's reaction is a silly, chest-beating exercise that is unlikely to impress anyone who has a heart for animals or who is bright enough to spot the difference between a bomb and a tofu cream pie."

HEADS OF THE CLASS
When Uncle John was in school, his teachers docked students one letter grade for term papers that were turned in on toilet paper or that were a day late. If Manitoba's government has anything to say about it, teachers in the province will no longer have that option. Students shouldn't be given lower grades for turning in work late, the Tories theorized, because such grades don't accurately reflect what students have learned or the amount of work they've done. It's all part of a larger issue, Manitoba's unwritten "no-fail" policy in which teachers in the province (speaking anonymously, of course) claim that they're pressured to find ways to pass even the most mediocre students so as to keep the kids with others in their age group. For now, the debate continues.

HAPPY HOLIDAYS!
In 2009, Canada's political leaders sent out holiday cards. That seems normal enough: Stephen Harper's had a picture of his family, and the Yukon's Liberal MP Larry Bagnell included a cute, piano-playing baby. But consider these: Defence Minister Peter MacKay posed with a group of soldiers; one is chugging a beer. And Trade Minister Stockwell Day featured his family and the note, "Another baby...now it's 13...Stimulus Package Working!"

Number of legal border-crossing points between the U.S. and Canada: 98.

HOPS & GLORY

Beer is Canadian!

THE BIG GUNS

How important is beer to Canada? The first commercial brewery opened in Quebec in 1668, but after that, more than a century passed before Canada's most famous brewing names began to appear. Here are the top five, in order of appearance:

1786: John Molson opened a brewery in Montreal. He'd never been a brewer, but had the confidence of youth and a copy of the book *Theoretic Hints on an Improved Practice in Brewing*. Today, Molson is Canada's oldest brewery and the second-oldest Canadian company of any kind (the Hudson's Bay Company is first).

1820: Scotsman Alexander Keith set up shop in Halifax. He also became the city's longtime mayor and highest-ranking Freemason. Every October 5 (his birthday), Haligonians celebrate by lovingly littering his grave with bottle caps and empty beer bottles.

1840: Thomas Carling was a farmer from Yorkshire who moved his family to Ontario in 1818. His home-brewed ales became popular among his neighbors, so eventually he gave up farming to sell beer on the streets of London, Ontario, from a barrel mounted to a wheelbarrow. In 1840, he moved his brewery into town, wisely locating it next to a military barracks.

1855: Originally from Ireland, John Kinder Labatt moved to Ontario in 1834. When his English investments faltered, Labatt sold his farm and bought half-interest in a brewery owned by one Samuel Eccles. Labatt slapped his name on the brewery when Eccles retired.

1867: Moosehead was the only major Canadian brewery founded by a woman. Susannah Oland first named her brewery S. Oland, Sons & Co. shortly after founding it in 1867 in Halifax. The Halifax Explosion of 1917 destroyed Oland's business and killed one of her sons, so she moved to New Brunswick. In the 1940s, the company officially changed its name to Moosehead, after one of its most successful beers (Moosehead Pale Ale). Moosehead is still run by the Oland family, making it the largest Canadian-owned brewery.

THERE GOES THE NEIGHBORHOOD

"While parents quail and children cry, the ghosts of the Donnellys will ride by, out on the Roman line." —Anonymous song

LIFE ON THE ROMAN LINE

In 1880, in the Biddulph Township of Lucan, Ontario, a long, violent feud caused a mass murder that nearly wiped out an entire family. Even though there were two eyewitnesses, no one was ever imprisoned for the crime. Instead, for more than a century, ghostly legends and stories have grown up around the famous victims of the crime, and the family became known as the "Black Donnellys."

James and Johannah Donnelly married in Ireland in 1840. Dreaming of a better life, they immigrated to Canada around 1842 with their baby, James Jr. A few years later, they had another child named William, and the family settled on 100 acres in Biddulph on a road called the Roman Line. There, the Donnellys had five more sons—John, Patrick, Michael, Robert, and Thomas—and finally, in 1857, a daughter named Jenny.

The Biddulph area began as a wild frontier where families settled grievances by fighting, killing livestock, torching barns, and burning homes. To make matters worse, old religious feuds in Ireland bloomed again in Biddulph. Violence erupted, not only between Catholics and Protestants, but also between anti-Protestant Catholics and Catholics who were considered friendly to Protestants—like the Donnellys.

When it came to feuding and fighting, James Donnelly certainly gave as good as he got...and so did his wife and their seven strapping sons. Even in their rough neighborhood, the family was feared for its tough ways. Brawling over religion and politics, however, didn't land James Donnelly in prison. That came from a quarrel over his land.

THIS LAND IS MY LAND

Like many other homesteaders, Donnelly never bought his acreage. He simply squatted—he built a log cabin and a barn, and took up farming. But in 1855, the land's absentee owner sold part of the property. Then, a man named Patrick Farrell rented it. Farrell wasn't happy that another family was living on land he was paying for. But the Donnellys insisted that they'd cleared and improved the place for nearly 10 years, so by the custom of the frontier, they had a claim to it.

Eventually, a court gave half of the disputed acreage to the Donnellys and half to Farrell. This left neither man satisfied, and one night, the two got into a drunken brawl. The fight ended with Farrell dead, a metal bar driven into his head.

Donnelly was arrested, convicted, and sentenced to be hanged. Luckily, his feisty wife Johannah worked for clemency and got his sentence commuted to seven years in prison. Some neighbors testified against James at his trial, claiming that Farrell's death was no drunken accident and that James had boasted that he should have killed him years ago. Whether or not that was true, the feud between the Donnellys and their neighbors grew deeper.

TAKING THE STAGE

James got out of prison in 1865, but there was no end to members of the family getting hauled before the authorities. They were (probably both rightly and wrongly) accused of attempted murder, assault, arson, and larceny. Eventually, Johannah was even charged with the crime of swearing at a constable.

Years passed, and the problems between the Donnellys and the community worsened. When William Donnelly started a successful stagecoach line that employed his brothers, a community rival tried to drive him out of business. On both sides, horses were killed, stables were burned, and equipment was sabotaged, leading to accidents and death. James Sr. began to fear that every crime in the area would be blamed on his sons. By 1879, the Donnellys and some of their neighbors had been feuding for decades. But that year, those neighbors gained a crucial ally: the new constable, James Carroll.

Osoyoos, BC, is home to Canada's only banana plantation.

AN UNHOLY MASS(ACRE)

On February 4, 1880, just after midnight, Constable Carroll came to arrest James Sr. and Tom Donnelly for some new infraction. Tom was in handcuffs when about 30 men from the town's newly formed vigilance committee broke into the Donnellys' house and beat the occupants to death. James Sr., Johannah, Tom, and their niece Bridget were all murdered. Somehow, the mob missed Johnny O'Connor, a 13-year-old who'd come to help with the animals and who was watching everything from a hiding place under the bed. After the vigilantes set fire to the house and left, Johnny escaped through the back door.

The mob wasn't done. Its next victim was William Donnelly (considered the leader of the brothers), who lived nearby. He and his family were awakened by shouting and calls for him to come to the door. When his brother John opened the door, he was instantly peppered with gunfire. He fell back into the house and died soon after. The mob left, believing that their job was done. But William Donnelly, the man they'd come to kill, was still alive, watching them from his window.

The slaughter ended there, but the aftermath was just beginning. Thanks to the testimony of William Donnelly and young Johnny O'Connor, six men were charged with the crime of murdering the Donnelly family. Finding jurors for the trial was difficult—especially after Johnny O'Connor's house was burned to the ground when the town found out he was one of the witnesses. Eventually, though, the men had two trials: the first ended in a hung jury, and the second with an acquittal. Feeling like they'd never be able to get a conviction for the crime, prosecutors gave up.

THE DONNELLYS FIGHT ON

You'd think that would've been the end of it, but over the years, legends arose that the Donnellys' ghosts were angry and out for revenge. On the 13th anniversary of the massacre, William Donnelly published a letter in which he wrote that 32 of the men he believed had taken part in the killings had suffered retribution. According to William, "several were killed by the London, Huron & Bruce train. More were found [dead] in bed without any apparent cause. More fell into a well. More dropped dead. More died suffering the agonies of a mad dog, and a few are in the asylum."

Q: What's a "grolar bear"? A: The hybrid grizzly/polar bear found in NWT in 2006.

William saw all this as a curse and heavenly justice, but others felt that the Donnellys were still fighting the feud from their graves. To this day, the people who live on the old Donnelly land believe that it is haunted.

International fascination with the Donnelly family continues. Books, plays, and a Web site tell their story. Lucan, the town that once denied them justice, now honors a more objective history of the family at the Lucan Area Heritage and Donnelly Museum. Maybe James and Johannah can finally feel that they've won a part of their battle at last.

* * *

"O CANADA!"

How many people does it take to create a national anthem?

• According to local legend, the first version of the lyrics for the Canadian national anthem were written by a Quebec lawyer in the late 1800s. The lawyer's name has been lost to history.

• In 1880, a Quebecois musician named Calixa Lavallée was commisioned to compose music to go along with those lyrics so that the complete song could be played during a celebration for Saint-Jean-Baptiste Day. But Lavallée didn't want to use the existing lyrics—he didn't want to be boxed in by another artist's words. So he created a melody and then got someone else to come up with new lyrics to fit his music.

• Enter Adolphe-Basile Routhier, a local lawyer, judge, and poet. Routhier put together most of the song, but his friend Ernest Gagnon (also an organizer of the festivities) wrote the first line, including the iconic phrase "O Canada!"

• Then in 1906, a Toronto doctor named Thomas Bedford Richardson translated the French lyrics into English. However, the song was slammed as "too religious" by the English-speaking parts of Canada and never caught on there.

• Two years later, *Collier's* magazine launched a contest to come up with new English lyrics. The winner: Mercy E. Powell McCollough of Toronto. Her lyrics never caught on either.

• Over the next 70 years, more than a dozen versions came and went. Finally, in 1980, politicians tweaked a poem by yet another lawyer, Robert S. Weir, and *those* became the song we know today.

The largest bird in Canada: the trumpeter swan, with a wingspan of up to 3 meters.

HODGEPODGE

Quick! Some facts about Canada.

• Great Slave Lake didn't get its name from slavery, but from the Slavey First People.

• Canada's 42 national parks cover about 2 percent of the country's entire land mass.

• Liddy's Bar in Torbay, Newfoundland and Labrador, claims to be the oldest drinking establishment in North America.

• Comedy legend Anna Russell began as an operatic soprano. Her transition to comedy is an "only-in-Canada" story: after she was hit in the face and throat with a hockey stick, she couldn't sing anymore, so she decided to become a comedian.

• The "Thousand Islands" in the St. Lawrence River actually have 1,793 islands.

• The southern parts of Canada are closer to the equator than the northern parts of California are.

• Canada has about 2 million lakes that cover more than 7 percent of the country.

• Birdwatchers have sighted more than 360 bird species in Point Pelee National Park.

• Per capita, there are more Tim Hortons in Canada than there are McDonalds and Starbucks in the U.S. combined.

• The cry of the Canada Jay sounds like "Poor Canada! Poor Canada!"

• An 1897 Newfoundland postage stamp was the first in the world to feature an image of miners mining.

• The United States bought parts of Alberta and Saskatchewan from France in 1803...and traded them to Great Britain in 1818.

• Canadians consume more Kraft Dinner (aka, Kraft Macaroni and Cheese) per capita than any other nationality on Earth.

DARK DOG DAYS

After a brutal defeat during World War II, Canadian survivors and prisoners of war took some cheer in telling tales about Gander the dog, a mascot that saved their lives.

A HEROIC TAIL

Locked for four years in a squalid Japanese prison camp, sick, ankle deep in mud, without enough to eat—that was the state of the Canadian survivors of the 1941 Battle of Hong Kong. They were ostensibly the lucky ones (they survived); more than 500 Canadians did not.

With the horrors the inmates had seen in battle and the tortures they experienced daily behind the barbed wire, there wasn't a lot to comfort them. So it's not surprising that they held on to small pleasures...like recounting the legendary exploits of a black dog named Gander who protected his companion soldiers and bested the Japanese army, even when it cost him his life.

THE DOG BEHIND THE MYTH

Gander started out as Pal. The dog was a Newfoundland, a breed that's known for its sweet disposition, strength, loyalty, and size (up to 68 kilograms/150 pounds when fully grown).

Pal was living with a family in the town of Gander in the early days of World War II. As he grew ever larger, the family started wondering if they'd chosen the right breed of dog, considering that they had children. When he exuberantly jumped on one of the kids' friends and accidentally scratched the little girl's face, the family started looking for a new home for Pal.

At the time, the Gander airport had been turned into an air base and was teeming with soldiers. Like most dogs in the town, Pal roamed freely. Plus, he was friendly, so he was well known by the townsfolk and soldiers. Hearing that he needed a home, members of a Quebec rifle regiment offered to take Pal on as a mascot. They changed his name to Gander and "promoted" him to sergeant, even affixing sergeant stripes to his collar. And when, in October 1941, they shipped out to Hong Kong, the soldiers took their now-beloved dog with them.

First Canadian city to offer free wireless Internet in its downtown: Fredericton, NB (2004).

Initially, life was good. Their military paychecks were enough for the men to live like kings in Hong Kong, and although there were reports of fighting elsewhere, the city was peaceful. There was no evidence of impending invasion, and the Canadian forces settled into the routine of garrison duty. They visited the sights, and Gander spent warm afternoons sleeping on a veranda in the sun.

PARADISE LOST

The Japanese military, though, had other plans for Hong Kong, and in the first week of December, they attacked. The Canadians and their allies were outnumbered three to one, and the Quebec soldiers ended up on the front lines, trying to save the British colony from becoming a Japanese one. Japanese ships shelled the island, and its troops started landing. Fighting got intense along the beaches, and Gander was right there, unafraid (the stories would say). The earsplitting sounds of rifles and explosions didn't make him flinch. All he wanted to do was take care of his men, like any good sergeant would.

As Japanese troops began landing on the beach, Gander ran at them, barking, snarling, and snapping at their legs, sending them back into the water and diverting them away from his men's position. Somehow, he didn't get shot.

One often-told story had Gander looking after wounded Canadian soldiers who were lying near a road. Japanese troops appeared and began walking toward where the men were partially hidden in the brush. Gander charged at the Japanese, barking and growling. They decided to change direction, giving Gander wide berth and saving the Canadians from discovery.

The most significant incident, though, sealed Gander's legendary status, and—in 2000—it also won him the animals-only Dickin Medal for "acts of conspicuous gallantry and devotion to duty in wartime." During close fighting, Gander's soldiers were pinned down. When a Japanese soldier threw a grenade into their midst, Gander didn't hesitate. He swooped up the grenade with his mouth and ran toward the man who threw it. Some people say he knew what he was doing and deliberately risked his own life for his men. But others argue it's likely he was just playing a game of fetch. Either way, it saved the soldiers' lives. Gander didn't make it, though. The grenade exploded as he ran, killing him instantly.

"I'm from Canada, so Thanksgiving to me is just Thursday with more food...

THE BLACK BEAST

Hong Kong fell to the Japanese just 18 days after the battle began, and all the surviving Canadian soldiers were sent to prison camps. And that bred one last, posthumous story about Gander triumphing over the enemy. According to the anecdotes, Canadian prisoners were interrogated about a special "weapon" that clearly concerned the Japanese: the fearless "black devils" or "black beasts" that had accompanied them to battle. The soldiers said nothing, simply allowing the Japanese to believe that Canada had bred some kind of super animal to fight in its army.

In 1945, the war ended, and the surviving soldiers went home. But they never forgot about Gander. In 2009, when a Hong Kong Veterans Memorial Wall went up in Ottawa, listing the 1,977 Canadians who served in the battle, survivors insisted that Gander's name be added.

* * *

ECCENTRIC GENIUS

When it comes to innovative (and wacky) pianists, a contest for the title of "world's greatest" would have lots of contenders: Rachmaninoff, Chopin, Beethoven. But for Canada, only one name comes to mind—Glenn Gould.

He grew up in Toronto's Beach neighborhood in the 1930s. By the age of four, Gould could already read music and had perfect pitch (the uncanny ability to recreate musical notes just by listening to them). At 15, he became a professional concert pianist. But like so many gifted artists before him, Gould also had an eccentric side that left many around him scratching their heads. For example...

• He showed up at Fran's Restaurant in Toronto every day between 2 and 3 a.m, always sat in the same booth, and always ordered the same thing: scrambled eggs.

• He rarely practiced his musical pieces. Instead, he spent hours studying the sheet music.

• Gould had a favorite rug and chair the he took with him to every performance.

• He hated to fly, but was happy to travel by boat, car, or train.

PIRATING MUSIC...
IN 1897

*Stealing music has been a problem for music publishers for a
lot longer than you'd think. As early as 1897, they were
complaining that Canada's "music pirates" were ripping
them off and putting their whole industry in jeopardy.*

DIRE WARNINGS
Music corporations warning that they're being driven out
of business by unauthorized recordings—it's something
we've gotten used to since the introduction of mp3-sharing soft-
ware in 1999. But it wasn't new then; in the 1980s, music compa-
nies had issued similar complaints about recordable audiocassettes:
"Home Taping Is Killing Music!" cried industry ads at the time.
Still, it's a surprise to discover that the music industry has been
making these complaints for more than a century. The rise of
radio in the 1920s brought more talk of looming bankruptcy, with
a record company spokesman saying that the "owners of receiving
sets wish to listen, but they are not willing to pay for the service
given."

But the great-grand daddy of industry complaints came in a
short news story from the *New York Times* on June 13, 1897. The
heading read "Music Pirates in Canada." And it has eerie parallels
to the present day.

THE GOOD OLD DAYS

First some background: Nowadays, sheet music is a specialized
commodity, selling relatively few copies to a small population of
musicians. But that wasn't always the case. Before Victrolas and
radio, most households contained at least one person who could
play a piano—and many homes had a baby grand waiting in a sit-
ting room or parlor for piano recitals and sing-alongs.

These pianists, of course, needed sheet music to keep up with
the latest songs. As a result, households across North America
bought a copious amount of sheet music at an astonishing rate.
According to the *New York Times* article, "fully 5,000,000 copies

From 1870 to 1923, Canada issued 25-cent bank notes to thwart the circulation of U.S. quarters

of songs were printed and sold in the month of May [1897]," retailing at 20¢ to 40¢ per copy.

So with that kind of market, what was the American Music Publishers' Association (AMPA)—the trade group in the United States responsible for producing and distributing sheet music—worried about? The *Times* reported that the AMPA's members were complaining that "spurious editions of the latest copyrighted popular songs...[which] sold at 2 to 5 cents per copy" were being printed in Canada and sold throughout the United States...a black-market operation that was costing them as much as 50 percent of their business.

MUSIC PIRATES

Implying that this piracy could drive them out of business before the turn of the century, the AMPA begged postal authorities from both countries to confiscate large batches of sheet music coming from Canada; since the legitimate music publishers were in the United States, these kinds of packages raised suspicion. Whether the tactic stemmed the tide is unclear, but we do know that the music industry somehow survived.

The AMPA still exists as well, protecting the publishers of sheet music from modern-day "pirates." A few decades back, the group went after people who made photocopies of the music; in recent years, the group has pursued lawsuits against Web sites that reveal lyrics and guitar chords of popular songs, calling the sites "no different than stealing"...as the war against music piracy continues into its third century.

* * *

GOING BATTY

Miles Nurse and Jennifer Plomt of Vancouver discovered in early July 2007 that they had some unusual housemates. Eighty bats had taken up residence in the walls of their condo. And if that wasn't bad enough, the couple were barred from removing the bats due to the B.C. Wildlife Act, which prohibits disturbing animals during their mating season. For the bats, that ended in late August, so for two months, the couple dodged the animals, which hung from the ceiling and doorframes...one even got into bed with them.

Reigning home-run king Barry Bonds used Canadian-made maple bats.

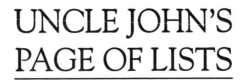

UNCLE JOHN'S PAGE OF LISTS

Some random information from the BRI's trivia files.

3 MOST POPULOUS CANADIAN CITIES
1. Toronto
2. Montreal
3. Vancouver

7 ORIGINAL SCTV CAST MEMBERS
1. John Candy
2. Joe Flaherty
3. Eugene Levy
4. Catherine O'Hara
5. Harold Ramis
6. Andrea Martin
7. Dave Thomas

4 TALLEST STRUCTURES IN CANADA
1. CN Tower (Toronto)
2. Inco Superstack (Sudbury, ON)
3. First Canadian Place (Toronto)
4. Commerce Court West (Toronto)

1 F5 TORNADO RECORDED IN CANADA
1. Elie, Manitoba (June 22, 2007)

6 WILD ROLLER COASTERS
1. Dragon Fire (Ontario)
2. Goliath (Quebec)
3. The Mindbender (Alberta)
4. The Tree Topper (Nova Scotia)
5. The Mighty Canadian Minebuster (Ontario)
6. Le Monstre (Quebec)

2 CANADIANS NAMED AS MLB MVPS
1. Larry Walker (B.C.)
2. Justin Morneau (B.C.)

2 HONORARY DEGREES AWARDED TO MICHAEL J. FOX
1. Doctor of Fine Arts (New York University)
2. Doctor of Laws (University of British Columbia)

4 POSITIONS IN CURLING
1. Skip
2. Vice
3. Second
4. Lead

3 MOST SELECTIVE CANADIAN UNIVERSITIES
1. McGill University (Quebec)
2. University of Toronto (Ontario)
3. Queen's University (Ontario)

Number of bodies of water in Canada called "Long Lake": 203.

SECRETS OF THE POSTAL CODES

It may look like gibberish, but those six letters and numbers divided by a space say a lot about you. (They are not, however, secret codes from the Illuminati… at least, not as far as we know.)

JUST THE FACTS, MA'AM

There was a time when Canada had no postal codes. It was a sparse country and everything was sorted by hand; individual postal workers were skilled at deciphering addresses and, in a split second, tossing the envelope into the right bin.

That started to change by the 1940s as the population of Toronto increased. The city got so big that Canada Post issued 14 postal codes corresponding to its different sections. Still, the codes weren't too hard to remember: they were only one or two digits, from 1 to 15 (excluding 7 and 11, and adding one called "2B"). Instead of just "Toronto, Ontario," you were expected to address it to something like "Toronto 3, Ontario."

The system worked well, but the sorting stations were getting swamped. So in 1968, Canada Post tried out a system with three digits, actually allowing a central location to presort each letter to the individual mail carrier who would deliver it. But as quickly as it began, that program was halted, and Canada Post announced that the entire country was going to get a six-digit, nationwide postal code system instead.

The new system was introduced in Ottawa in 1971. It was gradually rolled out through the rest of the country over the next three years.

NORTH AND SOUTH DECODER

There are potentially 7.2 million possible combinations of those six characters. So what do the individual letters and numbers mean?

• **First character:** It's always a letter, and it designates a wide area of real estate, like a province or territory—for example, S for Saskatchewan or Y for Yukon. But in the two most populous

provinces, the letter designates a region within the province. For example, Quebec is covered by three letters: G for its eastern part, J for the west and north, and H for metro Montreal. Ontario has five: K, L, M, N, and P. (O is skipped because it's too much like 0…zero. So are D, F, I, Q, and U because they resemble other numbers and letters.)

• **Second:** The second character is always a number. It indicates the city. For example, Moose Jaw has the number 6. Small towns may share a number with other small towns, which makes the next character important.

• **Third:** Always a letter. In a city, it tells what part. Moose Jaw has S6H, S6J, and S6K for its southeast, northeast, and western parts of town, respectively. The letter can also designate an entire town: S4A covers all of Estevan, and S4H all of Weyburn.

• **Fourth, fifth, and sixth:** The last three digits—always number, letter, number—indicate a bite-size part of a postal route. Perhaps one side of a street, an apartment or office building, a wall of post office boxes, or even just part of a university or hospital.

CODED HUMOR

Sometimes postal codes make interesting patterns and spell out words, although Post Canada seems to try to avoid the naughty ones (e.g., Alberta has postal codes spelling T1C, T1M, T1S and TIX, but not T1T; Saskatchewan avoids S0B). Some city codes read as if they're grave insults to the communities they represent (e.g., G0B, H1X, H8S, L1E, N1T, P0X…).

* * *

ONE PERSON'S TRASH…

In 2008, workers at a Toronto Goodwill found two paintings in their donations bin. The subject matter: canals in Venice. One employee, Helen Zhuang, noticed something unique about the paintings and set them aside. It's a good thing because they turned out to be original works by 19th-century Peruvian artist Federico Del Campo. No one knows who dropped off the paintings, but in June 2009, they sold at auction for $134,000. (All the money went to Goodwill.)

The arctic fox has the warmest pelt of any cold-weather animal…

SWEET & SAPPY

Take a minute to appreciate one of life's simple pleasures: maple syrup.

• It takes about 40 gallons of sap to make a gallon of maple syrup.

• If you taste the sap of the sugar maple tree, you'll probably be disappointed—it's watery and barely sweet. You have to concentrate the sap to get the syrup we know and love. For many years, syrup makers used to do that by boiling the excess liquid out of sap, but that took a lot of time and fuel. Then, in the 1970s, syrup producers discovered that a filtration process called *reverse osmosis* would remove 80 percent of the water before boiling, dramatically reducing the amount of energy they needed to use.

• Maple syrup predates European settlement in Canada. A First Nations legend says that the Creator first gave the world a maple tree that actually provided syrup straight up, but people ate too much of it, getting fat and lazy. So the Creator's second version of the tree came with the watery sap we have now. That way, people would have to work harder to get the syrup, and trees would produce smaller quantities.

• The Quebec region is the world's largest producer of maple syrup; it gives us about 75 percent of the world's supply. The rest of Canada combined adds another 5 percent.

• The world market for maple syrup has doubled in the last 10 years and is expected to do so again in the next decade.

• "The Maple Syrup Diet," made famous by a variety of Hollywood celebrities, consists of drinking a concoction of water, lemon juice, maple syrup, and cayenne pepper. Drinking 8–12 cups per day is supposed to cause a "cleansing reaction."

• A little terminology: A "sugar maker" is someone who collects maple sap and/or produces syrup. A "sugar bush" is the grove of trees a sugar maker uses. And a "sugar shack" is a vented building where the sap gets boiled into syrup.

• A century ago, sugar makers collected sap by gashing a tree and placing a bucket under it. Modern collection uses *spiles*—metal or

plastic tubing that transports sap directly to the syrup-making facility.

• Those taps don't damage maple trees if done right. Some trees have been tapped every year for decades.

• According to the "Ontario tapping rule," a 40- to 50-year-old tree with a diameter of about 2.5 centimeters (10 inches) can handle one tap. An additional tap can be added for every 12 centimeters (5 inches) in diameter. The idea is to get enough syrup to be useful, but not so much to harm the tree.

• Some other maples, such as the black maple and box elder, are just as good for producing maple syrup as the sugar maple.

• Sap flows best in "sugar weather"—when the temperature at night is still freezing but the days are mild. This is usually in late winter or early spring. Lately, though, climate change has been curtailing the already-short season of sugar weather in many areas.

• "The Jim Kelmun Protocol" was a home-remedy cancer treatment/prevention method promoted in the 1970s in the *Weekly World News*. It involved a patient consuming a mixture of maple syrup and baking soda, with the idea that the maple syrup would somehow invade the cancer cells and then the baking soda would kill them. (Before taking this remedy too seriously, keep in mind that other *Weekly World News* scoops have included the stories of Bat Boy, of postmortem appearances of Elvis, and that several world leaders are really extraterrestrials.)

• "Maple syrup urine disease"—an inability to metabolize amino acids—has nothing to do with real maple syrup. It's just called that because the patient's urine and sweat smell strongly of maple syrup.

• In May 2009, PETA called for a boycott of Canadian maple syrup to protest the killing of baby seals. Not because maple syrup producers have anything to do with seal slaughter, but because Canadian maple syrup is a hot commodity worldwide and it makes the country (which allows seals to be killed) lots of money. PETA figured that if the maple syrup industry's profits tanked because of people protesting the killing of baby seals, the government would have to take notice of their cause. (So far, it hasn't worked.)

THE CANADIAN RANGERS

They're the largest reserve military force in Canada, yet many Canadians don't know they exist. For more than 60 years, the Canadian Rangers have been instrumental in protecting the country's most remote and isolated areas from interlopers.

LONE RANGERS

A red-clad figure exhales a cloud of steam while gazing through binoculars across ice-packed seas, patrolling the northern border for ships that don't belong there. Another person in red searches wild terrain for a lost child or signs of life around a small airplane crash. Who are these hardy men and women?

Nope, not the Mounties. These are the Canadian Rangers, numbering in the thousands, yet barely known of by many Canadians. Combining traditional knowledge with military and lifesaving training, the Rangers are an organization uniquely positioned—by both skills and geography—to contribute to the security and welfare of the country. Their turf? Parts of Canada so remote that the regular Canadian military and law-enforcement teams have trouble getting there.

RANGERS IN THE NIGHT

The Rangers' origins go back to World War II when Canada declared war on Japan after the bombing of Pearl Harbor, Hawaii, in December 1941. It was a period of uncertainty about the country's security; years of the Great Depression had severely weakened Canada's defense capabilities. So you can imagine the frenzy that was triggered six months later when a Japanese submarine attacked Vancouver Island's Estevan Point lighthouse. True, there was no significant damage done—the sub fired 25 or so shells and missed the lighthouse every time—but this was the first hostile act on Canadian soil since the War of 1812. It spooked Canadians enough to demand action from the government.

The government responded first by extinguishing Pacific coast lighthouses, hoping to thwart Japanese submarine attacks but also

England's first overseas colony: Newfoundland.

making it more difficult for legitimate ships to navigate the coast. Next, more wisely, Canada created a new all-volunteer defense unit called the Pacific Coast Militia Rangers (PCMR), who were trained to watch out for enemy ships and aircraft and, in the event of a land invasion, to act as a stopgap until the army showed up. Eventually, PCMR volunteers numbered more than 15,000 men who watched the land and sea, day and night, for any suspicious activities.

NOT-SO-LONE RANGERS

Disbanded after World War II, the PCMR re-emerged in 1947 as the Canadian Rangers. The group's new beat was the remote, coastal region of Canada. Its mission: to provide a quasi-military and police presence in areas not easily supported by the regular Canadian Forces. Some notable features:

• Most of the Rangers are from the Inuit, First Nations, and Métis populations. Their specialized knowledge of the regions they monitor provides expertise to the regular Canadian Forces.

• Rangers are considered members of the Canadian Forces Reserve. They're paid for their work and for training in basic military skills, navigation, search and rescue, communications, and disaster relief.

• Membership is open to men and women over 18. Since there is no compulsory retirement age, some Rangers have served into their 80s.

• The Ranger uniform is as informal as it is distinctive, consisting of an insignia-imprinted red sweatshirt and baseball cap. Their gear includes a World War II–era rifle because the guns are reliable in extreme cold.

• There's also a Junior Canadian Ranger program for people ages 12 to 18. It teaches the traditional ways of making shelters, living off the land, and crafting sleds, boats, and canoes.

WARMING WORLD, CHANGING MISSIONS

In the late 1940s, Rangers monitored radar sites meant to detect encroaching Soviet ships, planes, and missiles. Today, they still report unidentified vessels within Canadian waterways, illegal attempts to enter the country, and the smuggling of drugs or other

When it freezes, Ottawa's Rideau Canal becomes the world's largest skating rink.

contraband. But the era of global warming has shifted some of the Rangers' duties. For example, they now also provide support to remote scientific expeditions and document the effects of climate change in their region.

One unusual mission involves flying the Canadian flag on remote islands and ice fields that the country claims as its own. Here's why that's important: Arctic thawing may open up far-north sea routes and make it easier to extract minerals, fish, and other resources. Other countries might like to establish claims to the area or declare new water passages as international waters. Canada's government, however, does not want to give up areas it considers Canadian. So to support its claims of ownership, the government sends Rangers out on frequent "sovereignty patrols"—some of which cover more than 5,000 kilometers (3,100 miles) in the harsh cold—to show a continuing Canadian presence in regions that might someday be disputed.

RANGER WILL, RANGER HARRY

Honoring the Canadian Rangers in a ceremony in November 2009, Prime Minister Stephen Harper expressed pride in the "great group of people who patrol our vast Arctic territory." He also presented the distinctive red sweatshirts and caps to Prince Charles of Wales, asking him to bestow honorary Ranger membership on Princes William and Harry. "I hope they fit," quipped Charles. To which Harper's wife Laureen responded, "One size fits all."

* * *

YOU'RE BETTER OFF WALKING

Parking is big business in Calgary; in 2009, the city brought in about $21 million from street meters alone. That's probably because, that year, the city's parking authority raised rates for street parking by $1, bringing the price to park on some city streets to a whopping $5 an hour. If you want a monthly space in a private lot, you'll shell out about $465. That makes Calgary the most expensive Canadian city to park in, and the second-most expensive city in all of North America. (New York is first.)

Until the 1960s, 95% of the milk consumed in Canada was delivered door-to-door.

A BERRY GOOD GADGET

*When asked what his IQ was, inventor Mike Lazaridis once replied
that he didn't know because "that's not what Canadians
do." But he ought to brag—this guy invented one
of the world's most-used mobile devices.*

RESEARCH IN MOTION

When he was 12 years old, Mihalis "Mike" Lazaridis won
an award for reading every science book in the Windsor
Public Library. But Mike not only liked to read about science, he
liked to apply it in the real world, too. He built rockets and radios,
and in high school, with his friend Douglas Fregin, he built a
solar-powered water heater that took first place at the Windsor
science fair.

In 1984, Lazaridis was two months away from graduating with
a degree in electrical engineering from the University of Waterloo
in Ontario when General Motors offered him $500,000 to develop
a message-scrolling display system for its factories. To get the job
done, Lazaridis teamed up with Fregin again. They dropped out of
college and formed an electronic and computer science consulting
company called Research In Motion (RIM).

Back in high school, Lazaridis's teacher and mentor, John Mic-
sinszki, had taught him that there was great potential in wireless
computer technology. Lazaridis never forgot the lesson: by 1988,
RIM was the first company in North America working on wireless
data technology. By 1996, RIM had developed pagers that could
send and receive messages, and a wireless device that would
receive and send e-mails from just about anywhere.

NEW AND IMPROVED

The first BlackBerry, introduced in 1998, was a two-way pager
that could also be used for e-mail messages of up to 16,000 charac-
ters. (A branding company came up with the name after someone
observed that the tiny buttons looked like seeds.) Meanwhile,
Lazaridis was working on a way to arm his mobile devices with a
tiny keyboard that users could type on with their thumbs. That
keyboard was integrated into the 1999 BlackBerry, which provided

The population of Dawson, YK, during the Klondike Gold Rush: 40,000...

access to e-mail, wireless Internet, a calendar, memo pad, and calculator.

It wasn't until 2002 that BlackBerry became the familiar "smartphone" that it is today, combining a mobile phone with all the earlier benefits. Users could talk on the phone, check and send e-mail, surf the Internet, and even transmit data back to their home computers. Corporations, executives, and techno-geeks took notice. By 2004, RIM had sold a million BlackBerrys.

PULL OVER, BUDDY!

Improvements made the BlackBerry so user-friendly that it began changing the way business was done. At first, the device was used mainly by stockbrokers, executives, and other professionals, but soon BlackBerrys proved that they were perfect for any mobile workforce. The London, Ontario, police who can't use laptops (because they patrol on motorcycle, foot, and horseback) use BlackBerrys to get instant access to federal and state police data-bases that store available information on suspect warrants, license plates, and driver's licenses.

ALL THUMBS

Some people love the technology that BlackBerrys provide, but others resent the access it gives to their employers after work hours. Love it or hate it, the device is now part of our culture and has even entered modern slang. Users can become so addicted that the device has been nicknamed the "Crackberry." Some addicted users have come down with a repetitive strain injury known as "Black-Berry thumb." For better or worse, BlackBerry thumb is spreading. In 2009, BlackBerrys helped make RIM one of the fastest-growing companies in the world.

* * *

STATISTICS SAY...

• The average Canadian family size is 3.1 people...including 1.2 children.

• 77 percent of Canadians live in cities or towns.

SAUCERS IN THE SKY

The phrase "Klaatu barada nikto!" saved Earth from annihilation by alien robots in the 1951 movie The Day the Earth Stood Still. *A Canadian bureaucrat then took flying saucer warnings to heart and convinced Ottawa to join him on a quest to find alien life.*

WAY, WAY OUT THERE

Flying saucers were just one more thing for shell-shocked, post–World War II societies to be scared of. If they're real, are they here to bring on the end of the world or to save our planet? Will they enslave or free us? Do they want to snack on cheap human protein, or do they just want to mess with our heads and see what happens?

Americans were in the vanguard of the UFO frenzy, with an escalating number of sightings as early as 1947. But it didn't take long for the excitement to spill over the northern border. For that you can credit, in large part, the untiring efforts of a Department of Transport (DOT) radio engineer named Wilbur B. Smith.

Given his job (and the time period), it's understandable why Smith wanted to know how spaceships worked, and he was intrigued by the possibility that they could be powered by tapping Earth's magnetic field. But Smith's interest wasn't just professional curiosity. He claimed to have received "mental messages from space people" since the 1940s. This may sound like grounds for a psychological evaluation today, but back then, Smith probably would've passed it. At the time, there was a keen interest in space exploration and the possibility of life on other planets. UFOs and aliens were showing up in novels, movies, TV shows, comics, and even on lunch boxes. The world was anxiously awaiting evidence that extraterrestrial visitors were among us, and Smith was determined to provide it.

"FLYING SAUCERS EXIST"

In 1950, Smith was just a government employee, but his life was about to change. At a radio engineering conference in Washington, D.C., he stumbled on two books. Both leveled accusations

that the American government was hiding what it knew about the many UFO sightings in the United States. These included a curious incident near Roswell, New Mexico, where witnesses claimed to have seen a UFO crash, scattering scrap metal and alien corpses across the desert. Within minutes, the witnesses said, mysterious government employees had cleared the site and taken all evidence behind the guarded gates of the Roswell Army Air Field.

One of the books, *Behind the Flying Saucers*, was soon discredited as a hoax that a couple of con men had perpetrated on the author. But the other, *The Flying Saucers Are Real*, was not as easily dismissed. In it, retired U.S. Marine Corps Major Donald Keyhole emphatically declared that the U.S. government was indeed hiding evidence of aliens and spacecrafts from the public.

This was so important that commenting on it couldn't wait until Smith got back to Canada. He beelined to the Canadian embassy to outline his theories about how the spacecraft might use magnetism as a power source, and he insisted that the Canadian government look into the matter. On November 21, 1950, he wrote a memo to Canada's controller of telecommunications:

> I made discreet enquiries through the Canadian Embassy staff in Washington who were able to obtain for me the following information:
>
> a. The matter is the most highly classified subject in the United States Government, rating higher even than the H-bomb.
>
> b. Flying saucers exist.
>
> c. Their modus operandi is unknown, but concentrated effort is being made by a small group headed by Doctor Vannevar Bush.
>
> d. The entire matter is considered by the United States authorities to be of tremendous significance.

PROJECT MAGNET

Smith didn't explain why, if the matter was classified "higher than even the H-bomb," U.S. authorities were blabbing about it to a low-level member of Canada's DOT. But no matter—the memo had the desired effect. Smith came back home and quickly sought the support of a higher-up in the Canadian Defence Research Board, Omond Solandt, to begin an official government study into UFOs. The pair dubbed it "Project Magnet" because of Smith's strong belief that magnetic energy was being used to fly the space-

crafts. Under the umbrella of the DOT and sponsored by the Defence Research Board, Project Magnet was set up and ready to go by the end of the year. Its sole purpose: discovering what technology powered UFOs.

After sequestering himself with any and all of the reports and documentation about UFOs that he could get his hands on, Smith released his own report in 1952. It concluded—surprise, surprise—that indeed, UFOs did exist. He asked for a bigger, better research center for his work. So with the full support of the DOT behind it, Project Magnet moved into a new facility on the shores of Ontario's Shirleys Bay that same year. Equipped with high-tech devices to measure everything from radio waves and gamma rays to gravity fluctuations and magnetic fields, Smith hired a staff of four to keep up his research. He also joined a separate UFO research project called "Second Storey," which consisted of a group of scientists and military officers who met regularly to assess whether UFOs were a threat and how the government should respond.

This was Smith's dream come true. He and his staff sat back in their Shirleys Bay digs and waited for the instruments to signal the approach of flying saucers…or any other unexplained phenomenon.

A MATTER OF GRAVITY

Finally, it happened. On August 8, 1954, researchers noticed one of their instruments going nuts. It was the gravimeter, designed to measure subtle differences in the Earth's gravitational pull. Smith and his staff ran outside to scan the skies, brandishing their cameras and detection devices. Unfortunately, low cloud cover made visibility difficult. The other instruments picked up nothing unusual, and the gravimeter quickly settled down to its normal state.

Gravimeters are used for a number of things, most commonly to find oil and other minerals. They're sensitive and susceptible to false alarms from minor earth tremors, floor vibrations, and even loud sounds. Still, it was data, and data needs to be recorded and reported, even if it's potentially faulty. So Smith put a call in to the DOT.

Somehow, the press found out about the unexplained occurrence. Newspapers began speculating about what happened, what it meant, and why the DOT had a secret UFO research lab in the

first place. Unaccustomed to frenzied public reaction and incessant phone calls from the media, the DOT caved, holding firm for just two days before officially shutting down Project Magnet.

E.T., PHONE HOME...PLEASE!

Smith, however, wouldn't be deterred. He got permission from the DOT to keep using the Shirleys Bay facilities on his own time to research his theories on magnetic energy and space travel. The agency agreed and also allowed him to continue using any equipment not needed elsewhere. Watching the skies at his own expense, Smith became more and more involved in the fringe aspects of UFO study. He reportedly even engaged in séances to communicate with aliens on spacecrafts.

Smith remained at Project Magnet's former facility, soldiering on until his death in 1962. Too bad he couldn't hold on for another five years, because that's when UFOs finally got around to visiting Canada.

Turn to page 286 for more UFO stories.

* * *

TRADE CANADA FOR GUADALUPE?

In late 1761, readers of the *London Chronicle* found themselves enmeshed in a running debate as to whether Canada (captured from the French two years earlier) was something worth keeping, or should be traded back to France for something more valuable— like, say, Guadalupe Island in the Caribbean. According to one reader, Guadalupe had already proven itself useful with its great location and bountiful supply of refined sugars. "As to Canada," the *Chronicle* reader wrote, "it is too early to form any judgment about what the amounts of the imports from, and the exports to, that acquisition will be." Other readers grumbled that the British should have taken Louisiana from the French instead of a cold land of dubious value.

After much discussion and debate, though, the argument that finally won the day was that England should hold onto any territories it got its hands on...no matter how much (or little) the territories seemed to be worth.

Former PM Lester Pearson once played semiprofessional baseball.

DOMESTIC DISTURBANCE

Gillette Bonne Bertault: was she a cold-blooded killer, or just a protective mother defending her daughter from a rotten husband?

A NOT-SO-IDEAL HUSBAND

Jacques Bertault believed in early marriages for his four daughters, no matter what they wanted. But it was his arrangement in 1671 with Julien Latouche to marry off 12-year-old Elisabeth "Isabelle" Therese that led to the first hanging of a woman in New France.

Isabelle protested the marriage, and her mother, Gillette, agreed it wasn't a good match. But Jacques prevailed because he thought Latouche had a promising future. So Isabelle reluctantly recited her wedding vows to Julien, age 29, at a small ceremony near the family's home in what's now Trois-Rivières, Quebec.

Julien soon showed himself to be an abusive alcoholic who couldn't keep a job as a farmer. Isabelle went hungry and was often badly beaten. Her parents despaired and felt guilty for arranging the marriage. Jacques tried to reason with Julien, but nothing changed. Although the Bertaults could have sought a way out of Isabelle's marriage through the courts, it was a difficult process in those days, so they chose not to.

MORE SOUP, JULIEN?

In May 1672, Julien agreed to join his in-laws for dinner. Unbeknownst to him, Isabelle and her parents had decided to kill him by poisoning his soup. Although Julien ate…and ate…at the meal, the plan failed.

The next evening, right after sunset, Madame Bertrault confronted Julien in the barn. After she greeted him with a snide comment, the two began a screaming match. At some point during the argument, Gillette grabbed a hoe and struck her hated son-in-law. He screamed for his life, and she called for Isabelle to come and help. Isabelle raced to the barn, but the girl couldn't bear to watch, much less participate in the killing.

Jacques, on the other hand, heard the commotion and came

running to help his wife, who struck Julien again, this time with more force. Then Jacques took the hoe from her and hit his son-in-law himself, while Gillette shrieked, "Kill him! Kill him!" After about an hour—and several more blows—Julien Latouche was dead. Gillette, Jacques, and Isabelle dragged his body to the river and threw it into the water.

HANG WOMAN

In the still of that spring night, Julien Latouche's cries for mercy had traveled across the river and were heard by neighbors. A group of four investigated; when they arrived at the Bertaults' farm, Jacques chased them off...his rifle at the ready. When the men sneaked back later and looked in the barn, they were horrified by what they saw: blood everywhere, bits of ripped clothing, even some teeth. They immediately turned in Monsieur and Madame Bertault to the authorities.

A police investigation followed, and then Jacques, Gillette, and Isabelle were all put on trial for murder. Jacques tried to shift the blame to Gillette and testified that she had nagged him many times to kill Julien. He also exposed Gillette's attempted poisoning the day before the murder. Ultimately, he said he had attacked Julien "in obedience" to his wife. For her part, Gillette admitted that she and her husband had indeed killed their son-in-law, but said they'd done it to protect their daughter. Isabelle backed up that story.

The judges didn't buy it, though. At the trial's end, Jacques, Gillette, and Isabelle were all found guilty and sentenced to death. Later, because of her age and the fact that she was pregnant with Julien's child, Isabelle was spared the death penalty. Instead, she was sentenced to witness her parents' deaths.

On June 9, 1672, Jacques Bertault was strapped spread-eagle to a wooden structure, strangled until he was dead, and then his body was beaten with an iron pipe...just for good measure. (It was the custom of the time.) After that, Gillette was hanged.

The rest of the Bertault family continued on, we assume; history doesn't say much more about them. Isabelle eventually remarried—twice—but apparently learned her lesson. She didn't kill either husband.

P.E.I. could fit in to Lake Ontario...three times.

SHIPBUILDER OF THE PLAINS

If you're traveling on Highway 2 about eight miles south of Moose Jaw, Saskatchewan, slow down and look for the reconditioned remains of Tom Sukanen's landlocked steamship. It's hard to miss. The ship has become a monument to a dream that became an obsession... and eventually swallowed the life of its creator.

LAND-LOCKED SAILOR

It's not clear why a no-nonsense guy like Tom Sukanen would take more than a decade and use his life savings to build an ocean-worthy steamer hundreds of miles away from open water. In fact, he was about as far away from access to the ocean as you can get in Canada: if you draw a circle that touches the inner shores of the Great Lakes, Hudson Bay, and the Pacific Ocean, you'll find that the center's not far from Sukanen's farm near the village of Macrorie, Saskatchewan.

In the early 1900s, neighbors who asked Sukanen why he was building the vessel got a variety of deadpan responses. Two of the most common were (1) he was afraid of rains and a biblical-grade flood (he said this to a neighbor during an extended drought); and (2) he was going to float the ship down the South Saskatchewan River in pieces to Hudson Bay, put it together in the water, and steer it to Finland.

LARGER THAN LIFE

In the early days, the opinion around town was that Sukanen had been driven wacky by a sad, hard, and solitary life. Since then, the consensus has become that he was also a strong, hard-working man who could do more with wood, steel, and mechanics than most people. There are stories of his homemade thresher, wheat puffer, sewing machine, water clock, and a self-customized automobile, complete with a hand crank starter inside the car. Not that these two faces of Sukanen are contradictory—history is full of examples of invention and insanity coming in the same container.

An icy road becomes less slippery the more the temperature drops below freezing.

Here's what we know of his life before he became the ship-builder of the plains: In 1898, at age 20, the Finnish-born Suka-nen joined a flood of about 360,000 Scandinavians migrating to the Americas to escape hard economic conditions in their home countries. He sought shipbuilding work, but jobs were scarce and he ended up, as did many other Scandinavians, on the plains of Minnesota. He took up farming and married. For 12 years, he lived a farmer's life—raising crops, as well as three daughters and one son.

In 1911, a drought hit Sukanen's Minnesota farm hard. He'd heard stories of free land being offered by the government in Saskatchewan, so he decided to investigate. Sukanen left his wife and children at the farm and trudged 600 miles north. There, he found good land and filed for a homestead about seven miles outside the town of Macrorie.

(BROKEN) FAMILY TIES

By 1918, Sukanen, through hard work and fanatical thriftiness, had received full title to his homestead and even saved $9,000 (worth more than $110,000 in today's money). His infrequent letters home to his wife had gone unanswered for years, so he decided to return to Minnesota and retrieve his family.

His trip there—again, on foot—brought only heartbreaking news. His wife had died during a flu epidemic, and his children had been separated and sent to foster homes. Able to locate only his son, Sukanen tried unsuccessfully on two separate occasions to spirit the boy away and sneak him across the Canadian border. Both times, he was caught and his son was returned to his foster home; the second time, Sukanen was threatened with jail if he tried again. He would have to continue on alone at his farm outside Macrorie, so he headed back to Canada. Not long after, Suka-nen began talking about building a steamship and steering it back to Finland.

HELSINKI IN A HANDBASKET

For a long time, his talk was just that. Sukanen continued living the agrarian life of a successful farmer, saving enough to make it through periodic droughts and crop failures. But as a farm depression hit in the late 1920s, crop prices dropped 40 percent, and the

Price of a suit of long underwear 100 years ago: 96¢. Today: about $30.

farmers around him went broke, a new sense of urgency motivated Sukanen, now in his fifties.

He constructed a sturdy rowboat, hauled it 17 miles to the Saskatchewan River, and rowed downstream more than a thousand miles to Hudson Bay...all to get to know the river. From there, he secured work on a freighter that returned him to his native Finland for the first time in 30 years. But before he left home, Sukanen had obtained a set of maps from the Regina Department of Archives to assist him in navigating Canada's waterways. He watched the ship's route carefully, marking his maps with notes. It appeared that the whole trip was a reconnaissance mission: he was laying the groundwork for an eventual return trip to his motherland in a vessel of his own.

While in Finland he had a pleasant time, meeting family and playing Canadian songs on a violin he had made. If getting there was the goal, he'd met it. Surely, a rational person would've just stayed, or gone home to tie up loose ends and come back via commercial transportation. But Sukanen had a different idea. Shortly after he returned to Saskatchewan, large supplies of steel, sheet metal, copper, and steel cable started arriving in the dusty town of Macrorie, addressed to Tom Sukanen.

SWEAT, TEARS, AND HORSE BLOOD

Sukanen worked tirelessly, day and night, with only a few hours' rest at a time. Neighbors watched, astonished and appalled at the amount of time and money he was spending on what looked like a fool's errand. His plans called for the ship to be built in three separate sections: hull, keel, and topside superstructure. The sections would be transported to the South Saskatchewan River, floated downstream on three flat-bottom barges (along the same route Sukanen had scouted in his rowboat), and put together on the shore of Hudson Bay.

But that wouldn't be for a while. There was more than a decade of hand construction to come first. Sukanen made the hull from double-planed strong oak, caulked and sealed with tar. That wasn't strong enough, though. After leaving the Hudson Bay and circling Greenland, his ship would surely collide with ice chunks. So he also covered the 13-meter (43-foot) long, 3-meter (10-foot) deep hull with a protective skin of sheet metal.

The keel—9 meters (30 feet) long and 2.7 meters (9 feet) high—was similarly constructed, but was also covered in galvanized iron laced together with steel wire. Following an old Finnish practice, Sukanen painted the keel in horse blood, believing that it would protect against the corrosive effects of saltwater.

The sleek design of the hull and keel contrasted sharply with the topside cabins. Divided into a wheelhouse in front and living quarters to the rear, the boxy structure looked more like an oversized farm shed than the top of an ocean-going vessel.

Easily spotted by the orange glow of the hot fire he used for shaping steel, Sukanen's solitary construction site attracted curious onlookers (and naysayers) from all over the country. Some of the younger ones even taunted him. But Sukanen, a man of few words, simply pushed on—the clanging of metal drowning out the taunts.

PROGRESS MEASURED IN WINCHES

When Sukanen finished the three pieces, he began to move them toward the river with the idea of installing the mechanical parts and engine after he got them down the river. He and his horses had little difficulty in dragging the cabin superstructure the 27 kilometers (17 miles) to the river. But it was a different story with the hull and the keel, each of which weighed several tons.

He employed a winching system that used willow tree logs and handcrafted wheels and was powered by Sukanen's horses and his own brute strength. Sukanen painstakingly inched both pieces toward the Saskatchewan River, dragging the hull and keel 6 meters (20 feet) at a time before he had to reanchor the winch and do it all over again.

For several months, "the Crazy Finlander," as his neighbors had begun to call him, carried on this way, moving only 20 to 30 meters (66 to 98 feet) a day. He made it 2.4 kilometers (1.5 miles) before the hull and keel got bogged down and he had to stop. When a neighbor with a steam engine not only refused to help but mocked him to his face, Sukanen moved into the ship's cabins, which were resting by the river. He abandoned his farm and focused his attention on building the ship's boiler and engine.

Sadly, the end was near. In 1941, vandals stripped the sheet metal off the ship's hull. Sukanen was crushed, out of money, and losing his sanity. Soon after, his distress and confusion convinced

authorities to commit him to a mental institution in North Battleford. Sukanen went along willingly, saying he wasn't feeling well.

FINISHING TOUCHES

On April 23, 1943, Tom Sukanen died in the hospital at the age of 64. Before that, though, he had related a prophecy of sorts to his sister: he said that after his death, three men would attempt and fail to assemble his ship, but that a fourth would succeed.

Sure enough, three different men tried and failed to raise enough money to put together the ship's pieces, which were weather-beaten but still intact and more or less where Sukanen had left them. Finally came a fourth man—a farmer from Moose Jaw named Laurence "Moon" Mullin. Long interested in the story of Sukanen, Mullin gathered the scattered sections of the ship and evicted both the people who were living in the hull...and their chickens, roosting in the keel. With a diligence not unlike Sukanen's, Mullin eventually assembled the ship with donations and a lot of volunteer labor. He discovered that the hull and keel fit together perfectly and probably would've made a seaworthy vessel had it ever made it as far as the water's edge.

It never did, and probably never will. Instead, the ship was permanently set up eight miles south of Moose Jaw, and in 1977, the nearby Sukanen Ship Pioneer Village and Museum opened for business. Not only does Tom Sukanen's masterpiece rest there, but so does Sukanen. Mullin built a traditional Finnish-style chapel on the site and relocated Sukanen's remains nearby.

Footnote: Sukanen also told his sister that the fourth man "will start the raising of my ship and it will sail across the prairies at speeds unheard of in this day and age, and will disappear in a mighty roar. My ship will go up and I shall rest in peace." That part of the prophecy hasn't come true...yet.

* * *

"I think of doing a [TV] series as very hard work. But then I've talked to coal miners, and that's *really* hard work."
—William Shatner

RUDOLPH THE RED-NOSED CARIBOU?

Reindeer are called caribou in North America, so if Rudolph came from Canada, would that make him a caribou?

THE SAME, ONLY DIFFERENT?

Any zoologist can tell you that reindeer and caribou are the same animal. They're both those stocky deer with the giant antlers that live in cold areas, and they both belong to the same species, *Rangifer tarandus*. The animals are generally called caribou only in North America, though; in most other places, they're referred to as reindeer. But more important than all that is, what would Uncle John say? Probably something like: if television Christmas specials reflect any approximation of reality (and there's no reason to believe otherwise), then yeah…Rudolph is definitely a Canadian caribou.

EXHIBITS ONE, TWO, AND THREE

Take, for instance, the cheesy but classic TV special *Rudolph the Red-Nosed Reindeer*, released in 1964. It turns out that, except for narrator Burl Ives, most of the talking and singing was performed by Canadians. The film was written in the United States and produced in Japan, but the entire sound track was recorded in a studio on Yonge Street in Toronto. And the main characters were voiced by three Canadians:

• Billie Mae Richards provided Rudolph's voice. She went from being a reindeer (or caribou) to playing Tenderheart Bear of the Care Bears, and a number of characters in the 1960s cartoon version of *Spider-Man*.

• Paul Soles voiced Hermey the Misfit Elf who really wanted to be a dentist. Soles has done Shakespeare at the Stratford Festival and cohosted *Take 30* for 17 seasons. He also won a Gemini Award for his role in the Canadian TV miniseries *Terminal City*.

• Larry Mann, a former disk jockey at CHUM in Ontario, was the voice of Yukon Cornelius. Mann also appeared in scores of movies

and TV shows, including *Get Smart*, *The Singing Nun*, *The All-New Scooby and Scrappy-Doo Show*, *Bewitched*, *My Favorite Martian*, *Howdy Doody*, and *Hill Street Blues*.

IS THAT YOUR FINAL ANSWER?

The evidence was mounting in favor of Rudolph being a caribou, but the Canadian Wildlife Service in the Yukon insisted on having the last word. It seems that you've got your wild Rangifer and your domesticated Rangifer. In North America, it's actually only the wild ones that are called "caribou." (We don't know who's domesticating all these reindeer/caribou, but plan to investigate.) And, let's face it—Rudolph is about as wild as Frosty the Snowman's top hat. So in the end, we had to relent: Rudolph is a reindeer after all, just like it says in the song.

Besides, everybody knows that caribou can't fly.

* * *

IN THE BEGINNING, THERE WAS...

When *Corner Gas* premiered in 2004, it revolutionized Canadian television—in 2006, it was the only Canadian-produced show (besides hockey) to break into the top 10. But before Canucks got to know Brent, Wanda, and the rest of the folks from Dog River, they had to suffer through years of bad sitcoms. Remember these?

Snow Job (1983–85): A group of characters tackled life and work at a posh ski lodge in the Laurentian Mountains. Wackiness ensued...or was supposed to. One reviewer wrote, "It's a good thing CTV chose to put a laugh track on the thing, or you wouldn't know where the jokes were."

Check It Out (1985): Don Adams of *Get Smart* fame headed this comedy set in a grocery store, which was produced by the same team that did *Three's Company*. It should've been a hit. It wasn't. *Check It Out* was quickly sunk by its stereotyped characters (Slutty Cashier, Dumb Stockboy, etc.) and lack of humor.

Gullage's (1996–98): This show's premise had potential: Calvin Pope was a driver for Gullage's Taxi service. He lived in St. John's, Newfoundland, with his mom and daughter, next door to his ex-wife. But in the end, more people found *Gullage's* "cute" than funny.

PUTTING THE "PUNK" IN PUNCTUALITY

The bank-robbing Stopwatch Gang—Patrick "Paddy" Mitchell, Stephen Reid, and Lionel Wright—were famous for their politeness, planning, and punctuality. Such nice boys…it's no surprise that they were Canadian.

FIRST, A FENCE

The Stopwatch Gang didn't ask for attention. In fact, the men didn't even come up with their name—it was given to them because one of their best robbery tools was a stopwatch hung around the neck of master planner Stephen Reid. During the 1970s and 1980s, they were credited with about 100 bank robberies (although Paddy Mitchell later swore that he could remember only 47), including one that netted $283,000 in San Diego, a California record. Their methodical effectiveness quickly put them on the FBI's most-wanted list in the United States.

Paddy Mitchell began his life of crime in Ottawa in a low-key manner: fencing goods that other people had taken the risk of stealing. Then in 1974, he got a tip about a shipment of gold bars being transported through the Ottawa airport to the Royal Canadian Mint and decided he'd like to take a more active part in the acquisitions branch of his business.

Mitchell recruited two calm, confident, intelligent, and methodical men to join him in stealing those bars: Stephen Reid was a great planner. Lionel Wright, a great executer. Their goals for the mission were threefold: get the bars, not hurt anybody if possible, and make a clean escape. Reid explained that all of those things were best accomplished by precise timing so that nobody wasted time standing around, wondering what to do next. His ideal for any job was to swoop in, take the goods, and be out the door within 90 seconds. He carried a stopwatch with him to call out the seconds if things started to go off schedule.

LEAVING ON A JET PLANE

The gang knew what they didn't want to do: go into the airport

with guns blazing. They needed a clever plan that required no confrontation with guards at all. A local thief Mitchell knew also worked at the airport, and Mitchell convinced him to help.

On the day of the heist, the inside man left a door open in the airport warehouse, and the trio slipped in. They surprised the guard in front of the secure room where the gold bars were being held, put a hood over his head, and handcuffed him to a steel railing. The clock was ticking, and the men were keenly aware that they had no idea how long it would be before someone stumbled onto the trussed-up guard. They also knew they'd attract attention if they pushed a heavy cart out of the airport terminal. So instead of escaping with the stolen gold, they quickly pasted new address stickers onto the boxes and dropped the packages into Air Canada's cargo area.

Within 90 seconds, the trio sauntered away in different directions. By the time authorities discovered the guard and figured out the gold was missing, the robbers were long gone, and the gold bars had been loaded into an Air Canada plane, heading for Windsor, where the gang would retrieve them.

THE TASTE OF MONEY

There's nothing like an audacious plan and a big score to whet a thief's appetite for more. It was time to try out their 90-second plan on banks. As the key strategist of the operation, Reid worked out every possible detail of the robberies in advance to be prepared for all contingencies, and he rarely robbed a bank without a stopwatch around his neck.

The gang's strategy was this: They burst in and took control of a bank before anybody could do anything stupid. In places that were too close to a police station for comfort, Reid discovered that calling in a bomb threat to an address across town drew most of the cops away and minimized the gang's risk. Reid even scripted out the gang's posture and words carefully so as to instill fear but not cause panic. He discovered that phrases like, "Reach for the sky," "This won't take long, folks," and "Stay where you are and nobody gets hurt" were effective. He also learned quickly to stay on script; one time, he made the mistake of ad-libbing—"Okay folks, imitate your favorite statue!"—and an elderly woman walked over and asked him to repeat what he'd said.

North America's oldest operating lighthouse (est. 1758) is on Sambro Island, NS.

CRIME PAYS, FOR A WHILE

In all, the Stopwatch Gang made off with about $15 million, hitting up to a hundred banks in Canada and the United States. Their biggest day came in 1980 in San Diego. They broke California's record for the single biggest take and came away with $293,000.

According to Paddy Mitchell, the greatest thrill in the world is "being back at the apartment after a successful job and counting the money." And like Wild West outlaws a century before, the Stopwatch Gang holed up in a hideaway in the Arizona mountains. Unlike most hideouts, however, this one was luxurious, built of cedar with wide expanses of glass, and surrounded by an active local community. The trio made friends with the locals. Reid and his girlfriend sometimes even played cards with the local sheriff and his wife. The men explained their long intervals away from home by telling their neighbors that they were concert promoters.

KINDER, GENTLER BAD GUYS

The Stopwatch Gang may have waved around a gun or two in the course of their work, but they certainly weren't trigger-happy. In fact, they never shot anyone. They were known for being matter-of-fact about the task at hand, calm, and usually downright polite. "Our number-one rule was: nobody gets hurt," Paddy Mitchell wrote in June 2000 in a series of articles for the *Ottawa Citizen*.

Eventually, their luck ran out, and all of them were arrested. That didn't stop their exploits, though. In the 1980s, Reid and Wright escaped from separate prisons and together showed up with a phony ambulance to take Mitchell away from his after he faked a heart attack. Another time, Mitchell wiggled to freedom through air-conditioning ducts.

But the men were always caught, and they all ended up back in prison for long stretches. Reid and Mitchell used some of the time to write books about their criminal lives. Reid married Candian poet Susan Musgrave and went straight for a little while but fell of the wagon; in 1999, he went back to prison for robbing a bank in Victoria. Mitchell died of lung cancer in 2007 while serving a 30-year sentence in North Carolina.

I ♥ NEW BRUNSWICK

*From crabs to covered bridges, here are 12 reasons
why you just gotta love New Brunswick.*

1. FIRST-PLACE TIDE. The Bay of Fundy's range between low
and high tide is the biggest in the world: 14 meters (45.5 feet). In
fact, so much water flows in and out of the Bay of Fundy each day
that nearby Nova Scotia actually tilts slightly under the pressure.

2. FORESTS. If you don't like them, you may not like New
Brunswick, since 80 percent of the province is covered with
trees.

3. THEY KNEW THEIR SHIP. In their heyday, New
Brunswick shipbuilders were among history's best. In 1851, the
town of Saint John launched the fastest clipper ship ever built,
the *Marco Polo*. After immediately getting stuck on mudflats for a
couple of weeks, the *Marco Polo* finally started breaking speed
records, including a round-trip between Liverpool and Australia
that took a mere five months, 21 days—the first time this trip was
completed in less than six months.

4. SURPRISE LOBSTER FESTS. In January 2010, residents in
Petit-Rocher, on coastal New Brunswick, received something bet-
ter than manna from heaven—thousands of lobsters washed up on
the beaches after a winter storm. According to Canada's Ministry
of Fisheries and Oceans (and the lobster fishermen who lost part
of their catch), picking up the lobsters on the beach was illegal; by
law, lobsters must be "harvested" in traps by licensed fishermen.
Anyone caught taking the lobsters could be fined $100,000. The
townsfolk didn't care, and even the mayor got in on the act. He
said, "If it's illegal, they are going to have to make a very, very big
prison for us all." (As far as we know, no arrests were made.)

5. MAGNETIC HILL. One area tourist brochure says of New
Brunswick's Magnetic Hill (just outside Moncton): "Take your foot
off the brake and be amazed as your vehicle rolls uphill!" Not
exactly, but it's a great natural optical illusion. The road is such

The word "toque" is a French alteration of *toca*...

that what looks to be downhill is actually slightly uphill, and vice versa. This allows barrels, free-flowing water, or a car in neutral to roll "uphill." Similarly, the magnetism also makes loonies roll out of your pocket and into the city's coffers, since nowadays drivers have to pay a $5 toll per car.

6. MAGNETIC RIVER. And speaking of mysterious uphill phenomena, consider the St. John River, on the Bay of Fundy. At the bay's high tide, the river rises some 7.5 to 12 meters (24 to 39 feet) from its average level, and a tidal wave rolls upstream, temporarily drowning rapids and reversing waterfalls. At least this one isn't an optical illusion. (And you don't have to pay a toll to see it.)

7. AN EXCLUSIVE CLUB MEMBERSHIP. Chaleur Bay in eastern New Brunswick is a member of the "most beautiful bays in the world club," a list that began in Germany in 1997 to highlight...well...the world's most beautiful bays.

8. VOUS C'EST BILINGUE, I SAY BILINGUAL. New Brunswick is comprised of about 65 percent native English speakers and 33 percent French speakers. Still, this province is fair. New Brunswick's constitution designates the province as bilingual, making it the only officially bilingual province in Canada.

9. THE "O'REENA." Fredericton's largest hockey arena is called Willie O'Ree Place, but has been nicknamed the "O'Reena" by locals. In 1958, O'Ree, born and raised in Fredericton, broke color barriers and became the first black player drafted into the National Hockey League.

10. PEAT MOSS. If you buy peat moss for your plants, odds are good that it came from New Brunswick. The Acadian Peninsula is the largest producer of peat moss in Canada, and the second largest producer in the world.

11. THEY HATED BENEDICT ARNOLD AS MUCH AS THE AMERICANS. Benedict Arnold betrayed the United States midway through the Revolutionary War. Before he switched sides in 1779, though, Arnold initiated two attacks against British-controlled Quebec City and one against Montreal. After the war, he settled in Saint John, New Brunswick, where for six years he alien-

ated his new hometown with shady business deals-and petty lawsuits. Finally, a large group of his neighbors burned his effigy on his front lawn, sending him packing to England.

12. GOT YOU COVERED. "Welcome," says the sign. "You are now entering the longest covered bridge in the world: 1,282 feet." That's how Hartland, New Brunswick, marks its 391-meter bridge over the St. John River. Opened on July 4, 1901, the bridge soon attained a tradition of being a place where local couples stopped their carriages and shared a kiss.

* * *

LAND SAKES, WHAT WOULD MARILLA SAY?

What do Quebec, Anne Shirley, and a sordid New York murder have in common? More than you'd think.

1. Sanford White was a famous New York architect who designed (among other things) Montreal's Mount Royal Club and the interior of the Banque de Montréal. In 1906, at Madison Square Gardens, White was shot in the face three times by Henry K. Thaw. The unstable young millionaire—whose mother once claimed his bizarre behavior started "in the womb"—was avenging the middle-aged architect's affair with Evelyn Nesbit, a showgirl (and Thaw's wife) a few years earlier when she was just 16.

2. After Thaw was committed to a mental institution for White's murder, he repeatedly attempted an escape to Montreal. And for awhile, repeatedly failed.

3. After five years of trying, though, Thaw actually made it to Canada, but only as far as Coaticook, Quebec, a few miles over the Vermont border. He was caught there and spent a few days in the Coaticook jail before being returned to the United States.

4. What does any of this have to do with Anne Shirley? During the two dramatic trials for Henry Thaw (in 1907 and 1908), magazines printed many photos of Evelyn Nesbit, the innocent-looking showgirl at the center of the case. In Cavendish, Prince Edward Island, author Lucy Maud Montgomery ripped out a photo of Nesbit and hung it over her writing desk, modeling the young Anne Shirley of Green Gables after the girl in the picture.

In the "Summer of '69," Bryan Adams was nine years old.

LOONY LAWS

Rotting fish, manhandling a mango, and measuring garbage—these are just some of the subjects covered by Canadian jurisprudence.

• Your money or your rights: It's illegal everywhere in Canada to pay for something with just pennies if the total is over 25 cents. You can't pay with only nickels for something over $5, or in all dimes if the cost is more than $10.

• Sure, you can fish in some of the lakes and streams of Canada's national parks, but if your catch rots, you've broken the law.

• Check in your old childhood closet: it's illegal to own any comic book that "exclusively or substantially" depicts crimes — real or fictitious.

• You can't "manhandle" fresh produce in British Columbia until *after* you've paid for it.

• Engaging in a duel is not specifically against the law in Canada. However, challenging someone to a duel, inciting another to challenge someone, or accepting a challenge is definitively breaking the law.

• You'll need a measuring stick to take out the garbage in St. John's, Newfoundland. Your trash must go out in a bag measuring at least 66 by 91 centimeters (26 by 35 inches), with a carrying capacity of 25 to 90 liters (6 to 23 gallons).

• Keep 'em in the backyard where they belong: Toronto forbids any crocodile or alligator, no matter how small or large, to be in private homes.

• See all those glossy ads for Viagra? An old Canadian law says you can be prosecuted if you advertise a product that enhances or improves sexual performance. There's a big loophole, however: you can skirt the law if you can prove that "the public good was served" by the advertisement.

• Got a wound? Don't consider changing your bandage in public or it'll cost you a pretty penny. (Literally—the maximum fine is one cent.)

THE AVRO ARROW

*Most Canadians know that the Avro Arrow was a kind of
high-tech plane, but do you know that it never even got
off the ground? Here's a classic from the BRI archives.*

HERE WE GO AGAIN

When the Soviet Union tested its first nuclear weapon in
1949, just four years after the end of World War II, it
began to seem like the next world war, this time a *nuclear* war,
might be just around the corner. The Soviets were also developing
long-range bombers—could they be planning to attack Europe and
North America?

Canada's response to the new threat was to develop jet fighters
that could intercept and destroy any Soviet bombers before they
could attack their targets. The first such aircraft, a jet fighter
named the Avro CF-100 Canuck, entered service in 1953. By then,
however, the Soviets were already working on a new generation of
jet-powered bombers, which would be able to fly higher and faster
than any they'd built before. The Royal Canadian Air Force felt
they needed a supersonic jet fighter to counter the Soviet threat.

DO IT YOURSELF

Specifically, the RCAF wanted a plane that could fly at Mach 1.5
(one and a half times the speed of sound), climb to 15,240 meters
(50,000 feet) in less than five minutes, and fly for 300 nautical
miles without refueling. It also had to be able to fly day or night in
any kind of weather. There were no planes in existence or even on
the drawing board that could meet those specifications, so in
December 1953, the Canadian government awarded Avro Canada
Ltd., the builder of the Canuck light aircraft, a $27 million con-
tract to begin work on developing just such a plane. When com-
pleted, it would be the fastest fighter plane ever built.

Building the Arrow, as the plane was called, was problematic
from the start. Avro's plan was to design the airframe and then buy
the engines, the weapons systems, and the other major compo-
nents from outside suppliers. But when its first and second choices
for jet engines were both discontinued, Avro decided to design the

engines in-house. The company encountered similar problems with its choices of missile and firing systems. All these setbacks caused the cost of the Arrow to soar, but the RCAF remained committed to the project. While this was happening, the Soviet Union detonated its first hydrogen bomb and rolled out two different kinds of jet-powered bombers. There was no time to waste—in 1955, the Canadian government awarded Avro a $260 million contract to build five test planes, followed by 35 production aircraft.

TURNING POINT

Avro had never built a supersonic aircraft before, yet it managed to design and build one of the world's most sophisticated aircraft in just under four years. It had accomplished a great deal in a very short period of time, but the timing couldn't have been worse: On the very day that the first flyable prototype was rolled out in front of 12,000 spectators in October 1957, the Soviet Union sent *Sputnik*, the world's first artificial Earth satellite, into space. If the Soviets were launching satellites, could nuclear-tipped missiles be very far behind? For a time, defense planners wondered if combat aircraft would become obsolete in the missile age. Meanwhile, the Arrow's cost kept climbing.

Earlier that year, Canada and the United States had formed the North American Air Defense Command (NORAD), and they'd already begun to coordinate their air defense. Cost: $270 million. NORAD's air defense system called for using Bomarc nuclear-tipped antiaircraft missiles, not fighter planes, to intercept enemy bombers. Could Canada afford both missiles *and* fighters?

In September 1958, the Canadian Department of Defence calculated that even after having spent $300 million on the Arrow, another $871 million was needed to finish the program. That was an astronomical amount of money in 1958. So the government decided that rather than build 40 planes as planned, it would commit only to finishing the handful of airplanes currently being constructed. The rest of the program was placed under review.

BLACK FRIDAY

Then, without warning, on the morning of February 20, 1959, the Canadian government announced it was scrapping the Arrow immediately. Avro employees learned of the decision 20 minutes

later, and at 4:00 that afternoon it was announced over the PA system that all 14,525 of them were out of a job. Another 26,000 Canadians working for Avro subcontractors lost their jobs, too.

WHAT'S THE PROBLEM?

The irony of the cancellation was that in spite of all the problems, Avro had managed to produce a very sophisticated aircraft that had performed exceptionally well in flight testing. At the time the program was canceled, the company was only two weeks away from fitting the aircraft with improved jet engines that would likely have made it the fastest fighter plane in the world.

Would the Arrow have broken the world speed record? We'll never know for sure, because shortly after the program was canceled, the Canadian government ordered everything associated with it—aircraft, models, tooling, spare parts, even blueprints and photographs—to be destroyed to prevent the technology from falling into the hands of Soviet spies.

Canadian taxpayers had pumped more than $300 million into the project by then, but had nothing to show for it. Avro closed its doors; Canada lost its edge in defense aviation and never built another fighter plane. Many of Avro's top designers and engineers went abroad to find work: some moved to Europe and worked on the Concorde, and more than 30 went to NASA and played leading roles in the effort to land *American* men on the Moon.

JET SET

All that survives today are a couple of engines, a cockpit, a nose cone, a few diagrams, odd parts, and some historical photos. This near-total destruction of the Arrow, combined with the fact that it was the most advanced fighter of its day, has elevated the plane to mythical status. "Arrow Heads," as fans are known, build replicas, trade conspiracy theories, and dream of what might have been. Wishful thinkers look at the 1959 photo showing the jets lined up outside the factory to be destroyed and note that one plane, RL-202, is not in the picture. Does that mean it's still out there somewhere, waiting to be found? University of Toronto historian Michael Bliss likes to tell his students it's in a barn in Saskatchewan: "It's taken out and flown once a year. By Elvis."

Scottish settlers in Alberta mistook elk for red deer, hence the city of Red Deer, AB.

THE TROPIC OF CANADA

Sunbathing on the balmy beaches of Ellesmere Island? Nunavut may not be so warm now, but you should've seen it back in its heyday.

GLOBAL WARMING, EOCENE STYLE

With its ice-covered ocean, treeless permafrost landscape, and subzero temperatures, the Arctic is probably not on any sun worshipper's list of top vacation spots. But at one time, the far north region was as warm and mild as any modern-day subtropical destination.

To experience that, you'd have to go way back, to the time before humans. And not just before humans settled the polar area, but before humans existed at all. That would be about 55 million years ago, at the beginning of the Eocene epoch, when the planet began warming up dramatically.

THE HEAT IS ON

Dinosaurs had been wiped out about 10 million years earlier, and new mammals and reptiles were moving into North America to fill the void. At the same time, the rising temperatures caused many species to go extinct; the ones that thrived tended to be small and heat-tolerant—early bats, rodents, marsupials, and ungulates (hoofed animals) that were about 60 percent the size of the mammals that had preceded them. And the oceans were bursting with sea life that included early ancestors of sharks and whales.

Unlike today, the temperatures at the equator and the poles weren't that different. Imagine palm trees growing in the northern part of the Yukon and Alaska, and swamp cypress and redwoods on Ellesmere Island, at the northern tip of Nunavut.

HERE'S THE DRILL

To gather evidence of this "prehistoric global warming," as scientists call it, a research team used two icebreakers powerful enough to penetrate ice sheets up to five meters (16.4 feet) thick and a drill ship that could reach nearly half a kilometer (0.27 mile) beneath the ocean floor. In 2005, geologists were able to determine the overall climate of the time periods in question by drilling below the seafloor and examining the plant and animal

fossil samples they found. And although the exact reasons for this natural greenhouse effect are still being debated, all evidence shows that it came about relatively quickly in geological time—less than 100,000 years.

The likeliest cause was an apparent buildup of carbon dioxide that may have heated the oceans enough to trigger a mass release of methane from the bottom of the sea, which raised temperatures even faster and higher. The Eocene warm spell lasted up to six million years before the earth slowly started to cool again. The average temperatures at both poles dropped below freezing more or less simultaneously about 45 million years ago.

WHAT'S AHEAD?
The data gathered in 2005 provided evidence about the earth's past—and vital information to help prepare for the future. "The evidence underscores the importance of greenhouse gases as a driver of climate change," observed Brown University geologist Steven Clemens, who analyzed the samples. "If you inject or remove large amounts of carbon in the atmosphere, you get truly global climate change."

Meanwhile, despite current evidence of rapid global warming, don't bother packing your tropical wear for a visit to Ellesmere Island. If it ever becomes that warm again, a lot of current life-forms, including humans, may not be around to see it.

* * *

SCHOOL DAZE
In 1987, *Degrassi Junior High* premiered on the CBC. It was one of the first Canadian TV shows to depict real-life teenagers and teen issues (like drug abuse, teen pregnancy, eating disorders, and racism). The show only lasted two years, but it won multiple Gemini awards and spawned several spin-offs. It also had some famous fans: Director Kevin Smith (of *Clerks* fame) once paid $8,000 to buy all the *Degrassi Junior High* episodes on videotape. He also paid homage to the show in the 1997 film *Chasing Amy*, when Holden (Ben Affleck) asks Banky (Jason Lee) what he wants to do one night. Banky's response: "Order a pizza and watch Degrassi Junior High."

THAT'S AN ICE WINE

Canada might not surpass California's Napa Valley, but the country can produce one wine that Napa will never be able to: ice wine.

ICE IS NICE

When life hands you frozen grapes, make ice wine. That's what Walter Hainle did after an early and unexpected frost hit his vineyard in British Columbia's Okanagan Valley in 1972. Hainle had lived in Germany and had seen *eiswein*, or ice wine, made from grapes that had frozen on the vine. So he picked the fruit and pressed it before it could thaw, yielding 40 liters (10.5 gallons) of ice wine.

Hainle's approach was a relatively new one...as far as history goes. The ancient Romans probably made something like ice wine, but its secrets were forgotten until the 1790s, when growers in Germany lost a lot of grapes to an early, severe winter. The dispirited farmers left the frozen fruit on the vine with the idea of picking it when they needed it to feed their animals later in the winter. But one winemaker decided to try pressing the frozen grapes anyway...and discovered that although the process yielded very little wine, the result was exceptionally sweet and delicious.

When temperatures drop below –8°C (17°F) or so, most of the water in the grape freezes. But sugars and other dissolved solids keep the last drops from freezing. So each grape yields only a little liquid—about 5 percent the amount you'd get if you pressed it unfrozen—but it contains all the grape's flavor and sugar in it. And because they're more concentrated, the taste is richer and sweeter.

THE CANADIAN CROP

The Niagara Peninsula's perfect convergence of good growing conditions for grapes and consistent freezing make it the world's most productive ice wine region. Inniskillin Winery in Niagara-on-the-Lake was a pioneer in Canadian ice wine, winning the 1991 Grand Prix d'Honneur at the prestigious Vinexpo held annually in Bordeaux, France. Since then, other Canadian regions have been challenging Ontario for its premier position, most notably

British Columbia and Nova Scotia. The Nova Scotia Winter Icewine Festival, held every February, features the region's wines and local cuisine.

Meanwhile, Icewine has become big business in Canada. (And by the way, that's "Icewine" with a capital I.) While the rest of the English-speaking world spells it the old-fashioned way—"ice wine"—the one-word name is a registered trademark in Canada. So don't be fooled: if it doesn't call itself "Icewine" and carry the VQA (Vintners' Quality Alliance) logo, it's not Canadian and it would be unpatriotic to drink it.

* * *

THE LAST SPIKE

The Canadian Pacific Railroad's "Last Spike" ceremony was supposed to feature pomp, the governor general, and a silver spike. It didn't quite work out that way. On November 7, 1885, in Craigellachie, British Columbia, railroad financier Donald Smith pounded in the last spike of the Canadian Pacific Railway (CPR), linking eastern and western Canada. The project had ended more than four years late. Still, all were smiling when Smith drove in the last spike. One man, though, and one important prop were missing from the occasion. Canada's governor general, Henry Petty-Fitzmaurice, had arrived months earlier from Ottawa with a ceremonial silver spike. But when he got to B.C., there was a still a 45-kilometer (28-mile) gap between the eastern and western tracks. Disappointed and a little angry, he took his silver spike and went home.

So, on that cold November day, when the railroad finally *was* finished, Petty-Fizmaurice was nowhere to be found and Smith pounded in the spike he was given. It wasn't silver or gold; it was just a standard-issue, iron railroad spike like all the others along the 3,000-mile track. Nonetheless, after the deed was done and the crowd dispersed, a railroad worker pulled out that spike, which had been slightly bent during Smith's efforts, and replace it with an identical (and straighter) one. The CPR cut pieces of the original spike to make jewelry for the wives of the railway's board of directors. Then, in 1985, it donated what was left of it to the Canadian Science and Technology Museum to commemorate the ceremony's 100th anniversary.

BULK SELLERS

*Joe and Ben Weider were two skinny Montreal kids who were
tired of being beaten up by neighborhood bullies. It wasn't
long before they started throwing their weight around.*

TURNING THE TABLES

Joe and Ben Weider were brothers who created a body-
building program that inspired a generation of comic book
readers to send away for a bodybuilding booklet. They founded
Tiger's Milk protein bars, the International Federation of Body-
builders, the Mr. and Ms. Olympia competitions (which brought
us the Terminator himself, Arnold Schwarzenegger), and a stable
of magazines, including *Shape* and *Men's Fitness*. Despite some
legal skirmishes based on the incredible claims for their equipment
and supplements, they became international successes. But their
drive to bulk up the world was inspired by their early years on the
mean streets of Montreal.

As kids, Joe and his little brother Ben were the neighborhood
bullies' punching bags, but they figured there had to be something
they could do to get even. First, they tried calisthenics, but that
didn't do much good. So 17-year-old Joe built a set of homemade
barbells from junked auto parts and started working out. In 1936,
he not only routed the bullies but won the Quebec Weightlifting
Competition, a prestigious event at the time. Seeing these bene-
fits, his younger brother Ben (just 12 years old) wasn't far behind
and started working out himself.

With only $7 to his name, Joe—a seventh-grade dropout—
decided to make some money by sharing his bodybuilding secrets
in a 12-page booklet that he sold to friends and fellow
weightlifters. He discovered there was a larger market too, and in
1938 began publishing a monthly newsletter, selling subscriptions
for $2 a year. Within two years, this grew into a full-fledged maga-
zine called *Your Physique*. It became *Muscle Builder* in 1966 and
Muscle & Fitness in 1980. The magazine continues to publish
under that name to this day.

Montreal's sister city is Hiroshima, Japan.

WORTH THE WEIGHT

Looking for more ways to make money, the brothers started hawking mail-order barbells in *Your Physique*'s pages. After World War II (and a stint in the army for Ben), the two expanded their operation: Joe moved to Southern California and focused on the U.S. side of their business with publishing, equipment, and food supplements. Ben stayed in Montreal, handled distribution, and became the founding president of the International Federation of Bodybuilders (IFBB), a job he held until 2006.

In 1946, the Weiders organized the first Mr. Canada bodybuilding competition, but it was their Mr. Olympia competition, which came almost two decades later, that led to their most lasting legacy. They created Mr. Olympia as a prestigious, well-paying contest. They wanted to legitimize bodybuilding, which—with its emphasis on bulging, oiled bodies in various poses—was generally thought of as a freakish exhibition, as opposed to a "real" strength sport like weightlifting. The goal of Mr. Olympia was to make the strength-training world take bodybuilding seriously, and the first competition took place in 1965.

PUMPING IRON IN THE MAINSTREAM

In 1969, Joe Weider invited a young Austrian bodybuilder named Arnold Schwarzenegger to compete in Mr. Olympia. Schwarzenegger came in second, but he tried again in 1970 and began a string of victories. As he gained more fame, he also gained some interesting endorsement deals with the Weider brothers. For example, comic book readers in the 1970s saw a long-running advertisement of Schwarzenegger lifting a bikini-clad woman and saying (via a comic book speech balloon), "I put 2 full inches on my arms, 3 inches on my chest, and trimmed 4 inches off my waist in just 7 weeks, thanks to the Joe Weider Musclebuilding Course—WHY NOT YOU?" A coupon in the corner invited readers to send away for a "free" (though they had to pay 25¢ for postage and handling) information booklet about the program.

It wasn't until 1977, though, when a documentary film called *Pumping Iron* hit the theaters that bodybuilding really went mainstream. The movie starred the sport's biggest star, Schwarzenegger, and showed his journey through training and competition. Not only did the film prove that the camera loved Schwarzenegger

(it got him a slew of movie offers), but it also gave a new sheen to the sport, making what was once considered freakish body modification part of the cultural norm.

Some of that legitimacy failed to fall on the Weider brothers' business, however. Throughout the 1970s and '80s, they became the target of investigations over "misleading" claims made in advertisements for their supplements. In one case, they claimed that Weider Formula No. 7 would help users gain a pound a day. (It didn't.) Another ad said that one of the Weiders' vitamin pack/supplements built new muscle and was an effective alternative to steroids. The Federal Trade Commission objected, and over the years, the brothers paid multiple fines to settle the complaints.

BIG BEN

Still, in 2006, Joe Weider was awarded the Venice Muscle Beach Hall of Fame's Lifetime Achievement Award, presented by his old protégé—now California governor—Arnold Schwarzenegger. The same year, Ben resigned the presidency of the IFBB and decided to pursue interests outside of bodybuilding. Still living in Montreal, he had become known as a formidable amateur historian of the Napoléon Bonaparte era of European history. Ben's collection of artifacts included one of the famous hats that Napoléon had worn during the invasion of Russia in 1812. He also coauthored several books on the French emperor, speculating in one that Napoléon had been secretly assassinated by a member of his entourage while in exile. (No one ever corroborated that, but many historians now agree that he was probably poisoned.)

During his later life, Ben received multiple honorary degrees and became a member of the Order of Canada and a Knight of the National Order of Quebec. In 2000, he was presented with the French Legion of Honor, the highest award given by the French government and established by Napoléon himself. Ben died in 2008.

* * *

"A lot of funny stuff happens in Canada."

—Samantha Bee, actress and comedian

...because no on will listen to you anyway." —Margaret Atwood

THE PEOPLE'S POET

*Writer Robert W. Service—better known as the "Bard of the Yukon"—
may have been born in Great Britain, but he was Canadian
through and through...at least, his poetry was.*

THE BARD ARRIVES

Young Robert Service arrived in British Columbia in 1894 with dreams of being a cowboy. Instead, he got a job as a clerk with the Canadian Bank of Commerce and headed for Whitehorse, Yukon, to work at a branch there.

Almost immediately, Service fell in love with the rough-and-tumble beauty of Canada's vast north and the grittiness of the miners who had overrun the area during the 1897 Klondike gold rush. He once said, "The only society I like is that which is rough and tough—and the tougher the better. That's where you get down to bedrock and meet human people."

Those "human people" became part of Service's language. He'd always fiddled with words, but in the Yukon, he became a poet, crafting piece after piece about the characters he met and the world they lived in: barmaids, barmen, drinkers, prospectors—they all showed up in Service's poems.

BIG BREAK

It didn't take long for the literary world to notice him. In 1907, a New York publishing company accepted a collection of his poems, published them, and made Service rich. That was just the beginning. Unlike most poets, Service found great success during his lifetime, publishing more than 1,000 poems. Over the years, he expanded his subjects to include Alaska, South Africa, and World War I, where he served as an ambulance driver. Eventually, he moved to France, where he died in 1958. But no matter where else he went or what other people he wrote about, Service is still best known for his witty prose and his clever take on the Yukon...a fact that earned him his best-known nickname: Bard of the Yukon.

For a look at Service's poetic prowess, consider the piece on the next page...inspired by a celebration at one of his favorite Yukon saloons.

Q: What is Joan O'Malley's claim to fame? A: She sewed the first Canadian flag.

"THE SHOOTING OF DAN McGREW"

Robert W. Service, "Bard of the Yukon," had a knack for capturing the lawless, Wild West aftermath of the Yukon gold rush. Below is one of his most famous poems, a classic published in 1907. (P.S. The poem is about a mysterious stranger who arrives in a Yukon saloon and clearly has a past with both Dan McGrew and the barmaid Lou.)

A bunch of the boys were
 whooping it up in the
Malamute saloon;
The kid that handles the music-
 box was hitting a jag-time tune;
Back of the bar, in a solo game,
 sat Dangerous Dan McGrew,
And watching his luck was his
 light-o'-love, the lady that's
known as Lou.

When out of the night, which was
 fifty below, and into the din and
the glare,
There stumbled a miner fresh
 from the creeks, dog-dirty, and
loaded for bear.
He looked like a man with a foot
 in the grave and scarcely the
strength of a louse,
Yet he tilted a poke of dust on the
 bar, and he called for drinks for
the house.
There was none could place the
 stranger's face, though we
searched ourselves for a clue;
But we drank his health, and the
 last to drink was Dangerous
Dan McGrew.

There's men that somehow just
 grip your eyes, and hold them
hard like a spell;
And such was he, and he looked
 to me like a man who had lived
in hell;
With a face most hair, and the
 dreary stare of a dog whose day
is done,
As he watered the green stuff in
 his glass, and the drops fell one
by one.
Then I got to figgering who he
 was, and wondering what he'd
do,
And I turned my head—and there
 watching him was the lady
that's known as Lou.

His eyes went rubbering round the
 room, and he seemed in a kind
of daze,
Till at last that old piano fell in
 the way of his wandering gaze.
The rag-time kid was having a
 drink; there was no one else on
the stool,
So the stranger stumbles across
 the room, and flops down there

The Toronto Maple Leafs were originally called the "Toronto St. Patricks."

like a fool.
In a buckskin shirt that was
glazed with dirt he sat, and I
saw him sway;
Then he clutched the keys with
his talon hands—my God! but
that man could play.

Were you ever out in the Great
Alone, when the moon was
awful clear,
And the icy mountains hemmed
you in with a silence you most
could hear;
With only the howl of a timber
wolf, and you camped there in
the cold,
A half-dead thing in a stark, dead
world, clean mad for the muck
called gold;
While high overhead, green,
yellow and red, the North
Lights swept in bars?—
Then you've a haunch what the
music meant…hunger and
night and the stars.

And hunger not of the belly kind,
that's banished with bacon and
beans,
But the gnawing hunger of lonely
men for a home and all that it
means;
For a fireside far from the cares
that are, four walls and a roof
above;
But oh! so cramful of cosy joy,
and crowned with a woman's
love—
A woman dearer than all the

world, and true as Heaven is
true—
(God! how ghastly she looks
through her rouge,—the lady
that's known as Lou).

Then on a sudden the music
changed, so soft that you scarce
could hear;
But you felt that your life had
been looted clean of all that it
once held dear;
That someone had stolen the
woman you loved; that her love
was a devil's lie;
That your guts were gone, and
the best for you was to crawl
away and die.
'Twas the crowning cry of a
heart's despair, and it thrilled
you through and through—
"I guess I'll make it a spread
misère," said Dangerous Dan
McGrew.

The music almost died away…
then it burst like a pent-up
flood;
And it seemed to say, "Repay,
repay," and my eyes were blind
with blood.
The thought came back of an
ancient wrong, and it stung like
a frozen lash,
And the lust awoke to kill, to
kill…then the music stopped
with a crash,
And the stranger turned, and his
eyes they burned in a most
peculiar way;

Last time a Canadian man won the Boston Marathon: 1977 (Jerome Drayton).

In a buckskin shirt that was
glazed with dirt he sat, and I
saw him sway;
Then his lips went in a kind of
grin, and he spoke, and his
voice was calm,
And "Boys," says he, "you don't
know me, and none of you care
a damn;
But I want to state, and my words
are straight, and I'll bet my
poke they're true,
That one of you is a hound of
hell…and that one is Dan
McGrew."

Then I ducked my head, and the
lights went out, and two guns
blazed in the dark,
And a woman screamed, and the
lights went up, and two men
lay stiff and stark.
Pitched on his head, and pumped
full of lead, was Dangerous Dan
McGrew,
While the man from the creeks
lay clutched to the breast of the
lady that's known as Lou.

These are the simple facts of the
case, and I guess I ought to
know.
They say the stranger was crazed
with "hooch," and I'm not
denying it's so.
I'm not so wise as the lawyer
guys, but strictly between us
two—
The woman that kissed him—and
pinched his poke—was the lady
that's known as Lou.

* * *

ADD VICE TO THE LOVED LORNES

You may have noticed that Canada has many more men named
Lorne than any other place in the world. That may be thanks to
John Campbell, Marquess of Lorne, who was appointed Governor
General of Canada in 1878. Married to Queen Victoria's fourth
daughter, Princess Louise, the Marquess impressed residents when
he and his royal wife tried to do Canadian things: ice skating,
tobogganing, fishing, visiting First Nations, that sort of thing. Both
he and Louise were artists: he painted and wrote poetry, and she
was a sculptor. But the marriage was not a satisfying one—he was
rumored to have what, back then, were called "vices" (i.e., gay
relationships). Still, the dashing young couple presented the image
of a loving pair in public, and the Marquess inspired many Canadi-
an parents to name their sons Lorne. By the way, what or where is
"Lorne"? It's a now-defunct district in western Scotland.

Nelson Mandela and the 14th Dalai Lama are both honorary Canadian citizens.

CELEBRITY 101

Get to know your Canadian celebrities.

• Ten-year-old Jim Carrey sent his resume to *The Carol Burnett Show,* hoping to land a job. (He didn't get one.)

• In 2003, singer Avril Lavigne got her very own computer virus. The "Avril virus" was so-named because it included photo attachments of Lavigne and opened a new browser that went to her official Web site. It also disabled the infected computer's antivirus software and hacked the user's passwords.

• Michael Cera's first acting role: a TV commercial for Tim Hortons...but he wasn't paid for it.

• When they decided to move from Ireland to Canada in 1912, Shania Twain's great-grandparents tried to buy tickets for the maiden voyage of the Titanic. Fortunately, they were too late, and the ship's third-class section (all they could afford) was already sold out.

• Mike Myer's had the idea for Wayne Campbell (from *Wayne's World*) for a long time. He first invented the character when he was 11 years old.

• Don't call Pamela Anderson dumb—she's written one novel (*Star Struck,* 2005) and co-written another (*Star,* 2004).

• Kiefer Sutherland was born in London...England; his actor parents were working there. After his parents divorced, he moved to California with his mother and sister. Sutherland didn't actually live in Canada until he was 10.

• In 1994, having just arrived from Toronto, 20-year-old Alanis Morissette was attacked on a street in Los Angeles. The muggers took her money, but left her bag. In it were a few lyrics for songs that ended up on her 1995 album *Jagged Little Pill.* She also wrote new songs for the album that were inspired by the attack. That album made Morissette famous, ultimately selling more than 33 million copies worldwide and becoming one of the most commercially successful records of all time.

The Miss Canada pageant was cancelled in 1992 after it was deemed degrading to women.

OLYMPIC HIGHLIGHTS: MONTREAL

Canada has hosted three Olympics. Here are some of the highlights, lowlights and even "relights" from the competitions. First up: Montreal, in 1976.

• Instead of carrying the Olympic flame across the ocean for the 1976 Montreal Summer Games, organizers "transmitted" it from Athens via satellite. An electronic signal generated by the flame's energy triggered an electronic fire starter in Ottawa that lit the torch on this continent.

• To the shock and dismay of spectators, a heavy rainstorm doused the Olympic flame along the running route from Ottawa to Montreal. Viewers were even more shocked when an overly helpful Olympic official whipped out his Bic lighter and relit it. After quick consultation, some other officials immediately doused the flame again, and relit it with what they said was the official backup flame, part of the original that they carried in a support van.

• Canada won no gold medals, the first time in Summer Olympics history that the host country failed to do that. However, Canadian team members did win five silver medals and six bronze, placing them 27th in the overall medal count that year.

• Taro Aso—elected prime minister of Japan in 2008—was a member of the 1976 Japanese shooting team. The team won no medals in Montreal. (Aso was also voted out of office after only one year.)

• Montreal included women competing in Olympic rowing, handball, and basketball for the first time.

• Romanian gymnast Nadia Comaneci, 14 years old, won three gold medals after scoring seven perfect 10.00s. But since Olympic officials hadn't anticipated perfection, the scoreboard had room for only the first three digits, giving the first impression that she had scored a shockingly low 1.00.

Until 1947, Newfoundlanders drove on the left side of the road.

- Fearing that he'd be disqualified from competing on the horse and rings, Japanese gymnast Shun Fujimoto hid the fact that he'd broken his knee during the floor exercise from everyone…including his coach. Fujimoto's triple somersault dismount from the rings had to be excruciating, but he managed to hide the pain and stay on his feet. He scored a 9.7, pushing his team on to victory, before collapsing into the arms of his coach. An Olympic physician observed, "How he managed to do somersaults and twists and land without collapsing in screams is beyond my comprehension."

- Shirley Babashoff, an American competitor, accused the East German women's swimming team of using anabolic steroids—citing their big muscles and low voices. The East German coach famously responded with sarcasm, saying, "They came to swim, not to sing." (It's since been proven that the team *was* using steriods after all.)

- One female competitor was exempted from having to take a gender test: Princess Anne, part of England's equestrian team.

- Russian competitor Boris Onishchenko was caught cheating during the fencing part of the modern pentathlon. His sword had been rigged to register a touch even when he missed. He was disqualified.

- Although Montreal's mayor boldly predicted that "the Olympics can no more have a deficit than a man can have a baby," the city proved him wrong. Montreal suffered crushing financial debt that took 30 years to pay off.

- Thirty countries boycotted the Montreal Olympics. Twenty-eight were African nations protesting the presence of the New Zealand rugby team, which had toured apartheid South Africa earlier that year. The other two were bitter enemies—the Republic of China (Taiwan) and the People's Republic of China. Neither competed because both were offended that the other was invited.

For highlights of the Calgary Winter Olympics, turn to page 356.
For Vancouver, check out page 437.

Reindeer can't live at the North Pole—it's too cold.

I ♥ NOVA SCOTIA

If you're a fan of blueberries and bluenoses, you already know what we're talking about. For everyone else, here are a dozen good reasons to love Nova Scotia.

1. NEW SCOTLAND. Nova Scotia (i.e., "New Scotland") lives up to its name. In the 2001 census, 31.9 percent of the population identified its ethnic group as Scottish. However, English was close behind (31.8 percent).

2. A BAD NICKNAME. Nova Scotians have been called "bluenoses" since the 18th century. Nobody quite knows why, and most of the theories sound pretty unconvincing. It may have been the name of a local tuber called an Irish bluenose potato, it may have had to do with noses turned blue from the cold, or it might come from fishermen's badly dyed gloves. No matter its origin, the name is still used proudly, including on the *Bluenose*, a famous Nova Scotian schooner that has been featured on postage stamps and the Nova Scotia license plate; its successor, the *Bluenose II*, can be seen docked in Lunenburg.

3. HOLLYWOOD BLUENOSES. Sure, Donald Sutherland and Ruby Keeler left Nova Scotia for Los Angeles, but in the summer, many other stars leave Hollywood for Nova Scotia: Jack Nicholson, Paul Simon, Billy Joel, Roger Moore, James Brolin, Demi Moore, and Alan Arkin have all reportedly owned summer homes there.

4. BOY SCOUTS. Port Morien, Nova Scotia, brags that it was home to the first Boy Scout troop in North America. The troop was founded in 1908, shortly after Robert Baden-Powell published the book *Scouting for Boys*, which inspired boys all over the world to form Scout troops.

5. COMING IN FIRST. Nova Scotia was the first European settlement north of Florida. The French arrived in 1604.

6. UNRIVALED BEAUTY. Alexander Graham Bell had a home

and laboratory in Cape Breton that he alternated with a home and laboratory in Washington, D.C. Bell has been quoted as saying, "I have traveled around the globe. I have seen the Canadian Rockies, the American Rockies, the Andes and the Alps, and the Highlands of Scotland; but for simple beauty, Cape Breton outrivals them all."

7. ELECTRICAL WAVES. Near the town of Annapolis Royal, the first tide-powered power station in North America generates electricity from the high tides of the Bay of Fundy.

8. BLUEBERRY MAN. What better way to honor your region's premier crop than representing it as a large, humanoid creature? Blueberry Man in Oxford is about four meters (13 feet) high—a giant blue ball with legs, arms, and a smiling face.

9. THE COAST. From the fluctuating tides in the Bay of Fundy to historic fishing villages to hiking trails and a hundred sandy beaches, Nova Scotia's coastline is its biggest tourist magnet.

10. HALIGONIANS. That's what people from Halifax are called. (We just like saying it.)

11. JAMBALAYA, GUMBO, DIRTY RICE, ETC. If the French Acadians (a.k.a., the *original* Cajuns) hadn't been kicked out of their homes in a ruthless exportation of about 10,000 people between 1755 and 1763, some of the Cajuns wouldn't have ended up in Louisiana to trade culture and cuisine with the Creoles and create a world-enriching gumbo of music, food, and colorful patois.

12. SEA MONSTERS. There have been hundreds of wild tales about Bay of Fundy sea monsters, including one from 1883 about fishermen finding a creature that stretched 28 meters (92 feet) and had eight partially digested sheep carcasses in it. (It was false.) In 2002, some of the rumors appeared to be confirmed, however, when a giant dead thing, 10 meters (33 feet) long, washed up on the Fundy shore. After much speculation in the news media and on the Internet, though, zoologists identified it as a basking shark.

TEST YOUR HOCKEY IQ

Hockey knows you, but how well do you know it? (Answers on page 452.)

1. Who was the only professional hockey player to have a career that spanned five decades?
a. Bobby Orr
b. Wayne Gretzky
c. Mark Messier
d. Gordie Howe

2. When was women's ice hockey added to the Winter Olympics?
a. 1978
b. 1988
c. 1998
d. It still hasn't happened

3. One brother was a champion center and Hockey Hall of Famer. The other was an equally renowned goalie, also in the Hall of Fame. Who were they?
a. Gordie and Syd Howe
b. Phil and Tony Esposito
c. Allan and Barney Stanley
d. Harry E. and Harry P. Watson

4. What did Gordie Howe get as a signing bonus when he joined the Detroit Red Wings in 1946?
a. A letterman jacket
b. A case of Moosehead lager
c. $25,000
d. Nothing

5. In the first seven Olympic hockey competitions, how many gold medals did Canada win?
a. Seven
b. Six
c. Two
d. None

Chances that a Canadian woman is interested in carolling on Christmas Day: 1 in 4.

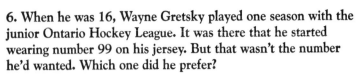

6. When he was 16, Wayne Gretsky played one season with the junior Ontario Hockey League. It was there that he started wearing number 99 on his jersey. But that wasn't the number he'd wanted. Which one did he prefer?

a. 9
b. 10
c. 19
d. 24

7. Before 1886, when the standard rubber puck became official, what was sometimes used in its place?

a. A croquet ball
b. A carved whalebone disk
c. A wooden square
d. A disk with spikes around its rim

8. What is done to the game pucks a few hours before an NHL game?

a. Locked in a safe
b. Put in the freezer
c. Painted
d. Weighed and measured in front of both team captains

9. What did the U.S. hockey team do after failing to win a medal in the 1998 Olympics?

a. Demanded a rematch
b. Went to Disneyland
c. Trashed their Olympic Village room
d. Went sledding in their underwear

10. In 1959, Jacques Plante revolutionized goaltending by being the first to wear what in a professional game?

a. Shin pads
b. Protective cup
c. Face mask
d. Skates

The average Canadian spends about one week each year waiting in line.

MILLION-DOLLAR NAMES, PART I

We've all spent our money with eponymous companies—like Kraft Foods or Tim Hortons. But how much do you know about the Canadians who gave us those brands?

ELIZABETH ARDEN

While working in a New York beauty salon in 1908, Florence Nightingale Graham (1881–1966) became known as "the little Canadian woman with the magic hands." An ambitious nursing school dropout from Woodbridge, Ontario, Graham borrowed "Elizabeth" from a former business partner and "Arden" from the Tennyson poem "Enoch Arden," and began formulating her own cosmetics as Elizabeth Arden. Her namesake company was reporting annual sales of $60 million when she died in 1966 and is still a major cosmetics firm today.

BATA SHOES

When Thomas Bata Jr. (1914–2008) moved his late father's shoe company to Ontario in 1939, he had to smuggle the equipment out of Czechoslovakia as the Nazis were moving in. Using modern assembly-line technology and a blitzkrieg of aggressive marketing, Bata created a shoe empire that now includes 33 factories, 5,000 shoe stores, and the Bata Shoe Museum in Toronto. The town of Batawa, Ontario, was once a company-owned commune for its workers and the site of the original Bata shoe factory. Eventually, though, it became too expensive to continue making shoes in Canada, and Bata moved overseas. The town of Batawa was absorbed into Quinte West, but the old factory building still stands.

CUNARD LINE

Halifax-born Samuel Cunard (1787–1865) had a dream: that the schedules of ships crossing the Atlantic would be as predictable as those of freight trains. That may not sound so amazing now, but it

Canada's first electric streetcar system was installed in Windsor, ON, in 1886.

just didn't happen in those days of wind-powered schooners. The idea was greeted with ridicule. That is, until 1833, when the Cunard-sponsored *Royal William* crossed the Atlantic; it was the first ship to sail from England to Canada entirely under steam power. Seven years later, Cunard's company began offering regular steamship service from Liverpool to Halifax, Quebec City, and Boston. The Cunard line had an unparalleled safety record for its first 65 years, with not a life lost…until 1915, when a German submarine sank the *Lusitania*, killing 1,200 people and becoming a major factor in the United States' decision to enter World War I.

FULLER BRUSH

"Fuller" wasn't a description of the bristles, but the last name of the company's founder, Alfred Carl Fuller (1885–1973). A self-described country bumpkin, Fuller grew up on a farm in Welsford, Nova Scotia. His career started disastrously: as a trolley conductor, he was fired for derailing the car, and his own brother fired him from his job as an express wagon driver because he delivered packages to the wrong people. Fuller didn't do as badly selling brushes door-to-door, though, so he borrowed $75 and started his own brush company. He sold everything from scrubbing brushes to hairbrushes. Eventually, he hired a fleet of traveling salesmen who became so famous they inspired two movies: *The Fuller Brush Man*, with comedian Red Skelton, and *The Fuller Brush Girl*, with Lucille Ball.

BUCKLEY'S MIXTURE

"It Tastes Awful. And It Works." It's hard to believe that would be a winning advertising slogan, but W. K. Buckley made it work, because he wasn't lying…it did taste awful. Buckley was a young pharmacist from Wallace, Nova Scotia, when the worldwide flu epidemic struck Canada in 1918. He mixed up an anti-cough concoction in a butter churn, tossing in ammonium carbonate, potassium bicarbonate, camphor, menthol, Canada balsam extract, pine needle oil, hot chili pepper juice, and a type of red sea algae commonly called Irish moss. It tasted, in Buckley's own assessment, "brisk." Still, it seemed to work. Buckley's Mixture sold for 75¢ per bottle. Long after his death and the sale of the company to a Swiss conglomerate, Buckley's awful concoction—now with a

decongestant added—still sells a reported 6 million bottles a year worldwide.

HARVEY'S

The Harvey's fast-food chain is actually named for an unsuccessful Toronto auto dealer. In 1959, restaurateur Rick Mauran wanted a simple name for his new operation. He considered "Humphrey's," but then ran across the name "Harvey's" in a newspaper ad for John Harvey's auto dealership. Mauran liked the name, especially when he discovered that the dealership was going out of business and that Harvey was willing to sell his "Harvey's" sign for cheap. Mauran bought it and put that sign outside his first restaurant on Yonge Street in Toronto.

MOORES CLOTHING FOR MEN

In 1980, Toronto-based entrepreneur Martin Prosserman was putting together a discount men's clothing chain looking for investors. Dave Moore had been in the men's clothing business for 15 years and thought a discount chain was a good idea. He had a modest amount of money to invest, so he became a minor stockholder in Prosserman's company. As plans moved forward, Prosserman called the investors together to decide a number of things, including what to call the chain. He wanted to give it a "shorter, sharper name" like Sears or Eaton's, which disqualified several possibilities, including "Prosserman's."

Finally, going down the list of investors, someone saw Dave Moore's name and threw it out for consideration. Moore's response: "Sure." Little did he know that, in just 14 years, his namesake chain would open 100 stores, allowing Prosserman to negotiate a $125 million dollar sale. Perhaps if Moore had had an inkling, he would've held onto the investment longer and gotten rich; instead, he cashed out after only two years and became a clothing wholesaler, which sold to retailers...including the chain that bore his name.

For more million-dollar names, turn to page 131.

Of all the provinces, B.C. holds the most Canadian weather records.

WIT & WISDOM:
DR. LAURENCE J. PETER

*Vancouver-born educator and writer Laurence Peter (1919–90) was
famous for his humorous book* The Peter Principle, *which said,
"In a hierarchy, every employee tends to rise to his level of
incompetence." Peter also had these thoughts about business.*

"Work is accomplished by those employees who have not yet reached their level of incompetence."

"Against logic there is no armor like ignorance."

"Bureaucracy defends the status quo long past the time when the quo has lost its status."

"Education is a method whereby one acquires a higher grade of prejudices."

"Democracy is a process by which people are free to choose the man who will get the blame."

"Don't believe in miracles—depend on them."

"Expert: a man who makes 3 correct guesses consecutively."

"Fortune knocks but once, but misfortune has much more patience."

"The man who says he is willing to meet you halfway is usually a poor judge of distance."

"An economist is an expert who will know tomorrow why the things he predicted yesterday didn't happen today."

"There is no stigma attached to recognizing a bad decision in time to install a better one."

"Men now monopolize the upper levels...depriving women of their rightful share of opportunities for incompetence. "

"Facts are stubborn things, but statistics are more pliable."

More Laurence Peter quotes on page 366.

A grave marker for Thomas Thompson, Toronto's first parks commissioner, reads...

CROSSING CANADA

*At 7,821 kilometers (4,860 miles), the Trans-Canada
Highway is the longest national highway in the world.
This list of facts isn't nearly that long.*

• The Trans-Canada Highway often confuses foreign travelers because most of it is not just one route but two (and sometimes even three) semiparallel highways. You could take 10 trips between Victoria and Toronto on the Trans-Canada Highway and not drive exactly the same way twice.

• The Canadian government never designated an "official" starting point for the highway, so the provinces took it upon themselves to choose one...or two. At the highway's western end, "Mile 0" is at the intersection of Douglas Street and Dallas Road in Victoria. At the eastern end, downtown St. John's, Newfoundland, also boasts a "Mile 0" sign.

• Why don't the signs say "Kilometer 0"? Because they were placed when the Trans-Canada Highway opened in 1962—Canada didn't begin the switch to metric until the 1970s.

• A marker near Thunder Bay, Ontario, commemorates the spot where Terry Fox abandoned his cross-country Marathon of Hope.

• Sleeping drivers are perfectly safe and legal on some parts of the Trans-Canada Highway: the ferry rides from Victoria to Vancouver; Wood Islands to Caribou, Nova Scotia; and North Sydney to Channel-Port aux Basques, Newfoundland and Labrador.

• At 1,643 meters (5,390 feet), the highest point on the highway is the Kicking Horse Pass along the border of Alberta and British Columbia. It goes over the continental divide.

• Don't get lost: the Trans-Canada Highway turns into the Autoroute Métropolitaine when it passes through Montreal.

• The highway bypasses one of Canada's most populated areas: Ontario's "Golden Horseshoe," which includes part of Toronto.

BASEBALL'S RISING SONS

As a Japanese-descent team playing against bigger, harder-hitting Canadian ball clubs, Vancouver's Asahi Tigers had to be smarter and better, and in doing so, they won the (sometimes-begrudging) respect of their opponents.

EYE OF THE TIGER

Baseball arrived in North America with British and Irish immigrants during the 19th century, and in 1838, Beachville, Ontario, was the location of the earliest documented game in Canada. But it was the United States that really went crazy for the game, codifying what became the modern rules and spreading baseball around the world. People in Japan were nearly as enthusiastic. Introduced by a visiting American in the 1870s, the game—called *yakyu* over there—spread to schools and universities across the country.

When Japanese settlers first came to western Canada in the late 1800s, they landed mostly in and around Vancouver, where the prejudices and persecutions that often plagued new immigrants were especially pronounced. Japanese immigrants were forbidden by law to vote or run for office. Yet thousands still came, finding employment only in the toughest jobs in the city's mines, lumber mills, and fisheries.

Despite the hard life, these early immigrants and their children were intrigued by Vancouver's burgeoning baseball teams, many of which included Japanese players. And in one story of perseverance and triumph over bigotry in the early days of Canadian history, the Asahi Tigers baseball team managed to become accepted in the city's league competitions and grew to become one of the most revered sports teams in Vancouver. But that would take a while.

LAND OF THE RISING SUNS

The "Nikkei"—as people of Japanese origin were known—ended up in segregated "Japan Towns" in cities throughout British Columbia. Unaccepted by the larger Canadian culture, these enclaves created their own institutions: Japanese-language schools, newspapers, and so on. In the early 20th century, Nikkei baseball clubs became a source of pride in any neighborhood or town that

had enough immigrants to organize a decent team.

In 1914, Harry Miyasaki, who owned a Vancouver dry cleaners, formed an all-Japanese baseball team. He called it the Asahi ("Rising Suns") Tigers. His goal? To play against the local Anglo-Canadian teams, beat them regularly, and win the Terminal City League championship. (Vancouver was nicknamed the "Terminal City" because it was the last stop on the Canadian Pacific Railroad.)

Two dozen applicants showed up for tryouts, including catcher Kunitaro Noguchi (one of the rare men who'd played on a team in Japan) and the two Kitagawa brothers—Mickey and Eddie—who formed the nucleus of the Asahi team.

BRAIN BALL

At first, the Tigers traveled widely, playing any Japanese group that could put together a nine-person roster. Built around speed and defense, the talented ball club earned a formidable reputation. Within seven years, the Vancouver Asahi were the most successful Japanese-Canadian team in the country. They even went overseas to play teams in Japan. But what they really wanted was to break into the white-led Terminal City League that dominated mainstream baseball in Vancouver. And considering their reputation, the Asahi's application to join wouldn't be easy to brush off.

It didn't take long for the team's talent to win fans, including Anglo Canadians. Although they didn't have many power hitters, the Asahi had speed, a wicked defense, and intelligent coaching by Miyasaki, all of which led them to victory. Because of their quickness, the Asahi often bunted and—even when the other team knew it might be coming—managed to move runners from base to base, sometimes scoring from second or third on a bunt. They once famously won a game 3–1 without getting a single hit: bunts, steals, and taking advantage of the other team's errors were enough to pull them through. Their style of play was nicknamed "brain ball" because they had to outthink their opponents, rather than outslug them.

STEALING HOME

Miyasaki's dream of winning the Terminal City League became a reality in 1926. But after that season, something else happened, something even Miyasaki probably never expected: despite the

prejudice against Japanese immigrants that still ran rampant throughout Vancouver, the Asahi were voted the most popular baseball team in the city.

The hard-hustling Tigers took that newfound reputation and ran with it, winning the Terminal League Championship again in 1930, 1932, and 1933. They also hit the road and won titles in other towns across British Columbia. Their success was so astounding that they even established their own farm teams to train young Japanese Canadians from throughout the country to play for them. And they began traveling to tournaments all over the Pacific Northwest, playing teams from the United States and Japan…and winning those games too. But as fast as the Asahi rose to success, the team's demise was more swift.

FOUL BALL

In late 1939, Canada entered World War II and found itself fighting Germany, Italy, and Japan. At first, Japanese Canadians, including Asahi team members, volunteered to serve in the country's armed forces, but they were turned down. Canada didn't trust anyone with Japanese heritage. Then, in 1941, when Japan bombed Pearl Harbor, Hawaii, the Canadian government followed America's panicked lead, fearing that an attack on the mainland was imminent. Although German Canadians and Italian Canadians were largely trusted as loyal citizens, the governments of both Canada and the United States for some reason believed all people of Japanese descent—men, women, even children—were potential saboteurs and traitors. Canada's government immediately closed the country's Japanese-language schools, impounded all boats owned by Japanese Canadians, and set a curfew that forbade them from being out of their homes after dark.

Not long after, the government took things one infamous step further and forced all people of Japanese descent living within 100 miles of the coast to give up their businesses and belongings and move to internment camps. About 22,000 Japanese Canadians were imprisoned in the camps, including the Vancouver Asahis.

AWAY GAMES

Internment ended organized baseball for the Asahi team, but individual players retained a love of the game, and their confine-

ment didn't stop them from playing. Although they were trapped in camps scattered throughout Canada's interior, former players organized competitions within their respective camps and setup games among the different camps. Eventually, the government allowed players and fans to travel from camp to camp so they could slug it out on the ball field and cheer each other on. These games became so popular that an entire league and championship game— the Slocan Valley Championship—emerged during internment.

In 1945, the Canadian government abolished its internment policy, and the camps were shut down. Unfortunately, this didn't create a celebrated Asahi reunion back in Vancouver. Many of the former players moved to different cities in search of work; others left the country that had imprisoned them unjustly and headed back to Japan. And thus, the saga of the Asahi came to an end.

But some people remembered the team. One of the original players joined the Montreal Royals, and others set up local leagues for young players. Then, in 2003, several members of the winning 1930s team traveled to the SkyDome in Toronto to watch the Asahi be inducted into Canada's Baseball Hall of Fame...and to cheer on their team one more time.

* * *

DOOMED FROM THE START?

The SS *Edmund Fitzgerald* sank in 1975 in Lake Superior's Canadian waters during a storm. The entire crew of 29 died, and the disaster has become one of the world's most famous accidents, thanks in part to the Gordon Lightfoot song "The Wreck of the Edmund Fitzgerald." But is it possible that the ship was doomed to its watery grave from the beginning? Maybe. During the ship's 1958 christening ceremony, it took three tries to break the champagne bottle, and defective keel blocks delayed the *Fitzgerald*'s launch for more than half an hour. When the ship was finally broken free, it leaned precariously sideways, slammed into the water, and crashed into a dock, leading some people to speculate in hindsight that there were too many bad omens to have launched the ship at all.

By the way, who was "Edmund Fitzgerald" anyway? In 1958, he was the president and chairman of the board for Northwest Mutual Life Insurance, the company that commissioned the ship.

WEIRD POLITICS

All's fair in love, war, and politics.

T**WEET-LE DUMB**
You wouldn't think that Canada's politicians would need a class in what to discuss on their Twitter pages and what to leave out. But apparently, they do. In 2009, members of the government received schooling in the dos and don'ts of social networking: Do use it to communicate real issues to voters. Don't use it to post messages about the bagel you had for breakfast or to talk trash about your fellow politicians.

IT WASN'T US!
In December 2009, a photo appeared on the Liberal party's Web site that showed Prime Minster Stephen Harper being shot. Since Harper was very much alive, shock and confusion were probably the first reactions of most viewers. On closer inspection, it turned out that an anonymous poster had superimposed Harper's face onto a famous photo of President John F. Kennedy assassin Lee Harvey Oswald being shot in Dallas, Texas, in 1963. And then the poster submitted the doctored photo to a contest on the Web site: the Liberals had asked for images that made fun of Harper (a conservative) for not wanting to attend a climate-change summit in Denmark. For their part, the Liberals claimed embarrassment over the assassination photo and absolved themselves of any blame, issuing a statement that said, "Though we do screen the pictures before posting them, it appears the Lee Harvey Oswald picture slipped through the cracks—it has since been removed. We apologize to those who took offence to the image." (For what it's worth, the Web site also took down an image submitted for the same contest in which Harper was shown with his arm stuck up a cow's behind.)

HEY, TORY...SAY SORRY
In November 2009, Conservative Nova Scotian MP Gerald Keddy referred to unemployed residents of Halifax as "no-good bastards." Keddy apologized, but that wasn't good enough for some. At least one of his colleagues in Parliament called for Keddy's resignation, and Halifax panhandler Rick Smith lamented, "I don't appreciate somebody not knowing me calling me a lazy bum."

WHERE'S STANLEY?

*The Stanley Cup has been through nearly as much rough
and tumble as the players go through to win it.*

THE COVETED CUP

Most famous sports trophies barely get handled, and some team members never even get within an arm's reach of them. But that's not the case with the Stanley Cup. The tradition with hockey's most-prized prize is that each member of the winning team gets the chance to take it home and show it off. It's a nice tradition, but there's just one problem: we're talking about hockey players here. For many of them, their time with the Cup has led to legendary stories of what essentially amounts to trophy abuse. Here are 12 ways the Stanley Cup has been (mis)used over the years.

1. Champagne cup: When it was first presented in 1892 by Lord Stanley, governor general of Canada and a rabid hockey fan, the trophy went to the country's best amateur club. And back then, the Cup really was a cup—a large silver chalice that cost Lord Stanley 10 guinea (about $50). In those days, it was easy to drink from, and many a celebration included some champagne—or something stronger—swigged directly from the Cup.

2. Holder of liquids: Drinking from the Stanley Cup became more difficult when a huge base was welded to the bottom, making it taller and heavier than before. The upgrade was necessary to make room for engraving more of the winners' names. That may have been when champagne was replaced by other liquids. For example, over the years, reports have surfaced that the Stanley Cup has been used as a baptismal font (by Colorado Avalanche defenseman Sylvain Lefebvre) and an accidental child's potty chair (by the young daughter of Detroit Red Wing Kris Draper).

3. Replaceable curiosity: While the Cup is touring or being man-handled by the players, a very good replica (let's call it SC#3) goes on display at the Hockey Hall of Fame in Toronto. This may sound like blasphemy, but not if you know that the official Cup the players get (let's call it SC#2) is also a replica. In 1969, Lord Stanley's

original Cup (SC#1) got too brittle to keep banging around in players' trunks, so it was replaced with the current Cup (SC#2), a fact that wasn't announced for another three years to avoid public outcry. Stanley's original Cup (SC#1) remains on permanent public retirement in the Hockey Hall of Fame. The current official Cup (SC #2) is on the road most of the year. And the official understudy Cup (SC #3) goes on display in its place. That may partly explain the cavalier attitude about the present-day Cup—players know that it already has a replacement ready and waiting.

4. Football: In 1905, one of the winning Ottawa Senators was dared to drop-kick the Stanley Cup into the city's Rideau Canal. Luckily, the player and his companions were too drunk to notice that the canal was frozen over. They figured it out when they heard the booted Cup bouncing and skidding across the ice into the distant darkness. Smart enough not to trust their own judgment or the ice, the men went home, sobered up, and came back the next day to reclaim the battered and newly dented Cup.

5. Flowerpot: At some point in 1907, the Cup was left at a photographer's house when the Montreal Wanderers wandered away without it. A little while later, somebody broke into the photographer's house and stole the Cup, leaving word that he was holding it until a ransom was paid. That demand was ignored. So were successive demands. Eventually, the thief gave up and left the Cup back at the photographer's house. Soon after, the photographer's wife, tired of it hanging around on the mantelpiece, decided to put the Cup to good use and planted some petunias in it. Eventually, the Wanderers came back to get it (and presumably got rid of the flowers).

6. Snowbank ornament: In 1924, a group of Montreal Canadiens got a flat tire on the way to a party. They had stashed the Stanley Cup in their car's trunk, and when they went to change the tire, they prudently sat the Cup on a snowdrift next to the road as they pulled out the jack and spare tire. However, they were less prudent after the job was done. It wasn't until well into the evening, when they were ready to drink champagne from the Cup, that they realized the last time they'd seen it was perched on that snowbank. Making a hasty break from the party, the players found the Cup still sitting in the same spot where they'd left it.

7. Swimming buddy: Penguins like to swim, even when they're from Pittsburgh. Silver, however, doesn't swim so well. In fact, the 35-pound (15.8 kilogram) silver Stanley Cup can be difficult to get out of a swimming pool after it sinks to the bottom and fills with water, as Penguins forward Mario Lemieux discovered when the Cup was tossed into his pool during a victory party in 1992. A year later, Patrick Roy learned the same lesson when some celebrating Canadiens threw it in his pool.

8. Pet dish: At least two players—the Anaheim Ducks' Sean O'Donnell and New York Islanders' Clark Gillies—have allowed the family dog to eat from the Stanley Cup. And New York Ranger Ed Olczyk gave Go For Gin, the 1994 Kentucky Derby winner, his dinner from the Cup as well.

9. Ashtray: Detroit Red Wing Chris Chelios took the Cup to Kid Rock's July 4, 2008, beach party in Malibu, California, and left it there, unattended for a while. In the meantime, clueless partygoers used it as an ashtray.

10. Bedmate: More than one player has taken the Cup to bed, presumably to cuddle with while sleeping. (Detroit Red Wing Steve Yzerman also took a shower with it.)

11. Strip club companion: Although many players just want to take the Cup to a restaurant, their old high school, or the graves of their dead parents, a number of players have also taken the Stanley Cup to see exotic dancers.

12. Protected ward: Nowadays, it's harder, but clearly not impossible, for players to get away with the worst of the cup-denting high jinks. Since Lemieux's 1992 pool incident, the Stanley Cup has usually been accompanied by a representative of the Hockey Hall of Fame whenever it goes home with players.

* * *

HOCKEY BUMPER STICKERS
- My other car is a Zamboni.
- Give blood. Play hockey.
- My goal is to deny yours.

The first Social Insurance Number was issued in 1964.

UNCLE JOHN'S PAGE OF LISTS

More random bits from the BRI's bottomless trivia files.

5 WAYS IN WHICH CANADA RANKS #1 WORLDWIDE
1. Fruit juice consumption
2. Uranium production
3. Average house size
4. Immigrants granted citizenship
5. Mushroom exports to the U.S.

7 "GREATEST CANADIANS" (PER THE CBC)
1. Tommy Douglas
2. Terry Fox
3. Pierre Trudeau
4. Frederick Banting
5. David Suzuki
6. Lester Pearson
7. Don Cherry

5 CANADIAN CHARACTERS ON AMERICAN TV
1. Terrance and Phillip (*South Park*)
2. Robin Scherbatsky (*How I Met Your Mother*)
3. Sheriff Bullock (*Deadwood*)
4. Eddie LeBec (*Cheers*)
5. Dudley Do Right (*The Rocky and Bullwinkle Show*)

5 DEFUNCT NHL TEAMS
1. Hamilton Tigers
2. Montreal Maroons
3. Montreal Wanderers
4. Quebec Bulldogs
5. The original Ottawa Senators

3 LACROSSE TRICK SHOTS
1. Around the World
2. The Back Breaker
3. The Kamikaze

5 WAYS IN WHICH CANADA RANKS LAST WORLDWIDE
1. Refugee population
2. Birth rate
3. Smokers
4. Length of prison terms
5. Population density

4 CANADIAN ACTS IN THE ROCK AND ROLL HALL OF FAME
1. Leonard Cohen
2. Neil Young
3. Joni Mitchell
4. The Band

18th-century French colonists used playing cards as currency.

ELSIE MacGILL

Sometimes it takes a hurricane to shatter glass ceilings.

TAKING OFF

Elsie MacGill is a legend in her field. The first woman to enter engineering school in Canada, she went on to a career in which she racked up a remarkable list of "firsts" for women, including becoming the first woman to oversee the production of fighter planes—World War II's Hawker Hurricane, which earned her the nickname "Queen of the Hurricanes." But behind all the accomplishments was a young woman who wasn't interested in making a fuss—she just wouldn't quit doing what she loved to do.

On March 27, 1905, Elizabeth "Elsie" MacGill was born into an unusual family in Vancouver, British Columbia. Her father was a successful lawyer, and her mother—at a time when most women stayed home to raise children—was the province's first female judge. The MacGills had two homes, one in the city and a vacation cottage outside Vancouver. The cottage and its grounds required a lot of upkeep, and young Elsie was so good at assembling and fixing the machinery that her family called her "Miss Fix-It." She never lost her interest in the way machines worked, and after graduating from high school, she headed off to study engineering at the University of British Columbia.

That didn't last long. The university decided that it wasn't ready to have a female engineering student, and the administrators asked MacGill to leave. Disappointed but determined, she tried again, this time at the University of Toronto. She got into that school's engineering program, but they weren't always prepared for her, either.

A NEAR CRASH AND BURN

MacGill liked to tell the story of being part of the rowdy, previously all-male crowd of engineering students. She said:

> One professor, who was unaware that his large class of men had, for the first time, been invaded by a "lady," began his opening lecture using the common engineering terminology: male and female fittings, flat bastard file, and bastard thread, to name a few of the

least offensive terms. At the first hint of a double meaning the men in the class exploded in laughter and the poor professor was reduced to confusion and blushes...However, none of this was enough to stop me from continuing my education.

After graduating in 1927 (the first woman to graduate from the school with an engineering degree), MacGill got a job at the Austin Automobile Company in Pontiac, Michigan. Among its many products, Austin manufactured airplanes, and MacGill soon was breaking new ground again, this time going for a master's degree in aeronautical engineering at the University of Michigan.

But just before graduation, MacGill contracted polio. Almost overnight, she became paralyzed, and doctors told her she coul not return to school and that she'd never walk again. MacGill refused to accept the diagnosis. She took her final exams in the hospital, graduated as the first female aeronautical engineer in North America, and though it took several years, she learned to walk with the help of two metal canes. Then it was back to school again...this time to the Massachusetts Institute of Technology for her doctorate.

FLYING HIGH

By 1934, MacGill was working as an assistant engineer for a company in Montreal, helping to flight-test aircraft. She'd also published several magazine articles about aviation and women's role in it. At that time, piloting a plane was considered to be a job for men only, but MacGill had always wanted to fly. Lingering disabilities from polio kept her out of the cockpit, but she still found ways of getting up in the air: "I always accompanied the pilots on all test flights—even the dangerous first flight—of any aircraft I worked on. It was the best way to assess the aircraft's performance."

Despite all her accomplishments, MacGill was still looking for her big break, the thing that would launch her career as an aviation engineer. It came in 1938, when she was hired at Canada Car and Foundry (Can Car) to design the Maple Leaf Trainer II, an airplane used to train pilots. With the Maple Leaf II, MacGill broke through yet another glass ceiling—she was the first woman in the world to design a manufactured airplane.

Meanwhile, Great Britain was expecting war with Adolf Hitler's Germany. In 1939, the Royal Air Force (RAF) contracted

Sea otters have the thickest fur of any animal...1.6 to 2.6 million hairs per square cm.

with Can Car to build Hawker Hurricane fighter planes. Dr. Elsie MacGill was put in charge of the project.

ALL HAIL THE QUEEN

The Hawker Hurricane was a single-seat fighter aircraft. It was the first RAF aircraft capable of flying more than 480 kph (300 mph). The Hurricane wasn't as fast or as good a climber as other fighter planes, but it was reliable and held up well in battle. It was the RAF's "go anywhere, do anything" fighter.

The Hurricane was constantly being improved, and part of MacGill's job was to winterize it. She designed de-icing controls and developed skis for the plane so that it could land on ice and in snow. She also supervised the plane's production, overseeing 4,500 workers, many of whom were women.

In 1940, the Hurricane found fame at the Battle of Britain—a campaign that lasted months and was mainly fought between the German Luftwaffe (Hitler's air force) and the British RAF. The Luftwaffe was on the attack, trying to destroy Britain's military defenses, and the Hurricane was the RAF's first line of defense. With these planes, the RAF managed to hold back the Luftwaffe and make the first break in Hitler's advance through Europe, a huge victory for the Brits. The Hurricanes accounted for more downed enemy aircraft than all the other defenses (including all aircraft and ground assaults) combined.

By 1943, MacGill had supervised the building of 1,451 of the planes that helped save Britain. Her work ensured that Canada played a central role in World War II aviation. She was also an inspiration to women who entered the workforce in great numbers during the war. The press took up her story, and MacGill got her most interesting "first" yet: she was the first female chief engineer to have her story told in comics. True Comic Books, a comic publisher at the time, immortalized MacGill in a publication called "The Queen of the Hurricanes."

FIRST IN WAR, FIRST IN PEACE

Canada stopped making Hurricanes in 1943; during the war, engineers had developed other types of planes that could outfly it. And Elsie MacGill found herself in a bit of hot water. She'd started secretly dating one of the men who worked for her, E. J.

Sigmund Freud's brother worked as a furrier in Toronto.

"Bill" Soulsby. Can Car had a strict "no fraternization" policy, and when their bosses found out, MacGill and Soulsby were fired. No matter. They married that year and set up their own aeronautic consulting firm in Toronto.

MacGill still wasn't done being a trailblazer. Over the next few years, she became the first female technical advisor to the United Nations' International Civil Aviation Organization, the first woman to chair a United Nations committee, and the first non-American honored by the American Society of Women Engineers. In the 1960s, MacGill turned her attention to working for women and children, and for her contributions to labor issues like maternity leave and the availability of day-care facilities, she received the Order of Canada in 1971.

Yet, despite all her awards and achievements, MacGill wasn't comfortable in the limelight. "I'm no hero. I was lucky," she once said. "I got a good education. So my mother was a judge; so what? I didn't think it was any more remarkable for a woman being a judge than it was for me to be an engineer." Not everybody agreed that MacGill was unremarkable, though. After she died in 1980, she was posthumously inducted into the Canadian Science and Engineering Hall of Fame and into the Canadian Aviation Hall of Fame.

* * *

CANADA'S BIGGEST OSCAR WINNER

Canada has produced hundreds of talented people, but which of them has won the most Academy Awards? If you guessed screen legend Norma Shearer, you're in the right family. Her older brother, Douglas, won 12 Academy Awards during his career. In the 1920s, Douglas left Montreal to visit Norma in Hollywood and ended up with a job as a camera assistant. When movie studios started experimenting with sound, Douglas became an expert and was appointed head of MGM's sound department, overseeing musicals and developing ways to synchronize sound with pictures. In 1955, he moved into technical research, co-developing MGM's first wide-screen system. Until his retirement in 1968, Shearer won five Best Sound awards (15 nominations), two Best Special Effects awards (six nominations), and five scientific/technical awards.

REAL OR RUMOR?
PART II

On page 8, we started uncovering the truths
about Canadian rumors. Here, we finish it up.

Rumor: Smugglers routinely hide drugs in Canadian vehicles parked in the United States, unknown to their innocent owners, and then unload them across the border.

True? No.

The story: Despite vivid stories that have circulated over the years, border officials consider this to be unlikely...mostly because they believe that no one would be willing to take the risk, effort, and time involved to load a vehicle in a public place, follow it around until its driver decides to head home, keep track of it until it reaches its Canadian destination, and then unload it in the owner's driveway or garage. There are easier ways to smuggle drugs into Canada.

Rumor: A watchman for the British Columbia Telephone Company accidentally roasted himself to death when he stood in front of a microwave to get warm.

True? No.

The story: As long as we live in a time of ever-changing and new technology, we'll have these sorts of rumors. While long-term and continuous exposure to microwaves may cause health issues, there are no known cases where a telephone-company worker has been cooked to death by one.

Rumor: In a Disney documentary filmed in Alberta, the filmmakers pushed lemmings off a cliff, creating the myth that lemmings commit mass suicide.

True? Yes.

The story: Although lemmings aren't even native to Alberta, that's where filmmakers created the lemming segment of *White Wilderness*, a nature documentary from 1958, using animals bought

Q: Which of the Great Lakes supports the most commercial fishing? A: Erie.

from Inuit children. At the end, the film crew herded the furry little actors to their deaths over a cliff and into the water, filming the "mass suicides."

Rumor: An American parent visiting Algonquin Park in Ontario smeared honey on his child's face to get a cute picture of a bear licking her face. Instead, the little girl was badly mauled.

True? No.

The story: Not just Algonquin, but just about every national park in the United States and Canada with bears has been cited as the site of this horrible occurrence. It never happened.

Rumor: In 1969, Bob Dylan, Mick Jagger, and the Beatles secretly got together "in a small town near the original Hudson Bay Colony" and recorded an album under the name the Masked Marauders.

True? No.

The Story: It sounds ridiculous, but in 1969, a prank *Rolling Stone* review of this nonexistent album set off a frenzy of record-buyers trying to find copies. Within a month, the joke got stranger when an unknown group claiming to be the Masked Marauders recorded an album with most of the song titles mentioned in the review... and sold 100,000 copies. Then in 1976, the Canadian group Klaatu benefited from similar confusion when rumors claimed that *they* were really the reunited Beatles. (They weren't.)

Rumor: In 1996, a tornado blew through southern Ontario, destroying a Can-View 4 drive-in theater in Thorold. Ironically, it was showing *Twister* that week.

True? Yes.

The story: Luckily, the tornado hit during the day, so nobody was hurt. But of course, later stories of the event included gross embellishments. One version had the real tornado hitting the theater during a climactic scene in which a movie tornado destroyed a drive-in theater and—until the screen fell down—everybody in the real audience thought it was all just Hollywood special effects.

I ♥ PRINCE EDWARD ISLAND

Islands can become insular and isolated over time, developing their own ways and even their own language. Despite—and because of—that isolation-bred strangeness, we offer 12 reasons that you have to love P.E.I.

1. ITS MAGNETIC HOMETOWN PULL...EVEN ON DEAD PEOPLE. Submitted for your consideration: the strange case of actor Charles Francis Coghlan, a native of P.E.I. who died in Galveston, Texas, in 1899. He was buried there in a lead-lined coffin. Less than a year later, a hurricane struck Galveston, bringing widespread flooding that washed Coghlan's coffin away. Fast-forward to 1908, off the coast of Prince Edward Island. Fishermen pulled a barnacle-encrusted coffin out of the Gulf of Saint Lawrence. Coghlan had hitched a ride home on the Gulf Stream.

2. POTATOES! Prince Edward Island is Canada's own private Idaho. The tiny province is responsible for a third of the country's total potato production.

3. IT'S GOTTEN "CLEVER" WITH ITS THREE COUNTY NAMES. Kings County, Queens County, and Princes County.

4. THEY'VE MILKED THE L. M. MONTGOMERY CASH COW FOR ALL IT'S WORTH. Lucy Maud Montgomery, author of the Anne of Green Gables series hails from P.E.I., and the province is proud of it. You can tour the Green Gables Farmhouse in Cavendish. Nearby, we have Avonlea Village, a 1999 replica of Montgomery's fictional town. There's an Anne of Green Gables Museum in Park Corner, on the homestead that reportedly inspired Montgomery's lesser-known Pat of Silver Bush novels. Scattered around P.E.I. are a number of hotels, barns, woods, stores, and churches that either inspired scenes in the books, were inspired by scenes in the books, or were used as sets in the popular Anne miniseries. (If you want to see the actual "Green Gables" house, however, you'll need to go to the outskirts of Toronto.)

And let's not forget *Anne of Green Gables*, the musical performed every summer since 1965 in Charlottetown, and its unauthorized "sequel," *Anne & Gilbert*, performed in Summerside.

5. BASIN HEAD'S SAND "SINGS." Because of a combination of sand-grain size and shape, silica, and humidity, romantic walks on the Basin Head's beach often take a slightly comedic turn. You may call it "singing," but others describe the noise that feet make on the sand as being like barking, squeaking, crunching, scraping, or that "zweet-zweet" sound people make when dressed in corduroy pants.

6. IT'S TINY AND CUTE. P.E.I. is Canada's smallest province in both population (140,000) and land area (5,684 square kilometers/2,194 square miles).

7. THE CAN BAN. In 1976, P.E.I.'s provincial legislature banned aluminum soft-drink cans as a way of cutting down on trash in landfills; drinks could only be sold in refillable containers. That lasted until May 2008, when the legislature decided to allow cans again. According to them, consumers really wanted to bring back cans, and "this province already has Canada's best recycling system and great cooperation from Islanders in making sure recyclables are dealt with responsibly. That allows Prince Edward Island to handle a greater variety of containers without a negative environmental impact."

8. EXTREME RECYCLING: THE BOTTLE HOUSES.
Three buildings on the coast of Cap-Egmont, including a tavern and chapel, are made out of 25,000 empty bottles. Credit goes to Edouard Arsenault, former keeper of the Cap-Egmont Lighthouse. He lost his job and lighthouse home to automation in 1957. In 1980, he found a new purpose in life, building a six-gabled structure by cementing glass bottles together. By 1984, he had finished three bottle buildings. The bad news is that he wasn't much of an engineer. The railroad ties he used for a foundation didn't last long in the ever-changing P.E.I. weather, and the houses had to be dismantled and completely rebuilt by professional bricklayers between 1992 to 1998.

9. THE WIND ENERGY INSTITUTE OF CANADA.
Located on North Cape at the northernmost tip of P.E.I., WEICan

is on one of the windiest spots in the country, thanks to the Gulf of St. Lawrence that surrounds most of it. The institute researches and tests power-generating wind turbines. Right next door is the North Cape Wind Farm, owned by the province of P.E.I., which generates 10.56 megawatts of power per year, about 18 percent of the island's total usage.

10. A PECULIAR COMBINATION OF NATURAL BEAUTY AND TRAVELER KITSCH. In P.E.I., you will find a giant fiddle, potato, strawberry (with arms, legs, and a face), egg beater, and sunflower mailbox...and a restaurant shaped like a ferryboat.

11. THE INN AT BAY FORTUNE. The century-old building housing the Inn at Bay Fortune on the east coast of P.E.I. has a storied existence. Playwright Elmer Blaney Harris built it around 1910 as a summer home and wrote several plays there, including *Johnny Belinda*. If *Anne of Green Gables* represented the light side of Prince Edward Island, the play and film adaptations of *Johnny Belinda* expressed the dark. Based on a real-life incident in nearby Dingwells Mills, the play was about the rape of a deaf girl, her subsequent pregnancy, rumors, lies, ruined reputations, betrayal, murder, and eventual justice. After Harris died, the home passed on to actress Colleen Dewhurst—who played Candice Bergen's tart-tongued mom in the 1980s TV show *Murphy Brown* and Marilla in *Anne of Green Gables*. She was also George C. Scott's wife (twice). After Dewhurst's death in 1991, the house became the Inn at Bay Fortune, made famous by its chef, Michael Smith, who hosted *The Inn Chef* from its kitchen for the Life Network and the Food Network Canada.

12. THE BIRTHPLACE OF CONFEDERATION. After hosting the Charlottetown Conference in 1864, which began the process of confederating Canada into existence, P.E.I. balked at actually joining. It considered staying a British colony, becoming its own country, or joining the United States as its northernmost state. Finally, Prime Minister John A. Macdonald bribed Prince Edward Island into joining Canada in 1873 by paying off its extensive railroad construction debts.

Dalhousie University in Halifax has its own nuclear reactor.

WHO'S THAT BAND?

*More stories behind the names of some of
Canada's most beloved musical groups.*

STEPPENWOLF: The "Born to Be Wild" group started out as a Toronto blues band called the Sparrow. When they got a recording contract, their producer—noting the popularity of Hermann Hesse novels at the time—suggested Steppenwolf after Hesse's creepily surreal book of the same name.

CHILLIWACK: The Collectors found some minor success as a 1960s psychedelic group, but luckily, the 1970s weren't that far away. Changing the group's name seemed like a good idea, and *Chilliwack*—a Native North American term from the Salish language meaning "going back up"—expressed their optimism about making it big. After several Canadian hits in the 1970s, the band finally had its first success in the United States in 1981 with "My Girl (Gone, Gone, Gone)."

SLOAN: This Halifax band got its name because of a friend's problems at work. Jason Larsen's French-speaking boss started referring to him as "Slow One," but it sounded like "Sloan" to his coworkers, and became his work nickname. Larsen agreed to let his friends Chris Murphy and Andrew Scott use it for their band, as long as they put him on the front of their first album—that's him on the cover of *Peppermint*.

THE POPPY FAMILY: "Which Way You Goin' Billy?" was the musical question posed in 1969 by the Vancouver psychedelic pop group the Poppy Family. Headed by Terry and Susan Jacks and backed up by two unrelated musicians, the oh-so-sixties name mirrored the popular Partridge Family and referenced the flowery source of heroin and opium. The family broke up when Susan left the marriage. Terry had a string of hits, including "Seasons in the Sun," before fading from the music scene; Susan still works in the music biz as a consultant, songwriter, and recording artist.

More bands on page 186.

Bugs Bunny's French-Canadian nemesis is named Blacque Jacque Shellacque.

PHANTOMS OF THE TUNDRA

Everyone loves a good ghost story. Luckily, Canada is a big country with lots of spooky sites and skilled storytellers. So turn out the lights, place a flashlight under your chin, and get ready for some ghastly tales.

WHO: The Blue Nun (and a priest of indeterminate color)

WHERE: St. Francis Xavier University, Nova Scotia

St. Francis Xavier University has its share of stories about disembodied voices and haunted elevators, but no ghost is as famous as the Blue Nun. There was this nun who leaped to her death from the fourth-floor balcony of the school's Gilmora residence hall. Every year, freshmen report a ghostly figure in a glowing blue habit drifting through their dorm rooms. They also claim to hear stifled giggling in the hallways.

Then there's the disgraced priest who haunts the stairwells. Supposedly, he was responsible for the nun's death. (Murder? A forbidden love affair? A secret meeting after Vespers?) So he follows her around, hoping to save her soul from the hellfire torment of living eternally among college freshmen.

WHO: Captain Colin Swayze

WHERE: The Olde Angel Inn, Ontario

The Olde Angel Inn, a popular tavern in Niagara-on-the-Lake, is home to the ghostly remains of British captain Colin Swayze. (You might notice that by coincidence his last name is shared with actor Patrick Swayze, the male star of *Ghost*. That fact is irrelevant to this haunting.) The story goes thusly: Captain Swayze was murdered in the cellar of the Harmonious Couch House Inn while searching for rum during the War of 1812. Or maybe he was bayoneted while making a valiant but hopeless last stand against detestable American soldiers who wanted to steal the rum. Regardless, he died. Then the Coach House burned to the ground, and the Olde Angel was eventually built on the exact same spot.

Most valuable vegetable crop in Canada: the potato.

These days, Swayze is said to wander the inn's halls and cause a ruckus every now and again. Guests hear fifes, drums, bagpipes, and loud partying echoing in the hallways, and sometimes things fall or get moved from their proper places. Apparently, though, Captain Swayze is a friendly ghost…as long as a British flag hangs in front of the inn. (The owner put one up a few years back.)

WHO: Lighthouse keeper John Paul Radelmüller
WHERE: Gibraltar Point Lighthouse, Ontario

No nation is complete without at least one haunted lighthouse, and among Canada's most famous is the Gibraltar Point Lighthouse on the Toronto Islands in Lake Ontario. It's supposedly haunted by the first (or eternal) lighthouse keeper John Paul Radelmüller.

Radelmüller, the story goes, brewed his own beer. On January 2, 1815, he refused to give beer to three drunken soldiers from Fort York in western Toronto, so they lured him to the lighthouse's cellar, killed him, and then hacked his body into pieces. After that, the soldiers buried the pieces of Radelmüller around the lighthouse. The ghost of John Paul Radelmüller has been reported to wander the islands ever since, probably trying to find his pieces and pull himself together. Strange mists, unidentified lights, and the sounds of a body being dragged up the lighthouse stairs are included in accounts from visitors, which are documented on a plaque at the popular tourist attraction.

WHO: A family of tourists, a long-lost bride, and a bellhop
WHERE: Banff Springs Hotel, Alberta

The Banff Springs Hotel opened in 1888 as a railway hotel with fantastic surroundings: the Rocky Mountains, Bow Falls, Mount Rundle, and even a thermal spring. In the years since, those surroundings were almost eclipsed by some even more fantastic occurrences inside the hotel itself.

The current Banff Springs Hotel is not the original structure. In 1926, a fire destroyed a large portion of the hotel, but legend reports some odd architectural finds. Supposedly, when the original hotel burned down, people discovered a previously unknown room that had no doors or windows. Plus, there's room 873, whose door is no longer visible; it was covered to blend in with the rest

of the hallway. The story goes that a family was murdered in the room and their little girl's fingerprints were smudged on a mirror. The fingerprints couldn't be washed off, so the room was closed for good.

This family still roams the hotel, along with myriad specters, including a bride who either tumbled down a staircase or had her dress catch fire, and Sam Macauley, a bellhop who died in 1978. People claim to have seen the bride floating up and down the stairs or dancing in her flaming gown in the hotel's ballroom. And Macauley helps out guests—carrying bags, unlocking doors, and turning on lights when no other hotel employees are around.

Despite these reports, the ghosts at the Banff Springs Hotel might not all be *entirely* supernatural. According to one local historian who looked into hotel records for some corroboration of the tales, there is no evidence that a bride died from burns or that a family was murdered on the grounds. He did find out that an elderly bellhop named Sam McCauley (with a slightly different spelling) once worked at the hotel. But he also uncovered accounts of a former public-relations director who thought ghost stories would be good for business, and a hotel manager who rigged a fishing line to make it look like empty bags were being carried across the lobby by a ghostly presence.

WHAT: A ghost train...we think
WHERE: Former railway between Prince Albert and St. Louis, Saskatchewan

This train's legacy is one of the most consistent examples of paranormal activity in Canada, although no one has ever seen an actual train. A light from an unknown source has often been reported following a dirt path that was once the location of railroad tracks between the cities of Prince Albert and St. Louis. Hundreds of people have claimed to see that light, but no one can give a clear explanation for it. Skeptics credit the glare to headlights from a nearby highway. Advocates suggest it may be the ghost of a conductor or brakeman. One story tells of a drunken railway worker who was decapitated while working on his locomotive. Maybe he now wanders the path in search of his lost head. However, why a man without a head would need a light and why the head isn't looking for the body, instead of vice versa, remain unexplained mysteries.

CIRCUS OF THE SUN

*"We're happiness merchants—giving people the opportunity to dream
like children." —Guy Laliberté, founder of Cirque du Soleil.*

LET THE SUN SHINE IN
We've all heard about it: that dazzling spectacle that com-
bines drama and comedy with pretzel-shaped acrobats.
Cirque du Soleil (French for "Circus of the Sun") is the world's
fastest-growing circus, but this huge entertainment powerhouse
had surprisingly humble beginnings—it was the brainchild of a
young street performer in the village of Baie-Saint-Paul, Quebec.
Here's the skinny on one of the world's greatest shows:

• In the early 1980s, Guy Laliberté, a Quebecois a college drop-
out who ran off to Europe to join the circus, found a new job; he
hooked up with Les Echassiers de Baie-Saint-Paul, a band of street
performers in Quebec. They toured the province, amazing crowds
with their ability to juggle, dance, play music, and eat fire—all
while walking on stilts.

• That job wasn't very lucrative; Laliberté and his colleagues
scraped by on whatever tips they got on the street. In 1984, they
finally got a big break. Quebec City was celebrating the 450th
anniversary of Jacques Cartier's discovery of Canada, and Laliberté
proposed creating a new type of circus for the celebration. Cirque
du Soleil had no animals or variety acts; instead, it featured a
combination of dramatic theater, thrilling acrobatics, and music.

• Things didn't go smoothly at first—the big top fell down on the
first day. Still, the performances were crowd-pleasers, so when the
Cartier celebration ended, Laliberté partnered with a fellow per-
former, Daniel Gauthier, and they took their circus show across
Canada.

• Canadians loved the show, but the partners wondered if there
was even more money in their venture. So in 1987, they decided
to risk all their savings and bring their blue-and-yellow Cirque du
Soleil tents to California. There, the show found stunning finan-
cial success. Today, Cirque du Soleil has 20 shows running concur-
rently all over the world.

Average number of hip replacements performed in Canada in a year: 23,000

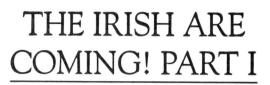

THE IRISH ARE COMING! PART I

In 1866, armed Irishmen marched over the U.S. border into Canada. Their lofty goal: to capture and hold one of the country's major cities, and from there launch an attack on Great Britain to force Irish independence. Here's the story behind one of North America's strangest military conflicts.

THE FENIANS AWAKE

Some ideas are so crazy they just might work. Many more ideas are so crazy that there's almost no chance they'd work. For example, let's say it's 1866 and you're the leader of the Fenian Brotherhood, a group of about 50,000 Irish Americans who want to win the independence of their homeland. What are the chances you'd decide that the best way to free Ireland was to invade Canada? Pretty good, believe it or not.

Founded in 1858 by John O'Mahony as the American arm of the Irish Republican Brotherhood—a military group aimed at ending British rule in Ireland—the Fenians recruited most of their members in Boston and other cities along the northeast U.S. coast. At first, the Fenians were more of a diplomatic organization. Problem was, many in the group weren't interested in negotiating or organizing—they were looking for direct confrontation, by force if necessary. So at a contentious convention in Philadelphia in 1865, O'Mahony lost control of the group when the members elected a man named William Randall Roberts as their chief executive.

Roberts was more confrontational than O'Mahony, but he was skeptical that his group would be able to mount a successful revolution in Ireland. So he hatched a bold plan: invade part of Canada, proclaim the occupied territory a new Irish republic, and use it as leverage to bargain for Ireland's independence from the British.

O'CANADA

From his home in New York City, Roberts met with his new "secretary of war," retired major-general Thomas "Fighting Tom" Sweeny, a one-armed vet of the Mexican-American War and the U.S. Civil War. Sweeny sketched out a multipronged attack for the

invasion: First, a 3,000-man unit from Chicago would cross the Detroit River, move into Windsor, Ontario, and battle northeast to London. Meanwhile, 2,500 men would cross Lake Erie from Cleveland, land at Port Stanley, and head north to attack London from another side. The combined forces would then join a third group from Buffalo, New York—2,500 men who would cross over the Niagara River and capture Hamilton. This combined force would then march 70 kilometers (43 miles) east and take Toronto.

By now, you're probably scratching your head and wondering why the Irish army would take such a long and complicated route to attack Toronto when there were more direct approaches—over Lake Ontario, for example. Wouldn't taking the time to march an army all those extra kilometers, while stopping to attack a series of nonstrategic towns, ruin the element of surprise and give the British army a chance to move in to defend the city? Why, yes it would.

A FEINT HOPE

It turns out that all of the above was meant to be a "feint," a way of diverting most of the British army away from the *real* point of attack…Montreal. Fighting Tom figured that there were at least 28,000 British soldiers and Canadian militia in Ontario and Quebec. He knew he'd never be able to gather enough Fenians to take them on directly, so his only hope was to draw the brunt of the troops to Ontario and then dynamite the railroad bridge over the Ottawa River, making a speedy return impossible. Meanwhile, another Irish force would swoop across the St. Lawrence River with 16,000 men and some ships to take Montreal. And, Sweeny theorized, the disgruntled Frenchmen in that city were bound to rise up against the British once the Irish forces arrived. It was such a good plan, how could it possibly fail?

BLESSINGS FROM BELOW

On February 19, 1866, Roberts received word from Ireland—the invasion plans had been given the green light by the leaders of the Irish Republican Brotherhood. He was also able to set up a meeting with U.S. president Andrew Johnson, who agreed—unofficially and ready to deny it—that the United States would recognize the new Irish republic if the Fenians managed to wrest a portion of Canada from the British.

Make no mistake: President Johnson wasn't on board because of some bond with the Irish. In fact, he never shared his real reasons for encouraging the Fenians with them. It all had to do with money. The British were refusing to pay reparations for their support of the Confederacy during the U.S. Civil War, even though there were treaties requiring that sort of thing. Johnson couldn't officially sanction the Irish invasion, but he could take his own sweet time in responding, giving them a chance to stir up trouble in Canada and give the British a taste of what they'd encouraged in the United States just a few years earlier.

BIG MOUTHS

Meanwhile, O'Mahony, still embittered and scheming after being deposed from Fenian leadership, heard about the plan. He had some supporters left and decided to round up his own army in a move that he hoped would regain him control of the larger group. In April 1866, his force of 1,000 men headed north toward New Brunswick. They were going to seize the island of Campobello; from there, they'd launch attacks on the British in Ireland.

It's hard to keep 1,000 excited men quiet, though. As the soldiers prepared to embark on their top-secret invasion, they couldn't help telling their friends, families, and pub mates. Before they even got on trains headed north, their "secret" was well known by the authorities in both the United States and Canada.

In Campobello, British forces were ready for the invasion, but they never fired a shot because U.S. soldiers stepped in and stopped O'Mahony's men well short of their target. They'd gotten their orders from President Johnson, who'd abruptly switched sides, deciding he could win some British support (and money) by making "a show of stopping the Fenian invasion by persuasion and without force of arms." In the end, the Americans prevailed, and O'Mahony's men were sent packing.

ONWARD, IRISH SOLDIERS!

Believing that O'Mahony's plan had been the rumored invasion of Canada by the Fenians and that it had been successfully quelled, the British let down their guard ever so slightly before the scheduled actual invasion on May 31, 1866.

Still, things didn't work out as planned for the Fenians. The armies that were supposed to divert the British to the east arrived in small numbers. Just 400 men showed up in Cleveland, only to be told that there were no boats to ferry them to Canada. They bunked in a warehouse for the night and, the next day, boarded trains to join the main force in Buffalo. There were only about 1,200 soldiers there, with word that another 4,000 were on the way.

The first wave crossed the Niagara River from Buffalo and captured the ruins of Fort Erie, which was no longer an active fort. They'd been detected en route, though, and their intended target, the railroad depot, had already been cleared of its cars and engines. Still, the Fenians kept going, heading west toward Hamilton, where they met up with 10 British rifle companies, who were no match for the battle-hardened Civil War veterans of the Fenian army. The Irishmen quickly pushed back the young and inexperienced British. The casualties of that battle were 20 British killed, 74 wounded; the Fenians lost 7 and had 17 wounded. It was a minor skirmish, but it was also the first Irish victory over British forces since the War of Austrian Succession's Battle of Fontenoy in 1745. Still, the Fenians had a lot of ground to cover and a lot of British soldiers to defeat before they could control a piece of Canada.

Want to know more?
The fight continues on page 267.

* * *

SNOWBALL EARTH

Scientists working in the Yukon have found some important evidence to support the so-called "snowball Earth" idea, the long-held theory that says millions of years ago, most of Earth's oceans were covered in snow and ice. The geologists discovered rocks in a Yukon mountain that they say date back 716.5 million years... about the time single-celled animals were just starting to evolve. The rocks contain glacial deposits (sand and gravel left behind by ancient glaciers) on top of coral reef deposits. Reefs? Aren't those in the tropics? Yep. Scientists think that, over eons, the snow-covered reef rocks moved from the tropics all the way to Canada as the Earth's tectonic plates shifted and pushed them north.

On October 14, 1979, Wayne Gretzky scored his first NHL goal against the Vancouver Canu

DOLLARS & NONSENSE

With something as important as money, you shouldn't believe the rumors. Except, of course, when they're true.

Rumor: On the first Queen Elizabeth $1 bill, the artist deliberately hid an image of a grinning devil in the queen's hair.
True? No.
The story: In banknotes issued shortly after Queen Elizabeth II was crowned in 1953, some people believed they saw the face of a grinning demon in her wavy hair. After some investigation, it appeared that Canadians were seeing things...though not necessarily through any fault of their own. Psychological tests have shown that humans are so attuned to other people that their minds tend to see "faces" in random patterns—this was probably one of those times. Still, enough people "saw" the grinning devil that the Bank of Canada ordered the highlights in the queen's hair to be darkened, exorcising the demon's face for good.

Rumor: When they were first issued, you could pop out the Toonie's gold-colored center with a hammer.
True? Yes.
The story: For a few months in the mid-1990s, popping out the center of this $2 coin became a national fad. The government wasn't amused—deliberately defacing any currency is against the law in Canada. So the Royal Canadian Mint quickly began attaching the centers more securely. Plus, people couldn't use the altered money and couldn't afford to keep destroying $2 coins, so the fad died out.

Rumor: The $10 bill misquotes the poem "In Flanders Fields."
True? No.
The story: The poem is printed correctly on the $10 bill. It really *does* read "In Flanders fields the poppies blow"...not "grow" as many people think.

Rumor: If you magnify the Parliament building on $2 and $10 bills, you'll see the American flag flying over it.

True? No.

The story: Actually, though, it does sort of look like it. That's because the image is old. The old Canadian flag is what's shown, but to be fair, it's not that hard to mistake the Union Jack in the flag's top left quadrant with the blue field of stars on the U.S. flag.

Rumor: The Loonie dollar design was a last-minute substitution when the Royal Canadian Mint lost its original die-cast in transit.

True? Yes.

The story: In 1987, the new dollar coin was supposed to just update the "two-guys-in-a-canoe" design that had long graced the silver dollar. The Royal Canadian Mint called a courier service to carry the new stamping dies from Ottawa to the production plant in Winnipeg. A fellow in uniform showed up and took the package away. Nobody thought to check his ID, though, and he (and the dies) disappeared. Rather than risk that somebody out there might use those dies to make their own dollars, the mint retired the design and used their second choice: the loon.

* * *

BATHROOM BREAK

• The Canadian Toilet Organization is an activist group working on an agenda to promote low-flow toilets; increase the number of public toilets in urban areas; achieve "toilet parity" between men and women in office buildings, schools, and other public buildings; and help the millions of people in Third World countries who are burdened with inadequate and unsafe disposal of human waste.

• Although you wouldn't want an airplane without a toilet, the two have combined to produce the occasional newsworthy event: CBC News reported in 2008 that a large chunk of ice from a leaking airplane toilet fell out of the sky and crashed through a woman's house, leaving a 30-centimeter (12-inch) hole in her roof and landing directly on her bed. Although frightened and a little nauseated, the woman wasn't hurt.

THE ARTISTS' NATURE

Around the beginning of the 20th century, a group of Canadians shook up the art world and created Canada's first national art movement.

EUROPEAN WANNABES

Today, it's hard to imagine landscape painting as controversial. What could be more traditional than painting the world around you? So it's strange to discover that an upstart band of landscape painters known as the "Group of Seven" started a movement in the early 1900s that brought international recognition to Canadian art for the first time. Adding to their mystique was the sudden and mysterious death—accident, suicide, murder?—of Tom Thomson, one of their most promising young associates.

In order to understand the significance of Thomson and the Group of Seven, it's important to understand mainstream Canadian art in the early 20th century. The national galleries were full of Canadian-themed art that tried very hard to pretend it had not been painted in Canada. Most of the early painters eagerly packed up their brushes and easels and headed for European academies to learn to paint like the French or English. At the time, European landscape painters were focused mostly on pastoralism, an artistic genre that emphasized idealism instead of realism (and included a lot of shepherds and pastures, hence the name). But there were no verdant pastures and moors in Canada; there were angry cliffs, rugged mountains, vast prairies, and freezing tundra. Yet rather than embrace those natural features, many Canadian painters stuck to the pastures. In some cases, they even went so far as to declare Canada's dramatic landscapes unsuitable for painting.

There were exceptions, of course. Paul Kane (1810–71) was as much a mountain man as an artist, tramping across the wilds of Upper Canada, sketching and painting the forests he saw and the First Nations people he met. His work influenced Lucius Richard O'Brien (1832–99) and others. But even these men based much of their success on idealized landscapes painted in the European tradition.

POOR TRAITS OF THE ARTIST AS A YOUNG MAN

Ontario native Tom Thomson spent his young adulthood in the late 19th century bouncing around with little ambition. Eventually, he managed to find work as an engraver in Seattle, dabbling in fine art on the side. Thomson might have stayed there for good, engraving and dabbling, if not for an overreaction to a woman he loved.

Alice Elinor Lambert was an American high school senior who later went on to fame as a writer of romance novels. However, she clearly wasn't very familiar with romance in 1904 when Thomson got down on a bended knee, declared his love, and presented her with an engagement ring. He expected a loving response. Instead, she giggled. Ever the sensitive artistic type, Thomson not only fled the room—he left Seattle entirely, never to return.

But what was mortally embarrassing for Thomson turned out to be great for Canadian art. Once he'd relocated to Toronto, Thomson joined the design firm of Grip, Ltd., a company that had been founded in 1873 by J. W. Bengough, one of Canada's finest cartoonists. Grip designed and published Bengough's weekly humor magazine, *Grip*, and designed a limited number of books, pamphlets, and advertising on the side. Eventually, Grip came into its own as an important design firm, providing artwork for advertising and other commercial uses.

It was in this atmosphere that Thomson began his association with most of the artists who became the Group of Seven: J. E. H. MacDonald, Arthur Lismer, A. J. Casson, Frederick Varley, Frank Johnston, and Franklin Carmichael. Challenged by Grip's art director to try landscape painting as a way of improving their skills, it wasn't long before the artists were heading off for the unspoiled natural beauty of Algonquin Park, paints and canvases in hand…and their expenses covered by an heir to the Massey-Harris farm-equipment fortune.

THE CANADIAN SPIRIT

From his first trip in 1912, Thomson started spending as much time as possible in Algonquin, eventually quitting his day job, taking a position as a park ranger, and living in a lakeside shack. Joanne Kates of the *New York Times* later wrote, "His early work was dull and timid, but after Thomson went on his first canoe trip north of Toronto, his eyes were opened and his palette exploded with color."

Yum: Canada is home to Donut Lake (MB), Donut Bay (ON), and Coffee Cove (NF).

As his artistic skill blossomed, Thomson traded tips and inspiration with his friends, pushing them to create their own exciting new visions of Canada's wilderness. Over five years, Thomson himself produced hundreds of sketches and dozens of paintings, including masterpieces such as *The Jack Pine* and *The West Wind*, described by fellow artist Arthur Lismer as "the spirit of Canada made manifest in a picture." Many of those paintings went on display at the National Gallery of Canada in Ottawa, and Thomson was considered one of the country's most promising painters.

But his career came to an abrupt end on July 8, 1917. As he had done many times before, Thomson took his boat onto Canoe Lake. That afternoon, the boat was spotted floating overturned. Eight days later, Thomson's body turned up, a fishing wire wrapped 17 times around one leg and a large bruise on his temple. Despite that, the local coroner ruled it a case of accidental death due to drowning. Thomson was buried within 48 hours.

What exactly happened that day on Canoe Lake has stumped art historians and armchair detectives ever since. Theories involving murder or suicide have been most popular—there were rumors that Thomson owed money to a local lodge owner who killed him during a fight to get it back. Supposedly his girlfriend (she never copped to the relationship) was pregnant and he'd borrowed the money to marry her…or killed himself because he couldn't. Even his burial site came under scrutiny: originally, Thomson was interred in his beloved Algonquin Park, but two days later, his brother had the body exhumed and moved to a family plot.

ARTISTIC AGITATORS

What we do know is that Thomson's paintings greatly influenced the other men he'd worked with at Grip. Those paintings owed little to pastoralism and traditional European landscapes. Their style was rooted instead in design concepts taken from the Art Nouveau and Postimpressionist movements, which emphasized color, flowing curves, and simple authenticity. In taking a new approach to traditional landscapes—and by putting Canadian landscapes unmistakably before their audience—the Group of Seven (as the painters eventually came to be called) intended to use their art as a declaration of national pride.

By 1919, the remaining artists had added to their numbers A. Y.

Jackson and Lawren Harris (a Massey-Harris heir and an artist in his own right), and they had begun a campaign of artistic confrontation, provoking public battles with prominent art critics who wanted nothing to do with this new style of painting. The publicity attracted important supporters like noted art critic Barker Fairley and Eric Brown, director of the National Gallery of Canada in Ottawa. Brown took the group's paintings overseas to exhibitions in Europe, where they were met with approval, providing vindication that at last Canadian art was worth serious attention.

By the late 1930s, the once-revolutionary Group of Seven had split up, and their landscapes had in turn come to be seen as the old guard, inspiring the next generation of artists who painted in opposition to their work. "Les Automatistes," based out of Montreal, rose up in a new revolution with their 1948 manifesto *Refus Global* ("Total Refusal") and ushered in an era of abstract and surrealist art. But the Group of Seven remained a historical landmark in the art world, the first who could really stand up and say (proudly), "We're Canadian artists!"

* * *

BARYSHNIKOV BAILS

On the night of June 29, 1974, a 26-year-old Soviet ballet dancer named Mikhail Baryshnikov bolted out of the O'Keefe Centre in Toronto. It was the last night of the Kirov Ballet's Canada tour, and Baryshnikov was the company's star. The show ended with him dancing a spectacular pas de deux, and while his Soviet "escort" (a.k.a., a KGB agent assigned to make sure the dancer didn't do exactly what he did) waited for him to sign some autographs, Baryshnikov slipped out a side door and into a waiting sedan. The car disappeared into the night, and Baryshnikov became one of the most famous defectors of the Cold War.

Baryshnikov later said that he chose to seek asylum in Canada (and later moved to the United States), not to reject his homeland but to take advantage of dance opportunities in the West. In the years after his defection, Baryshnikov went on to work with famed choreographers like George Balanchine and Twyla Tharp and danced with the American Ballet Theater and the New York City Ballet. He also served as the artistic director of the American Ballet Theater and eventually began his own company.

MILLION-DOLLAR NAMES, PART II

On page 93, we introduced some eponymous Canadian companies. Here are five more.

GRAND & TOY

At age 25, James Grand (1857–1922) started a stationery "store" in Toronto—he took orders and sorted out the products on his mother's kitchen table, and then delivered supplies door-to-door from a wagon. In 1883, he teamed up with his brother-in-law, Samuel Toy, and started a real store with 12 employees, including his son Percy. In 1904, when much of the city's downtown burned during the Great Toronto Fire, Percy Grand saved the business by standing on the store's roof and dousing flaming debris with water, leaving Grand & Toy as the only office supplier still standing in the city's core. (Percy is also credited with, in 1927, being the first to round the sharp corners on hexagonal pencils, making them more comfortable while still retaining their non-roll feature.) Grand & Toy now has 90 locations across Canada.

TIM HORTONS DONUTS

What does hockey have to do with doughnuts? In most ways, not much, except that Tim Horton, a Hockey Hall of Famer from Cochrane, Ontario, helped start the now-famous doughnut chain. Tim Horton was a defenseman who played for the Toronto Maple Leafs from 1952 to 1970. After 18 seasons, Horton was traded to the New York Rangers, then to the Pittsburgh Penguins, and finally to the Buffalo Sabres. Throughout his career, Horton tried a number of business ventures to capitalize on his fame, including an auto dealership and an unsuccessful chicken-and-burger chain in the Toronto area. It wasn't until he and a partner opened Tim Hortons Donuts in 1964 that he achieved business success. It didn't last long. In 1974, during his second season with the Sabres, he flipped his Italian sports car after a game and died in the crash. He was 44.

KRAFT FOODS

James Lewis Kraft (1874–1953) from Stevensville, Ontario, was one of 11 children raised on the family's dairy farm. At 18, he entered the retail grocery business by working at a food store in Fort Erie. Jumping the border in 1903, Kraft moved to Chicago, where he bought cheese wholesale and then resold it to local merchants from a rented horse and wagon. Eventually, he started making his own cheese. In 1916, wanting to extend the shelf life of cheddar, he invented processed cheese (cheese blended with other dairy and nondairy ingredients), which allowed him to ship his cheeselike product throughout North America without fear of it spoiling. By the 1930s, Kraft was selling more than 450,000 kilograms (1 million pounds) of the stuff every day. His company also came up with Velveeta, Jell-O, Kraft Dinner, Miracle Whip, and dozens of other household staples.

LEPAGE GLUES

You could say that Prince Edward Island's William Nelson Le Page (1849–1919) had a great deal of stick-to-itiveness. He put his mind to creating something that didn't exist yet: glue that didn't have to be heated. Rather than boiling discarded cow parts (the standard way to make glue in the late 1800s), he tried using something he could get cheaply—fish skins. He ended up with an industrial-strength glue that had a good shelf life and worked at room temperature. Expanding into the home market with Le Page's Liquid Fish Glue, he sold 50 million bottles between 1880 and 1887.

Le Page left the company in the 1890s and sold his shares, but maintained rights to his name. His partners ignored those rights and added insult to injury by altering the spelling of Le Page to LePage, omitting the space in the official company name. After a lengthy court battle, the LePage Company won, and William Nelson Le Page—lacking the commercial use of his name and a good part of his fortune—retired to Vancouver.

NEILSON DAIRY

William Neilson of Almonte, Ontario, had been trained as a small-town machinist, but in 1890, he moved to the big city of Toronto and opened a grocery store, figuring a can-do man like

himself could make it even if without much experience or knowledge. Three years later, he was bankrupt and working in North Dakota at a $4-a-day job on his brother Jesse's farm. Eventually, though, William saved some money and returned to Toronto, where he bought seven cows and some used, hand-turned ice cream makers. His son Morden went work as the churner, a tedious and strenuous job. (On the other hand, Morden later became Canada's amateur wrestling champion from 1900 to 1903, and he credited his muscle-building churning with helping him win the title.)

This time, William's business was an instant success. By 1915, it was selling a million pounds of ice cream and half a million pounds of candy a year. William also died that year, and Morden took over as company president...and made some great decisions. Morden Neilson didn't invent the Eskimo Pie, but in 1922, he was smart enough to buy the rights to it. Two years later, he introduced the Jersey Milk chocolate bar with a mail-in contest that offered an actual Jersey cow as the first-place prize. We don't know what the winner did with the cow, but we know that the Jersey Milk bar became the company's all-time bestseller.

For the last installment of "Million-Dollar Names,"
turn to page 411.

* * *

DIGESTING THE NEWS

Maggie, 76, from Edmonton, Alberta, eats paper. But not just any paper...only the *Edmonton Sun*. She began the diet in 2000 and does it every day. When asked why, Maggie said, "I can't explain it. It just tastes so good." (She claims to have tried the *Edmonton Journal* as well, but says it just doesn't have the same flavor.) In 2007, though, Maggie ran into some trouble: a wad of paper got stuck in her esophagus, and she couldn't swallow. So she went to see Robert J. Bailey, a doctor at Royal Alexandra Hospital, who was "able to advance the ball out the esophagus and into her stomach." And what was the doctor's reaction to the situation? Bailey noted that Maggie didn't seem to have any vitamin deficiencies or mental problems. Apparently, he said, "She just likes to eat newspaper."

In 1940, Sudbury, ON, became the first Canadian city to install parking meters.

SKIRTS & TILLS

Newspaper columnist Valerie Gibson once said, "A British politician is usually caught with his hand up a woman's skirt, while a Canadian politician is usually caught with his hand in the till." With all due respect, Canadian politicians aren't as predictable as all that. If fact, they seem able to multitask pretty well, often mishandling both skirts and tills with alacrity. As evidence, we offer the following.

EMMERSON SCANDAL
Year: 1907
Category: Skirt

Background: In 1904, Liberal leaders appointed member of parliament Henry Robert Emmerson as minister of railway and canals. Although he supported strong bridges, good track beds, and women's suffrage, he had his weaknesses. Increasingly exasperated party leaders warned him that his alcoholism and womanizing would lead to his downfall.

What Happened: That prediction came true in 1907 when a newspaper in Montreal reported that he'd been thrown out of one of the city's hotels with "two women of ill-repute."

Aftermath: Emmerson blustered and filed an unsuccessful libel lawsuit, but still quickly resigned.

PACIFIC SCANDAL
Year: 1873

Category: Till

Background: Canada's first prime minister, Sir John A. Macdonald, and other Conservatives were accused of accepting $350,000 in donations in exchange for steering Canadian Pacific Railroad building contracts to an American consortium headed by shipping and railroad magnate Sir Hugh Allan.

What Happened: Macdonald denied wrongdoing...until a telegram surfaced in which he demanded that Allan send another $10,000 before the election.

Aftermath: Macdonald resigned. Liberals won the 1874 election.

A Halifax curling rink became a temporary morgue for bodies recovered from the *Titanic*

GERDA MUNSINGER SCANDAL

Year: 1966

Category: Skirt

Background: Gerda Munsinger was a pretty East German who moved to Canada in 1955 and became hostess at the Chez Parée club in Montreal. She quickly cultivated "relationships" with several cabinet members in the Progressive Conservative government of John Diefenbaker. Believed to be a Soviet spy, she was quietly deported in 1961. The government breathed a sigh of relief that the scandal had been hushed up successfully.

What Happened: In 1966, three years after the Diefenbaker government was replaced by the Liberals, parliament was engaged in a heated debate. The Liberal minister of justice, Lucien Cardin, angrily blurted out, "Yeah, but what about Munsinger?" What had been an old piece of tightly held gossip suddenly catapulted into the newspapers.

Aftermath: A lot of scandal, censure, and a field day of headlines, but since the Tories were out of power, it all ended up as sound and fury, signifying not much of anything.

TUNAGATE

Year: 1985

Category: Till (sort of)

Background: Health inspectors from the Ministry of Fisheries and Oceans inspected a batch of tuna from the StarKist Tuna plant in St. Andrews, New Brunswick, and found it to be so substandard that it wasn't even fit to be used for pet food. The ministry quarantined a million cans of tuna from the plant.

What Happened: The plant's owners called John Fraser, the minister of fisheries and oceans, threatening to close the plant if the tuna couldn't be sold. Fraser ordered the cans released to consumers. When the story became public, Fraser said he'd sent cans for testing beforehand…but the testing labs made sure that everyone knew he'd released the cans before they actually sent him any results. (In fact, they discovered the tuna was edible, but it looked, smelled, and tasted below Canada's acceptable standards.)

Aftermath: Prime Minister Brian Mulroney demanded Fraser's resignation. It didn't seem to hurt Fraser's career—he became speaker

American immigrants to Canada were not recognized as a distinct ethnic group until 1991.

of the House of Commons shortly after. StarKist closed the plant, putting 400 people out of work.

DUPLESSIS ORPHANS SCANDAL

Year: 1940s–60s

Category: Till

Background: Quebec premier Maurice Duplessis discovered what he thought was a brilliant loophole in Canadian law: orphanages were to be funded from the budget of the province, but mental institutions were funded by the national government. So why not certify that all of Quebec's orphans were mentally ill, thus letting the province escape the cost of caring for them? Duplessis found some cooperative psychiatrists who made the necessary diagnoses, and the poor kids were shipped to Catholic orphanages (now relabeled as mental health facilities) and existing insane asylums. The province received tens of millions of dollars in funding.

What Happened: It was absolutely disastrous to the kids. Thousands were labeled as insane and mentally deficient; as a result, they were neglected, abused, deprived of decent schooling, forced to work long hours caring for adult patients, and even used for drug testing and medical experiments.

Aftermath: In the 1990s, 3,000 survivors of the abusive treatment agitated for public awareness and reparations. After several decades of stonewalling and denial, the Quebec government finally offered a nominal settlement of about $15,000 each to orphans who had been labeled mentally deficient. Urged to accept the money by their lawyers—who received substantial legal fees in the settlement—and threatened with an alternative of no compensation at all, many of the survivors accepted the offer. Nobody has been prosecuted.

HONORABLE MENTION: DAR HEATHERINGTON PUBLIC MISCHIEF SCANDAL

Year: 2003–04

Category: Unknown

Background: Darlene "Dar" Heatherington was a 39-year-old member of the Lethbridge, Alberta, city council when she made international headlines. How? She mysteriously disappeared from a

As a 10-year-old playing pee-wee hockey, Wayne Gretzky scored 378 goals in 72 games.

conference in Great Falls, Montana. After three days of searching and police bulletins, she turned up in Las Vegas wandering around a casino in a daze, saying first that she had been kidnapped and raped, then that she had met an old friend and had traveled with him, and finally that she had been drugged and kidnapped after all.

What Happened: Police in Las Vegas doubted her story as it changed, but officers back in Lethbridge began reviewing other statements she'd given about being stalked and receiving obscene letters.

Aftermath: Heatherington recanted her stories...and then recanted her recantations. She was charged with public mischief for making up the stalker stories and fabricating the evidence, convicted, and removed from the city council.

* * *

MASTER OF TIME AND DISTANCE

Let's all raise our watches to engineer and inventor, Sandford Fleming of Peterborough, Ontario. Not only did he propose both Greenwich Mean Time and the worldwide time zone system—consider these other accomplishments:

• He designed Canada's first postage stamp, depicting a beaver in an oval frame, known by collectors as the Threepenny Beaver. The stamp spawned a long-running bit of Canadian slang that meant "really great." (e.g., "That song is a threepenny beaver!")

• He engineered all of the Intercolonial Railway (in Nova Scotia, New Brunswick, and Quebec) and most of the Canadian Pacific Railway.

• In 1849, Fleming founded the Royal Canadian Institute, now the oldest science organization in Canada. In 1882, he was a founding member of the Royal Society of Canada, an association of scientists and scholars.

• After he "retired," he advocated tirelessly for the All Red Line, an underwater system of telegraph cables that would link all of the British Empire. It was completed in 1902.

• Knighted by Queen Victoria in 1897, Sir Fleming proved himself to be a real "threepenny beaver."

CURLING THE LAWS OF PHYSICS

In the topsy-turvy world of curling, spinning the stone makes it curve the "wrong" way on ice, at least according to the basic laws of physics. It took years of research and an expert to figure out why.

A CURIOUS QUESTION

Take a curling stone and deliver it across a hard, smooth surface with a clockwise spin and it will curl to the left, the *opposite* direction of the spin. That seems backward, but because of some very tricky physics laws, it's true for any object. Now, if you take the same stone and deliver it exactly the same way across ice, it will curve *into* the direction of the spin: to the right.

Why does it behave differently on ice? Explaining that has long been one of those minor mysteries of life. So much so that an amateur curler and associate physics professor at the University of Northern British Columbia took a good look at the phenomenon. Dr. Mark Shegelski wrote several papers about the curious effect, and here's what he found.

HOW DOES IT WORK?

It all has to do with friction. First of all, think about what happens when you push *anything* across a surface. Because of friction from sliding along, the top of the object—the part that's not in contact with the surface—moves more freely than the bottom, tilting the object forward. This shifts more weight to the front of the object than the back, meaning the front has more friction than the back. (This effect also explains why your car's front brakes get more wear than its back brakes, and why the fronts of sled runners and skis get more wear than the back.)

So now let's take a look at the curling stone on a smooth floor. When you launch it, the stone's weight shifts toward the front. With the stone tilted forward, there's extra friction on its front surface, which is spinning clockwise. But the stone actually goes to the left because that side has less friction and moves more freely. Still with us?

OKAY, FAIR ENOUGH. BUT THEN WHY DOES THE STONE CURL TO THE RIGHT WHEN ON THE ICE?

Shegelski and his associates think it has to do with the response of ice to friction. Their research indicates that the friction in the stone's front side is enough to immediately melt the ice into a microscopic layer of water, about as thick as a bubble's skin. The ice thaws when the stone rubs it, but then refreezes in a split second. Wet ice is much more slippery than ice that's dry, and that split second of thawing and slipping is just enough to change the direction of the stone.

HOW DOES THIS AFFECT THE SPIN?

The heavy front end melts the ice, creating a slippery zone. Since the weight of a tossed stone is in the front, the lighter back end doesn't melt the ice as much, if at all, so it actually gets more traction on the ice than it would on a hard surface. But the rotating stone, which on other surfaces is pushed in the direction of its lead side (which is coming into the leftward part of its spin), is now pushed in the direction of its trailing side on ice (which is heading into the right-sided portion of the spin). Mystery solved.

* * *

THE CANADIANS WHO RULED HOLLYWOOD

• When did Canadians win the Oscar for Best Actress three years in a row? In 1929, Toronto's Mary Pickford won for *Coquette*. She was followed by Montreal's Norma Shearer in *The Divorce* in 1930. Finally, Marie Dressler (of Coburg, Ontario) won for *Min and Bill* in 1931.

• What Canadian director has won the most Academy Awards? Norman Jewison. His films—including *Fiddler on the Roof, Jesus Christ Superstar, Moonstruck,* and *Agnes of God*—and the actors in them have received a total of 46 Academy Award nominations and 12 Oscars. One, *In the Heat of the Night,* was nominated for seven awards and won five: Best Picture, Best Actor, Best Film Editing, Best Sound, and Best Writing Adapted Screenplay.

Because of his name and his association with *Fiddler on the Roof,* people are often surprised to discover that Jewison isn't Jewish. He was raised Protestant.

ISN'T IT ROMANTIC?

Romance novels make up a third of all adult mass-market paperback books, and the giant in the market is Harlequin. Around the world, day and night, this Canadian publisher sells four books every second.

AHHH...ROMANCE

Despite a popular misconception, romance novels are not all exactly the same. For one thing, there are genres and subgenres: "NASCAR romance," "Christian romance," "medical romance," or "science fiction romance." For another, the books have gotten more explicit over the years: no longer are the characters limited to a kiss and a marriage proposal at the end. And finally, although many other companies have gotten into the act, the powerhouse in the field of romance is Toronto publishing house Harlequin.

The first romance novel might've been *Pamela, or Virtue Rewarded* (1740) by Samuel Richardson. The title pretty much sums up the plot, which could serve as the template for romance novels over the following centuries: after a rocky beginning, a virtuous virgin gets her man and finds happiness forever after. Romance writers also like to cite Jane Austen's *Pride and Prejudice* as a masterpiece in their genre, and the writing of the Brontë sisters as a continuation and extension of the tradition. In fact, these books make their era sound so romantic that a good proportion of 20th-century romantic fiction was historical, harkening back to the mid-1800s...almost as if the authors and readers wanted to believe the romance lacking in their lives was just a matter of having been born in the wrong century.

STANDING OUT FROM THE PACK

Until the 1930s, romance novels were considered just novels like any other, albeit ones aimed primarily at women. Finally, though, one publisher realized that there was a huge and hungry market for fantasy romance and that readers would buy the books as fast as a publisher could get them off the press and onto the shelves. That publisher wasn't Harlequin, which didn't exist yet.

Q: Why do Canadian and American beers taste different? A: U.S. brewers use more corn.

It was the England-based Mills & Boon, which realized that cheap fantasy romances would sell well in a population eager for escape during the Great Depression.

So Mills & Boon focused solely on romances and began pumping out cheap hardbacks in brown covers. The company also quickly discovered that readers didn't want surprise endings, complex characters, or even necessarily believable circumstances. Sales were better for pure fantasy, so Mills & Boon developed a stable of writers who could churn out books with similar plots, themes, characters…even the page counts were the same, which also allowed the company to standardize production and printing.

LOVE FOR SALE

In 1949, Canadian businessman Richard Bonnycastle formed a consortium that established Harlequin Enterprises Limited in Winnipeg, Canada. His first order of business: picking up the Canadian rights for books that had already been published in the United States and England—westerns, cookbooks, crime novels… and romances. He quickly noticed that the romances did best of all—in fact, there seemed to be an insatiable demand for them. So in 1957, he negotiated to become Mills & Boon's sole North American distributor. He also toned down the product for the American market. The stories still mostly took place in Europe, but behavior that was okay there was often too racy for U.S. readers. So Bonnycastle kept the languid looks and sexual tension but, with some editing help from his wife and secretary, deleted anything that suggested actual sex.

That was probably just as well because the sex in Mills & Boon was never consensual. Why? The publisher was sure that readers would be shocked and horrified if an unmarried heroine actually said yes to it. So, as in *Gone With the Wind*, the hero in a Mills & Boon romance novel always took the heroine by force. She fought him to no avail, was crushed under his manly insistence, was raped by him, enjoyed the experience, and married him. Happy ending.

SOAPS AND SUPERMARKETS

While the Bonnycastles were establishing Harlequin's style and identity, another man found its marketing strategy. W. Lawrence Heisey had worked for Procter & Gamble, had a Harvard MBA,

The character of James Bond is based on William Stephenson, a real-life spy from Winnipeg.

and liked to describe himself as just a soap salesman. That description was apt because, in the 1970s, he went about selling the Harlequin romances as if they were consumer products instead of books. Unlike most publishers, he did extensive market research to determine who romance readers were and what they looked for in a title, a cover, characters, and a plot. He emphasized the Harlequin logo to get readers looking for the brand, put sample copies in boxes of laundry detergent, bought advertisements on soap operas, and placed the books in supermarkets because "that's where the women are."

The company may have been content reprinting British bodice-rippers forever, except a trend was stirring. A big American publishing company, Simon & Schuster, started copying the Harlequin brand and formula, but used American writers and heroines. They called their romance line Silhouette, and it was so successful that Harlequin lost sales in the United States. Not wanting to miss out on the lucrative American market, Harlequin changed its model: In 1980, the company hired its first American writer to copy the Mills & Boon formula, but to create an "original" product. When that got a good response, Harlequin slowly began generating an increasing amount of original material for Americans, dictating plot points and paying authors very modest wages...while selling truckloads of books.

Having regained its luster, Harlequin attracted suitors. The one that won the company's heart was Torstar, the corporate owner of the *Toronto Star*, which engulfed Harlequin in an embrace, pulled it close, and whispered, "May I buy you?" Like Harlequin's heroines, the answer was a breathy yes. And then, in good measure, Torstar also wooed Harlequin's romance competitors, having its way with Mills & Boon itself and seducing Silhouette away from Simon & Schuster in 1984.

READING & WRITHING

Today, Harlequin is still owned by Torstar and is located in the suburbs of Toronto. The company has published books by more than 1,300 authors and received solicitations from hundreds of thousands more. Every month, it receives about 1,000 unsolicited submissions from wannabe writers. Editors read every one.

Of the people who have written for Harlequin, almost all are

women. The exceptions: a few men have partnered with their wives or other women, and there's a retired Air Force colonel somewhere in Texas who writes under a pseudonym.

The guidelines are surprisingly specific for each of the various romance series lines. For example, the Silhouette Desire line requires a length of 50,000 to 55,000 words. And the author must insert a conflict between the hero and heroine before the end of chapter one. And what of the characters themselves? The criteria have changed since the early days of brutish men and passive women. Today, a heroine must be "complex and flawed," "strong-willed and smart," yet "capable of making terrible mistakes in matters of the heart." The hero must be "an alpha male with a sense of arrogance and entitlement," but "never physically cruel." The hero "should own the ranch, not work on it," or "be the company CEO, not a handyman." The books should be rife with "classic" plots such as "revenge, secret pregnancies, marriages of convenience, and reunion romances." And when you're writing, absolutely don't forget the three P's of Harlequin success: "powerful, passionate, and provocative."

* * *

HARLEQUIN BY THE NUMBERS

0: Number of nights an unmarried couple can stay together in the same building without a chaperone in a Harlequin Steeple Hill Romance, marketed to conservative Christians.

29: Number of languages in which Harlequin romances have been printed.

40–49: Primary target age for Harlequin romances.

120: Number of different books Harlequin publishes each month.

240: Number of cover models needed per month, assuming two per cover.

2002: Year Harlequin got its first female president and chief operating officer.

5.8 billion: Total number of books sold since Harlequin's founding.

American athletes playing for Canadian pro sports teams receive Medicare coverage.

I ♥ LOVE ALBERTA

An oversized Easter egg, dinosaurs, cowboys, and safety from tsunamis—we offer 12 reasons to love Alberta.

1. CITY NAMES. The province's 10 largest metropolises include places like Red Deer, Medicine Hat, and Wood Buffalo. Things get even weirder as you get into Alberta's small towns: Hairy Hill, Driftpile, etc.

2. BUFFALO BASHING. For almost 6,000 years, First Nations people living in what became southern Alberta used a spot in the foothills of the Rocky Mountains as a buffalo jump. A what? Blackfoot hunters drove buffalo from their grazing grounds over a 10-meter (33-foot) cliff in order to kill them for food and furs. Today, the area is called Head-Smashed-In Buffalo Jump, and it's one of five UNESCO World Heritage Sites located in the province.

3. BURIED TREASURE. Alberta is often called the "energy province" because of its many oil, coal, and natural gas deposits.

4. A FLESH-EATING LIZARD. That's not a legendary creature but the translated name of a real thing: the *Albertosaurus sarcophagus*, the first known Canadian dinosaur. In 1884, Joseph Burr Tyrrell, a 26-year-old geologist working for the Geological Survey of Canada, stumbled on the animal's skull while doing research near the Red Deer River Valley. Tyrrell knew nothing about dinosaurs, but he knew enough to bundle up the curious artifact and transport it to Calgary for further research. That discovery ultimately set off the Great Dinosaur Rush of 1910–17, in which wild-eyed paleontologists seeking fame and fortune dug up the surrounding area looking for bones. (They found many.) For his discovery, Tyrrell got the Royal Tyrrell Museum of Paleontology in Drumheller named after him; it opened in 1985 just a few kilometers from where Tyrrell unearthed his find.

5. COWBOYS. How many working cowboys are there in Calgary? Not many. But just as everybody's Irish on St. Patrick's Day, everybody's a cowboy during the annual 10-day Calgary Stampede rodeo. Alberta has romanticized the once-menial job of

herding cattle more than just about anywhere else in the world. Check out the dude ranches, cowboy singers, a cowboy poetry association, and enough western boot and clothing stores to outfit a stampede of cowfolk. Heck, you might even see a real working cowboy—you'll be able to pick them out because they're likely to be the only ones not wearing cowboy duds.

6. GLACIERS. There are glaciers in Alberta, most notably in Jasper and Banff national parks. Unfortunately, the glaciers are dwindling with global warming, so see them while you still can.

7. NATIONAL PARKS. Alberta has five of them. One is the first-established and most-used national park (Banff); another is the only Canadian national park fully surrounded by a fence (Elk Island).

8. VEGREVILLE'S GIANT PYSANKA. Ukrainians settled heavily near Vegreville in central Alberta. *Pysanky* are Ukrainian Easter eggs, famous for their intricate geometric designs and vivid colors. In 1974, Vegreville decided to celebrate the 100th anniversary of the Royal Canadian Mounted Police, as well as its own heritage, by building the world's largest Easter egg, a 7.8-meter (26-foot) pysanka prominently situated near Highway 16. The egg, described by the city as "an immense jigsaw puzzle containing 524 star patterns, 1,108 equilateral triangles, 3,512 visible facets, 6,978 nuts and bolts, and 177 internal struts," was the subject of a "Roadside Attractions" postage stamp in 2009.

9. SOME ILLEGAL ALIENS WELCOME. Alberta has a reputation for friendliness to strangers, and perhaps the stranger the better. In 1967, the town of St. Paul built a UFO landing pad to attract tourists from all over. Next to the raised platform is a sign that designates the pad area as an international territory and "a symbol of our faith that mankind will maintain the outer universe free from national wars and strife…All visitors from Earth or otherwise are welcome to this territory and to the Town of St. Paul."

10. BIBLE BILL AND THE SOCIAL CREDIT PARTY. In 1935, Alberta citizens were drowning under the weight of the Great Depression. Farmers especially were suffering from a prolonged drought and lots of debt. Enter William "Bible Bill" Aberhart, a radio evangelist, high school principal, and member of the

The word "Canuck" originated in the mid-1800s as a derisive term for French Canadians.

Social Credit Party. Their platform? All Albertans should share in the province's wealth by earning dividends on its profits; Aberhart campaigned on a promise to give every Albertan $25 per month. That approach earned the Social Creditors a landslide victory in the 1935 election and control of the province until 1971. But once Aberhart got into office and saw the mountain of debt facing the province, he realized that Alberta didn't really have any profits to share, and he never was able to keep his $25-a-month promise. No mater. Albertans liked him anyway—Aberhart served as the provincial premier until his death in 1943.

11. HOODOOS. Dinosaur Provincial Park in southeastern Alberta is home to dinosaur bones, yes, but also some unique rock formations. Hoodoos are tall, thin rock spires that jut skyward in a badland. They're formed by eons of wind erosion and look sort of like natural totem poles.

12. SAFETY FROM TSUNAMIS. Of the 13 territories and provinces, landlocked Alberta is one of only two that can guarantee 100 percent safety from disastrous oceanic fluctuations.

* * *

DYNAMIC DUO

If you ever watched *Kids in the Hall*, you know that Canadians are funny folks. But that programs would not have been possible without the antics of a pair of comics from Ontario who inspired *Kids in the Hall*'s creators: Johnny Wayne and Frank Shuster.

Wayne and Shuster met in the 1930s in a grade 10 history class. They went on to study at the University of Toronto, where they started writing plays and comedy sketches. In 1942, they enlisted in the Canadian army, performing shows for troops serving in World War II, before returning home and landing their own CBC television show. On that program, they used camera tricks to amaze audiences. (In one skit, Wayne and Shuster seemed to defy gravity while painting Italy's Tower of Pisa.) They also spoofed movies like *Star Trek* and even Shakespeare's plays—one sketch called for a baseball game starring Hamlet and Macbeth. But their comedy was uniquely Canadian; they refused to do "cruel humor." And, despite lucrative offers, they refused to turn American, keeping their lives and families firmly rooted in Toronto.

The southernmost point in Canada is Middle Island, ON, in Lake Erie.

THE MERRY WAVES OF WINDSOR

In its glory days—the early 1970s—CKLW radio had 62 million listeners in Canada and the United States, making it the eighth most-listened-to station in North America.

THE BIG 8

Walk along any beach in Ontario, Michigan, or Ohio during the summer in the 1960s and 1970s and you'd probably hear the same song playing from all directions on a hundred transistor radios. Just about every teen growing up then listened to 800 on the AM dial: CKLW, a.k.a. "The Big 8."

Based in Windsor, Ontario, CKLW was about as far south as you could go and still be in Canada. And although the "LW" in its initials stood for London and Windsor, the bulk of the station's listeners lived outside Canada. Its tower on the edge of the Detroit River broadcasted at the highest legal power of the time (50,000 watts), booming through the Detroit metropolitan area, into Ohio during the day, and—on a clear night—all the way into America's Deep South and east to the Atlantic coast. Sometimes, even people in Scandinavia and ships in the northern Atlantic could tune in to CKLW.

THE TOWER OF POWER

It was the sheer volume of listeners, though, that made the station a force. CKLW's call-in contests, for instance, could cripple local phone services by jamming up the lines in both Canada and the United States. That overwhelming popularity gave CKLW a lot of say in determining what songs would be successful—and most of that power rested in the hands of music director Rosalie Trombley. She had a knack for knowing what listeners wanted, and time and again, her picks became hits. Artists from Alice Cooper to Anne Murray to Elton John have acknowledged her influence.

But Trombley's brusque manner and her ability to make or break a song bugged some people, too—so much so that in 1972, Detroit musician Bob Seger recorded "Rosalie," a scathing "tribute" song:

Norman Breakey of Toronto invented the paint roller (1940).

"She makes her choices
And you best be smilin'
when it's choosin' time…
She's got the power, she's got the tower—
Rosalie!"

Detroit stations gleefully played Seger's single, but CKLW refused. Trombley reportedly threatened to quit if anyone put it on the air. As a result, the song never made it big.

But that almost didn't matter. CKLW's hit-making power was at the beginning of a downward slide. In fact, all the AM music stations were in trouble because droves of listeners were deserting them for the better sound of FM.

THE REAL KILLER

Even so, technology wasn't CKLW's biggest problem. It was the new Canadian Content law, or "CanCon," enacted in 1971, that did the most damage. The law required that 30 percent of all music on Canadian airwaves be performed by Canadian artists—known or unknown. CKLW tried to make the best of it, playing hits from the cream of Canada's musical crop: Joni Mitchell, Gordon Lightfoot, Neil Young, the Guess Who (the first Canadian rock band to have a number-one hit outside of Canada with "American Woman"), and its spin-off group, Bachman-Turner Overdrive. Even Canadian one-hit wonders like the Five Man Electrical Band ("Signs") got their chance at stardom.

With these playlists, CKLW maintained the top position in its markets for several years, but after a while, the station began to lose one of its core audiences, black teens, because the CanCon-required percentage of Canadian artists diluted the number of soul songs the station could play. For similar reasons, CKLW was also playing fewer oldies, so its older audience started to tune in elsewhere, too.

LIKE A ROLLING STONE?

It didn't take long for competitors to take advantage of the situation. American stations stopped playing Canadian artists altogether and added more oldies, soul music, and new American and British hits to their lineups. Naturally, when offered the choice

between the latest song from the Five Man Electrical Band and one from the Rolling Stones, music fans went with Mick.

The station never really regained its mojo. The end came in 1984 when CKLW fired 40 staffers...including hit-maker Rosalie Trombley. It closed its Detroit area sales office and changed its format to 1940s and 1950s pop standards and big band music. Soon after that change, the station was sold. In its current incarnation, CKLW is a news/talk radio station serving a mostly Ontario audience.

*　　*　　*

THE MULRONEY TAPES

In 2005, author Peter C. Newman released a book of transcripts of his interviews with former Canadian prime minister Brian Mulroney (1984–93), best known for the 1988 Free Trade Agreement (and for being extremely unpopular when he left office). Here's some of what Mulroney had to say:

On Pierre Trudeau: "Very, very inept. He has a streak of malice in him that is most unbecoming. He conducted himself like a cruel dictator. This guy was a bully with people when he became prime minister, he was dishonest intellectually, and his record is absolutely mediocre."

On Joe Clark: "He never knew how to manage men and women. I'm not so sure that he does today, although if he hasn't learned anything over the last few years, he'd be a very stupid man."

On Jean Chretien: "He came into politics in 1963 and hasn't had a new idea since. He's not an impressive guy at all. He thinks he's a stand-up comedian. I was out of politics for seven years, reading and working and thinking and learning new things, and new approaches. He hasn't read a book in 20 years."

On his treatment by the media: "You will not find one favourable adjective about me in 10 years. Even Hitler had someone writing one good adjective."

On his own leadership skills: "You have to understand people. You have to like people. You would fail as a leader if you allowed vindictiveness or mean-spiritedness to enter your judgment or your personality."

APRIL FOOL'S!

Canadians enjoy a bit of tomfoolery, and the often-staid CBC is no exception, playing April Fool's jokes on its listeners, viewers, and, at times, even its own presenters and reporters.

• **1978:** On April 1, 1978, environmentalist and radio reporter Dr. David Suzuki was assigned to interview a "shark expert" without having time to prepare. He was told that a prehistoric—and unbeknownst to him, imaginary—shark called a *Carcaridon*, which was 20 to 30 meters (80 to 100 feet) long, had survived to present day, and researchers were attempting to catch one using a smaller shark as bait.

• **1979:** The CBC radio show *The Food Show* offered a recipe for what it called "Polly on a cracker"—parakeets basted with paprika and lightly roasted. The show's host interviewed a woman who said she supplied frozen, chestnut-stuffed parakeets (or, budgies) to gourmets in Toronto and Vancouver. For their part, the "gourmets" admitted that the birds didn't offer much meat, but "the incredible thing about them is you can eat the bones as well—they just crunch. They are juicy, but they need a lot of spice."

• **1980:** Radio reporter Karin Wells was fooled when she interviewed two men who claimed to be introducing romance novels for men that featured traditional male activities like industrial jobs, gambling, hunting, fishing, and sports. The idea, they said, was that after a football game, men "will want to see a little romance, a little lyricism, a little sensitivity in the locker room instead of the shouting and yelling."

• **1988:** During a radio broadcast, Dr. Frederick Farben (really a CBC radio employee) shared his "research" on color allergies—people allergic to red, yellow, blue, or other colors across the spectrum. His prescription for a color allergy? Avoid that color or, if that's impossible, wear tinted lenses (e.g., rose-colored glasses). The good doctor claimed that 2 percent of all Canadians may be affected by color allergies, and that the affliction wasn't necessarily only in people allergic to other things. He said, "You may

have no reaction to pollen or ragweed, but you may come in contact with something that is ochre or puce and it may throw you off completely." (The Inuit seemed to have immunity, he said, possibly from living so much of the year in monochromatic, white surroundings.)

• **1990:** A CBC broadcast covered, with all the conventions of a television news story, a new craze among kindergarteners: "Last week Tanya did something in school that most of us were told never to do when we were children: She ate worms." Included in the story were interviews with nutritionists, school officials, and outraged parents. Also included was a helpful recipe, allegedly from the Ontario Science Center, in case the viewer wanted to try the dish at home: "The worms were grown organically, boiled in lemon juice, then baked for 10 minutes" at 175°C (340°F).

• **1996:** CBC radio included a fake documentary about a disease that was supposedly common in Ontario in the early 1800s, believed by some to have been caused by eating meat from bears that were near hibernation time. Called Sarner's disease, its victims appeared stone-cold dead without a detectable heartbeat, breathing, or other signs of life for days or even weeks...and then revived, as if they'd been hibernating like bears. According to the broadcast, as a result of the disease, hiding dead relatives became a widespread practice.

* * *

THE FESTIVAL OF FESTIVALS

According to *Variety*, the Toronto Film Festival (TIFF) is "second only to Cannes in terms of high-profile pics, stars, and market activity," which makes TIFF a really big deal and earns it the nickname the "festival of festivals." In 2008, TIFF received 4,209 submissions; it chose to screen just 312 films...a 7 percent acceptance rate. That means it's harder to get into TIFF than Harvard University (which accepts 9.3 percent of applicants). Some movies screened at the festival that went on to box-office glory: *Slumdog Millionaire, Precious, American Beauty, Hotel Rwanda, The Big Chill, Strictly Ballroom, Chariots of Fire,* and *Ray*.

(VERY) COLD CASE

While on an expedition in the Arctic channels between Canada and Greenland in 1871, explorer Charles Francis Hall may have been a victim of a murder. The chief suspect? Respected physician and scientist Dr. Emil Bessels.

TROUBLE FROM THE START

In 1871, American explorer Charles Francis Hall was ready to leave for his third expedition to the Arctic on a ship called the *Polaris*. His knowledge and reputation had made him the most likely to achieve what nobody had so far: reach the North Pole. He had received a grant from the United States Congress to finance the journey. However, part of the deal was that he had to take along a scientific team headed by the Smithsonian Institute's Dr. Emil Bessels. The scientists would take samples of flora and fauna, and record whatever data they could.

Shortly after the ship left New York City, though, conflict arose. Bessels didn't think Hall was qualified to lead the expedition, and the 25 shipmates took sides, depending on where their loyalties lay (with Bessels or Hall). The simmering resentments boiled up into mutinous behavior as the ship sailed on and the weather got colder. By the time the group reached St. John's, Newfoundland, they were in real trouble. Bessels and his scientists lost their nerve and wanted to turn back to the safety of more temperate waters. Hall wanted to push on to the pole, his stated plan from the beginning. Since he was officially in charge of the voyage and the "captain" of the ship, he made the decision: It was September. They would winter in a safe harbor just off the Greenland coast and then would continue on toward the North Pole in the spring.

A POISONOUS ATMOSPHERE

Hall didn't have any real sailing experience, though, and some of the crew didn't like the decision or his being in charge. Soon, insubordination became official mutiny. Parts of the ship's equipment disappeared, apparently tossed over the side, and its boilers were sabotaged. In response to the tensions and conflicts, Hall's

second-in-command started drinking in secret, depleting the jars of alcohol that had been brought along for preserving specimens.

October arrived. One clear day, Hall went on a hunting and exploratory dogsled journey over the ice with Hans Hendrik, an Inuit interpreter and the namesake of Hans Island, located between Greenland and Canada (*more about that on page 297*). When they returned, cold and tired, Hall eagerly drank a cup of hot coffee. Too sweet, he complained—acidic too, like it was burning his throat. That should've been a warning. Within a few hours, he went into convulsions, started vomiting, and became delirious.

Bessels supervised the care of the captain, getting him into bed and offering some soothing "medicines." Over the next few days, the good doctor sat by Hall's bed and tended to him. However, in a coherent moment, Hall accused Bessels and his allies of poisoning him and sent the doctor away. From then on, he refused any food and liquid not prepared by a trusted Inuit aide.

Remarkably, Hall improved. After a few days, he was on his feet again and able to make his way onto the deck for short intervals. Bessels, though, told the ship's chaplain that he was worried about the captain, despite the apparent recovery. He convinced the chaplain to talk with Hall about letting the doctor continue medical treatment again. Hall reluctantly agreed. Almost immediately, his health went into decline, and the convulsions and delirium returned, worse than before. Four days later, he was dead, buried in Greenland's frozen permafrost.

INQUEST

In 1873, the U.S. Navy held an inquest into Hall's curious death. They discovered that his records and journals had disappeared from the ship. They also found that the journals of other crewmen included mysterious gaps and missing pages for the time period of Hall's sickness and death.

The naval inquiry asked Bessels to give his professional opinion of Hall's death. The doctor responded by repeating a folk belief of the time: "He had been exposed to very low temperature during the time that he was on the sledge [sled] journey. He came back and entered a warm cabin without taking off his heavy fur clothing, and then took a warm cup of coffee. And anyone knows

what the consequences of that might be [ie, death]."

The inquest panel bought it. Without a body, records, or journals, and with the doctor's assurances that he had done everything possible, the inquiry reported that Hall died of natural causes and "apoplexy" (a stroke), and that Bessels's care "was the best practices under the circumstances."

CALLING IN CSI

But was it? The fact that Bessels and at least two of his cohorts expressed relief over Hall's demise was not necessarily incriminating, nor were the missing journals. Still, those facts raised suspicions that an autopsy might have allayed or confirmed. In 1968, a Hall biographer decided he wanted to settle the issue once and for all. Professor Chauncey Loomis of New Hampshire's Dartmouth College traveled to Greenland to exhume Hall's body. Although it was nearly 100 years later, the permafrost's deep freeze had preserved Hall's flesh, clothes, and coffin quite well, and Loomis was able to take samples of hair, bone, and fingernails to analyze.

The results: arsenic—large doses of it administered in the last two weeks of Hall's life. In fact, the symptoms reported by the crewmen were consistent with arsenic poisoning. And the suspicion that Hall's coffee had been poisoned was also consistent with the account that he'd found the coffee overly sweet and that it burned his esophagus and throat going down.

Even if the results are accurate, though, we'll probably never know for sure who doctored the coffee. We'll also never know for sure how someone kept Hall dosed with arsenic for most of the last two weeks of his life. However, we do have a pretty good suspect.

* * *

BENEATH THE CAP

The next time you drink a beer from the Victoria, B.C., Phillips Brewery, look under the cap—you'll see this warning: "Remove cap before drinking." It's good advice, although information you probably wouldn't have seen unless you'd *already* removed the cap.

THE ARCTIC THERMOMETER

What do you do when your normal thermometer routinely freezes solid? Here's a handy homemade invention created by "Yukon Jack" McQuesten. All you need are four bottles...

BRRR!
For centuries, people in most climates found that mercury thermometers worked well enough to keep track of the temperature outside. But what about the times when the weather is so cold that even mercury freezes? Such was the challenge in the Yukon during the early days of European settlement. It wasn't just a matter of idle curiosity, either—the weather often got cold enough that a person outside could quickly die of hypothermia. So it was important to know what you were up against before you left your cabin.

Enter "Yukon Jack" McQuesten. Born Leroy Napoleon McQuesten in Maine, he had gone west for the California gold rush, and when that didn't pan out, he headed north. Eventually, he ended up about 10 kilometers (six miles) south of present-day Dawson City where, in 1874, he established a trading post called Fort Reliance. It was there he invented a thermometer that saved the lives of many people. He called it the "Sourdough Thermometer," after the local nickname for prospectors who ate a lot of sourdough bread. It was surprisingly simple, yet brilliant.

LITTLE OF THIS, LITTLE OF THAT
The thermometer consisted of four small bottles. The first contained mercury; the second, coal oil; the third, 150-proof Jamaica ginger; and the fourth, a medicine called Perry Davis' Painkiller—a well-known and much-used elixir at the time, made of ethyl alcohol, opiates, and other unknown herbal ingredients.

How did it work? By paying attention to the freezing points of each liquid. The bottles were set outside in a row where they could be seen from a window. When the mercury froze, the temperature outside had reached –40°C (–40°F). If the coal oil

also froze, it was –45°C (–49°F). The Jamaica ginger froze at –51°C (–59°F), but it was the painkiller that you needed to watch for the really cold temperatures: it turned white at –51°C (–60°F), crystallized at –57°C (–70°F), and froze solid at –60°C (–76°F).

If the mercury hadn't frozen, everyone knew it was safe to go outside wearing normal arctic furs. (If the mercury did freeze, most people went outside as little as possible.) But if the Perry Davis' Painkiller froze, it was unsafe to be outside unless you were within range of a roaring fire.

FAME AND FORTUNE

This lifesaving invention made Yukon Jack a legend. Prospector and young author Jack London considered it an honor to call him a friend. Years later, London wrote characters based on Jack and his wife Kate—an Athabascan native—in his Yukon stories, *The Wife of a King.* Another honor of sorts came in the 1970s when American alcohol producer Heublein Spirits named a whiskey "Yukon Jack" and put a picture of McQuesten on the front of its bottle.

Jack and Kate did okay, too. They operated trading posts up and down the Yukon River for 20 years, amassing a $2 million fortune before retiring in 1894 to a Victorian mansion in Berkeley, California.

* * *

HERE TODAY, GONE TOMORROW

An ice shelf is a thick, floating platform of ice created where a glacier flows into the ocean. The largest one in the Northern Hemisphere is the Ward Hunt Ice Shelf on the northern coast of Ellesmere Island, Nunavut. It formed about 3,000 years ago and encompasses 400 square kilometers (155 square miles).

In 2002, scientists began noticing that Ward Hunt and others in the area were breaking apart. Today, Canada's arctic has five large ice shelves left, and they cover just 10 percent of the area they did 100 years ago, leading scientists to worry that global warming may make the shelves disappear completely in the next few years.

At rest, a human body gives off as much heat as a 74-watt light bulb.

DON'T FORGET THE BARREL, PART I

Just after the dawn of the 20th century, the first person went over Niagara Falls and lived. Since then, other thrill seekers and fools have attempted similar feats—some successfully, some not. And they've chosen some wacky ways to do it.

THE FALLS

Canada claims Horseshoe Falls, the only part of Niagara Falls that gives at least a slight chance of surviving an "over-the-falls" attempt since it dumps directly into deep water instead of onto rocks below. Every attempt, successful or not, has taken place on the Canadian side of Niagara Falls, although it took a while before Canadians decided to get into the act. Here are a few of the brave (crazy) souls who've tried.

ANNIE EDISON TAYLOR: THE ORIGINAL

Date: October 24, 1901

Method: Wooden and iron barrel

Result: Survived, first person to live after going over the falls

You wouldn't suspect that Annie Edison Taylor would be one to go over Niagara Falls in a barrel. In 1901, Taylor was a Civil War widow and an aging music teacher from Bay City, Michigan. But this was also during a time before Social Security, and Taylor had no savings, no pension, and no children to take her in. As her 63rd birthday approached, she came up with an audacious idea—go over Niagara Falls with the hope that the stunt would earn her enough money to live out her days comfortably. (However, her unspoken thought may have been that death might be the second-best alternative to her dismal financial prospects. One historian reported rumors that before she came up with her Niagara scheme, she considered throwing herself into the Saginaw River.)

On her 63rd birthday, Taylor crawled over the side of a rowboat and strapped herself into a cramped barrel. It had been made back in Michigan by the West Bay City Cooperage Company from

oak, iron, and a mattress, and was weighted at one end with a 90.7-kilogram (200-pound) anvil in the hope that it would keep the barrel upright at least some of the time. On the shore, her newly hired manager talked to a small group of reporters and onlookers, most of whom believed they were watching the prelude to a suicide. In fact, the manager himself had reason to be concerned beyond his financial interests—authorities on both sides of the river threatened him with manslaughter charges if she died.

A friend screwed down the lid, wished her good luck, and cast her adrift. For 18 long minutes, Taylor floated in the dark…her heart pounding, the barrel spinning and toppling her in all directions amid the ever-growing turbulence of the rapids. Suddenly, stomach-turning weightlessness and her own disembodied scream were followed by a hard and sudden blow that bruised her body, gashed her head, and briefly knocked her out.

Dazed and disoriented, Taylor floated, came to, and breathed deeply, wondering if she'd be saved before she ran out of oxygen. Finally, she heard knocking and muffled voices. Then came a welcome stream of light and the face of a man squinting down at her. He shouted, "My God, she's alive!" Spectators along the shore cheered and applauded. Taylor said, "Nobody ought ever to do that again."

But of course they would. Taylor's successful stunt inspired many others over the coming years. And what of her dreams of wealth? Alas, they didn't come true. Her manager disappeared with her barrel (he wanted to use it to find fame himself), and she spent most of her existing savings trying to track him down and get it back. She made some money posing for photos and selling souvenirs to tourists at a small stand near the falls. She also tried to write a book and considered taking a second plunge but died in poverty in 1921 at age 82.

BOBBY LEACH

Date: July 25, 1911
Method: Steel barrel
Result: Survived
New York restaurateur Bobby Leach had been a performer with the Barnum and Bailey Circus, so he figured he knew enough

about stunts and bragged for nearly a decade, "I can do anything Annie can!" On July 25, 1911, he finally tempted fate in a custom-made steel capsule. He survived the trip, but not without fractures and contusions that kept him in a hospital for six months. Unlike Annie Taylor, Leach actually made a pretty good living for a while after his barrel ride, recounting the experience and letting spectators inspect his barrel. Fifteen years after his stunt, though, he died in a freak accident while touring New Zealand—Leach slipped on a discarded orange peel and broke his leg. The man who survived a tumble over Niagara Falls ultimately died of...gangrene.

JEAN LUSSIER
Date: July 4, 1928
Method: Inflated rubber ball
Result: Survived

"Smiling Jean" Lussier was a machinist born in New Hampshire to French-Canadian parents. He spent his childhood in Quebec before moving to Massachusetts. Although he was capable of making a barrel out of metal or wood, he decided to take a radically different approach: a 1.8-meter (6-foot) rubber ball reinforced with steel bands. Inside, he also reinforced the bottom edge with 68 kilograms (150 pounds) of solid rubber padding and ballast, then lined the inside floor, walls, and ceiling with more than 30 inflated inner tubes, leaving a little space in the center for himself.

Lussier survived the fall and moved to Niagara Falls, New York, to sell photos and souvenirs...including "genuine pieces" of his rubber ball, which went for 50¢ each (about $7 in today's money). Local residents wrying noted that he continued selling pieces of discarded inner tubes long after the original ball was gone.

For part II, turn to page 273.

* * *

"Canadians were the first antiAmericans, and the best. Canadian antiAmericanism, just as the country's French-English duality, has for two centuries been the central buttress of our national identity."

—Jack Granatstein, historian

WHATEVER HAPPENED TO UNCLE TOM?

For the title character of her groundbreaking book Uncle Tom's Cabin, *Harriet Beecher Stowe needed a real-life model. That's when she "borrowed" from the autobiography of Josiah Henson, an escaped slave living in Canada.*

GOOD ARTISTS COPY

"So you're the little woman who wrote the book that made this great war!" Supposedly, that was what Abraham Lincoln said when he met Harriet Beecher Stowe. He was talking about her antislavery novel, *Uncle Tom's Cabin*. The book fired up antislavery sentiment in the northern United States, Canada, and Great Britain while angering slaveholders in the American South.

Stowe knew she needed a good slavery story to really make people support abolition, but she was an affluent white woman from Connecticut. She'd never owned slaves or lived under slavery, never escaped, never had to travel undercover out of America's South or through the North, where slave catchers had the right to capture suspected runaways. For that, she borrowed from a book with one of the long, unwieldy titles that were popular at the time: *The Life of Josiah Henson, Formerly a Slave, Now an Inhabitant of Canada, As Narrated by Himself.* (Readers back then didn't seem to mind if a title gave away a book's ending.)

HENSON'S STORY

Born in Maryland in 1789, Josiah Henson worked as a field slave for most of his first 41 years and managed to save $350 to buy his family's freedom…only to be told—after he'd paid the money—that the price had risen to $1,000. He didn't have the rest. Under the threat of being separated from his family and being "sold down the river" to harsher conditions in the Deep South, Henson eventually gathered up his wife and four children and, in the dark of night, headed for Canada. Henson wrote:

> When I got on the Canada side…my first impulse was to throw myself on the ground, and giving way to the riotous exultation of

my feelings, to execute sundry antics which excited the astonishment of those who were looking on. A gentleman of the neighborhood, Colonel Warren, who happened to be present, thought I was in a fit, and as he inquired what was the matter with the poor fellow, I jumped up and told him I was free.

Over the following few years, Henson flourished in Canada. The family settled in Ontario, and he became a furniture maker. He was getting paid for his labors, and his family could afford some small comforts. He learned to read...with his 12-year-old son as teacher. While in Canada, he also met some of his old friends and acquaintances, who asked him to begin preaching on Sundays. It was a skill he'd acquired while living in the American South. Henson later wrote:

I hope it is no violation of modesty to state the fact that I was frequently called upon, not by blacks alone, but by all classes in my vicinity, the comparatively educated, as well as the lamentably ignorant, to speak to them on their duty, responsibility, and immortality, on their obligations to their Maker, their Saviour, and themselves.

THE DAWN SETTLEMENT

As the center of a growing community of several hundred black people in the area, Henson began noticing that the others had done essentially what he'd done: fled to Canada, settled in the place where they arrived, and made their living working for others. Many were inexperienced, though, and didn't make good business decisions or negotiate fair deals for themselves. So Henson started preaching about the importance of "raising their own crops, saving their own wages, and securing the profits of their own labor."

He also began thinking about establishing a collective farm for former slaves, where they could learn skills and thrive in their new country. To help him make the idea a reality, Henson received donations from supporters in the United States and England. With the money, he bought 200 acres in Dawn Township near Dresden, Ontario, and named his venture the Dawn Settlement The commune had a slow start, but eventually it prospered, becoming a major exporter of lumber to the United States and Great Britain, and home to 500 people. It included a farm, a lumber mill, a brickyard, and a school. It was also around this time that Henson wrote *The Life of Josiah Henson*, published in 1849.

O'Leary, PEI, is home to Canada's only potato museum.

STOWE-AWAY

The timing of Henson's autobiography was perfect for Harriett Beecher Stowe, who eventually acknowledged that she loosely based her characters' experiences on the life of Henson. She wrote *Uncle Tom's Cabin* first as a 40-week series in an abolitionist newspaper and then, in 1852, sold it as a novel. The first printing sold out quickly, and within four years, 2 million copies had sold. *Uncle Tom's Cabin* ultimately became the second-best-selling book of the 19th century (after the Bible).

Some people might have objected to having their story appropriated, but Henson seized the opportunity. In 1858, he came out with an expanded edition of his own book that included an introduction by Stowe and which had a new title: *Truth Stranger than Fiction: Father Henson's Story of His Own Life.* Later on, in 1876—seven years before his death at the age of 93—Henson made the Stowe connection even clearer with another edition: *Uncle Tom's Story of His Life: An Autobiography of the Rev. Josiah Henson.*

DAWN'S SLOW SUNSET

Henson's Dawn Settlement didn't have that kind of lasting success, though. It had been founded as a demonstration project to prove that former slaves could make the transition to self-sufficiency and freedom. But new arrivals came faster than the community's modest profits could support. Henson—the symbolic head, spiritual leader, and a well-known literary figure—made a number of lecture tours through the United States and England in the 1840s and 1850s to raise enough money to keep Dawn going. Eventually, though, even hard work wasn't enough to keep it afloat. The school closed in 1868, and within a few years, nearly all the settlers had moved on...all but two. Henson and his wife stayed until their deaths.

Today, several of the original Dawn Settlement buildings, including Henson's house, are still standing and have been preserved as part of the Uncle Tom's Cabin Historic Site in Dresden. For his part, Henson became one of the best-known and most famous escaped slaves in North America, and to honor his life and accomplishments, in 1983, the government in Ottawa made him the first black man to appear on a Canadian postage stamp.

Documents at China's national library claim that Buddhist monks visited...

GOOD NEWS

Who says the news is all bad?

ONE HOLE OF A WEDDING
The Tim Hortons on King Edward Street in Winnipeg doubled as a wedding chapel in September 2009 when locals Al Rutherford and Verna Williams tied the knot. The pair had met at the doughnut shop 10 months before, and Rutherford—with either a flair for the romantic or a concern for his wallet—suggested they get married there. Said Rutherford, "We're here all the time, so it just made sense." After the ceremony, the newlyweds celebrated with family and friends...and wedding cake made out of Blueberry Bloom doughnuts.

TOUCHED BY AN ANGEL
Two days after New Year's 2010, 11-year-old Austin Forman headed to the forest behind his home in Bar Boston, British Columbia, to gather firewood. His golden retriever Angel kept him company. Just before the two reached the trees, Austin noticed a figure in the twilight. First, he thought it was a dog, but quickly realized it was a cougar. The animal lunged for him and would have landed a solid bite if not for Angel, who threw herself between cat and kid. After some shouting, screaming, and serious cat/dog fighting, a Mountie who lived nearby shot and killed the cougar. Austin had not a scratch, and Angel—though suffering serious bites and bruises—was patched up by the vet and sent home after a few days. According to Austin, "She was my best friend, but now she's even greater to me."

HOME IS WHERE THE COLOR IS
Manon Leblanc of Chelsea, Quebec, likes bright colors. In July 2009, she painted one of the buildings she owns a vibrant magenta in the hopes that it would attract renters. The town's council, however, was peeved: Chelsea requires that owners get the okay from the council before making any "major" improvements, and even though Leblanc had filed a request, she didn't wait for the decision before she started painting. In the end, though, the council voted to let her keep the magenta. Why? They felt it was "better than the pink [she] had before."

THE GUY WHO BEAT LEWIS & CLARK

History didn't record the words of explorer Alexander Mackenzie
when he got to the end of his first expedition in 1789. But it may be
just as well, because that was the day Mackenzie discovered that,
on his quest to find the Pacific Coast, he'd not only arrived in
the wrong harbor—he'd also ended up in the wrong ocean.

GO WEST, YOUNG MAN

In 1803, U.S. President Thomas Jefferson hired Meriwether Lewis and William Clark to explore the western part of North America. The men crossed the continent and were hailed as heroes...but they weren't the first to do it. More than 10 years earlier, on June 3, 1789, Canada's Alexander Mackenzie—an employee of a fur trader called the North West Company—pushed his canoe into the Northwest Territories' Great Slave Lake. He was accompanied by four French-Canadian voyagers, their various native slaves and wives, and a Chipewyan translator. As they paddled around the ice chunks blocking the lake, Mackenzie relied on his map (the only one of the area) to navigate their course.

Mackenzie was on a mission from his employer to find a route to the Pacific Ocean. He'd gotten the map from his predecessor on the project, a man named Peter Pond, who spent years gathering data from trappers and First Nations people and mapping out what they told him about waterways and lakes. Pond sketched and re-sketched his map until (according to him) it was clear that there was a river route from Great Slave Lake to Alaska, through Russia, finally arriving in Europe.

England was the main market for the company's furs. Wealthy Brits had an insatiable appetite for beaver, polar bear, and ermine skins to make hats and coats. But this demand had nearly wiped out those animals in eastern Canada, so trappers were moving farther west. An easy route to England from North America's west coast would save fur traders the time they'd normally spend carrying the furs back across the continent to Atlantic harbors.

A RIVER CALLED DISAPPOINTMENT

When Mackenzie made it to the west end of Great Slave Lake, he must have felt relieved. Sure enough, there was a river leaving the lake and heading west, just as Pond's map showed. Mackenzie and his crew took off down the rapid river, averaging better than 120 kilometers (75 miles) a day. The river took a northward bend, and after two weeks, the intrepid group emerged into open waters. Success! Not really. They hadn't found the Pacific. It was the Arctic Ocean…about 1,200 kilometers (750 miles) east of where they'd hoped to be.

According to some, Mackenzie named that waterway Disappointment River. Others say he called it the Grand River. (It was later dubbed the Mackenzie in his honor.) Whatever the river was called, though, the trek out, which followed the river's current, was a lot easier than the way back. Mackenzie's group began the return trip on July 16 and didn't reach their starting point until mid-September.

GETTING HIS BEARING STRAIGHT

In retrospect, there were reasons that Mackenzie should have distrusted Pond's map from the start. First of all, Pond had become a little unstable after years in the wilderness, sometimes erupting unpredictably with rage. (In fact, there were rumors that he'd murdered two rival fur traders.) Also, Pond had never actually traveled the route. He'd depended on the recollections of others, often filtered through a language barrier and the fog of time. In the process, he made several faulty conclusions. First, he believed that Great Slave Lake was farther west that it actually was. Second, he was under the impression that the Mackenzie River traveled due northwest, instead of a little bit west and straight north. And third, he thought the river's outlet was an inlet in Alaska.

After figuring those things out, Mackenzie realized there were no reliable maps of the area. He needed to learn more about the land and how to determine accurate latitude and longitude so he could pinpoint exactly where he was and where he wanted to go. That required the right instruments and an expert knowledge that few in the New World possessed. So he went to England in the winter of 1791–92 to get the equipment and learn how to use it.

First Canadian-born prime minister: Sir John Abbott.

SECOND TRY

By late 1792, Mackenzie was ready to try again. This time, he decided to go southwest, putting in at the Peace River in Alberta, near his home base of Fort Chipewyan, and heading upstream toward the Rocky Mountains. He set out in October with some of the same crew from his first attempt. They got as far as they could before the snow came, and then hunkered down to wait out the winter. Six months later, the ice had thawed enough for them to continue on.

The wintertime had not been a total waste, though. During the cold months, the group built a birch canoe. This was not just any canoe—it was huge, big enough to fit the whole crew and all their equipment. Mackenzie described it in his journal:

> Her dimensions were twenty-five feet long within, exclusive of the curves of stem and stern, twenty-six inches hold, and four feet nine inches beam. At the same time she was so light that two men could carry her on a good road three or four miles without resting. In this slender vessel, we shipped provisions, goods for presents, arms, ammunition, and baggage, to the weight of three thousand pounds, and an equipage of ten people.

TAKE A LEFT AT THE PARSNIP

An old native had told Mackenzie to continue upstream on the Peace River until it split in two. From there, he should take the portion heading southwest (now called the Parsnip River) because, near its glacier-fed headwaters, there would be a spot where he and his crew could hike over the mountains. On the other side, they'd find a navigable river that flowed west.

This all turned out to be true, but the trail was harder than it sounded. For three weeks, Mackenzie's expedition slogged up small rivers and streams and carried the mammoth canoe up, over, and around narrow ledges, thick brush, ragged rocks, and rushing rapids.

Finally, the group found a modest tributary heading in the right direction, which led them to what's now called the Fraser River. This river wasn't on any of Mackenzie's maps, so he optimistically decided that they'd reached the headwaters of the mighty Columbia, which he knew flowed all the way to the Pacific Ocean. It turned out that he was wrong, but for the time being, spirits rose.

GREASE...

The group rode the Fraser downstream and stopped at an native village. There, the tribe issued a warning: turn around. Parts of the river ahead were impossible to reach. And even if they did somehow get through, the river went a long way south before it hit the ocean. Instead, the group should turn around, head back up the Fraser, and keep their eyes peeled for the Grease Trail.

Naturally, the crew didn't want to turn back, but they decided to heed the warning. It took 12 days of paddling upriver, but finally, they found the trail. They parked their canoe and set off with their gear and provisions on their backs. As they slipped and slid along, the group discovered that the Grease Trail lived up to its name. It was the route that the coastal Dakelh and Tsilhqot'in people had used for centuries to carry fish grease harvested from spawning eulachon. (The fish are also sometimes called "candlefish" because they're so fatty that if you dry them, they'll burn just like candles.) The tribes traded the fish grease with other First Nations communities along the route, and over the years, grease had been tracked up and down the path.

...AND CANADIAN GRAFFITI

Mackenzie's crew carried on. They climbed over a 2,000-meter (6,500-foot) high mountain (now called MacKenzie Pass) and then went down into the gorge of British Columbia's Bella Coola River. As they approached the mouth of the Columbia, they met the Bella Bella tribe. Mackenzie wrote in his memoirs that the tribe exhibited "an air of indifference and disdain." One man explained their hostility: a ship had come through six weeks earlier, carrying white people, one of whom had shot at him and another who had struck him on the back with a sword. It turned out that Mackenzie had just missed George Vancouver, who was mapping the Pacific coastline...and apparently alienating the locals at the same time.

Just to be safe, Mackenzie and his group paddled out to a large rock in the Dean Channel, where they slept. The next morning, Mackenzie mixed some vermillion with hot grease and used it to paint an inscription on the rock: "Alexander Mackenzie, from Canada, by land, the twenty-second of July, one thousand seven hundred and ninety-three." Then they hightailed it out of there, heading for home. They made the 1,850-kilometer (1,150-mile)

Canada is home to 10 species of maple tree.

trip in just 32 days. Unfortunately, the trip was pretty much for nought. The North West Company didn't have an immediate, practical use for the knowledge Mackenzie had gained, so his report of the journey was filed away, to be reviewed at a later date that never came.

AFTERMATH

On August 31, 1803, exactly 10 years and one week after Mackenzie arrived back at Fort Chipewyan, Meriwether Lewis and William Clark began their expedition across North America. They garnered attention and international acclaim, and sometimes were credited as the "first" to cross North America. If Mackenzie cared, his reaction wasn't recorded. Besides, he'd already left the continent. He experienced some kind of nervous breakdown in 1799 and moved to England, where he died in 1820.

That he faded into obscurity may not seem fair, but consider this: Mackenzie wasn't the first to cross the continent, either. In 1536, more than 250 years earlier, Spaniard Cabeza de Vaca and three others arrived on the Pacific Coast after a journey called the Narváez Expedition. They were all that remained of 300 men who'd begun the trek in Florida. The Spanish explorers had so angered the natives along the way—by plundering their villages for food, women, and slaves—that only those four completed the voyage alive.

*　　*　　*

HAPPY BIRTHDAY, BABY!

In 2008, Leap Year babies all over the world got the chance to celebrate their actual birthdays: February 29. It's a party that comes around only once every four years, and for some, keeps them young. (One grandfather of 10 celebrated his 18th birthday in 2008.)

It's not easy to become a Leap Year baby. Worldwide, the odds of being born on February 29 are 1 in 1,500, and since 1980, only 6,746 Canadian babies have gotten the title. But it's quite a club to belong to. According to Peter Brouwer, who cofounded the Honour Society of Leap Year Babies (and who "turned" 13 in 2008), "People born on Leap Day have a lot more fun."

The world's strongest current is the Nakwakto Rapids at Slingsby Channel, B.C.

THE NORTH POLE

*We're talking about the north magnetic pole,
not the place where Santa lives.*

TRUE NORTH

Until 1600, when English physician/philosopher William Gilbert proposed the idea that the earth is a giant electromagnet, people thought there was a magnetic mountain somewhere near the North Pole that attracted compass needles. Gilbert's theory was confirmed by explorer James Clark Ross, who, in 1831, followed his compass until it stopped pointing north. By circling around, he found the magnetic sweet spot at Cape Adelaide on Nunavut's Boothia Peninsula.

AS THE WORLD TURNS

In 1903, polar explorer Roald Amundsen (figuring that Ross might have been sloppy) found the north magnetic pole in a location that was slightly more northern and western. Finally, a series of expeditions sponsored by the Canadian government discovered that they were both right: the north magnetic pole is moving continuously in a northwestern direction.

In fact, during the 20th century, it moved a total of 1,100 kilometers (684 miles), accelerating all the while, from 9 kilometers (5.59 miles) per year in 1970 to 60 kilometers (37 miles) per year by century's end—roughly a speed of 7 meters (22 feet) an hour. If the movement continues at this rate and direction, the north magnetic pole will be in Siberia by 2050.

There's a reason the earth's magnetic field won't stay put. Like liqueur-filled chocolates, the earth has a liquid center—a core of molten iron and nickel that's almost as big as the moon. The earth's rotation keeps the liquid moving. As it churns against itself, the molten metal produces electricity, making the earth a huge electromagnet and creating a powerful but constantly shifting magnet field.

OPPOSITES ATTRACT

If you've ever played around with magnets, you know that a mag-

It's against the law to use the name "Parliament Hill" for commercial purposes.

net has two poles. If the poles are the same, they'll repel each other; if they're different, they'll snap together. A compass needle is itself a magnet: one end is attracted to the earth's north magnetic pole, the other to its south magnetic pole (which, by the way, is also shifting, staying on the opposite part of the world from its northern counterpart.)

In 2007, the hosts of the U.K. television show *Top Gear* decided to see if it were possible to drive to the north magnetic pole. Jeremy Clarkson and James May set out in a pickup truck. It was way below freezing, but that was a good thing...because magnetic north is in the Arctic Ocean. They made it, becoming the first—but probably not the last—to perform such a crazy stunt.

*　*　*

CANADIAN VS. AMERICAN FOOTBALL

Both American and Canadian football developed out of rugby and evolved into very similar games—players from the CFL regularly join the NFL, and vice versa. But there are still some major differences between the two sports. Here are a few:

• A CFL field is 110 yards long by 65 yards wide with a 20-yard deep end zone. An NFL field is 100 yards by 53.3 yards with a 10-yard deep end zone.

• The goal posts in the CFL are located on the goal lines. In the NFL, they're placed at the back of the end zones.

• The offensive team has four attempts or "downs" per scoring drive in the NFL. In the CFL, they get three downs.

• When the ball is snapped by the center on each play in a Canadian game, it has to go through the center's legs. Not so in America.

• Distance between the line of scrimmage (where the ball is set at the beginning of each play) and the team playing defense in the CFL is one yard. In American football, it's just 28 centimeters (11 inches).

• In the NFL, each team gets 11 players on the field at a time. In the CFL, it's 12.

• CFL game balls have a white stripe around each end; there are no stripes on NFL game balls.

ARGH, MATEYS!

Pirates and privateers, both require the same skills: looting, murdering, plundering, and kidnapping. The only real difference is sponsorship—a pirate works for himself and his crew, but a privateer is sanctioned by his own government as long as he pays a portion of his loot and attacks (mostly) its enemies' ships. Here are some of the most legendary Canadian swashbucklers to hit the high seas.

ROBERT CHEVALIER DE BEAUCHÊNE

How he lived: Even before Robert Chevalier de Beauchêne became a privateer, he lived a storied life. Whether the stories were true is another matter—Chevalier had a reputation of exaggerating. In 1693, at the age of seven, Chevalier ran away from his home near Montreal (or maybe was kidnapped…no one knows for sure) and was adopted by an Iroquois tribe. His parents retrieved him a year or two later, but Chevalier had already gotten a taste of adventure. He soon ran away again, this time attaching himself to a band of Algonquins who had sided with French colonists fighting British invaders. While helping to defend the settlement of Louisbourg, Nova Scotia, Chevalier met up with a group of Acadian privateers. He was so dazzled by their tales of life on the high seas that he joined their crew. After an apprenticeship spent pillaging English colonies along the North American coast, he got a ship and crew and struck out on his own.

What became of him: Canada remained his home port, but Chevalier died in France in 1731 while dueling for a woman's affections.

PETER EASTON

How he lived: Not all pirates start out bad. Peter Easton was a naval officer from a distinguished military family. In 1602, Queen Elizabeth I gave him three warships and sent him to Newfoundland to protect its fishing fleet from pirates and the encroachments of the Spanish. Easton had a great year in Newfoundland piloting his ship, the *Happy Adventure*, through a series of lucrative encounters. Unfortunately, the next year something terrible happened: peace

broke out. When James I succeeded Elizabeth, he promptly negotiated a treaty with Spain and canceled all privateer commissions. Easton, suddenly out of a job, decided to ignore his new orders. Over the next few years, he bought more ships and "recruited" large crews. (Actually, he press-ganged Newfoundland fishermen to work on his ships.) He continued to attack Spanish vessels, but also decided to diversify, demanding protection money from English ships as well. He even blockaded the busy Bristol Channel in southwestern England, demanding tolls from any ship that wanted to pass through. Eventually, Easton became one of the most successful pirates of the 17th century.

What became of him: Sometimes crime *does* pay. Around 1610, after several years of pirating, Easton retired to Savoy in southern France with about 2 million pounds' worth of gold. There, he married a noblewoman, attained the title of Marquis of Savoy, and lived for at least another 10 years before apparently dying peacefully.

JOHN NUTT

How he lived: John Nutt became a pirate without going through the legal pretense of first being a privateer. Born in England, Nutt visited Newfoundland as a gunner on a ship in 1620. He loved the town of Torbay and resettled his family there before embarking on a life of piracy in the Gulf of Saint Lawrence and the Irish Sea. Nutt was an equal-opportunist who offered protection to English and French settlements alike...for a price. He also recruited sailors by offering regular wages and commissions, a pay and benefit package that lured many men away from the Royal Navy.

What became of him: We don't know. He almost died by hanging in 1623, but George Calvert, an English politician who had been one of Nutt's protection clients, intervened and had him released. Nutt was still pirating as of 1632, but after that, he disappeared.

PIERRE LE MOYNE D'IBERVILLE

How he lived: He was born in Montreal, but had family ties to France. As a sailor and privateer, d'Iberville became renowned for siding with the French to drive English settlers out of Newfoundland. Despite a 1687 "live-and-let-fish" treaty, which allowed the English and French to coexist and fish in the Grand Banks,

d'Iberville led raiding parties that terrorized towns along the coast. Over four months in the winter of 1696–97, d'Iberville and his men destroyed 36 settlements. For his splendid work, the French government sent him to the area that's now Louisiana so he could set up a garrison to ward off English ships. Then in 1706, d'Iberville captured the English-held Caribbean island of Nevis and made plans to attack the Carolina colony on the North American mainland. He traveled to Havana, Cuba, to recruit Spanish aid for that venture.

What became of him: In Havana, he caught yellow fever and died. Colonists up and down the North American coast breathed a sigh of relief.

JOSEPH BAKER

How he lived: Some pirates weren't worthy of waving the Jolly Roger. Take Canadian-born Joseph Baker. In 1800, he signed on to the merchant schooner *Eliza*. With two other crewman he'd recruited for his plot, Baker attacked the first mate during a night watch and tossed him overboard. Then the men went after the captain, William Wheland, wounding him in a brief skirmish and taking him hostage. But during a discussion of where to sell the ship's cargo, the mutineers realized that none of them actually knew how to navigate the ship. Sensing an opportunity, Wheland offered to sail them anywhere they wanted...if they spared his life. Baker agreed, but he wasn't an honorable man. When Wheland learned that Baker intended to murder him as soon as they sighted land, he locked the other conspirators in the hold, caught Baker by surprise, and chased him up the mainmast.

What became of him: Wheland kept Baker up there, lashed to the mast, until they landed on St. Kitts in the West Indies, and then turned him over to the authorities. After a four-day trial in April 1800, Baker and his pals were hanged.

HONORABLE MENTION: THE SALADIN MUTINEERS

How they lived: During the mid-1800s, Peruvian guano (excrement from seabirds) was a valuable commodity for manufacturing fertilizer and gunpowder. In 1844, the *Saladin*, a three-masted British ship, sailed from the coast of Peru carrying a huge load of guano and a small fortune in silver. Onboard were a man named

George Fielding and his 12-year-old son. The elder Fielding, it turned out, was a guano smuggler on the run from Peruvian authorities. He convinced a half-dozen crewmen to take control of the ship and kill the captain and five others. Later, though, the mutineers became suspicious of Fielding and threw both him and his son overboard. Near Country Harbour in Nova Scotia, they decided to run the ship aground and make off with the cargo.

What became of them: Soon after, Canadian authorities caught the six men and put them on trial. Four were found guilty and hanged, but two others were acquitted—the jury believed they'd only joined the mutiny out of fear that they'd be killed.

*　　*　　*

CANADIAN ON THE ROCK

The prisoner who spent the most time in the notorious prison on San Francisco's Alcatraz Island was Canadian. Alvin "Old Creepy" Karpis was born (without the nickname and with Karpowicz as his last name) in Montreal in 1908. By his 10th birthday, he'd fallen in with a bad crowd that corrupted his morals and shortened his last name. First arrested for burglary in 1926, Old Creepy got hired into an entry-level position in the murderous Barker Gang and quickly worked his way up the ladder to an upper management position, increasing gang profits by innovating a successful strategy of kidnapping industrialists for ransom. Victims included William Hamm Jr. of the Hamm's Brewing Company (netting $100,000, the equivalent of $1.5 million in modern money) and Edward Bremer, president of a Minnesota bank ($200,000/$3 million). As proof of his commitment to the organization, Karpis had his fingerprints surgically removed so he couldn't be traced easily.

Unfortunately, United States bureaucrats caught him anyway and arrested him in 1936, sending him briefly to Leavenworth prison in Kansas, and finally to Alcatraz. When Alcatraz closed in 1962, Karpis was transferred to McNeil Island Penitentiary in Washington where he taught a young Charles Manson (whom Karpis called "lazy and shifless") how to play guitar. In 1969, he was deported to Canada. He died in 1979.

Q: What's the difference between a Canadian and a canoe? A: Sometimes a canoe tips.

FOOD FOR COMEDY

Some regional Canadian foods just sound funny. Here are a few that we feel a little awkward requesting in a public place.

Lassy Mogs
Small, cakelike cookies ("mogs") sweetened with "lassy" (molasses), originally from Newfoundland.

Jiggs Dinner
Salty beef mixed with cabbage, boiled potatoes, carrots, and turnips.

Figgy Duff
A boiled-in-a-bag pudding from Newfoundland, rich with butter, sugar, eggs, and raisins…but no figs.

Scrunchions
Pork rinds.

Fish and Brewis
Newfoundland classic made with dried, salted cod, hard tack, and scrunchions (see above).

Chinois
Very similar to shepherd's pie, this French-Canadian dish features layers of ground beef, corn, and mashed potatoes. Despite the "Chinois" in its name (in French, *pâté Chinois* means "Chinese pie"), it's not Chinese. The dish probably gets its name from two towns in Maine (China and South China), where men from Quebec went to work in forestry camps around 1900. Cooks at the camps probably served it, and the men brought the dish back to Quebec with its new name.

Sea-Moss Pudding
Irish moss boiled in water, mixed with milk and sugar. A dessert made in the Maritimes from its copious harvest of Irish moss…which is not really moss, but Canada's most valuable seaweed crop.

Jambuster
What people in Manitoba call a jelly doughnut.

Son-of-a-B**-in-a-Sack Bugger-in-a-Bag**
Also called *poutine en sac*, these European-origin puddings are steamed inside a cotton bag.

Crimcoe
Chocolate milk on Cape Breton Island.

Donair
A pita with spiced meat and sauce made popular in Halifax.

May West
The crème-filled, chocolate-frosted snack cake was originally named Mae West after the buxom actress, but the name changed in the 1980s to avoid lawsuits from the actress's estate.

Toutin
Also known as "damper devils." Similar to pancakes, but made by deep-frying dough.

Duck
A huge, tasty clam—the geoduck—found on Canada's west coast.

Bokkepootjes
This chocolate-dipped cookie's name is Dutch...for "goat feet."

Newfie Screech
A strong, harsh, popular Newfoundland rum.

Vi-Co
Chocolate milk in Saskatchewan. The Vi-Co brand was originally American and came to Canada in the 1950s. But pretty soon, Co-op Dairies bought it and made Vi-Co wholly Canadian.

* * *

CANADA'S FIVE DEADLIEST TORNADOES

1. Regina, Saskatchewan: June 30, 1912
(28 people killed)

2. Edmonton, Alberta: July 31, 1987
(27 people killed)

3. Windsor, Ontario: June 17, 1946
(17 people killed)

4. Pine Lake, Alberta: July 14, 2000
(12 people killed)

5. Valleyfield, Quebec: August 16, 1888
(9 people killed)

WILD, WILD WEST, PART I

Canada's western frontier had its share of colorful outlaws.

RATTLESNAKE DICK BARTER
Sometimes people get themselves a bad nickname and end up living down to it. That was the case for "Rattlesnake Dick" Barter, who started out honest enough but became the ornery sidewinder his name implied. In 1850, Barter, an educated teenage son of a British army officer, left his home in Quebec with two relatives, hoping to strike it rich panning for gold in California. They arrived at Rattlesnake Bar, a small mining area along the American River, but within a few days, Barter's companions decided mining was too much work for too little gold, and they left Barter alone in California.

Although he tried hard, Barter didn't do well as a miner. Some said that was because Dick's spot at Rattlesnake Bar was already "placered out"—all the easy gold on the surface of streams and rivers had been found. Still, around town in the saloons, the young man bragged about how much gold he was finding. And all that exaggerating earned him the nickname "Rattlesnake Dick."

It also made him more enemies than friends. Twice he was arrested for crimes he didn't commit. First, a store owner accused him of stealing merchandise, but Barter was acquitted. After that, he was accused and convicted of stealing a mule. But while Barter was on his way to jail, the mule was found with a man who admitted to the crime, so Barter was set free.

Pirate of the Placers: Hoping to start a new life, Barter began to call himself Dick Woods and moved to Shasta City, in northern California. But once there, he ran into a few miners from the old days and was again saddled with his nickname and bad reputation. So it seems Barter finally just decided that if he was going to be called a criminal, he might as well become one, and he started working hard at building up that bad reputation. After mugging his first victim, he reportedly made a point of saying, "You have just been robbed by Rattlesnake Dick, the Pirate of the Placers."

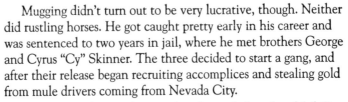

Mugging didn't turn out to be very lucrative, though. Neither did rustling horses. He got caught pretty early in his career and was sentenced to two years in jail, where he met brothers George and Cyrus "Cy" Skinner. The three decided to start a gang, and after their release began recruiting accomplices and stealing gold from mule drivers coming from Nevada City.

For a while, they made enough to keep sheltered and fed. But finally, they got the opportunity for their biggest heist yet. A drunken mining engineer talking big in a tavern let it be known that a Wells Fargo mule train was coming, and it was loaded with $80,600 in gold bullion—the equivalent of a few million dollars in today's money. The gang split into two. Most of them planned to ambush the well-guarded convoy, but Barter and a cohort were supposed to steal some mules to replace the branded (and easily recognizable) Wells Fargo animals. That part of the plan went seriously awry—Barter and his buddy were caught in the act and thrown in jail, making them unable to help the others.

Lost treasure: Meanwhile, back at the robbery site, the convoy approached, and the Skinner brothers couldn't wait for the long-overdue mules. Things started out okay—after the brothers threatened the guards, the men meekly handed over the gold. But the Skinners didn't want those incriminating Wells Fargo mules, so they decided to unload the gold. What they discovered, though, was that all that gold was too heavy for their horses to carry, making a speedy getaway impossible. George Skinner made an executive decision on the spot: he decided to bury half of the loot somewhere on Trinity Mountain and would come back later to dig it up.

That never happened. When the Wells Fargo posse caught up with the group, the ensuing shootout killed George Skinner and, with him, the details of where he buried the gold treasure. The bags of gold bullion have never been recovered.

Jailbird: Dick Barter was never convicted of the holdup. He got out of prison for mule thievery, continued his life of crime by robbing stagecoaches, and was sent to jail often…only to escape each time. In July 1859, while riding with his gang outside of Auburn, California, Barter was shot in a confrontation with law-enforcement officials. He managed to ride away, but was mortally wounded. The next morning, he was found dead by the roadside. He was 26.

PEARL HART

Pearl Taylor came from a solidly middle-class, educated Ontario family, and her initial downfall came in 1888 when (at age 16) she fell in love with a handsome guy named Fred Hart. They eloped. Fred worked as a bartender, but his wages went to feed a wicked gambling addiction. He was also a mean drunk, making Pearl's life miserable. Still, the two traveled to the World's Columbian Exposition in Chicago in 1893 to work whatever jobs they could find there. Fred became a sideshow barker; Pearl sold tickets and toured the fair's exhibitions.

Chicago exposed Pearl to many new ideas. She became enthralled by Annie Oakley's Wild West Show performance and heard a number of female speakers, including Julia Ward Howe, a noted women's activist famous for writing the blood-stirring song "The Battle Hymn of the Republic." It was in Chicago that Pearl got her first taste of independence and her first inkling that she ought to leave Fred.

The couple separated several times. The first time, Pearl was pregnant, so she made her way back to Canada, where she dropped off her son with her mother before heading to Arizona. In 1895, Fred found Pearl living in Phoenix, and the two reconciled. After Pearl gave birth to another child, Fred decided he'd had enough of domesticity and left to join the Spanish-American War. Once again, Pearl left her baby in Canada with her parents and returned to Arizona, where she hooked up with a miner named Joe Boot.

Taking care of Mom: Months later, she received word that her mother was ill, possibly dying, and in need of money for medical bills. Pearl and Joe decided they needed to make a lot of money fast, so they came up with a con: she would lure men to a hotel room, Joe would knock them out, and the two would take the men's money to help out Pearl's mom.

That, however, turned out to be too much trouble for the small amount of money they grossed, so the couple decided to think bigger—they figured that robbing a stagecoach would prove more cost-effective. Pearl cut her hair and dressed in Joe's clothing. The two staked out a suitable spot and waited for the Globe-to-Florence (Arizona) stage. When it arrived, they stopped it; Joe threatened the passengers with a gun, and Pearl relieved them of almost $450 and two revolvers.

Disappearing act: As well as the robbery was planned, the escape wasn't so easy. Pearl and Joe were quickly caught and thrown in jail. Pearl briefly escaped before the sheriff's posse brought her back, but eventually, she spent 18 months in jail for the crime. And that made her famous. As one of only a few female stagecoach robbers, Pearl became well known in the United States and Canada. Reporters from both countries clamored to tell her story and take her picture. Pearl Hart had no taste for fame, though. When she got out of jail, she disappeared. Apparently, she died in the United States sometime after 1928.

* * *

THE CASE OF STEVEN TRUSCOTT

Canada abolished the death penalty in 1976, and one of the cases that inspired the decision was that of Steven Truscott. He was 14 years old in 1959, when he gave 12-year-old Lynne Harper—a classmate in Clinton, Ontario—a ride on his bicycle. Two days later, Harper was found raped and strangled in some nearby woods. Because Truscott had been the last known person to see her alive, police zeroed in on him as a suspect almost immediately even though there were no witnesses and no physical evidence linking him to the crime. The boy was arrested within two days of the body's discovery, and the subsequent trial lasted only two weeks. Truscott was found guilty and sentenced to death by hanging, making him Canada's youngest death row inmate ever.

People all over the world were outraged that a child would be sent to his death. England's *Guardian* newspaper called the sentence "shocking," and Canadian prime minister John Diefenbaker said he had no intention of allowing the boy to be executed. Weeks before Truscott was scheduled to die, he received a stay of execution. Then his sentence was commuted to life. Finally, in 1969, Truscott was paroled. He changed his name and quietly reasserted himself into regular life.

The conviction remained on Truscott's record until 2007, when Ontario's court of appeals reviewed the case, decided the original trial had been unfair, and acquitted him of Lynne Harper's murder. The next year, Ontario awarded Truscott $6.5 million in damages. Finally, a victory of sorts—Truscott called the ruling "bittersweet." (Lynne Harper's murder has never been solved.)

"If all politicians were like Pierre Trudeau, there would be peace." —John Lennon

SHAT FACTS

William Shatner is one of Canada's most cherished actors. Although his most beloved character—James T. Kirk—won't be born until 2233 in Riverside, Iowa, Shatner hails from Montreal.

• Before he went Hollywood, Shatner played Shakespearian roles in Ontario's Stratford Festival and appeared as Ranger Bob in the Canadian version of the *Howdy Doody Show.*

• He appeared on *Alfred Hitchcock Presents* and The *Twilight Zone,* including the famous episode where a former mental patient sees a gremlin on an airplane wing. He also appeared on an episode of *The Man From U.N.C.L.E.* in 1964 with Leonard Nimoy, the future Spock.

• In the early 1970s, between the *Star Trek* television show and the *Star Trek* movies, acting roles dried up, and Shatner lived in a camper in California's San Fernando Valley.

• In 2006, Shatner auctioned off his kidney stone for $25,000 and gave the proceeds to Habitat for Humanity.

• Shatner breeds American saddlebreds and quarter horses on his ranch in Kentucky.

• He suffers from tinnitus, brought on by a too-close explosive charge while filming *Star Trek.*

• In 1965, he starred in the horror movie *Incubus,* which was filmed entirely in the Esperanto language (created by L. L. Zamenhof in the 1800s as the world's first "politically neutral" and universal language). Shatner learned his lines phonetically and spoke them with a French accent, a language he learned from his childhood in Montreal. (The movie bombed.)

• Shatner is of Jewish descent. His grandfather, Wolfe Schattner, anglicized his last name when he moved to Canada from Eastern Europe. As a teen, Shatner worked at Camp B'nai B'rith in Quebec's Laurentian Mountains.

Only prime minister with a PhD: W. L. Mackenzie King.

NAME CALLING

*How did Canada and its provinces
and territories get their names?*

IT TAKES A VILLAGE

Canada: In 1535, explorer Jacques Cartier landed in what's now Canada and, gesturing around him, asked an Iroquois named Donnacona, "What do you call this place?" Apparently thinking Cartier was asking about their community, Donnacona said "Kanata," meaning "village." Cartier, believing that he had just been told the name of the entire area, dutifully wrote the word on his map.

It's not a bad name, though. According to National Resources Canada, some of the other names considered in 1867 included Albertsland, Albionora, Borealia, Britannia, Cabotia, Colonia, Efisga (a combination of the first letters of England, Ireland, France, Scotland, Germany, and Aboriginal lands), Hochelaga, Norland, Superior, Transatlantia, Tuponia (an almost-acronym for "The United Provinces of North America"), and Victorialand.

COLLECTING ROYALTY

New Brunswick: The Duke of Wellington called him "the worst man he ever fell in with his whole life, the most selfish, the most false, the most ill-natured, the most entirely without one redeeming quality." He was talking about the namesake of New Brunswick: the Duke of Brunswick-Lüneburg, who later became King George IV. As both duke and king, George was known to be a profligate, a wastrel, a glutton, a bigamist, and (some say) an abusive husband. When he died in 1830 after 10 years as king, even the staid *London Times* noted, "There never was an individual less regretted by his fellow-creatures than this deceased king. What eye has wept for him?...If he ever had a friend—a devoted friend in any rank of life—we protest that the name of him or her never reached us."

Alberta: This province was named after Princess Louise Caroline Alberta, fourth daughter of Queen Victoria. When the princess was born, the queen predicted that the girl would turn out to be "something peculiar." A sculptor, dancer, and painter who was

The copyrights for all of Margaret Atwood's novels are held by O. W. Toad...

often constrained by her royal position, Louise strove for independence and became a supporter of the 19th-century feminist movement. In 1878, her husband—John, Marquess of Lorne—was appointed governor general of Canada, and Louise Alberta spent time living in Ottawa, learning to ride a sleigh, skate, and fish before returning to England. Lake Louise, the village of Caroline, and Mount Alberta were also named after her.

Prince Edward Island: When the French owned the island, they called it Île Saint-Jean (Island of Saint John). After the British conquered it in the late 1700s, they renamed it to honor Prince Edward, son of George III and a lieutenant-general in Canada's British army. No sooner had the island been renamed but the 32-year-old prince was promoted to commander-in-chief of British North America. He stayed in that post until 1802 when he became the governor of Gibraltar, but his harsh treatment of soldiers there boiled over in a mutiny on Christmas Day of that year, effectively ending his military career.

EXPLORERS AND SETTLERS

British Columbia: An American actually named this province... well indirectly. Captain Robert Gray, a ship-merchant from Rhode Island, named the Columbia River after his sailing ship (the *Columbia*), and Canada's western-most province took its name from the river that ran through it. After the border with the United Stated was defined, most of Columbia ended up south of the U.S.-Canada border. So to keep things unconfused, the Canadians helpfully attached "British" to "Columbia" for their parcel.

The United States, meanwhile, did its best to muddy everything up. When applying for statehood, people living in American Columbia had to change their state's name because the federal government feared there would be confusion between Columbia and the District of Columbia. The state's citizens settled for Washington. Shortly thereafter, someone decided to add "Washington" to the name of the District of Columbia. So instead of a Columbia/ District of Columbia confusion, the poor state was left with an even worse Washington/Washington confusion.

Newfoundland: John Cabot went looking for Indochina in 1497 and aimed his ship far north to avoid Christopher Columbus's

unfortunate earlier run-in with land down south while on a similar search. As it turned out, Cabot hit his own obstacle, a little land mass we now call Canada. Since it wasn't on the maps, he sketched it in and marked it "New Found Land" as a place marker until somebody could explore it properly. Instead, the name stuck.

Labrador: As was customary in 15th-century Portugal, explorer João Fernandes affixed the word "Lavrador" (which means "landowner") to his name to show his status as a man of property. In 1499, King Manuel I hired Fernandez Lavrador to claim new lands in the Americas for Portugal. He came upon a big island just off the mainland. Eventually, it came to be known as Labrador after Fernandes.

Nova Scotia: The name means "New Scotland" in Latin. In early European settler days, the area changed hands at least nine times in battles and treaties between the British and French (and once, briefly, by the Americans). In 1755, the British expelled 12,000 French inhabitants as a way to strengthen its precarious hold on the region. An influx of Scottish people followed, making theirs the largest ethnic group in the province and cinching its name.

NATIVE TONGUES AND LAPPING WATERS

Manitoba: "The straits where the Great Spirit lives" is the meaning of the Cree word *manito-wapow*, and it refers to the middle of Lake Manitoba, where a narrow straight produces rushing water. The Cree believed that the sound made by the water crashing against rocks was their god Manitou beating his drum and communicating with them. When it came time to name the province, Canadian leaders dubbed it Manitoba, or "the God who speaks," in honor of this story.

Quebec: There have been several names used for the area that is now Quebec, including Canada East, Lower Canada, New France, and even just plain Canada. None of these worked for lawmakers, though, so when they had to choose a name for their province, they looked outside of the old standards.

The word *quebec* means "narrow passage" or "strait" in the Algonquin language. This was the aboriginal name for the Saint Lawrence River area, now Quebec City, where the river narrows.

This name made sense: it was one of the earliest-named spots in the region, and it honored the native people who had lived there for generations.

Ontario: The province is named for the large Lake Ontario, and the name comes from the Wyandot word *onitariio* ("beautiful lake"). In translation, though, things get redundant: "Lake Ontario" actually means "Lake Beautiful Lake."

Saskatchewan: Say "swift-flowing river" in the Cree language and it comes out *kisiskatchewani sipi*. The Saskatchewan River is formed where two large branches hook up around the city of Prince Albert, right in the middle of the province. The European settlers agreed that this river was a big enough landmark to name the surrounding region after it. But pronouncing the word properly wasn't as simple, so they shortened it to "Saskatchewan."

Yukon: When Hudson's Bay Company employee John Bell asked Yukon's native residents what the big river nearby was called, they answered, *yu-kun-ah*. In their native tongue, that simply means "a great river." Bell, however, thought it was a good name, and the simplified "Yukon" was added to the map. The region was also named after the "great river."

Nunavut: This one's easy: *nunavut* means "our land" in Inuktitut. The Inuit make up more than 85 percent of the province's population and have been calling the area Nunavut for generations. When the Northwest Territories were finally divided in 1999, the region officially became known as Nunavut by the rest of the country and the world.

WELL, DUH!

Northwest Territories: In English, this name means "territories in the northwest," which, in relation to the whole of Canada, they are exactly.

* * *

KNOW YOUR ICE

If you're floating on a chunk of ice shorter than 10 kilometers (6 miles) long, it's an ice floe. If it's bigger, your on an ice field.

Canada's southernmost town: Kingsville, ON.

WHO'S THAT BAND?

*More stories behind the names of some of
Canada's most beloved musical groups.*

FIVE MAN ELECTRICAL BAND: The Staccatos were a moderate success in the Ontario area in the early 1960s, but as the hippie era bloomed, that name proved to be out of touch. Bands like Big Brother and the Holding Company and the Nitty Gritty Dirt Band were popular, so why not adopt a similar-sounding name that literally told what they were? Their one hit—"Signs"—catapulted Five Man Electrical Band to success. The band still tours on the power of that hit, but today it has six members.

HEART: American draft expatriate Mike Fisher formed this band with a group of his Seattle friends (including Ann and Nancy Wilson) who had trickled up to Vancouver. First signed to the city's Mushroom Records, the band had its first hit singles, "Crazy on You" and "Magic Man," in 1976. Its name—originally White Heart—was inspired by *Tales from the White Hart*, a collection of sci-fi short stories by Arthur C. Clarke.

APRIL WINE: According to the group's Web site, "April Wine" was chosen in 1970 "simply because they were two words that sounded good together." Born in Halifax but raised in Montreal, the group celebrated its 40th anniversary in 2010 with honors from the Juno Awards and the Canadian Music Hall of Fame.

MAHOGANY RUSH: The band's leader, Frank Marino, thought up this name during an acid trip that put him in the hospital. He was trying to explain the nature of his LSD exhilaration—the "rush"—and figured that "mahogany" described it best.

RUSH: When the Toronto band formed hastily in 1968, drummer John Rutsey's older brother suggested Rush, both because of the psychedelic connotations (see Mahogany Rush) but also to reflect the band's frenetic scrambling for a name before its first performance at a church-sponsored coffeehouse.

More bands on page 239.

Joni Mitchell's real name: Roberta Joan Anderson.

AN ICE PLACE TO VISIT

"You can never step into the same river twice," observed Greek philosopher Heraclitus, describing a river's constant changes. At the Hôtel de Glace near Quebec City, you can never stay in the same room next season.

THIS ROOM IS FREEZING!

In the world of cool places to stay, the Hôtel de Glace is one of the coldest. Enjoy your room, because soon enough, it will melt away. So will the lobby, art gallery, tables, chairs, bed frames, and even drinking glasses and serving dishes. All are made of ice and snow.

Canada's only ice hotel, the Hôtel de Glace resembles its European sister ice hotels in offering strictly seasonal (January to April) accommodations. When the spring sun arrives, the hotel self-destructs...only to rise again in a completely different design the following winter.

The Hôtel de Glace first offered its less-than-warm hospitality on January 1, 2001. In that edition, the hotel had 22 rooms. More recent versions of the hotel have had up to 85, as well as an ice café, nightclub, art gallery, and even a wedding chapel that Ireland's *Independent* newspaper rated as one of its top-10 "Dream Wedding Locations"...which may be true if your dream location involves indoor temperatures of about –5°C (28°F).

ICE SPECS AND OTHER COOL FACTS

• In all, some 15,000 tons of snow and half a million tons of ice go into the hotel's construction. Machines produce customized snow, adjusting the mix to control humidity. Workers also use a lot of "snice"—a mixture of sticky snow and ice—as the equivalent of mortar and cement.

• Ice shelters have a reputation for promoting deep, refreshing sleep—writer Herman Melville called heated rooms one of the discomforts of the rich. He advised those wanting a good night's sleep to "have nothing but the blanket between you and your snugness and the cold of the outer air. Then there you lie like the one warm

Canada's largest native land animal: the bison.

spark in the heart of an arctic crystal." You'll find that relaxing cold at the Hôtel de Glace…plus walls that are 1.2 meters (4 feet) thick, which dampen outside sounds to almost nothing.

• The beds are made of ice, but they're lined with deerskins and covered with mattresses and arctic sleeping bags.

• The cost of a one-night, one-bed stay during the 2010 season can run between a few hundred and $1,000, depending on the extras and amenities you choose.

• In the one comforting exception to the all-ice rule, the bath-rooms are located in a separate, heated building not made of ice.

WORLD'S BIGGEST ISLANDS

Of the world's 100 largest islands (Greenland being the biggest), 22 are Canadian. They are…

• Baffin Island, #5

• Victoria Island, #8

• Ellesmere Island, #10

• Newfoundland, #15

• Banks Island, #24

• Devon Island, #27

• Axel Heiberg Island, #32

• Melville Island, #33

• Southampton Island, #34

• Prince of Wales Island, #40

• Vancouver Island, #43

• Somerset Island, #46

• Bathurst Island, #54

• Prince Patrick Island, #55

• King William Island, #61

• Ellef Ringnes Island, #68

• Bylot Island, #71

• Cape Breton Island, #76

• Prince Charles Island, #77

• Anticosti Island, #89

• Cornwallis Siland, #95

• Graham Island, #100

DAVID THOMPSON'S NOTEBOOK: FLORA & FAUNA

In the late 18th and early 19th centuries, explorer David Thompson traveled all over western Canada, recording what he saw in a series of leather-bound notebooks.

THOMPSON'S STORY

David Thompson arrived in Manitoba from England in 1784, when he was just 14 years old. His father had died a few years before, and Thompson spent some time living at a London charity school because his mother couldn't afford to take care of him. But at 14, he was apprenticed to the Hudson's Bay Company and set sail for Canada, where he spent the rest of his life.

During his seven years with Hudson's Bay and several more with the North West Company, Thompson worked as a scribe, clerk, and surveyor. He explored what's now Saskatchewan, Manitoba, Alberta, and British Columbia and mapped more than 3 million square kilometers (1.2 million square miles) of North America, a feat that earned him the title "greatest land geographer who ever lived."

But Thompson wasn't just a fur-trader's hack. He was keenly interested in the land, people, and animals he encountered during his travels, and he kept notebooks with him at all times. Between 1784 and 1812, he filled 77 of them and was writing a book about his experiences when he died in 1857. That volume wasn't ever published, but in 1916, Canadian geologist Joseph Burr Tyrrell collected Thompson's notebooks and published them under the title *David Thompson's Narrative*.

We were fascinated by Thompson's observations, and in this first installment of several, we've excerpted his thoughts about the native wildlife and plants he came upon during his trips through Canada's western wilderness. Thompson writes...

POLAR BEARS

"The steady enemy of the seal is the polar bear. How this awkward animal catches the watchful seal, I could not imagine. The Esquimaux [Eskimos] say he prowls about, examining the ice holes of the seals, and finding one close to high broken ice, there hides himself, and when the seals are basking in the sun and half asleep, he springs upon them, seizes one, which he hugs to death, and as fast as possible, with his teeth cuts the back sinews of the neck. The Seal is then powerless and Bruin feasts on him at his leisure.

MOSQUITOES

"After passing a long, gloomy, and most severe winter, it will naturally be thought with what delight we enjoy the spring and summer. Of the former we know nothing but the melting of the snow and the ice becoming dangerous; summer such as it is, comes at once, and with it myriads of tormenting musketoes; the air is thick with them, there is no cessation day nor night of suffering from them. Smoke is no relief: They can stand more smoke than we can, and smoke cannot be carried about with us. The narrow windows were so crowded with them, they trod each other to death in such numbers we had to sweep them out twice a day.

Different persons feel them in a different manner: Some are swelled, even bloated, with intolerable itching; others feel only the smart of the minute wounds. Oil is the only remedy and that frequently applied; the Natives rub themselves with sturgeon oil, which is found to be far more effective than any other. All animals suffer from them, almost to madness; even the well feathered birds suffer about the eyes and neck.

While these insects are so numerous they are a terror to every creature: the dogs howl, roll themselves on the ground, or hide themselves in the water; the fox seems always in a fighting humour: he barks, snaps on all sides, and—however hungry and ready to go a birdsnesting, of which he is fond—is fairly driven to seek shelter in his hole. A sailor finding swearing of no use, tried what tar could do and covered his face with it, but the musketoes stuck to it in such numbers as to blind him, and the tickling of their wings were worse than their bites. In fact oil is the only remedy.

The cold nights of September are the first, and most steady

Canada is home to Sausage Lake (ON), Pork Peninsula (NU), and Tenderloin Mountain (BC).

relief. In America there always has been, and will be, woods, swamps, and rough ground, not fit for the plough, but admirably adapted to produce musketoes. The cows turned out to graze, when they return to be milked, bring with them more than enough to plague the farmer.

WILD RICE

"The wild Rice is fully ripe in the early part of September. The natives lay thin birch rind all over the bottom of the Canoe, a man lightly clothed, or naked, places himself in the middle of the Canoe, and with a hand on each side, seizes the stalks and knocks the ears of rice against the inside of the Canoe, into which the rice falls, and thus he continues until the Canoe is full of rice; on coming ashore the women assist in unloading. A canoe may hold from ten to twelve bushels. He smokes his pipe, sings a song; and returns to collect another canoe load.

And so plentiful is the rice, an industrious man may fill his canoe three times in a day. Scaffolds are prepared about six feet from the ground made of small sticks covered with long grass; on this the rice is laid, and gentle clear fires kept underneath by the women, and turned until the rice is fully dried. The quantity collected is no more than the scaffolds can dry, as the rice is better on the stalk than on the ground. The rice when dried is pounded in a mortar made of a piece of hollow oak with a pestle of the same until the husk comes off. It is then put up in bags made of rushes and secured against animals. The natives collect not only enough for themselves, but also as much as the fur traders will buy from them; Two or three Ponds of water can furnish enough for all that is collected."

For more flora and fauna, turn to page 432.

* * *

THE CASE OF THE MISSING PRIME MINISTER

A group photo of world leaders during the 2009 G-20 summit in London, England, had to be taken a second time when someone noticed that Canada's prime minister, Stephen Harper, was missing. Where was he? Harper had stepped away for a bathroom break.

Saskatchewan's official sport: curling.

A COLD ONE IN THE YUKON

During long, cold winters, there's great comfort in greeting
friends in a tavern, getting absolutely plastered, and
drinking a beverage with a human toe at the bottom.

TOE-NIGHT'S THE NIGHT

Since 1973, the Sourdough Saloon in Dawson City has offered the Sourtoe Cocktail, a stiff drink with a stiffer garnish—a genuine, pickled human toe. The macabre tradition started when the owners of the bar were considering the idea of giving tourists "Honorary Sourdough" certificates, named after the slang term for gold prospectors because they baked and ate so much sourdough bread in the wilderness. But the bar owners decided that would dishonor the tens of thousands who actually braved bone-chilling winters and abject disappointments during the late 19th century in the unforgiving Yukon gold rush.

"Well, how about a 'sour toe,' then?" suggested local Dick Stevenson, who happened to be in the bar listening to the conversation. He suggested offering a drink with an actual toe in it and giving certificates for patrons who were brave (or foolish, or drunk) enough to drink it down to the bottom.

"THE LIPS HAVE GOTTA TOUCH THE TOE"

Stevenson wasn't joking. He'd recently bought a cabin nearby, and in the leftover stuff inside, he found a grisly souvenir—a jar containing an alcohol-pickled big toe. After a little asking around, he discovered that the previous occupants had been two brothers who made a living smuggling booze into Alaska during Prohibition. While dog sledding a shipment one winter, the brothers ran into a group of Mounties and took off, fleeing from the law. They got away, but one of the two got his feet wet. His big toe froze, and with no doctor available, he had his brother chop it off and preserve it in alcohol.

The game was afoot. Stevenson's drink idea got a toehold on the menu: a beer stein filled with champagne and garnished, like an

olive in a martini, with Stevenson's pickled big toe at the bottom.

To everyone's surprise, it didn't take long before someone ponied up the $5 pricetag and tried it to become a member of the Sourtoe Cocktail Club. To join, there's only one rule: "You can drink it fast, you can drink it slow—but the lips have gotta touch the toe." Those who fulfill that requirement earn a certificate, and so far, it's estimated that more than 24,000 people have chugged the cocktail down.

BUT...WHERE DO THEY GET THE TOES?

Pickled toes aren't so easy to get your hands on, but it's not completely impossible either. For one thing, most Sourtoe Cocktails reuse the toe. If a patron accidentally swallows one, it's considered a major faux pas, but it does happen. Stevenson's original contribution was accidentally swallowed in 1980, and several others have been lost that way since. So the saloon always has replacement digits on hand, as many as 12 piggies at a time, just waiting to step forward and take their place in the cocktail. Luckily, worldwide notoriety has helped boost the number of donations. One even arrived unsolicited from Virginia, complete with a cautionary explanation: "Don't wear open-toed sandals while mowing the lawn."

* * *

THE PLAINS OF ABRAHAM

This region with the biblical-sounding name was the spot of a crucial battle during the Seven Years' War. For most of 1759, the plains of Abraham were just grazing land outside Quebec City. But on September 13, the English surprised French forces there, defeated them quickly, and seized control of the city...the beginning of the end for the French in the New World. Today, it's a historic park.

But where does the name come from? That goes back to a 17th-century farmer named Abraham Martin. He was one of the first Europeans to arrive in New France (around 1620) and eventually settled near Quebec City. Martin became a farmer and fisherman and lived on the land that came to bear his name.

MORE CELEBRITY 101

Let's get to know a few more Canadian celebrities.

• Newscaster Peter Jennings got his start in broadcasting in 1947 when, at the age of nine, he began hosting *Peter's People*, a Saturday morning kids show on the CBC. (He got the gig because his dad worked at the station.

• Folksinger Joni Mitchell was supposed to perform at the famous Woodstock Music & Art Fair in 1969, but she was also scheduled to appear on the *Dick Cavett Show* (a popular talk show in the 1960s and '70s) on the same day. The traffic in and out of the festival was so bad that her manager didn't think she'd make it to Cavett's show on time, so he urged her to pull out of the Woodstock line-up. She did, appeared on *Dick Cavett* as scheduled, and wrote a song in homage to the festival—it was entitled (surprise, surprise) "Woodstock."

• On April 1, 1997, *Jeopardy* host (and Sudbury, Ontario, native) Alex Trebek swapped jobs with *Wheel of Fortune* frontman Pat Sajak as an April Fool's Day joke.

• Back in 1990, when Celine Dion recorded her first English album, the Quebec music industry gave her its Anglophone Artist of the Year award. But having been born and raised in Charlemagne, Quebec, Dion was insulted to be called an "anglophone artist." She refused to accept the prize, saying, "I am not an anglophone artist, and the public understands that. Everywhere I go in the world, I say that I'm proud to be Québécoise."

• Today, musician Sarah McLachlan mostly sticks to the piano and guitar, but the first instrument she learned to play was the ukulele.

• Neither NBC president Brandon Tartikoff nor producer Gary David Goldberg thought Michael J. Fox had the right look for the role of 1980s heartthrob Alex P. Keaton on TV's *Family Ties*. Tartikoff even went so far as to explain his concern by saying that Fox just "didn't have a face you'd see on a lunchbox." After the show became a hit, Fox glued a picture of himself onto a lunchbox and sent it to Tartikoff with a note that basically said, "Eat crow!"

k. d. lang's full name is Kathryn Dawn Lang.

GRAVEYARD OF BURIED HOPES

Author L. M. Montgomery led a life of quiet desperation. Details of her emotionally wrenching private world—and possible suicide— give extra poignancy to her beloved character's most famous line, "My life is a perfect graveyard of buried hopes."

MAUD OF CAVENDISH

The author of the Anne of Green Gables series, Lucy Maud Montgomery earned the love and admiration of millions of fans for more than a century. Her first book, *Anne of Green Gables* (1908), has inspired adaptations to film, TV, and stage, charming children and adults with the life of misplaced orphan Anne Shirley and her life on Prince Edward Island.

Readers familiar with the story of Anne Shirley—an orphan girl sent to live with a strict, morally upright elderly foster brother and sister—will undoubtedly see similarities between Anne and her creator. As a young child, Montgomery was sent to live with a strict older couple—her maternal grandparents—after her mother died and her father left to seek work in Saskatchewan. Living in the small town of Cavendish on Prince Edward Island, Montgomery found herself isolated, lonely, and constantly under the disapproving gaze of her grandparents.

Like Anne, Montgomery also completed a teaching certificate course in one year and went on to teach before studying literature at Dalhousie University in Nova Scotia. And like Anne, she began writing for publication in her early 20s. Unlike her heroine, though, Montgomery seemed unable to rise above her surroundings and forge her own happy life.

That wasn't clear from the surface. Three years after the publication and immediate success of *Anne of Green Gables*, Montgomery married a Presbyterian minister named Ewan Macdonald. When Macdonald took a position in a church in Leaskdale, Ontario, the couple moved into the church rectory where, over the next 15 years, Montgomery wrote most of her tales about the people living in the fictional town of Avonlea.

JOURNEY'S END

Before Montgomery's death in 1942 at "Journey's End"—her home in Toronto—she'd published 20 novels and more than 500 short stories and poems. But it turned out that there was much more of her writing that hadn't seen the light of day: her journals. It wouldn't be until the 1980s that the journals first appeared in print, giving an intimate view of the author's internal life.

Those journals reveal a woman who, near the end of her life, was worn down: the demands of a 31-year loveless marriage to a husband who suffered terrible depression, and the disappointment in her son, Chester, who had moved back home after losing his position at a law firm, fathering a child out of wedlock, and then marrying and subsequently divorcing the baby's mother. By the standards of the time, all these "scandals," particularly her husband's shaky mental health, would have been seen as unacceptable to talk about in public, especially for a minister's wife. So Montgomery was left to suffer in silence.

A month before she died, Montgomery declared, "I shall be driven to end my life." A week before she died, an old friend from Leaskdale visited. At the end of the visit, the friend remarked that she would come back the next week; Montgomery responded cryptically that she had doubts she'd still be there to visit.

Lucy Maud Montgomery was found dead on April 24, 1942, at the age of 67. Her death was ruled to be the result of congestive heart failure.

BUT WAS IT SUICIDE?

In the reports of Montgomery's death, no mention was made of a scrap of paper found at her bedside, a handwritten note that spoke of the writer losing her mind in stages, asking for forgiveness from God and everyone else "even if they cannot understand," and alluding to circumstances "too awful to endure and nobody realizes it." The letter finished with this poignant summation: "What an end to a life in which I tried always to do my best."

In September 2008, Montgomery's granddaughter Kate Macdonald Butler went public with a bombshell that she said her father, Stuart Macdonald—Montgomery's younger son—had revealed to her. Shortly before dying, Stuart told his daughter that he'd found the bedside note and suspected suicide from the start.

He told no one of his suspicions, though, silenced by the same stigma that had isolated his mother.

Butler went public with the secret, she said, in an effort to encourage discussion about depression and suicide, and to help "sweep away the misconception that depression happens to other people, not us—and most certainly not to our heroes and icons."

NO ABSOLUTE ANSWERS

Despite this information and other anecdotal evidence, debate still lingers over the exact circumstances of Lucy Maud Montgomery's death. Understandably, her admirers are mostly unwilling to admit to such a disturbing possibility, but even among scholars, the matter hasn't been closed. For example, Mary Henley Rubio at Ontario's University of Guelph (and author of a Montgomery biography and coeditor of her published journals) says other possibilities should be considered. For example, says Rubio, Montgomery was taking several medications that, if mixed, could cause an unintended drug overdose. It's also possible that what sounded like a suicide note might have been intended as a journal entry.

No matter what the details are, though, Montgomery seemed to have led a life of emotional isolation and depression. Although spunky Anne Shirley could always bounce back, her creator appeared to be more like supporting character Miss Lavender Lewis in *Anne of Avonlea*, who said...

> I'm just tired of everything...even of the echoes. There is nothing in my life but echoes...echoes of lost hopes and dreams and joys. They're beautiful and mocking. Oh Anne, it's horrid of me to talk like this when I have company. It's just that I'm getting old and it doesn't agree with me. I know I'll be fearfully cranky by the time I'm sixty. But perhaps all I need is a course of blue pills.

* * *

BAD JOKES
Q: Why did the Canadian cross the road?
A: To get in the middle.

Q: How do you stop bacon from curling in a frying pan?
A: Take away its brooms.

I ♥ THE NORTHWEST TERRITORIES

Before they started carving it up, the Northwest Territories was about the biggest thing in North America. Oh well, it's still got its musk oxen and pingos, and at least it didn't get renamed "Bob." Here are 12 reasons to love it.

1. THE IBYUK PINGO. At 49 meters (161 feet), the Ibyuk pingo is Canada's tallest, and growing (about 2 centimeters/0.8 inches a year). Also called *hydrolaccoliths*, pingos are earth-covered ice bulges. After growing for up to a thousand years, they eventually burst open, their ice melting in sunlight and collapsing into a crater sometimes called an *ognip* ("pingo" spelled backward). The Mackenzie Delta is home to not just Ibyuk but 1,350 other pingos—about a quarter of the world's total.

2. MULTIPLE PERSONALITY. "The Northwest Territories" has a plural construction, yet it's always referred to as a singular (e.g., "The Northwest Territories *is...*" not "The Northwest Territories *are...*").

3. MEET ME AT THE CORNER. Although the Northwest Territories shares land borders with five provinces/territories, there are actually six you can touch with one foot while your other foot is in the NWT. This is thanks to the spot where the NWT's southeast corner meets Manitoba's northwest corner. And if you have really big feet, it's also the one spot in Canada where you can stand in four different political regions at once (since Nunavut and Saskatchewan have corners that meet there, too).

4. A GREAT BIG LAKE. The NWT's Great Bear Lake is the biggest lake entirely inside Canada. It's also the fourth-largest lake in North America. The three that are larger: Lake Superior, Lake Huron, and Lake Michigan.

5. ICE ROAD TRUCKERS. Who could imagine that a reality TV show about truckers who drive on NWT's "ice roads" (winter

routes laid out over frozen lakes and rivers) would be popular? Well, the History Channel did. According to the station, *Ice Road Truckers* "charts two months in the lives of six extraordinary men who haul vital supplies to diamond mines and other remote locations over frozen lakes that double as roads." They're probably the only truckers who actually *hope* for consistently freezing temperatures and thick icy roads, considering this fact from the History Channel's Web site: "If a rig breaks through the ice and sinks into the freezing water, the trucker has less then a minute before they will freeze to death."

6. POLYMORPHICALLY POLYGLOT. The Northwest Territories has 11 official languages, more than any other political entity in all of the Americas. Three-quarters of its 43,000 residents call English their "mother tongue." Dogrib and South Slavey were second and third at about 2,000 and 1,300 people, respectively, beating French, which claims just under 1,000 speakers. Several of the official languages are spoken by fewer than 200 people.

7. IT COULD'VE BEEN CALLED BOB. In a 1996 poll about what to rename the Northwest Territories after Nunavut split off, keeping "Northwest Territories" was the first choice. The second most popular choice, originally suggested by a prankster, was "Bob."

8. SOMBA K'E. In the Dogrib language, that's what the city of Yellowknife is called; it means is "where the money is." Makes sense, considering the number of gold and diamond mines in the area.

9. A TREELESS NATIONAL PARK. Aulavik National Park on Banks Island has the highest concentration of musk oxen on earth, and they're pretty well protected—there are no roads leading into the park, so to visit, you'll need to charter a plane. Also, Aulavik has no trees, not even one, because it's above the tree line. Past the tree line, trees can't grow because of lack of moisture, cold temperatures, or other inappropriate conditions

10. WATCH THE SKIES. In 1978, Yellowknife nearly got hit by pieces of Cosmos 954, a nuclear-powered Soviet satellite. It

CM (the world's leading maker of hockey equipment) stands for Canada Cycle and Motor Company

crashed beyond the town's outskirts apparently without hurting anybody. The satellite did, however, release some pretty nasty radioactive fuel. Canada billed the Soviets $6 million for cleanup costs; the Soviets paid half of that.

11. IT'S COOOLD. The northern coast and islands of the Northwest Territories have what's called a "polar climate." That means the sun shines 24-hours-a-day in the summer, rarely shines in the winter, and the highs (in summertime) don't go above 10°C (50°F).

12. NIRVANA. Who'd expect to find Nirvana in the Northwest Territories? Mount Nirvana is the highest mountain in the region. In 1965, climbers Bill Buckingham and Lew Surdam became the first people to reach its summit, and Buckingham called it Nirvana. Although the name has become commonly used among the alpine crowd, Statistics Canada still refers to it as an "unnamed peak."

* * *

OUT LIKE FLYNN?

Errol Flynn was one of the most famous swashbucklers of the 1930s. He made a name for himself with movies like *Captain Blood* and *The Adventures of Robin Hood*. But his private life was one of chaos: he had trouble with the IRS, made bad business investments, and became a raging alcoholic. He died on October 23, 1959, while visiting Vancouver, and despite the fact that he'd complained of back and leg pain that same day, his friend George Caldough drove them (and Flynn's 16-year-old "traveling companion," Beverly Aadland) to a party. According to Caldough, a doctor was supposed to be there, but rather than take it easy, Flynn regaled party goers with glamorous stories about his early years in Hollywood and the stars—like John Barrymore and W. C. Fields—that he hung out with. Eventually, Flynn disappeared from the group, and Aadland found him on the bathroom floor, his skin blue and his hearbeat weak. Finally, he was rushed to a hospital, but it was too late. The official causes of death: myocardial infarction, coronary thrombosis, coronary atherosclerosis, liver degeneration, liver sclerosis, and diverticulosis of the colon.

The Canadian side of Niagara Falls has a flow of 155 million liters of water per minute...

MOVING DAY

Most housing leases in the province of Quebec renew on July 1, which just happens to be Canada Day. That means hauling furniture instead of reveling has become the activité du jour for many Quebecers. How did the tradition get people moving, and why is it still around?

MAY DAY! MAY DAY!

Most Canadians commemorate July 1 in traditional holiday fashion, with parties and outdoor barbecues. The people of Quebec celebrate an annual event of another kind: Moving Day...or, in the local vernacular, *Fête du Déménagement* (the Moving Holiday). This is especially true in Montreal, where more than a third of the city's residents lease their homes and have to re-sign (or move) every July 1.

It wasn't always this way, and it wasn't always on this particular day. In the 1700s, the government of colonial New France wanted to prevent landlords from evicting tenant farmers before winter snows melted, so it set the earliest legal eviction date each year at May 1. The rural practice of annual lease agreements ending at midnight on April 30 eventually became the practice in urban leases as well. Province-wide, May 1 became "Moving Day" and remained so until the 1970s.

SCHOOL'S OUT

As times changed, though, modern tenants became more concerned about the school year than about spring planting schedules. Transferring students in and out of school a few weeks before the term ended (simply because the government had declared that all leases came due on May 1) became a major headache for educators and families alike. To address this, a new Quebec law in 1974 decreed that leases would be valid until midnight on June 30. "Moving Day" pulled up stakes and relocated to July 1.

The intentions behind the date shift appeared straightforward enough, but many Quebecers suspected that provincial politics were also involved. Thousands of people exchanged living spaces en masse, and at a time when Quebec was grappling over whether

or not to leave the Canadian Confederation, some thought that the new date was a deliberate attempt to tamp down Canada Day celebrations. That theory, however, requires ignoring the fact that the man who introduced the bill, Jérôme Choquette, was a federalist-leaning national assembly member...of the Quebec Liberal Party.

SPRING BACKWARD

Although the July 1 date has generally gained acceptance in the province, there are occasional rumblings by traditionalists intent on moving Moving Day back to May 1 so that all Quebecers can participate in Canada Day celebrations like everyone else. An online petition posted in May 2008 contained an inspiring comment: "This public holiday [Canada Day] should be celebrated by holding up a flag of our country, not by moving furniture." However, in a year and a half, the petition garnered just 42 signatures.

* * *

WE ALL FALL DOWN

In 2003, two researchers from Nova Scotia's Dalhousie University (Sarah Shea and Sarah Giles) published a satirical study in the *Canadian Medical Association Journal* arguing that children's nursery rhymes "portray head injuries as inevitable events that do not require medical follow-up." Some of their evidence:

• The severity of the injuries sustained by Jack (falling down and breaking his crown) and Jill (who "came tumbling after") are unclear, thus making it impossible to decide whether medical attention was necessary.

• No one seemed to care that the elderly man in "It's Raining, It's Pouring" "went to bed and bumped his head and couldn't get up in the morning." The reason for bumping his head (foul play, an accident, a seizure, etc.) was never investigated.

• The kids in "Ring Around the Rosie" (who "all fall down") may live during the time of the bubonic plague, but according to Giles and Shea, "It is absurd to think that a pneumonic process could take an entire group of children from the joyous noise of a game to the silence of death this quickly. Clearly, something happened that led to physical—and probably cranial—disaster."

Q: Who was the first baby born on Canada's centennial (July 1, 1967)? A: Pamela Anderson

CANADA'S FIRST SUPERSTAR EXPORT

*It's become a cliché—a talented Canadian achieves international
fame and ends up living in America. But someone had to
do it first, right? We think we've found her.*

DRAMA QUEEN
In 1875, 13-year-old Georgina May Campbell of Whitby,
Ontario, changed her name to May Irwin and, out of
necessity, went into show business. Her father had died suddenly,
and her mother needed money. So Mrs. Campbell decided that
May and her younger sister Flo should hit vaudeville's stages as a
singing act. By the time May was 15, the pair was playing the
Tony Pastor's Theatre in New York, one of the most highly sought
gigs on the vaudeville circuit.

May and Flo stayed at the Pastor Theatre for six years, becom-
ing a well-known act (and getting rich). Then, when May turned
21, she set out on her own, bouncing between vaudeville and
comedic theater in London and New York for nearly four decades.

For all her comedic talent, though, May Irwin was renowned for
her melodic voice, strong and loud enough to fill a theater. She
wrote some of her own songs, and made others her own just by the
power of her voice. Her hits included "The Frog Song," "The
Bully Song" (also called "I'm Looking for the Bully of the Town"),
"Crappy Dan," and "Hot Tamale Alley," a song she wrote with
George M. Cohan, a popular Broadway star known as the "father
of American musical comedy."

THE KISS SEEN 'ROUND THE WORLD
But singing and dancing and making people laugh weren't enough
for Irwin—she was provocative, too. And Irwin was making a
name for herself just as one of Thomas Edison's most important
inventions—the phonograph—was revolutionizing entertainment.
And thanks to Edison, Irwin achieved what's probably her
longest-lasting claim to fame: she appeared in the first-ever movie

University of Toronto professor Daniel Wilson coined the term "prehistoric" (1851).

kiss. Thomas Edison saw her perform in a musical called *The Widow Jones* on Broadway in 1896. The play ended with a sweet and very long, lingering kiss between the two stars, Irwin and John C. Rice. Edison was so enchanted that he hired Irwin and Rice to come to his studio and perform the kiss for his cameras.

The resulting 18-second film, *The Kiss*, titillated and scandalized many; it resulted in brisk ticket sales as well as stern newspaper editorials. Some people demanded that the film be confiscated and its exhibitors arrested. But others were more offended by aesthetics than morality. One critic wrote, "Neither participant is physically attractive, and the spectacle of the prolonged pasturing on each other's lips was beastly enough in life size on the stage but magnified to gargantuan proportions and repeated three times over, it is absolutely disgusting." (Irwin was considered "pretty" in that buxom, big-boned, 19th-century way, and Rice was almost 40, balding, and sported a bushy mustache.)

Back in Canada, though, *The Kiss* became the first film to be publicly shown in Ottawa, and only the second film ever exhibited in the entire country. (The first had premiered in Montreal less than a month earlier.). And 100 years later, in 1999, the U.S. Library of Congress called *The Kiss* "culturally significant" and choose to preserve it as a national resource.

EXIT STAGE LEFT

May Irwin's last professional hurrah was a 1922 Broadway run. After that, she retired and split her time among several homes, including a winter home in Florida and a vacation house on Club Island in Ontario's Thousand Islands area. Irwin wasn't done with fame, though. One day, at a restaurant on Club Island, she was served a salad topped with a type of dressing that was unique to the area. She liked it so much that she bought the recipe and started serving it to guests at her various homes. She called it "Thousand Islands dressing," a name that stuck. She died in New York City in 1938.

* * *

"There are no rules here—we're trying to accomplish something."
—**Thomas Edison**

COMEDY CENTRAL

How many Canadians does it take to screw in a lightbulb? Keep reading.

FOR THE LOVE OF THE GAME

It's game seven of the Stanley Cup Finals and a man in the cheap seats sees an empty one at center ice. He skulks down and asks if anybody is sitting there. The woman sitting next to it sighs sadly and says, "My husband was supposed to be sitting there. We attended every playoff together since 1987, but he died and this is the first time I've come alone."

"That's so sad," said the man. "Maybe you should've brought a friend or a relative this time?"

"I couldn't," she said. "They all went to the funeral."

AND THEN THERE WAS CANADA

On day six of the Creation, God announced to his archangel underlings, "Today we're creating a place called Canada. Pull out all the stops. Give it beautiful mountains, lakes, plains, forests, and sandy beaches. Underground, give it oil, gold, etc. Oh, and plenty of fish and wildlife."

"Sir," interjected an archangel, "aren't you being overly generous to these Canadians?"

"Don't worry, I'll balance it out," said God. "Wait 'till you see the neighbors I'm giving them."

LET THOSE AMERICANS LOOSE?

An American couple gets hopelessly lost while driving through Canada. Over the objections of her husband, the wife calls out to a pedestrian, "Hey buddy, can you tell us where we are?" The pedestrian smiles sympathetically and says, "Saskatoon, Saskatchewan."

After she rolls up the window, her husband says, "I told you it wouldn't do any good. They don't even speak English up here."

THE LIGHTBULB MOMENT

Q: Okay, really—how many Canadians does it take to change a lightbulb?

A: None. We don't try to change them. We accept them as they are.

Arctic hares have black eyelashes that protect their eyes from the sun, like sunglasses.

WARE A LEGEND IS BORN

Alberta cowboy John Ware was an impressive man, both in stature and nature. He was also a curiosity, a fact that led many people to embellish his true accomplishments.

BACKGROUND
John Ware was an African American born in the southern United States in 1845. After the Civil War, he migrated west, learned cowboy skills, and began working for various ranchers. Eventually, he arrived in what became Alberta and helped to pioneer the ranching industry in that region.

Ware was a novelty in Canada's Wild West. It wasn't just the color of his skin that made him stand out—in the rough-and-tumble culture of the time, his kindness and honesty were as renowned as his cowboy skills. He soon became a beloved member of the community and a symbol of tolerance in the all-white ranching world. He eventually started his own successful cattle ranch, married, and had six children.

Not surprisingly, John Ware became a legend in the area. But he was also a real man, and his accomplishments were genuine enough that two creeks, a mountain, a ridge, a school, and other things were named in his honor. In that spirit, we take a moment to set the record straight about one of Canada's most famous cowboys.

LEGEND: John Ware could stop a steer dead in its tracks and bring it to the ground in one move.

FACT: Ware was an amazing roper, regularly wowing colleagues with the lasso tricks that he'd picked up in Texas. He was also a superior steer wrestler. Although it's a common sight in today's rodeo shows and competitions, in Ware's day, it's likely that few Canadians had seen a man wrestle a steer to the ground. In fact, Ware was so skilled that, in the summer of 1893, he won the steer wrestling competition at the Calgary fair.

LEGEND: John Ware took his cattle across the Bow River without getting a single one wet.

FACT: This may be true. When Ware set up his own ranch in

Turner Valley, Alberta, in the late 1890s, he had to move his cattle to the other side of the city of Calgary, which was split by the Bow River. Some sources say he waited until nightfall, ran his cattle through the city's streets, over a river bridge, and onto his new ranch. If he really used this relocation method, it would explain how his cows stayed dry.

LEGEND: John Ware discovered the Turner Valley oil field when he lit a match and the ground caught fire.

FACT: The Bar U Ranch, located about 100 kilometers (62 miles) south of Calgary, was one of a few large corporate ranches in the area during the 1880s, and one of the most profitable. John Ware worked there for several years before moving on to another ranch—the Quorn in the Rocky Mountain foothills. At the Quorn, he grazed his boss's cattle on land that later became the Turner Valley oil field. But he didn't find oil there. Credit for that discovery goes to a local farmer named William S. Heron in 1913.

LEGEND: The Blackfoot people gave John Ware the name *Matoxy Sex Apee Quin*, or "Bad Black White Man," because of his admirable strength and courage.

FACT: John Ware's Blackfoot name was *Matoxy Sex Apee Quin*, but not because the group admired him. (Remember, "bad" didn't mean "good" in those days.) According to Ware biographer Grant MacEwan, the Blackfoot saw Ware as an outsider who often treated them harshly as he policed the local lands with fellow ranchers. The name "white man" just meant "outsider," but "bad" described their opinion of him.

LEGEND: There wasn't a horse he couldn't ride, and John Ware was never thrown from a horse.

FACT: According to Ware's daughter, this came straight from the horse's mouth, as it were. When asked to tame horses, Ware usually accepted, boasting that he'd never been thrown. But even though he was a respected broncobuster with an uncanny horse sense, in the end, a horse killed him. While out herding cattle in September 1905, Ware's horse fell on him and crushed him to death. Ware's funeral was one of the largest, if not *the* largest in the young city of Calgary, and people of all races turned out to pay their respects.

YOU CALL THAT ART?

*Canadians are as artistic as the next guy, but
sometimes, they get a little too creative.*

STILL LIFE
In 2008, artist Michael Fernandes put together an odd
exhibit in Halifax, Nova Scotia: a banana in a window.
Some called it just a piece of fruit on a windowsill, but Fernandes
argued that it was art...and eventually set its price at $2,500. A
few buyers were interested, but most people were unimpressed.
Still, Fernandes changed the piece of fruit each day—adding a
slightly greener banana and eating the previous one. The goal?
To show that humans are "temporal, but we live as if we are not."

FRED FLINTSTONE THROWBACK
Quebec artist Michel de Broin is known for his playful creations,
so it's no surprise that in 2008 he rigged the shell of an old Buick
Regal to run on pedal power. De Broin attached a four-seater
bicycle to the Buick, installed hand brakes, and let some friends
in Toronto take it out for a drive. A police officer spotted them
plodding down the road, pulled them over, and cited the group
for driving an unsafe vehicle. At the court hearing that followed,
de Broin defended his creation as an artistic pursuit. (Plus, the car
was technically a bike, which is allowed on Ontario's roads.) The
judge bought the argument and threw out the case.

SAY IT, DON'T SPRAY IT
In 1996, an art student from Toronto made a splash by spewing
hatred on two famous paintings. In May, Jubal Brown ingested
red paint and then vomited it onto *Harbor of Love*, a piece at the
Art Gallery of Ontario. Six months later, he did it again, this
time hurling blue paint onto Dutch painter Piet Mondrian's
Composition in Red, White and Blue at New York's Museum of
Modern Art. A museum spokesperson called the Mondrian inci-
dent "unfortunate" and "a fluke," but Brown told the *New York
Times* that he did it on purpose to protest "oppressively trite and
painfully banal" art. Museum officials considered filing charges
for vandalism, but worried Brown's claim of "artistic protest"

Lake Ontario has frozen over twice: in 1875 and 1934.

might weaken their case. Eventually, they just let it go; Brown eventually became an art gallery manager and video producer.

SWEET REVENGE

The *New York Times* once called Hungarian-born Toronto performance artist Istvan Kantor "Canada's leading shock artist," and he wears the title with pride. Since the 1970s, Kantor's work has included wearing the bloody carcasses of dead animals and painting Xs in his own blood on the walls of the National Gallery in Ottawa and the Museum of Modern Art in New York. He was arrested for vandalism in 1988 after the New York incident because he accidentally got some paint on a nearby Picasso. He's also a wacky guy (all the clocks in his home are set to 6:00 p.m., what he calls "Happy Hour") and is one of the creators of Neoism, an artistic movement that began in Canada in the 1970s and pushes the limits of artistic expression. (Kantor says there are no limits.)

After years of being reviled and criticized for his outrageous performances, the Canadian art world finally legitimized Kantor in 2004 with one of its top honors, the Governor General's Award in media and visual arts. It came with a $12,000 prize, and many people criticized the decision to give the prize to a man considered to be so offensive. For Kantor, though, it was a validation of his life's work. He said, "I went back as king! It's a revenge for me. My work was always anti-establishment, anti-art art, anti-authoritarian, and now suddenly I have been recognized by the same people who at certain times put me in jail."

A LITTLE SOMETHING TO CHEW ON

Jason Kronenwald got an art degree from the Queen's University in Kingston, Ontario, but made a name for himself with something a little less erudite: chewing gum. In 1996, Kronenwald made his first "Gum Blonde," a portrait of a blond woman created entirely out of chewing gum. Today, he has more than 20 Gum Blondes on his Web site, and many are of celebrities: Avril Lavigne, Paris Hilton, Britney Spears, etc. Each is crafted from chewed gum on a plywood canvas. He doesn't use any paint or dye and includes only high-class gum, freshly chewed by friends. Says Kronenwald, "I'm not into picking it off of seats in the theater."

The Scarborough Suitcase (a 12-pack beer carton with handles) was invented in 1957.

BORDERLINE INTEREST

You probably know that the Canada/United States border—8,891 kilometers (5,524 miles) long—is the longest boundary between any two countries in the world. But do you know these facts?

• Unless you count the disputed Hans Island, which might be half Danish (*more about that on page 297*), Canada ranks first in the category of "largest country in the world that shares a land border with only one other country."

• Determining the border on the 49th parallel was remarkably accurate for its time: today's surveying methods show that it varies just a few hundred meters from the true latitude. Despite that, there are no plans to relocate the border.

• What if the 49th parallel were Canada's border all the way across North America? The country would lose its two biggest cities (Montreal and Toronto), its capital (Ottawa), and the capital cities of all the provinces except Alberta, Manitoba, and Saskatchewan. Plus, 72 percent of all current Canadians would suddenly be waving red, white, and blue flags and asking ignorant questions about Canada.

• There are some buildings, constructed before the border was defined, that straddle the Vermont/Quebec border, so some of the people living there cross from one country to the other anytime they move from the northern to the southern rooms of their homes.

• Which province has the longest international border? Ontario (2,760 kilometers/1,715 miles).

• Which province has the shortest? It's a tie between Prince Edward Island and Newfoundland; neither borders another country.

• Alaska is the state that has the longest border with Canada (2,475 kilometers/1,538 miles), but which state comes in second? Michigan (1,160 kilometers/721 miles).

John Lennon and Yoko Ono's infamous "bed-in" took place in a Montreal hotel.

I ♥ THE YUKON

Yes, it's cold. Yes, it's too dark in winter and too light in summer. It doesn't matter, the Yukon has a colorful history and incredible landscapes that trigger the imagination. Here are 12 reasons you gotta love it.

1. DEMSTER HIGHWAY. It is 734 kilometers (456 miles) long, is Canada's only public road in the Arctic Circle, and follows an old Gwitch'in hunting and trapping trail.

2. GREAT HEIGHTS. The Yukon boasts the highest mountain in Canada: Mount Logan stands 5,959 meters (19,550 feet) tall.

3. THE COLDEST TEMPERATURE EVER RECORDED OUTSIDE OF ANTARCTICA. On May 26, 1991, the thermometer on Mount Logan read –77.5°C (–107.5°F).

4. NICE SUMMERS. Sure, it's chilly in the winter, but average summer temperatures in the Yukon hover around 20.5°C (69°F).

5. THE KENO CITY PUBLIC LIBRARY. Once home to Canada's largest silver mines, Keno City now mostly gets its silver from tourists. And where do they go for top-notch Yukon entertainment? The public library, of course. Not only is the library located in an old Anglican church (great architecture), it also hosts the town's main theater. And if it's books you seek, the library is open 24 hours a day and operates on the honor system. Anybody can take out any of the library's 2,000 books with the expectation that they'll bring them back…eventually.

6. "SKOOKUM" JIM MASON, KATE CARMACK, AND GEORGE CARMACK. Although there's some controversy about which of the three it was, one of them discovered gold at Bonanza Creek in 1896, setting off the Klondike gold rush. Mason was in the Yukon looking for his sister Kate and her husband George (he found them fishing in the Klondike River) when the trio stumbled on gold. That single find sent tens of thousands of people to the Yukon and put the area on the map.

7. GREAT CREATIVE FODDER. The Yukon's vast landscape

and exciting history make it an inspiration for many writers. The 1897 gold rush alone inspired James Michener's *Alaska*, Jules Verne's *The Volcano of Gold*, and Jack London's *White Fang*, *The Call of the Wild*, *Burning Daylight*, and *To Build a Fire*. On film, it inspired the highest-grossing silent comedy, Charlie Chaplin's *The Gold Rush*, and other films such as Mae West's *Klondike Annie*, James Stewart's *The Far Country*, and even a 1978 *Peanuts* special called *What a Nightmare, Charlie Brown!* But perhaps best of all, the Klondike gold rush was revealed to be the source of the fabulous fortune held by Scrooge McDuck, Donald's rich uncle.

8. OLD CROW. The only Yukon community that can't be reached by car, Old Crow is also the only Yukon town north of the 60th parallel. Being well within the Arctic Circle, its 250 residents experience a full 24 hours of darkness in late December and 24 hours of daylight in June.

9. CANADA, DRY. Whitehorse is the driest city in Canada. It gets only about 145 centimeters (4.7 feet) of snow and 163 millimeters (6 inches) of rain every year.

10. LOTS AND LOTS OF SPACE. Whitehorse, the Yukon Territory's largest city, is home to about 25,000 people. It's second-largest town, Dawson City, has only 2,000 residents. (You don't get a lot of traffic in the Yukon.)

11. REALLY ANCIENT ANCESTORS. In the Bluefish Caves in northern Yukon, archaeologists have found evidence of human habitation that dates back 25,000 years…or so some of them think. In 1985, scientists discovered what look like bone tools, but not all scientists believe the bones *are* tools; they could've just been worn down from time and scavengers. But if the discoveries are real, the Bluefish Caves are the site of the world's oldest human settlement.

12. THE FLAG. How many places have a flag with a malamute on it?

* * *

"This is the Law of the Yukon, that only the Strong shall thrive;
That surely the Weak shall perish, and only the Fit survive."
—**Robert W. Service, poet and "Bard of the Yukon"**

WHO LET THE DOGS OUT?

There's no doubt about it: Canadians love their dogs. Canucks spend nearly $2 billion each year on them. And judging by the fact there are many breeds native to the Great White North, it's clear that this bond between human and canine has been around for a long time. Let's take a brief walk into the world of Canadian dogs.

NEWFOUNDLAND

Then: The Newfoundland dog probably developed in the 1500s from mastiffs that were brought by Europeans and bred with native canines. Newfoundland was a natural fit to the small fishing village life, so dogs with traits that could aid the people living there were the ones that prevailed: large size, strength for hauling carts and equipment, and webbed toes for strong swimming were the ticket to favored status.

Now: Today, the Newfoundland is more of a pet than a worker. However, the dog has long been long known for its heroism in rescuing people from drowning, so Newfoundland dog clubs often teach water rescue courses.

Fast Fact: Nana, the dog in J. M. Barrie's *Peter Pan*, was likely based on Barrie's real and beloved Newfoundland, Luath.

CANADIAN ESKIMO DOG

Then: This is one of the oldest dog breeds still in existence in Canada. The Inuit used them for about 1,800 years for hunting and sledding, and the animals have been part of the native culture for as far back as their oral history goes. These dogs were also used early on by European explorers and worked as hauling dogs in both the Arctic and Antarctica. Because the dogs howl like the American wolf (and have some similar markings), many early European explorers and scientists thought the Canadian Eskimo dog was a wolf mix. Recent genetic testing has disproved that theory.

Now: In 1950, estimates put the Canadian Eskimo dog's population at more than 20,000. Today, that number has fallen into the

Only mammal found exclusively in Canada: the Vancouver island marmot.

hundreds. The introduction of snowmobiles eliminated the need for sled dogs, and by 1970, the breed had nearly died out. But tourism to the Canadian Arctic may actually save the breed from extinction. With more and more visitors wanting a "real-life" dogsled experience, the demand for Canadian Eskimo dogs has increased in recent years. In 2000, the government of Nunavut made this dog its official territorial animal in an effort to bring more attention to the plight of Canada's oldest native dog.

Fast Fact: Despite "Canadian Eskimo dog" being the breed's common name, "Eskimo" is considered derogatory by many of Canada's First People. The Inuit prefer to use the name *Qimmiq*, which means "dog," or "Canadian Inuit dog" instead.

NOVA SCOTIA DUCK-TOLLING RETRIEVER

Then: This breed first came on the scene in Yarmouth County, Nova Scotia, in the early 1800s. Its origins aren't completely clear, but the dog looks to be a blend of Irish setter and cocker spaniel. Unless you're a hunter, you may not know that tolling is a specific hunting technique that lures bird prey. In the case of the Nova Scotia duck-tolling retriever, a hunter hides near a body of water and tosses objects out in the open for the dog to play with. The dog's swishing tail, flopping ears, and contrasting white chest draw the attention of nearby ducks. As the ducks come closer to the shore to check out the dog's frolicking, the hunter appears, startling the flock and sending them skyward. Then he shoots them down, and the dog retrieves the fallen birds.

Now: Nova Scotia duck-tolling retrievers today are mostly kept as pets, but duck hunters still use the dog's innate ability to lure and retrieve. In 1995, the Nova Scotia duck-tolling retriever was declared the provincial dog of Nova Scotia.

Fast fact: People may have gotten the idea to use dogs to hunt ducks after watching the red fox do it. One fox hides while the other romps and dances, mesmerizing nearby waterbirds. When the birds come closer, the playful fox disappears, and they curiously follow up onto land…where the hidden fox is waiting to attack.

TAHLTAN BEAR DOG

Then: Canada's only native West Coast dog comes from the Tahltan people of northern British Columbia. The Tahltan bear

dog was bred for hunting, particularly bears. The dogs were small to medium in size, with medium-length hair, pointy ears, and a bushy tail. On the hunt, they were carried in sacks until the hunters found prints in the dirt or snow. The dogs were then released to chase the bear, confusing and cornering it with their incessant yapping. Hunters followed and slew the confused bear.

Now: Today, this breed is officially considered extinct. Although some groups are trying to bring back a dog that's physically similar, there's no way to re-create the bear dog breed without some of the original purebred animals, the last of which is believed to have died in the 1970s.

Fast Fact: The Tahltan people loved dogs in general but held their bear dogs in especially high esteem. Some hunters were said to carry the smaller bear dogs almost lovingly in packs on their chests during hunting expeditions, and many people allowed the animals to sleep indoors with the family. That said, they also had a spiritual ritual of shallowly stabbing their dogs' haunches with animal bone at the onset of a hunt.

LABRADOR RETRIEVER

Then: This is another breed that originally hails from Newfoundland. It's difficult to pin down the exact lineage, but Labrador retrievers probably came from the St. John's dog—the smaller offspring mating Newfoundlands and European water dogs. The breed probably showed up in the late 1700s on the boats and shores of Newfoundland, working and keeping constant companion with the fishermen. By the late 1800s, Labs went to England, where they were used primarily for hunting. (Because the breed was further developed in England, many don't consider the Labrador retriever to be truly Canadian.)

Now: More Canadians keep Labrador retrievers as pets than any other breed of dog, and the breed's exceptional intelligence has made them the number one choice to train as service dogs for people with disabilities. They also have a keen sense of smell and are used often as trackers in investigative work. The Labrador retriever has been known to perform heroically in emergency situations, too, protecting injured owners or even putting itself in harm's way to save the life of its master.

Fast fact: Endal, a yellow Lab from England, won nearly a dozen

Canada's first prison: Kingston Penitentiary in Ontario (est. 1835).

major awards for rescue, service, and charity work before his death in March 2009. As a result of his achievements, he was dubbed "the most decorated dog in the world."

DOG GONE...BUT NOT FORGOTTEN

There have been many more native purebred dogs in Canada's history, but centuries of development has made several breeds obsolete. Here are three early ones, documented by western explorers and settlers, that are no longer with us:

• **Coast Salish wool dog:** Similar in size and coat to a Pomeranian, this small, furry dog was bred for its soft fur, which was used by the Salish peoples of the West Coast to make clothing.

• **MicMac Indian dog:** MicMac hunters trained this breed to prance around, luring ducks close enough for a kill.

• **Hare Indian dog:** This dog resembled a large fox and was used to chase prey around the Mackenzie River. This breed rarely barked, but when it did, it sounded like a wolf howling.

*　　*　　*

THE YEAR THEY CANCELED THE STANLEY CUP

Some things are usually too important to cancel, regardless of the disaster. One of those is the Stanley Cup. Since 1892, through both world wars and the Great Depression, the games were played.

Except one year. In 1919, the Spanish flu was raging through the world, eventually killing 50 million people. Still, the National Hockey League was not going to cancel games just because of a little pandemic. That year's Stanley Cup began as an exciting series, and after the fifth game, the Montreal Canadiens and the Seattle Metropolitans each had won two games, with one tie. The sixth and final game would be crucial.

The day of the game, however, five Canadiens were so sick they couldn't even wobble onto the ice. The team asked to bring in substitutes from Victoria, but Seattle refused to agree to that, so officials canceled the final game, leaving the series unfinished. (Things got worse for Montreal. Defensive player Joseph Hill, a veteran who had won the cup three times in his 15-year career, was rushed to a Seattle hospital, where he died from the flu.)

With a high point of 140 m above sea level, P.E.I. has the lowest elevation of all provinces.

FIRST LADIES

*Let us now praise the Canadian women who—
sometimes in the face of great resistance—
accomplished firsts in their fields.*

EMILY CARR (1871–1945), PAINTER
She's sometimes called "Canada's Georgia O'Keeffe" for her talent and her perseverance in the face of an indifferent culture, though the best of her painting career occurred after she hit age 57. Frankly, though, Emily Carr should probably just be called "Canada's Emily Carr," because she was unique on her own terms. She may also be the only Canadian painter who has a crater on Venus named after her by the International Astronomical Union.

Carr was raised in British Columbia when it was still pretty wild and untamed. She studied art at the California School of Design in San Francisco (the closest place to study art at the time) and at the Westminster School of Art in England. After spending time abroad, Carr moved back to western Canada in 1913.

Carr was an artistic pioneer, painting the First Nations through a modern view—landscapes and depictions of what remained of their villages, homes, and totem poles. For decades, she had trouble selling her art, so she ran a boardinghouse in Victoria called the "House of All Sorts." Other jobs she held during that time included selling hens and fruit, breeding English sheepdogs, and caring for her pet monkey, Woo. She also drew cartoons for a women's weekly magazine and created "native pottery" for the local tourist trade, collecting the clay herself from cliffs near her house.

Eventually, though, her persistence paid off. Carr's paintings came to the attention of the National Museum in 1927. It was there that she met some of the influential "Group of Seven" painters (*for more about them, turn to page 127*), who encouraged her: "You are one of us," Lawren Harris told her. That re-energized her, as did the fact that her art was finally becoming recognized, first nationally and then internationally.

Carr was given her first solo exhibition at the Art Gallery of Toronto in 1937, when she was 66. Two years later, she suffered a stroke that limited her mobility, so she moved into her sister's

Northern lights displays can impair the navigating abilities of homing pigeons.

house and turned her attention to writing, turning out seven mostly autobiographical books before her death in 1945.

FRANCES MOORE BROOKE (1724–89), NOVELIST

After a year or so in the wilds of Quebec, Francis Moore Brooke became bored with the life of a British military chaplain's wife. So over the next four years, she wrote a novel called *The History of Emily Montague*, about a Quebec woman adapting to the transition from French rule to British. It was the first novel written in Canada—and possibly the first written in North America because the Puritans thought novels were a waste of time (and that fiction, being by definition untrue, was also therefore a lie…and a sin).

After Brooke returned to England, she published several more of her "books of lies," gaining critical acclaim and popularity with readers. She died in England in 1789. Almost 200 years later, in 1985, she also got a crater on Venus named after her.

EMILY JENNINGS STOWE (1831–1903), DOCTOR

When Emily Jennings applied to Victoria College in 1852, she was turned away because she was a woman. But she kept looking until she was granted admission to Toronto's newly launched Normal School for Upper Canada in 1853. She graduated a year later with honors and a degree in education that left her well positioned for her first mention in history…as the first female principal of a public school in Upper Canada (in Brantford, to be specific).

Emily Jennings married John Stowe in 1856, and the couple had three children before John developed tuberculosis. The disease changed the direction of all of their lives. Emily's desire to care for her husband led her to study homeopathic medicine and herbal remedies, which in turn led her to want to become a medical doctor. She applied to medical schools, but quickly learned that there was no medical school in Canada that was open to female students ("or ever will be," one school administrator told her emphatically).

Finally, Emily Stowe headed south and, in 1867, earned a medical degree at the New York Medical College for Women. However, there was a problem—in the interim, the Canadian medical association had started requiring that graduates from American colleges take some specific Canadian courses to apply for a license. This created a dilemma: Stowe couldn't legally practice without

the courses, but no Canadian schools would accept her. So she illegally opened an office in Toronto, becoming the first woman to practice medicine in Canada, even though she didn't have a license; her patients were mostly women and children.

She kept trying to get into Canadian schools too. Finally, in 1871, the University of Toronto relented, accepting Stowe and another female aspirant, Jennie Kidd Trout, as special cases. The faculty and the other students were unwelcoming and harassed the women. Trout stayed and finished the program, but Stowe—fed up with the ill treatment—left school without taking the licensing exam and went back to her clinic as an unlicensed doctor…but as a newly minted feminist.

In 1879, she was charged with giving a pregnant girl herbs to help her induce an abortion. At the time, one of the medical profession's arguments against allowing female doctors was the "concern" that they'd be more likely than male physicians to help pregnant girls get abortions, a procedure that had been outlawed in Canada in 1869. In Stowe's case, the pregnant girl was found dead shortly after visiting her clinic, so Stowe was charged with culpability in the death and with providing a "poison with the intent to procure a miscarriage." The case went to trial and Stowe was found not guilty. But she always believed she'd been the victim of discrimination. Stowe said, "My career has been one of struggle, attended by that sort of persecution which falls to the lot of everyone who pioneers a new movement or steps out of line with established custom."

Finally, in 1880, others in Canada started to recognize her contribution to the field of medicine. The College of Physicians and Surgeons of Ontario issued Stowe a license based on her education and experience, making her the second licensed female physician in Canada. (The first was her classmate at the University of Toronto, Jennie Trout.) The door was cracked open for women to enter the profession. Three years later, Stowe was in the audience when the first woman graduated from a Canadian medical school. There was good reason for that (besides wanting to support a new female doctor): that first graduate was Emily Stowe's daughter, Augusta Stowe-Gullen.

For more women who were first in their fields, turn to page 277.

Color TV signals were first transmitted in Canada in 1966.

AUTOS TO OTTAWA

Real Canadian car companies never quite got off the ground. Instead, the ones that made it were American subsidiaries…and their Canadian partners.

CANADIAN FORDS?

Gordon McGregor had a strong baritone voice that made him a popular singer at parties and a convincing speaker when he talked business. One day in 1904, he was talking to two of his partners—who were also his younger brothers—in the offices of the Walkerville Wagon Works in Walkerville, Ontario, now part of Windsor. "There are men in Detroit, like Henry Ford, who say every farmer will soon be using an automobile," McGregor intoned, with all the self-assuredness of an older brother. "I don't see why we can't build autos right here."

His brothers were ready to listen, party because it sounded like a good idea, but also because they knew their company was in dire straits. Their father had died the year before, and the wagon works he had founded and passed on to them was spiraling down the drain of insolvency. It seemed doubtful that their business of making horse-drawn wagons was ever going to be as profitable as it used to be, what with these new horseless carriages exciting the public imagination. Bold action was called for. If they failed, the worst that could happen was that they'd go out of business, and they were already on the verge of that.

The brothers looked at each other, shrugged, and decided that yes, Gordon should get in touch with his acquaintance across the Detroit River. Maybe that Henry Ford fellow would want some sort of partnership that could benefit both companies. After all, what were automobiles but wagons with motors added on?

Soon after, Gordon made an appointment with Henry Ford. But just to hedge his bets, he also scheduled another meeting with auto magnate Henry Leland about the possibility of making Canadian Cadillacs.

NOT YET A BIG WHEEL

It wasn't that Ford was doing *that* much better than the McGregor

Q: What do Pierre Trudeau, pianist Glenn Gould, and Nazi henchman…

brothers. In fact, none of the American carmakers were doing terribly well. There were too many of them, and they were chasing too few customers. There weren't many people who could afford to buy a luxury item like an automobile. Thus far, the Ford Motor Company had manufactured two models of cars, and neither had been successful. But McGregor believed in Ford's vision to build a moderately priced, reliable car for the common man. If Ford could pull it off, it would be a refreshing contrast to the high-priced autos of the day.

At the meeting with Gordon McGregor, Ford made it clear that he had long wanted to tap into the mostly untapped Canadian car market. He immediately saw the benefits in having a factory in Canada. For one, he could circumvent Canada's stiff import tariffs, which were 35 percent on manufactured goods. Best of all, being in Canada as a "Canadian" business would give Ford access to a much juicier plum: the entire British Commonwealth. And it didn't hurt that hooking up with a willing Canadian partner meant that the development costs could come out of someone else's pockets. Ford could reap much of the profit, while letting McGregor worry about raising the capital to make it happen.

The two struck a deal: the American Ford Motor Company would own 51 percent of McGregor's newly created the Ford Motor Company of Canada. In return, McGregor would have the right to manufacture cars using Ford's designs, patents, and parts. Ford Canada would get the exclusive right to sell Fords in almost all of the British Empire—Canada, India, Australia, etc. But there was one big exception: Henry Ford would keep the United Kingdom for himself.

McGregor was excited (and desperate) enough to agree to those terms. He needed $125,000 for start-up costs and immediately began looking for investors. He rounded up enough brave—or foolish—men to get the business going. Although they eventually got many times the return on their investment, for the next few years it looked as if breaking even was a doubtful possibility.

0 TO 16 MPH IN TEN SECONDS

In October 1904, McGregor drove the first Ford Canada car out of the factory and down Windsor's Sandwich Street. Automobiles were still something of a novelty then; their clouds of smoke,

...Rudolph Hess have in common? A: All have been portrayed by Canadian actor Colm Fiore.

horse-spooking noise, and dangerously inexperienced drivers made them largely unpopular, especially in a region that hadn't yet been acclimated to them. Perhaps that was the reason that Ford Canada had trouble at first.

By the summer of 1905, the 17 wagon-works employees had hand-assembled and the company sold just 107 Ford Model Cs and seven Model Bs...not the 400 that McGregor hoped would be sold by then. The next year was worse: 101 cars. McGregor was nervous...and his investors, even more so.

They became more heartened in 1908 when things started turning around. Demand tripled, overseas sales finally started getting a foothold, and at the end of the year, the company showed a profit of $19,000. The investors, with their modest dividends in hand, quieted. McGregor offered to buy out any that had cold feet about the venture; none took him up on the offer. Smart move, because pretty soon they were going to be rewarded many times over. In 1909, Henry Ford unveiled the Model T. This was it—the car that would change everything and would get the middle class and farmers into automobiles.

SUCCESSFUL FORMULA...TO A "T"

It's hard to overexaggerate the Model T's impact. Instead of building luxury cars by hand one by one, Ford was offering a barebones design "in any color they want, as long as it's black," built by the hundreds on an ever-moving assembly line. Despite this, his no-frills car was sturdy, dependable, and half the price of other cars, starting at $850 Canadian (about $19,000 in today's money). People didn't know it at the time, but with increased efficiency and the economies of scale, Ford would reduce the price each year—down to $300 by 1920—and offer payment plans so almost anybody could buy a car, even if it took years to pay it off.

The Model T became a necessity in rural areas. Not only did it make traveling easier, but from Ford, farmers could buy plans and parts to turn the car into a tractor. They could also use the car's engine power to run shredders, flour grinders, butter churns, pumps, and anything else normally powered by horse, hand, or a strong back.

In 1909, Ford Canada sold 1,200 Model Ts—by 1915, that had grown to 18,700. Both Ford and McGregor became extraordinarily

Anne Murray's hit "Snowbird" was inspired by snow buntings she saw on a P.E.I.. beach.

rich, and Windsor became the "automotive capital of Canada," as General Motors and Chrysler followed Ford across the Detroit River.

2-DOOR TUDORS AND 4-DOOR FORDORS

For whatever reason, even if it were to just assert some independence from the mother company, Ford Canada's versions of the American-designed Fords usually ended up being a little bit different. For example, the first Model Ts in the United States had an open-air design without car doors; passengers just stepped over the car's side panel into the car. Ford Canada, on the other hand, provided actual doors from the start.

A few years later, when the American model became more enclosed, Ford America offered two doors—both on the passenger side. (Henry Ford resisted putting a door on the driver's side because he feared the danger of the driver stepping into traffic.) Ford Canada did away with that nonsense by offering a four-door design, two on *each* side, justifying it to the home office by pointing out that (at the time) some Canadian provinces drove on the left side, some on the right, and it wouldn't be worth the added expense of making two different body designs.

The names were different, too. A 1923 Model T was called the Roadster south of the 49th parallel, but it was the Runabout north of it. Both countries called the two-door sedan a Tudor, but the Canadians played a sly joke by coming out with a four-door version called the Fordor.

The tradition continued into the 1960s. Canadian models like the Monarch, Frontenac (named after Louis de Buade de Frontenac, a governor of New France in the late 17th century), Victoria, and Mercury (two years before Ford America released a different car with the same name), provided different brands and models from the American lines.

THE BOTTOM FALLS OUT

Over the ensuing decades independent Canadian companies— like Gray-Dort and the Canada Cycle and Motor Company in the early years, and Bricklin later on—tried to compete with the American-based Canadian giants, but all eventually failed. Then when the Great Depression hit in 1929, the Canadian companies

While in office, PM W. L. Mackenzie King sought advice through séances.

suffered along with their American counterparts. Canadian car production plummeted from a high of more than 200,000 a year—nearly half of them exported to other markets—to a paltry 60,000, less than 10,000 of which were exported.

Canadian car factories shrunk to minimal operations with skeleton crews. They wouldn't become fully active again for a decade. And they had no idea that when their factories did get busy again, they wouldn't be making cars.

WAR...WHAT'S IT GOOD FOR?

In 1939, Canada joined Great Britain in declaring war against Germany and its allies. Suddenly, the car companies got an order they couldn't refuse: produce Canadian military pattern (CMP) vehicles, military trucks that were to be made to British army specifications.

Under pressure and down to bare-bones staffing, Ford and GM pooled their engineers and designers. Working together, they created an ugly but rugged design with a blunt snout and a windshield that slanted downward to reduce glare to both the driver and enemy planes flying overhead. Their plants also combined efforts and produced more than 400,000 of the sturdy beasts that were put to good use by Commonwealth troops during—and after—the war.

THE IMPORT QUESTIONS

After the war, the Canadian auto industry returned to civilian production, experiencing prolonged growth as new cars, replaced every year or two, became part of the new suburban existence. Between 1946 and 1954, Canadian production increased from 92,000 to 375,000 cars a year; employees, from 22,000 to 29,000. Cars for export began rolling onto ships in huge numbers, aided by the fact that postwar England, Italy, and Germany were in no condition to produce their own cars. Ford Canada opened a huge new headquarters and plant in Oakville, Ontario; GM became the country's largest employer.

But it couldn't last. By the mid-1960s, Canadian carmakers were struggling again with flagging exports, outdated factories, and a small, mostly saturated domestic market. In 1965, Canada's prime minister Lester Pearson negotiated an agreement with

American president Lyndon Johnson that eliminated tariffs and essentially merged the two countries' auto industries into one. This sparked a wave of investment by American firms in Canadian plants, increasing production, employment, and the number of models available to Canadian consumers. But it also marked the end of the Canadian car industry as a distinct entity.

By the 1970s, even these consolidated car companies were suffering. An oil embargo and a tsunami of imports challenged North American car companies. Decades later, they're still having trouble—the economic recession caused the country's carmakers to request government help in 2008 and 2009. But somewhere, among Canada's businessmen and industry folk, there's an entrepreneur like Gordon McGregor keeping an eye out for the next big thing.

* * *

THE GOLDEN CURSE

Have you heard the legend of the Lost Lemon Mine? It goes like this: In 1870, two prospectors broke off from their group searching for gold in the hills of southwestern Alberta. Lemon and Blackjack, as the men were known, spotted small bits of gold in a mountain stream and followed the water until they found the gold's source... and nuggets as big as their fists. Eureka! But that night, after the men argued about whether to keep searching or to return home, Lemon crept over to his sleeping partner and drove an axe into Blackjack's head. A group of natives (probably Stoney) were camping nearby and saw the crime. When they told their chief about it, the man put a curse on the entire area. Most people couldn't find the mine after that, but those who did (including Lemon) suffered terrible consequences...insanity, alcoholism, and grisly deaths. Today, gold hunters are still looking.

Most historians and geologists think this story is just that...a campfire legend from the frontier. They contend that gold is usually associated with volcanic activity, and Alberta doesn't have a lot of that. (Now if the men had come upon a huge concentration of oil, there might be some truth to the tale.)

Only Canadian player in the Baseball Hall of Fame: Ferguson Jenkins (Chicago Cubs).

GOD SAVE THE QUEEN

Let's get to know the woman on the money.

• Elizabeth II is a "queen regnant" because she's got all the powers and duties of a ruling monarch. A "queen consort" is someone who's married to a king but has no official power.

• Also among Elizabeth's official titles is "Queen of Canada," which means that technically, she's the employer of the country's government workforce, owner of all companies that the government owns, the legal guardian of Canada's foster children, and the Honorary Commissioner of the Royal Canadian Mounted Police.

• Elizabeth learned to drive a car when she was 19 years old.

• She met her future husband Phillip for the first time in 1939, when she was just 13 years old. (He was 18.) She started sending him letters, and the two kept in touch, eventually marrying in 1947. Their marriage is the longest-lasting of any British monarch.

• When World War II ended in 1945, Elizabeth and her sister Margaret asked their parents—the ruling monarchs—to let them go outside and walk among the ecstatic Londoners celebrating the victory in Europe. There were some security concerns, but the two weren't recognized. Of the experience, Elizabeth said, "I remember lines of unknown people linking arms and walking down Whitehall [Road], all of us just swept along on a tide of happiness and relief."

• Queen Elizabeth and Prince Phillip traveled to Canada for the first time in 1951, two years before her coronation. She's come more than 20 times since, making Canada the most-visited country in the commonwealth.

• In 2002, the last time a poll was taken, about half of all Canadians thought the monarchy Elizabeth heads was outdated, but only 41 percent wanted to abolish it.

• According to British law, all the whales and sturgeon in British waters belong to Queen Elizabeth. The animals are called "fishes royale" because of a law passed in the 14th century that said, "The [monarch] shall have...whales and sturgeons taken in the sea or elsewhere within the realm."

THE HALIFAX EXPLOSION

Here's a classic from the BRI archive. In late 1917, World War I raged in Europe. Back in North America, the port of Halifax, Nova Scotia, was the hub of Canada's war effort. Most ships heading out to the Atlantic brought prosperity to the small town…but two also brought disaster.

TWO SHIPS NOT PASSING IN THE NIGHT

In December 1917, the French cargo ship *Mont-Blanc* took on 3,000 tons of explosives in New York, including more than 181,436 kilograms (400,000 pounds) of TNT, for the war effort. The 97.5-meter (320-foot) ship was headed into Halifax Harbour to await a convoy of ships that would accompany it to England. The *Mont-Blanc's* captain, Aimé Le Médec, should have been flying a red flag to warn other ships of the dangerous cargo, but he was afraid that enemy ships might see the flag and start shooting at him.

At the same time, a 134-meter (440-foot) Norwegian ship called the *Imo*—much faster and larger than the *Mont-Blanc*—was leaving Halifax. The *Imo's* captain, Haakon From, knew he was behind schedule and ordered the ship full speed ahead.

Halifax Harbour has a rough hourglass shape. The "waist" of the hourglass is a slim channel of water called the Narrows. Halifax is on the south side of this channel; the town of Dartmouth sits on the north side. During World War I, the waterway was one of the busiest in North America. Two ships passing through the Narrows had to do so with caution—as the *Imo* and the *Mont-Blanc* were soon to learn.

COLLISION

On the cold, clear morning of December 6, sometime before 9:00 a.m., the *Imo* and the *Mont-Blanc* both entered the Narrows: the *Imo* going east toward open sea (too fast, some said). The *Mont-Blanc* was going west to moor up. Harbor rules say that ships must pass port to port—left side to left side—just like cars on the road. But the *Imo* was veering too far north and was headed directly toward the *Mont-Blanc*. Captain Le Medec, aboard the *Mont-Blanc*, signaled the other ship, but, strangely, Captain From didn't

Sockeye salmon get their name from *sukkai*, a Coast Salish word meaning "red fish."

stop—instead, he signaled that he was continuing farther north. After repeated and confused attempts to communicate with horns and flags, Le Medec finally steered his ship southward...but Captain From did the same thing at the same time. Result: The smaller ship was broadsided. The collision sent the *Mont-Blanc* straight toward the city of Halifax.

The impact started a fire on the deck of the *Mont-Blanc*. Its crew, knowing the ship could blow up at any second, went straight to the lifeboats...without alerting the harbor patrol of the dangerous cargo. They rowed north toward Dartmouth, leaving the floating bomb heading straight for Halifax.

It was an astounding sight: a flaming ship drifting slowly toward shore. All morning, people stopped to watch. The *Mont-Blanc* drifted for about 20 minutes until it came to rest against Pier 6 in the Richmond district, the busy, industrial north end of Halifax. As firefighting crews rushed to put the fire out, the flames moved closer and closer to the massive stores of TNT on the lower decks.

EXPLOSION

Then, shortly before 9:05 a.m., a blinding, white flash filled the harbour. The *Mont-Blanc* exploded into bits and a giant mushroom cloud rose up over the town. More than 1,600 people on shore were killed instantly. Thousands more were injured. Schools, homes, factories, and churches were leveled by the ensuing shock wave. An 18-meter (59-foot) tidal wave swept away what was left of the waterfront, drowning many of the initial survivors and sinking dozens of ships in the harbor. Shattered pieces of the *Mont-Blanc* were hurled as far as three miles away. A tugboat was thrown from the middle of the harbor onto the Dartmouth shore. The wave also rushed over the shores of Dartmouth and up Tufts Cove, where it completely washed away a Micmac First Nations settlement.

The blast was so strong that it could even be heard in Charlottetown—217 kilometers (135 miles) away. At the time, it was the largest man-made explosion in human history, and its size and devastation wouldn't be eclipsed until the first atomic bomb was dropped on Hiroshima in 1945.

More than 1,600 homes were gone; 12,000 more were damaged from the fires that spread through Halifax after the explosion. At least 6,000 people were left homeless at the onset of a powerful

winter storm that dropped more than a foot of snow within the next 24 hours. Hundreds who had survived the blast, the tidal wave, and the ensuing fires ended up freezing to death.

RELIEF

Rescue efforts were slow at first. Power, water, gas, telephone, telegraph, and railroad lines were all obliterated. The dead and dying crowded the streets, and thousands were buried under debris. Making things worse, medical supplies were in pitifully short supply. But help was on the way.

Money started pouring in from all over the world; even places like China and New Zealand sent money. For its part, the Canadian government appropriated $18 million for relief efforts, and surrounding towns donated shelters, blankets, and other necessities. But much of the immediate help came from America, especially from Massachusetts. A train full of supplies and medical personnel left Boston for Halifax the day of the explosion. In all, Bostonians donated $750,000 through the Massachusetts-Halifax Relief Committee. (To this day, Halifax sends an annual Christmas tree to the City of Boston in gratitude.)

THE BLAME GAME

Survivors of the explosion were stunned. Something this horrible had to be somebody's fault. First, they blamed the Germans—if Germany hadn't started the war, the disaster wouldn't have happened. Every surviving German in town was rounded up and arrested, in spite of the fact that they had suffered like everyone else. But as rebuilding began and cooler heads prevailed, people realized that if anyone was to blame, it was the ships' captains.

Captain From and most of the crew of the *Imo* perished in the blast; Captain Le Medec of the *Mont-Blanc* survived and was brought to trial. After months of inquiry and many civil suits, there was insufficient evidence to establish criminal negligence. Captain Le Medec's license was revoked, but in the end, no one was ever convicted.

On January 22, 1918, Canada appointed the Halifax Relief Commission to handle insurance claims, pensions, rebuilding, and the rehabilitation of survivors. The extent of the damage was so great that the commission remained open until 1976.

NBA star and proud Canadian Steve Nash was actually born in South Africa.

RADIO STAR

Some Canadians do great things and find fame.
But others remain in obscurity…like this guy.

MERRY CHRISTMAS!
In 1906, radio operators on ships in the Atlantic Ocean had only ever heard dots and dashes from their radio receivers. So you can imagine their shock, late on Christmas Eve, when a man's voice came through the headphones. He was talking to them loud and clear, followed by a violin playing "O Holy Night" with the same man singing along on the last verse. Then, after reading a series of Bible passages, the male voice extended wishes for a merry Christmas and signed off. The night was silent again, and radio operators asked themselves: What *was* that? Had they imagined it?

The voice and violin belonged to Canadian Reginald Fessenden, as did the radio transmitter and related patents. Being the first public broadcast of voice and music by radio, the experimental Christmas Eve transmission was a triumph for Fessenden after he endured many disappointments over the previous half decade.

MARCONI WINS

Fessenden boasted a great résumé—he had worked as Thomas Edison's chief chemist, then made instruments and machines for George Westinghouse. He'd also been designing and testing new ways of using radio waves and wireless radios to send Morse code messages (the only means of radio communication in those days) over long distances. However, in the race for success, he kept coming in second.

In 1896, an Italian named Guglielmo Marconi successfully transmitted some clicks across a short distance in England, winning a huge grant from the English government. That was a setback for Fessenden, who'd hoped to be the first, but even more disappointing was the fact that, a couple of years later, he found out the Canadian government had put a great deal of money behind Marconi and provided him with an experimental radio

Q: Who is the only princess born in Canada? A: The Netherlands' Princess Margriet (1943).

station at Cape Breton Island, Nova Scotia. That the Canadian government would support an Italian inventor instead of one of their own was a blow to Fessenden.

It was also during this time that Fessenden took a vacation to Peterborough, Ontario. Lounging next to a quiet lake, he threw rocks into it and watched the rhythmic ripples spread out in ever-growing circles. "What if...?" he asked himself. What if radio waves were like those ripples? Could *sound* waves be broadcast over radio waves? Was it possible that Marconi's Morse code clicks were actually a dead-end, and that the real challenge would be to turn sound waves into radio waves that could travel in all directions—like ripples—to any transmitter nearby?

FANTASY ISLAND

After returning from vacation, Fessenden got another blow: he'd been turned down for an electrical engineering teaching job at McGill University. He headed to the United States instead to work on his new radio idea. But even the most serious inventor needs a steady job...and paycheck. So after a stint at the Western University of Pennsylvania in Pittsburgh, Fessenden convinced the United States Weather Bureau to hire him to develop radio as a way to improve weather forecasting. He also convinced his new employer to invest in the equipment he needed and let him keep the patents on his inventions.

Fessenden set up a transmission station on the Potomac River—on Cobb Island, Maryland—and a receiving station 50 miles away in Arlington, Virginia. On December 23, 1900, a year before Marconi made the first transatlantic Morse code radio transmission from Cornwall, England, to Newfoundland, Fessenden and a technician in Virginia readied their equipment. Then Fessenden attached a microphone and spoke into it to the technician 50 miles away: "One, two, three, four, is it snowing where you are, Mr. Thiessen? If so, telegraph back and let me know." Within seconds, Morse code came clattering back to him: it was Thiessen informing him that, yes, it was indeed snowing. Excited, Fessenden wrote in his journal: "This afternoon here at Cobb Island, intelligible speech by electromagnetic waves has for the first time in world's history been transmitted."

MARCONI WINS...AGAIN

Fessenden's employers at the weather service were pleased—in fact, perhaps too pleased. Immediately, the boss started pressuring the Canadian inventor to share the radio patents. When the pressure got to be too much, Fessenden quit his job and teamed up with two millionaire investors. The trio started a Canadian company—Fessenden wanted to work from his home country—and set about trying to get funding from the Canadian government. Fessenden not only was turned down, but learned that Canada had granted Marconi the right to build radio stations there. Disappointed and furious, Fessenden went back to the United States.

One reason for all the back-and-forth was that Fessenden's approach to radio was different from Marconi's, and from the other inventors who were inspired by the Italian. They employed a "whiplash" method, using on-and-off clicks as a way of signaling. What they didn't seem to realize was that it was possible to generate a continuous electromagnetic wave that could be used to carry more than clicks: voices, music, sounds of all kinds. Fessenden was on to something big and was unwilling to let it go. He set up a transmitting station at Brant Rock, Massachusetts, near Boston and a receiving station in Scotland and started amassing patents.

Soon after, he got "accidental" confirmation that his theory could work over long distances. A registered letter arrived from his engineer in Scotland that said, on January 3, 1903, "at about 4 o'clock in the morning I was listening in for telegraph signals from Brant Rock when to my astonishment I heard instead of dots and dashes, the voice of Mr. Stein [one of Fessenden's associates]...At first I thought I must be losing my senses, but I'm sure it was Stein's voice for it came in as clearly as if he were in the next room."

CHRISTMAS AT SEA

Still, there were bugs to work out. To pay the bills and finance further research, Fessenden needed a steady income. So he took at job at the U.S.-based United Fruit Company, setting up a radio system to make sure its ships and mainland stations could transmit Morse code. But he also kept at the radio work, and in 1906, on Christmas Eve—sure his system was ready for a public demonstration—Fessenden tuned up his violin and sent a message in Morse code to the dozen United Fruit Company ships in the Atlantic,

"International" Ontario town names: Ireland, Poland, and Siberia.

telling them to listen for "something different" at 9:00 p.m.

That transmission revolutionized radio research, and it would be nice to be able to say that Fessenden's triumph brought him fame, fortune, and the respect of the scientific world. But it didn't. Instead, he ended up mired in legal battles after one of his partners illegally sold his patents to American corporations. Fessenden eventually moved to Bermuda and died in relative obscurity, remaining just a footnote in the annals of the development of broadcasting.

* * *

CREAM OF THE CRIMINAL CROP?

The most notorious criminal in English history may be Jack the Ripper, a serial killer who terrorized London between 1888 and 1891. Prostitutes in the city's Whitechapel district lived in fear of the mysterious man who cut his victims' throats and mutilated their bodies. Five murders have been identified as the work of Jack the Ripper, but there could be many more. Yet, the killer was never caught, and his identity remains a mystery.

Could a *Canadian* have been Jack the Ripper? It doesn't seem likely, but some people think so. Thomas Neil Cream was a doctor from Quebec who graduated from McGill University in 1876. He spent most of the 1880s in a Chicago, Illinois, prison for poisoning Dr. Daniel Stott. (Cream and Stott's wife were having an affair and wanted to do away with the pesky husband.) In 1891, Cream moved to London, England, where he began a poisoning spree, killing prostitutes with strichynine. The next year, he was caught, tried, and hanged for one of those murders. But just as the trapdoor opened and the noose tightened, Cream shouted, "I am Jack!" And detectives (both licensed and armchair) have been a flutter ever since.

But Cream was in jail during most of Jack the Ripper's spree, you say. Yes, he was...*supposedly*. But there are theories: Maybe he had someone take his place in Chicago. Maybe he bribed the guards to release him earlier than reported. Maybe he had an accomplice. All this would just be wild speculation if not for one bit of evidence: Cream's handwriting very closely resembled that of some notes known to be left by Jack the Ripper. And so the mystery continues.

"All pro hockey athletes are bilingual. They speak English and profanity." —Gordie Howe

WIT & WISDOM: MARGARET ATWOOD

"A word after a word after a word is power," wrote author Margaret Atwood—most famous for her award-winning The Handmaid's Tale. *A "word after a word after a word" can also be entertaining and enlightening, as illustrated by these Atwood quotes.*

"I've never understood why people consider youth a time of freedom and joy. It's probably because they have forgotten their own."

"The beginning of Canadian cultural nationalism was not 'Am I really that oppressed?' but 'Am I really that boring?'"

"In the spring, at the end of the day, you should smell like dirt."

"A ratio of failures is built into the process of writing. The wastebasket has evolved for a reason."

"A divorce is like an amputation: you survive it, but there's less of you."

"A voice is a human gift; it should be cherished and used, to utter fully human speech as possible. Powerlessness and silence go together."

"Put yourself in a different room, that's what the mind is for."

"For years I wanted to be older, and now I am."

"Little girls are cute and small only to adults. To one another they are not cute. They are life-sized."

"Gardening is not a rational act."

"Never pray for justice, because you might get some."

"War is what happens when language fails."

"If the national mental illness of the United States is megalomania, that of Canada is paranoid schizophrenia."

"Everyone else my age is an adult, whereas I am merely in disguise."

World's most northerly grain-growing area: Peace River Region, AB.

SAINTS, PRESERVE US!

How do you get to be a Catholic saint? Step one: Move to a wild new country. Step two: Get slaughtered in the line of duty.

SPREADING THE BLESSINGS

In 1639, Jesuit missionaries from New France arrived at a site near modern-day Midland, Ontario, to spread the benefits of Christianity and civilization to the Native populations. They built a mission called Sainte-Marie-au-pays-des-Hurons ("Sainte-Marie-Among-the-Hurons") near a large Huron settlement and set up a working town—chapel, houses, blacksmith shop, and kitchen—to show the blessings of modern European living.

Their intentions were good. Although soldiers stopped by on their way to other places, the Jesuits disdained a permanent military presence, fearing that soldiers would "bring the worst of Europe" with them.

Despite all that, the presence of the mission had a devastating effect on the Huron living nearby. Bitter intertribal conflict developed between believers in the tribal gods and the new Christian converts. And the diseases that the Europeans brought were devastating. Smallpox in particular ravaged the Huron settlement, and the neighboring Iroquois, seeing an opportunity for an advantage against their weakened rivals, bought guns from Dutch traders and began encroaching on Huron territory. Then, the conflict started picking off Jesuits as well. Here are the earthly ends of the saintly eight.

ISAAC JOGUES AND JEAN DE LALANDE

In 1642, Isaac Jogues headed an expedition back to Quebec to gather supplies. On the return trip, the group was captured and tortured by Iroquois. Jogues was brutalized—his beard, hair, and nails were ripped out, and parts of his fingers were bitten from his hands—but he survived as a slave for more than a year. During that time, he tried to convert his captors, until finally Dutch traders helped him escape and make his way back to France. There, as a "living martyr," the pope allowed Jogues—who lacked the necessary digits—a special exemption from the rule that the

Toronto-born Art Irwin invented the baseball glove.

bread and wine be touched only by the priest's thumb and forefinger during holy communion so that he could still conduct mass.

Jogues wasn't done with Canada, though. In 1646, he and another Jesuit, Jean de Lalande, traveled back to the Iroquois camp to try to make peace between the tribes. The Iroquois, now suffering horribly from both smallpox and crop failure, accused Jogues of being a sorcerer, causing their tribulations in revenge for his earlier treatment at their hands. This time, the Iroquois beat Jogues and Lalande to death and decapitated them.

RENÉ GOUPIL

René Goupil had studied to be a surgeon, which came in handy when he traveled to Canada to work in a hospital there. On the way back from Jogues's 1642 supply trip to Montreal, Goupil was also captured by the Iroquois, but he wasn't as lucky as Jogues. When Goupil made the sign of the cross above a child's head, the adults went from thinking he was a spy for the French military to believing he was putting a curse on the kid. The Iroquois beat Goupil so severely that his face was mutilated nearly beyond recognition. Goupil didn't take the hint, though, because he was later discovered teaching the sign of the cross to children. The Iroquois had had enough; a warrior killed Goupil with a tomahawk to the head. (Goupil, for his pains and medical training, is the patron saint of anesthetists and anesthesiologists.)

ANTOINE DANIEL

Antoine Daniel also worked with the Huron, but was in Teanaostaye, near present-day Hillsdale, Ontario. When Iroquois attacked the mission village in 1648, Daniel gathered the Huron women and children, quickly baptizing them and giving them general absolution. Then he calmly marched out to meet the invaders, carrying a crucifix. The Iroquois were taken aback for a few seconds by his brazenness, but then they killed him in a volley of arrows and bullets, set the chapel on fire, and threw his lifeless body into it. During this deliberate distraction, most of the Huron women and children escaped.

JEAN DE BRÉBEUF

Jean de Brébeuf was the uncle of the poet Georges de Brébeuf; he

was also the author of the "Huron Carol," a song still sung at Christmas today. Brébeuf spent time with the Hurons, learning their language and reputedly writing their first dictionary. (He was also said to have given us the name of the Native American sport of lacrosse; he thought the stick looked like a bishop's crosier.) Brébeuf's charismatic presence was responsible for many of the conversions that split the Hurons into feuding factions.

When the Iroquois did attack in 1649, Brébeuf and a fellow Jesuit, Gabriel Lalemant, were captured. According to church tradition, Brébeuf stayed calm during the assault, preaching until he was gagged. His nose and lips were torn from his face and boiling water was poured over his head in a mock baptism. Impressed by his courage and lack of crying out, some Iroquois cut his heart from his chest and ate it in the hopes of attaining his stoic courage. When the Jesuits reclaimed his body, they did something similar, dissolving his flesh in lye to save his bones as church relics. The bones now rest in a reconstructed mission near Midland, Ontario.

GABRIEL LALEMANT

Not much is known about Gabriel Lalemant, not even the definitive spelling of his name. (Lallemant is also used). He had been at the Huron mission only six months before being captured and tortured to death with Jean de Brébeuf. His torments were captured vividly, however, by the people who collected his body. According to one account, Lalemant "had received a hatchet blow on the left ear, which they had driven into his brain, which appeared exposed: we saw no part of his body, from the feet even to the head, which had not been broiled, and in which he had not been burned alive—even the eyes, into which those impious ones had thrust burning coals." His bones were also kept as relics.

CHARLES GARNIER

When Iroquois attacked on December 7, 1649, Charles Garnier was the only priest left living among the Hurons. He reportedly did his best to baptize children and grant absolution as quickly as possible. While trying to reach out and help a dying man, Garnier was shot by a musket and then killed by a hatchet that penetrated his skull.

NOEL CHABANEL

Noel Chabanel had vowed never to leave the mission...and he was still there after the other seven were killed. But on December 8, 1649, his turn came: Chabanel was killed by what one Jesuit described as "a renegade Huron."

WHAT BECAME OF THEM?

When the eight Canadian martyrs were sainted in 1930, the pope collectively named them patron saints of both Canada and North America. And what happened to the mission? The remaining Jesuits burned Sainte-Marie to the ground to keep it from being overrun and desecrated. Then they relocated to a new mission, which they named Sainte Marie II and which they hoped would be more defendable. It wasn't. After less than a year at the new location, the missionaries were running out of food. That and the constant threat of Iroquois attacks sent them back to the safety of New France.

* * *

WEIRD RESTAURANTS

• The **Spirit Lounge**, a vegetarian hotspot in Montreal, may look avant-garde: tinsel streamers hang in the doorways, walls are painted gold, the chairs are a blue leopard print, and the wine list is written with a glitter pen. But it's got some old-fashioned rules: Food is not to be wasted. If you don't finish your dinner, you're required to donate $2 to charity and you don't get to order dessert. If you don't finish your dessert, you're banned from returning...ever.

• Do you like garlic? You better if you want to dine at **Garlic's** in London, Ontario. They've got garlic ice cream, garlic martinis, a garlic and onion soup, and chocolate-dipped garlic bulbs, among other things.

• The food at the **Cave** restaurant in Saskatoon isn't much to write home about: sandwiches, ribs, pasta, the usual. What sets the place apart is that it's designed to look and feel like you're inside an actual cavern.

• And then there's **Brothers** in Vancouver...where all the waiters dress like monks.

WHO'S THAT BAND?

*The stories behind the names of some of
Canada's most beloved musical groups.*

ARCADE FIRE: This Montreal indie band's Win Butler explained that as a child he heard a story that haunted him: an account of an arcade burning down with kids trapped inside. "It's probably something that the kid [who told me the story] made up, but at the time I believed him."

BACHMAN-TURNER OVERDRIVE: Bachman and Turner, of course, were people in the group, but where did Overdrive come from? The band was going home to Winnipeg from an Ontario job and stopped for gas in Windsor. On a magazine rack, one of them saw a magazine for truckers called *Overdrive*. The band liked the word and thought it would describe their sound. (By the way, although the world would pronounce Bachman as if it were "bockman," the family pronounced it "bakeman"…and so did the band when referring to itself.)

MEN WITHOUT HATS: According to a Web site dedicated to the band's song "The Safety Dance," founder Ivan Doroschuk and his two brothers refused to wear hats during Montreal's cold winters, calling themselves "the men without hats."

THE TRAGICALLY HIP: When the 1960s made-for-TV Monkees split up, member Michael Nesmith embarked on his own projects, trying to reclaim his sense of artistic integrity. In 1981, he made a movie called *Elephant Parts* that included music interspersed with comedy bits. One of those bits was called "The Tragically Hip," and a group of musical guys from Kingston, Ontario, who watched the film thought it was the perfect name for a band.

CRASH TEST DUMMIES: We prefer their original name—Bad Brad Roberts and the St. James Rhythm Pigs—but they came under the sway of a medical student friend who suggested Crash Test Dummies instead.

Name of the first complete dinosaur specimen mounted in a Canadian museum: *Edmontosaurus.*

I ♥ NEWFOUNDLAND & LABRADOR

The northeastern seaboard is not a place for the weak at heart:
the winds blowing off the North Atlantic bring in more than
their fair share of cold, fog, rain, and snow. But the
area also has a rugged natural beauty and people
to match. Here are 12 reasons to love it.

1. A FULL NAME ALMOST NOBODY USES. Despite its official name change in 2001, most people still refer to the whole province as "Newfoundland," and the mainland region as "Labrador."

2. CONTRARIAN TOURIST FESTIVALS. Most places schedule their tourist festivals during their best weather. Just to be unusual, the town of Mount Pearl celebrates its Frosty Festival in early February during its coldest and snowiest time of year. Promising "music, magic, dancing, great food, laughter and good sportsmanship," the festival activities include just about any contest that will get you through the first weeks of February: video-game competitions, ice hockey, lip-synch contests, bowling, indoor soccer, a film festival, skating, drinking, swimming (indoor, we hope), and—for the hardy—"Sno Pitch Softball" and "Wild Winter Games." All activities are presided over by that jolly snowman himself, Frosty.

3. NEWFIES. We love Newfoundlanders...and Newfie jokes. (It's all in good fun.) Like this one, for example: A Newfie's wife died so he called 911. The operator said they'd send someone over right away and then asked where the man lived.

"At the end of Eucalyptus Drive," he said. The operator asked, "Would you spell that for me?"

After a long pause, the Newfie replied, "How 'bout if I drag her over to Oak Street and you pick her up there?"

4. A HAVEN FOR ALLERGY SUFFERERS. There is no rag-

The first recorded Christmas celebration in Canada took place in Quebec City in 1535...

weed pollen in Newfoundland and Labrador; the province doesn't
have the right growing conditions for the plants. (There are also
no snakes, poison ivy, poison oak, chiggers, or spotted ticks.)

5. DILDO. One story says that this town got its name from the
pegs on a rowboat that slide into the pivot holes of the oars, keep-
ing the oars from sliding out of your hands. 'Nuff said.

6. MISERABLE ENGLISH WEATHER. St. John's brags that
it's the oldest English-founded settlement in North America.
Apparently the settlers were looking for a place that reminded
them of home—or at least had its miserable weather. Of all major
cities in Canada, St. John's is reportedly the cloudiest (1,497 hours
sunshine per year); the wettest (151.4 centimeters/59.6 inches of
rain a year); the windiest (24.3 kilometers/15.1 miles per hour
average speed); the foggiest (124 days); and the snowiest (359
centimeters/11.9 feet).

7. ISLANDS...7,000 OF THEM. The largest, of course, is New-
foundland. The smallest is Landsat, measuring only 25 by 45
meters (82 by 148 feet). It got its name in 1976 when it showed
up on images coming from the Landsat 1 satellite. To make sure
the island wasn't just a speck of dirt on the lens, final visual verifi-
cation of its existence fell to Frank Hall of the Canadian Hydro-
graphic Service. While being lowered by helicopter onto the
surface of the ice-covered island, Hall discovered just in time that
he was about to land on top of a polar bear that had been all but
invisible on the ice. The startled bear reared up and took a swat at
Hall, and the helicopter crew hurriedly pulled him back up again,
figuring the near-death experience was verification enough.

8. ST. JOHN'S. Ever wonder how the province's capital city got
its name? According to legend, explorer John Cabot first set foot
on Newfoundland in 1497 on the feast day of St. John the Baptist.
He named the region after that event.

9. INVASIVE SPECIES. There were no squirrels on Newfound-
land until 1963, when some "helpful" scientists introduced the
first ones to the area. It didn't seem like too big a deal, except the

squirrels liked to eat the seeds of the blue spruce tree...and so did red crossbills, a type of bird native to the island. The squirrels out-ate the birds, leaving few seeds behind for the red crossbills and leading to a huge decline in their population.

10. A NEIGHBORLY BORDER FEUD. Quebec and Labrador have both claimed a broad swath of land at the southern border of Labrador. In one corner: the federal government, courts, the Con-stitution Act of 1982, and the world's mapmakers agree that it belongs to Labrador. In the other: the Quebec government and its mapmakers say the area belongs to them. So far, it's unresolved.

11. GROS MORNE NATIONAL PARK. A UNESCO World Heritage Site, the park's name comes from its high spot, Gros Morne ("great somber") Peak on Newfoundland island. Ship-wrecks, sea caves, twisted coastal trees, mountains, fjords, water-falls, dangerous animals—you'll find them all there.

12. A HEART-TUGGING MEMORIAL. Above Gander Lake is a life-size bronze statue of an American soldier holding the hands of two children as he stares north over the lake toward the United States. It's a memorial for 248 soldiers who, on their way home for Christmas in 1985, died in a fiery plane crash at the spot.

* * *

THE MUD BOWL

A football game where someone almost drowned? It happened in 1950 at the Grey Cup final between the Toronto Argonauts and the Winnipeg Blue Bombers. The game was the first sold-out Grey Cup ever, and fans had high hopes for the hometown team (Toronto) to claim victory. But as temperatures climbed to 10°C (50°F) that November day, the snowpack on the field started to melt. By kick-off, it was thick mud. But the game must go on—so the Argonauts and Blue Bombers slipped and slid through four quarters of play, with Toronto ultimately winning, 13–0. And that player who nearly drowned? He was a Blue Bomber who took a hit just before halftime and fell facedown into a deep puddle. (He lived.)

The world's largest dump truck (the Terex Titan) resides in Sparwood, BC.

FREEZE FRAME

*In a time of bulky movie cameras, Robert Flaherty made
a film about Inuit life in the icy regions of north Quebec.
It was the first feature-length documentary to achieve
popular success, and it was filmed in one of
the most extreme locations possible.*

IRON MAN

Nanook of the North depicted a year in the life of an Inuit family living near Inukjuak, Quebec, on Hudson Bay. On its release in 1922, the film spread images of the majestic Arctic landscape and "Eskimo" culture (which were not entirely accurate—more on that below). Cold-weather anorak coats, nose-to-nose "Eskimo kisses," kayaks, igloos—for most people at the time, *Nanook* was their first exposure to all of these things. In those days of silent films, the documentary was a smash hit, earning more than $40,000 (about 80 percent of its budget) in its first week of release.

Director, producer, and general force of nature Robert Flaherty began his improbable movie career as an iron prospector for Sir William Mackenzie. Mackenzie built railroads, and one thing railroads need a lot of is iron. Finding new and cheap sources of iron ore required prospecting in previously unexplored locations. As a result, Flaherty went on several extended trips to the Arctic region around Hudson Bay to seek out iron ore deposits.

During his travels, Flaherty developed a keen curiosity about the Inuit people and an appreciation for their ability to survive in an unforgiving environment. He figured others would find them interesting as well, and wanted to preserve a record of their traditional life, even as incursions by outsiders (including himself) were beginning to change it.

In 1913, before his third prospecting expedition to the Hudson Bay, Flaherty bought a movie camera with the idea of capturing some footage of the icy expanses and the Inuits. He figured that "armchair traveler" societies would pay him to screen and narrate an Arctic travelogue for their members—people who were curious about other lands but were too busy, too poor, too unwilling, or too infirm to actually make the journey themselves.

Canada's fastest mammal: the pronghorn antelope. It can run at speeds up to 100 km/h.

FIRED WITH ENTHUSIASM

Flaherty came back from the wild with a limited amount of footage that he spliced together and showed to audiences in Toronto. Their exuberant applause encouraged him to buy up all the film he could find before his next prospecting trip. In 1915–16, he returned to the Arctic and shot 30,000 feet of film, totaling more than six hours of footage. Unfortunately, he didn't do much prospecting, and Mackenzie—who had previously supported Flaherty's film dabbling—fired him.

But that might've been the least of his troubles. When Flaherty returned to Toronto, he accidentally dropped a cigarette on the film. The nitrate-covered stock, made of the same explosive ingredient as guncotton, burst into flame. Flaherty was lucky to escape the blaze. He later claimed that he was glad it happened, though, because it gave him a another chance to get the movie right.

TAKE TWO

Knowing in his gut that a story about the Inuit could have everything that made for a successful movie—action, danger, heart, and a walrus or two—Flaherty began shopping for potential financial backers. Finally, he found Revillon Frères, a fur-trading company with several outposts around Hudson Bay, which agreed to provide money and logistics help.

Flaherty bought two more cameras, a lighting kit, a semiportable movie developing and printing machine, a projector, and 75,000 feet of film stock. In June 1920, he headed north. Traveling by canoe and schooner, it took him two months to reach his destination: Cape Dufferin on northeastern Hudson Bay.

CASTING CALL

There, Flaherty met an Inuit named Allakariallak. In the tradition of Hollywood screen names, Flaherty dubbed him Nanook, which means "polar bear" in the Inuit language. Allakariallak had a wife and family, which was good because Flaherty knew audiences would feel a kinship with a hardworking family man. But Allakariallak's real wife, Cunayou, didn't have that certain something for film, so Flaherty cast a prettier woman named Alice Nuvalinga to play "Nyla," Nanook's wife. (Apparently, Nuvalinga had more than a little of that certain something because Flaherty reportedly

fathered a child with her during filming.) Cunayou appears in the movie as Nanook's second wife.

All of this would've been okay in a feature film, of course, but today it would be considered questionable conduct in what was supposed to be a documentary. In the 1920s, though, the documentary business was all but nonexistent, so Flaherty was able to make up the rules as he went along.

LIGHTS, CAMERA, BREAK OPEN THE IGLOO

With his cast lined up, Flaherty turned his attention to the set...that is, the environment, which arguably is the real star of the movie. Flaherty's cameras were the best he could get in those days for cold-weather work, allowing him to film without too many freeze-ups and glitches.

But the cameras were big, and igloos are small and their insides aren't well lit. How to record typical family life inside? Flaherty had an idea. He got Allakariallak and his friends to build an igloo with a cut-away wall, and he shot all the interior scenes—even the nighttime ones—during the day to allow light and high enough temperatures to avoid freezing the talent.

Flaherty had a very specific vision for the film: he wanted to record the Inuit culture before European influences destroyed it. The problem was that, by 1920, Europeans had already been in the region for some time, trading goods for furs.

So Flaherty staged scenes. In one case, he created a scene in which Nanook goes into a trading post and pretends to encounter a gramophone for the first time, laughing excitedly and even playfully biting a record. In reality, though, the Inuit were already familiar with gramophones and other modern technology, and they were intensely interested in it. In particular, Allakariallak and his friends were fascinated by Flaherty's production equipment. The men became adept at disassembling and reassembling the camera when it jammed or took on moisture. They even created a drying reel out of driftwood and helped Flaherty improvise when his equipment proved inefficient at processing film in the cold.

CUE THE WALRUS

A more serious problem for Flaherty's "realism," though, was that Allakariallak was accustomed to using a rifle for hunting, which

was not in character for Nanook. Flaherty was firm in his insistence that Nanook use traditional harpoons and ivory knives as hunting tools, a requirement that almost proved fatal.

Flaherty and Allakariallak, who had become an enthusiastic partner in dreaming up scenarios, decided to film a hunt in which the men killed a walrus with harpoons. They piled the equipment in a kayak and headed to Walrus Island, a journey that took more than three days, and then got set up to film.

Things went bad quickly. When the men harpooned a walrus, it scampered toward the sea...dragging Nanook and two other hunters with it. For more than 20 hair-raising minutes, the hunters struggled to pull the 2,000-pound walrus bull out of the surf, while its herd members menaced them. Flaherty said later that the men were crying and shouting to him to let them use a rifle to finish it off, but he continued hand-cranking the camera, pretending to not understand them.

Despite the danger, when Flaherty developed and screened the footage, all was forgiven. Allakariallak was so pleased that he persuaded Flaherty to film a polar bear hunt, an expedition that required an overland trek of 600 miles. This venture went even worse than the walrus hunt. The group got lost and ran out of rations, sled dogs died of starvation, and when the men did find polar bears, they were too weak to hunt them. The group managed to kill some seals and somehow made it back to base with all human lives intact, 55 days after starting out. After that episode, Flaherty kept production close to camp.

COLD REALITY

So much of the film's "reality" was faked or simulated: the three-sided igloo, the staged encounter with the gramophone, a seal hunt in which Nanook gamely struggles against the rope of a harpooned seal (actually an off-camera crew person). At the end, Nanook and his family were portrayed as being alone, possibly facing death from exposure even though the production crew (small though it was) was right there. With so much of the film being staged, how could a viewer believe anything? Flaherty argued that the essential message of his film was true—a people's indomitable will to survive—and that he recorded real Inuit doing real tasks, including hunting real wild animals.

But even after filming, Flaherty spun romantic fiction that sometimes conflicted with the truth. For example, when reports surfaced a couple of years after the film's release that Allakariallak had died, Flaherty told the press that the man died from starvation, further demonstrating the extreme life depicted in his movie. In reality, Allakariallak died of disease, probably tuberculosis.

IT'S A WRAP

Still, *Nanook of the North* was a hit, and in 1989, it was one of the first 25 films inducted into the U.S. National Film Registry. Some fast facts:

• Based on the movie's incredible commercial success, Flaherty had the chance to film similar docudramas, including one set in Ireland's Aran Isles. The shark hunt in *Man of Aran* is remarkable, and Flaherty had to bring in an Inuit to teach his Irish actors how to hunt sharks in the traditional manner, since the Irish no longer hunted that way themselves.

• The success of the film led to a cultural fad of plastering the image of Inuits on everything from refrigerators to Eskimo Pies. There was even the song "Nanook," a 1922 "novelty foxtrot."

• Allakariallak's children survived, and a grandson even played Allakariallak in the movie *Kabloonak*, a 1994 film about the making of *Nanook of the North*.

• Alice Nuvalinga, who played Nanook's wife Nyla, had a baby a few months after Flaherty left. She named him Joseph Flaherty. (Joseph was Robert Flaherty's middle name.) In 1953, Joseph was relocated by the government to Grise Fiord, Nunavut, during the High Arctic Relocation Program—a controversial government migration program that sent 87 Inuit, mostly welfare recipients from Quebec, to live in the Arctic so Canada could claim sovereignty there. The Inuit claimed the migration was forced; the government called the participants "volunteers." Eventually, in 1994, the Canadian government set up a $10 million trust fund as a reparation to the families.

A McGill chemistry professor invented the green dye used on American dollars.

MOUNTIE MADNESS

The Royal Canadian Mounted Police has had its share of bad press over the years. But have a heart. Look at some of what they have to deal with.

WELL, THAT'S ONE EXPLANATION

In November 2009, an RCMP officer in Ontario sat through two traffic light cycles; the car in front of him hadn't moved. When he investigated, he found the driver of the car chatting on her cell phone. He asked why she hadn't gone on the green, and she explained that it would have been illegal—talking on a cell phone and driving weren't permitted. After a lecture on the law, he "encouraged" her to hang up and move along.

RIGHT PLACE, WRONG TIME

A Mountie in Surrey, British Columbia, responded to a burglary call in August 2009. He pulled right up in front of the store being robbed at 72nd Avenue and Scott Road ready to catch the bad guy, but before he could climb out of his patrol car, a minivan with California plates slammed into him. Was it the robbers on the run? Nope, just a drunk American driving recklessly on Surrey streets. The Mountie and the driver were both treated at the hospital, and a second officer was dispatched to attend to the robbery. But it was all to no avail. Amidst all the noise and commotion, the thief got away.

TEAM EDWARD TO THE RESCUE!

In March 2009, the cast and crew of *Twilight: New Moon* descended on Vancouver Island to film a few scenes. Hordes of teenage girls followed, aching to get a glimpse (or a piece) of Robert Pattinson, who plays Edward, the lead vampire. The film's producers were so concerned that the girls would cause trouble, they hired two Mounties to guard the actor. Said one constable, "It was an unusual mission, but our remit was to keep the fans off the set." He also noted that "it was raining really hard the whole time but the producers loved that because it helped to make their scenes much more gloomy and atmospheric. This is a beautiful part of the world, but when it gets cold and wet even a vampire would get the chills."

50 millionth song downloaded from iTunes: "The Path of Thorns" by Cape Breton's Rita MacNeil.

TAKING A BITE OUT OF CRIME

RCMP officers got an odd call in September 2009: A 20-year-old Vancouver man phoned his parents from Cancún, Mexico, where he claimed he'd been kidnapped, forced into a fight, shot at, and then dumped in a lagoon...only to be gnawed on by crocodiles. His family, understandably upset, called in the Mounties to investigate. After talking with the man and the Mexican authorities, though, the police came to a different conclusion. As it turned out, the man had been drunk and stumbled to the lagoon to go to the bathroom. There, he tripped, fell into the water, and was bitten by several crocodiles. Oh, and those crocs? They were each only about 25 centimeters (10 inches) long, and the lagoon was plastered with signs warning that they were there.

INK NOW, THINK LATER

When police arrived at the Saskatchewan home of David McKay to serve an arrest warrant, they were confused by the man who answered the door: he claimed to be "Matthew," not David, but said he had met David once and the man was a "badass." The Mounties took "Matthew" down to the station anyway because he matched McKay's description. Once there, the man answered questions while officers debated what to do. Finally, while "Matthew" was being processed, the Mounties caught a break: he had a tattoo on his back that said "David McKay." The criminal was processed and charged with obstruction for failing to give the police his real name.

BEE-ATTLE ROYALE

In 2007, Mounties were dispatched to round up a group of honeybees that had flown the hive in Shelbourne, Nova Scotia. Beekeeper Rodney Dillinger said that half of the hive (about 30,000 bees) had gotten into a fight with the other half over their queen and then buzzed off. According to an RCMP spokeswoman, Dillinger told the Mounties that the bees "were last seen near a Tim Hortons on the edge of town. He wanted us to help him round them up." According to Dillinger, the bees weren't dangerous, "but they look ugly to people who are not familiar with bees, and I'm worried someone may attack them with a broom or a stick." Last we heard, the bees were still missing, but people in Shelbourne had their brooms at the ready.

Only Canadian on the cover of the Beatles' *Sgt. Pepper* album: child actor Bobby Breen.

TRUTH, JUSTICE, AND A CANADIAN...EH?

He's billed as an American hero, but Superman has more Canadian connections than you can shake a maple leaf at.

• Joe Schuster, the artist and co-creator of Superman, was born in Toronto and lived there until his family moved to Cleveland, Ohio, in 1929, when he was 10. The fictional town of Metropolis was modeled on Toronto.

• Schuster got interested in comics because his dad read him the funny pages from the *Toronto Star*. Later, he got a paper route and delivered the same paper. When Schuster first drew his *Superman* comic, he named Clark Kent's newspaper the *Metropolis Daily Star* in tribute, but an editor at DC Comics made him change it to the *Daily Planet*.

• Superman's secret Fortress of Solitude is under the ice at the North Pole. Canada has put in a claim that the North Pole is Canadian, so Superman may be a resident...whether legally or illegally.

• *Smallville*, the TV show based on the life of young Clark Kent, films mostly in and around Vancouver, the city that doubles for Metropolis. Smallville's Main Street is made up of a combination of locations in Merritt and Cloverdale, B.C. A farm in Aldergrove is used as the Kents' farm, and Victoria's Hatley Castle acts as Lex Luthor's home. Many of the show's interiors are filmed at BB Studios in Burnaby.

• Scenes from the *Superman* movies were filmed at Alberta locations, including Barons (Clark Kent's grade school) and High River (Lana Lang's house and most of Smallville, including its town square).

• Joe Schuster was not only Canadian—his cousin was Frank Schuster of the long-running comedy team Wayne and Schuster.

The arctic tern has the world's longest migration route—about 35,000 km a year.

NATURE'S LIGHT SHOW

*There's a spot in the Yukon where spectacular and mysterious
colored lights shimmer across the night sky. Welcome to
the wonderful world of the aurora borealis.*

THE BARD'S BALLAD

In the poem "The Ballad of the Northern Lights," Robert Service wrote about a mining team slowly going crazy under the *aurora borealis*: two of the men committed suicide, and the third staked a worthless claim on what he believed was the lights' source: a mountain filled with radium.

The northern lights have that kind of reputation—a phenomenon so mind-boggling that it drives mere mortals bonkers. We know it works that way on electronic equipment: when the northern lights are brightest, radio and satellite transmissions are disrupted, and GPS guidance systems can send you off to unexpected places. Here's some more of what we know about those magical lights.

WHAT'S IN A NAME?

A French philosopher named Pierre Gassendi gave the lights their best-known name in 1621: *Aurora* after the Roman goddess of light, and *Boreas*, Greek for "north wind." The Cree call the northern lights the "Dance of the Spirits," and tribal legends say the lights are either spirits in the sky playing catch with a walrus skull, or the torches of the spirits of the dead as they go to the afterlife.

BEN GETS IT WRONG

For centuries, people considered the lights to have religious or magical origins, but Benjamin Franklin wasn't having any of that. In 1778, he claimed to have solved the mystery of the northern lights: they were, Franklin said, merely electrical charges caused by snow and moisture. Although a step closer than most who came before him, Franklin was wrong.

Modern scientists believe that magnetically charged plasma from the Sun is the cause. The Sun shoots out streams of ionized gas, or the "solar wind." When this solar wind comes in contact

with the Earth's magnetic field, the ions are captured and pulled toward the magnetic north and south poles. Some of the ions also get pulled down into the Earth's ionosphere—about 100 to 130 kilometers (62 to 80 miles) overhead—where they collide with gases, creating a huge neon light without a glass tube to contain it. And as with a neon light, different gases give different colors. At the highest altitudes, oxygen emits dark red and green; at lower altitudes, you get blues and brighter reds from nitrogen.

AURORAS IN SPACE

The lights usually look like a curtain when viewed from the ground, but from space, they've been described as looking like a "monk's haircut"—a giant oval surrounding each of the magnetic poles. And they don't just appear on Earth but on other planets as well, and even on some of the planets' moons. Space probes and the Hubble Space Telescope have recorded vivid aurora activity on Mars, Venus, Saturn, Jupiter, and on three of Jupiter's largest moons: Io, Europa, and Ganymede.

BEST LIGHT SHOW EVER

The amount of solar wind is always changing, so sunspots—intense magnetic activity that appears on the surface of the Sun and leaves a visible dark spot—can launch great amounts of plasma into space, sometimes hurtling toward Earth. This magnetic intensity creates much bigger aurora light shows at our poles. The spring and autumn equinoxes are a time when the lights are most common because that is typically when we receive more of the Sun's plasma spews. The Sun also has magnetic fluctuations that occur in pre-dictable 11-year cycles. According to the CBC, the last light show peak occurred in 2001; the next will be in 2012, so book your reservations early.

But, where to go? The aurora borealis is the northern version, and the *aurora australis* ("of the south") is the southern equivalent. Both offer great shows, but don't even think about trying to get down to see the aurora australis. It doesn't offer quite the same viewing experience because most of the best viewing areas down there are covered with water or ice.

In the north, the town of Yellowknife, Yukon, claims to be the capital for aurora borealis tourism, and the farther you get from

cities, towns, and outdoor lighting, the better the light's performance. But you'll face stiff competition for lodging during the next big show. Newlywed Japanese couples typically flood Canada during peak times of northern lights activity due to a Japanese legend that says, "A child conceived in the spell of the lights will be fortunate in life."

LIGHT READING

The closer you get to the North Pole, the better chance you have of seeing the northern lights. But once in a shimmering blue night, the aurora borealis appears even to folks closer to the equator. For example, on November 5 and 6, 2001, the northern lights were seen vividly throughout most of the United States, even as far south as Texas. But that was nothing compared to September 2, 1859, when a massive solar storm brought the nighttime colors to the United States, Europe, Japan, Australia, and thousands of ships at sea. In Boston, according to the *New York Times*, the light was "so brilliant that at about 1 o' clock [in the morning] ordinary print could be read by the light."

And, in case you were wondering: even though you can't see them, the lights are there in the sky during the daytime as well.

* * *

SPEAKING TOURIST

Some people say there are no dumb questions. Based on the things some tourists to Canada have asked, we're not so sure.

• If the Columbia Icefield (Alberta) melts before we get there, can we do a different excursion?

• Will I see polar bears in the street?

• We're going to British Columbia, so do we need to change our money to pounds?

• Where is the rocky mountain?

• What time do they turn off Niagara Falls?

• How much does it cost to get into Canada, and are children a different price?

The Skydome's retractable roof weighs 11,000 tons.

ELVIS LIVES!

*Have you seen Elvis lately? If so, be sure to let
them know at "Elvis Lives Lane" in Ottawa.*

IS THERE AN ELVIS IN THE BUILDING?

The semiserious Elvis Sighting Society (ESS) in Ottawa celebrates the life and music of the King of Rock 'n' Roll "until he went into exile" on August 16, 1977 (the day most of us think he died). And appropriately—considering Elvis's well-known love of food—the society's headquarters is housed in the Newport Restaurant, a sit-down burger and pizza place located in an alley called Elvis Lives Lane.

The Newport's owner, Moe Atallah, is a huge fan of the King's music and has decorated the Newport with Elvis paintings, photographs, and memorabilia. But it wouldn't be the Elvis *Sighting* Society, of course, if it didn't concern itself with the phenomenon of posthumous Elvis sightings. So, sure enough, the ESS maintains a log of Elvis sightings on its Web site, and Canada has been the location of many of the King's most "credible" appearances. Here are some of our favorites. (It's funny, Elvis seems to spend a lot of time in Ontario.)

• Elvis spotted standing in the audience at a Joe Cocker concert in Toronto. He looked the same, except with grey in hair and sideburns.

• Elvis seen browsing CDs in a West Edmonton Mall music store.

• Elvis performed Beatles songs on karaoke night at a hotel bar in Coboconk, Ontario.

• Elvis sipped a glass of Uzo at the King's Arms Pub in Oakville, Ontario. (He had reportedly lost weight.)

• Elvis seen talking with a one-legged man in Mystic, Quebec.

• Apparently hard-up for cash and "in the ghetto," Elvis seen shoveling snow in Cambridge, Ontario, for $5 per driveway.

• North of Minaki, Ontario, a hungry Elvis scared off a pair of bears and took the pork chop they were fighting over.

"I would rather have played for the Leafs than be prime minister of Canada." —Lester Pearson

CLEVER CANADIANS, PART I

*If, as Mark Twain once suggested, accidents are the greatest
of all inventors, then Canadians should keep being careless.
Whether accidental or on purpose, these inventions
have proved to be both innovative and useful.*

BLOWING IT THE FIRST TIME

In 1870, New Brunswicker Robert Carr Harris took out a patent for the first snowblower. It didn't really work, and over the years, several other people tried to improve on the machine. But none of those worked well enough, either. Finally, in 1925, Arthur Sicard of Montreal developed a blower that actually worked. Although Sicard's contraption would be considered cumbersome by today's standards, it was downright innovative at the time. A truck fitted with a tractor motor pushed a snow scooper. Attached to the vehicle were movable chutes that blew the collected snow away from streets, driveways, and sidewalks. Not surprisingly, Canadians laid down their shovels and cleared a path for the Sicard snowblower.

SKI-DOO FROM A SKI-DOG

Many people assume that Bombardier (the company that makes the Ski-Doo and Sea-Doo...and jets) got its name from bomber planes. Not so. Instead, credit Quebec-born Joseph-Armand Bombardier (1907–64), who in 1937 began making vehicles that could run on roads thick with snow. His first invention: a buslike vehicle that carried up to a dozen people. That was a great help to residents in Quebec because most towns in that province didn't plow their roads in winter. By 1949, though, Quebec lawmakers mandated that towns at least plow their main roads, so Bombardier set about inventing the personal off-road snowmobile. Originally dubbed the "Ski-Dog," a typo in the first promotional literature called it the "Ski-Doo," and the name stuck. (Bombardier also went on to manufacture airplane and railroad parts. The recreational piece of the company split off in 2003 from its parent.)

The first covered shopping mall in Canada: Park Royal (est. 1950) in West Vancouver, BC.

FROM CANE TO ABLE

British Columbia resident Norm Rolston was tired of watching his aunt struggle with two unwieldy canes to help her walk, so he decided to come up with a better option. Rolston experimented with a stroller and a shopping cart, and settled on a hybrid—the Able Walker, which he patented in 1986. Initially, doctors hesitated to prescribe the walkers. Similar wheeled walkers at the time were precarious, often tipping and causing falls. But the Able Walker had fully pivoting wheels that allowed users to turn corners easily. It also employed easy-to-apply brakes. Rolston and his wife marketed the device the old-fashioned way with flyers and legwork, and within two years, the Able Walker had raked in more than $5 million.

BLOWING HOT AND COLD

During the 1800s, indoor spaces (in Canada and elsewhere) were difficult to cool in the summer and heat in winter. In particular, available heat sources—mostly fireplaces and wood-burning stoves—were risky to home and health due to poor ventilation. So what was a train passenger to do but swelter or freeze? Much to the delight of North American rail riders in the mid-1800s, Canadian military colonel and politician Henry Ruttan decided to change that. Utilizing the natural airflow of a train's forward motion, he invented a system whereby outside air was forced into a series of ducts. Ruttan first focused on a cooling system—air was cooled, cleaned, humidified, and then circulated through the carriages. Then he modified the system to provide heat, creating the world's first air-conditioning/heating system.

WHISTLE WHILE YOU WORK

Before the 1980s, athletic whistles usually came with a small ball (called a "pea") inside; the rolling ball created an attention-getting warble. The problem was that the peas could jam, turning the whistle into a whisper. Professional basketball referee Ron Foxcroft became tired of faulty pea whistles after an embarrassing moment at the 1976 Montreal Summer Olympics. Witnessing a foul during the gold-medal basketball game between the United States and Yugoslavia, Foxcroft blew his whistle but couldn't pro-

In 1910, it cost 2¢ to mail a letter in Canada.

duce a sound—the pea had jammed. The game went on, the uncalled foul outraged the crowd, and Foxcroft vowed he'd never be at the mercy of a pea whistle again. Back at home in Ontario, Foxcroft developed a whistle that warbled loudly using a series of tuned chambers instead of a moving pea. Today, the Fox 40 Pea-less Whistle, introduced in 1987, is used by sports referees, police departments, and military units around the world.

CUTTING THROUGH THE FOG

Robert Foulis, a Scotsman turned Canadian, invented the first automated, steam-powered foghorn in 1859. Inspired by the resounding bass notes of his daughter's piano playing, Foulis discovered that a loud, consistent low note could carry through the fog. He erected the world's first steam-powered foghorn on Partridge Island in New Brunswick's Saint John Harbour that same year. But despite the importance of Foulis's invention, he never got around to patenting his foghorn, so he never earned a cent from it.

SYMBOL FOR YOUR THOUGHTS

In the mid-1980s, 12-year-old Ontario student Rachel Zimmerman needed an idea for her school science fair. Already something of a computer geek, she knew about Blissymbols, a series of pictograms invented by linguist Charles K. Bliss in the 1940s. Bliss had intended for the symbols to be used to surmount language barriers—he'd hoped that the group of pictograms would be universal, recognized by all no matter a person's native language. Zimmerman thought, why not create a Blissymbol computer program and interface so people of any language could communicate with each other via computer? Using a custom touch pad and a printer, Zimmerman invented the Blissymbol Printer, which allowed users to choose images that matched their thoughts. The computer then translated the symbols into written words that could be stored for later use, printed, or even sent by e-mail. The Blissymbol Printer went on to compete in Canada's World Exhibition of Achievement of Young Inventors, and Zimmerman won a silver medal.

More clever Canadians on page 294.

Shortest term for a PM: Charles Tupper, who served for 69 days in 1896. (He was fired.)

HIGHWAY PETROL

*In 2004, Canada officially jumped from number 20
in world oil supply to number 2, second only to
Saudi Arabia. How did that happen?*

OIL IN THEM THAR SANDS

When oil prices went sky-high in the mid-2000s, Alberta's oil sands suddenly became a valuable commodity. The cost of extracting petroleum from sand or clay can run up to $20 a barrel—generally too expensive compared with the few dollars it takes to simply pump it from the ground. But suddenly, as oil prices jumped from about $25 a barrel to $45 in 2004 (and then to $147 in 2008), that production cost became bearable. Almost overnight, Canada's estimated reserve of extractable oil went from 5 billion barrels to an astonishing 180 billion, second only to Saudi Arabia's 262 billion and knocking Iraq's 115 billion barrels into third place.

Not bad considering that Canada was long thought of as an also-ran in the oil business...ironic, considering the country drilled the first oil well in North America.

WELL ENOUGH

Popular histories—particularly those written in the United States—tend to give credit for North America's first oil well to the 1859 strike at Edwin Drake's well near Titusville, Pennsylvania. But that's wrong. Four years before, Canadian James Miller Williams struck black gold in what's now the town of Oil Springs, Ontario.

In 1855, Williams purchased the International Mining and Manufacturing Company, Canada's first commercial petroleum company. Its founder, Charles Nelson Tripp, had chartered the company in 1854 to look for oil deposits in the land around Enniskillen Township, Ontario. The ground was marshy and prone to flooding, though, and the venture quickly turned into a money pit. Disgusted and broke, Tripp was happy to cash out.

After Williams took over the site, his workers complained about a lack of fresh drinking water in the marshes. In 1858,

while digging a water well, Williams accomplished—20 meters (65.6 feet) down—what Tripp had gone bankrupt trying to do: he hit oil.

WHY PETROLEUM BEFORE CARS?

Back then, oil didn't mean what it means today—the primary source for gasoline. Before the internal combustion engine, gasoline was considered a waste product. So why were men like Williams and Drake so interested in finding oil? Because even before cars, petroleum-based products were important.

"Rock oil" (from which we get the word petroleum; in Greek *petra* = "rock," and in Latin, *oleum* = "oil") had been used from ancient times for a variety of things. The Chinese were the first to refine crude oil for fuel, and the ancient Greeks, the first to invent a petroleum-based weapon—"Greek fire," a type of primitive napalm. Petroleum seeping up from the ground had also been used for waterproofing, paving, and medicine. And First Nation canoe-builders used Canada's coal tars to waterproof their vessels.

Before the mid-1800s, people used crude oil as a fuel and lubricant, but in the 1850s, thanks to the Industrial Revolution, demand began to climb significantly. Canadian inventor Abraham Gesner synthesized coal into a lamp oil that he called "keroselain" (what we know today as kerosene). Then, in 1855, American Benjamin Silliman discovered that Gesner's process also worked with oil, laying ground for a boom in North American oil industries. (Before that, lamp oil had come from whales, making it an expensive commodity that cost the equivalent of about $60 per gallon today.)

OIL AND BRIMSTONE

With James Miller Williams's 1858 discovery of oil in Ontario, speculators and entrepreneurs descended on the area to sink their own wells around a new boomtown dubbed Petrolia. Equipment was still primitive and often homemade, resulting in "refineries" that looked more like backwoods whiskey stills, distilling kerosene with simple equipment in rickety shacks.

One problem developed. The Ontario "sweet crude" was soured with sulfur compounds. Even with refining, its kerosene retained a faint rotten-egg smell that made the oil less desirable to buyers.

Q: What's the difference between water and American beer? A: You can get water for free.

Worse, the wells in Ontario were not producing as much oil per well as were those in the United States and eastern Europe, adding to the costs of exploring and drilling. Then, in the 1880s, electrical lamps started to replace kerosene lamps. As Montreal, Ottawa, and Toronto went electric, the Canadian oil industry, already ailing, seemed destined for a long decline.

GASEOUS CLAY
But then, with the appearance of the internal combustion engine, Canada's oil industry received a stay of execution. By 1913, there were 50,000 registered cars in Canada, up from just a few dozen a decade earlier. That sent oil producers scrambling for new and better oil fields.

Alberta showed early promise in the late 1800s with an accidental natural gas strike. A team from the Canadian Pacific Railroad, drilling for water, hit a pocket of natural gas, which is often a sign of oil below. After a substantial oil strike in 1914 at Turner Valley, southwest of Calgary, investors formed more than 500 oil companies within a few days. (Three years later, most of them had gone out of business.)

By the 1930s, the Turner Valley wells were showing signs of playing out. So in 1946, the Imperial Oil Company dug 133 "wildcat" wells around Alberta and Saskatchewan. Wildcats are exploratory wells; there is no guarantee that they'll produce anything. That was certainly the case for Imperial—all 133 came up dry. In desperation, the company also tried an unpromising site 15 kilometers (9 miles) west of Leduc, south of Edmonton. There, they struck oil—a lot of it—and that was the birth of Canada's modern oil industry.

The Leduc fields were the great reservoir of petroleum the Canadian oil industry had been searching for. By the time the Leduc No. 1 site played out in 1974, it had produced 50,300 cubic meters (320,000 barrels) of oil and 9 million cubic meters (320 million cubic feet) of natural gas. What was next?

STRIP-MINING ALBERTA
What came next was oil sand, and Alberta has a lot of it. Under the province's forests and peat bogs lie 140,200 square kilometers (54,132 square miles) of oil sand, containing an estimated 1.7

As part of their training, *Apollo 16* and *17* astronauts took field trips...

trillion barrels of oil. Getting it out, however, can be problematic. Only about a tenth of the total amount is close enough to the surface to make it economically feasible to extract, though on paper it sounds easy: scrape away the topsoil, strip-mine the oil sand, send it off to the refinery, replace the topsoil, and plant some trees to replace the old forests. No problem!

Well, not really. There are obvious environmental concerns about strip-mining that much land, not to mention using the extra water and energy needed to process the oil sand. Added to that problem is the fact that the United States is Canada's biggest customer. And since about 40 percent of America's oil consumption goes to transporting passenger cars, many Canadians wonder if it's worth despoiling the Alberta countryside and releasing pollution and greenhouse gases just to enable American SUVs to release even *more* pollution and greenhouse gases. And so the debate over Alberta's oil sand continues…probably just until the next spike in oil prices, though.

* * *

CANADA'S HARD OILERS

For more than 50 years, starting in 1874, Canada's drillers exported their expertise around the world. Calling themselves "hard oilers," they sank some of the first wells in Egypt, Turkey, Borneo, Burma, Peru, and Russia. They also lent their expertise to American ventures in California, Oklahoma, and Texas.

These men got to travel the world and lead lives of adventure seldom seen outside of books and movies. It wasn't unusual for hard oilers to find themselves moving equipment with elephants instead of trucks, or coming face to face with armed locals and three-meter (10-foot) cobras. During World War I, hard oilers in the Middle East occasionally had to set their tools aside to help defend their drilling sites from hostile raiders.

Why did they do it? The pay was great. An oiler's typical wage in the 1920s was $4,500 a year…at a time when the average Canadian made about $1,000 annually.

SYMBOLIC OVERVIEW

Do you know all of the official symbols of the provinces and territories? Some of them surprised us. Test your national knowledge with these stumpers. (Answers on page 453.)

1. What's Quebec's provincial symbol?
a. The pom de terre
b. The fleur-de-lis
c. The nom de plume

2. What's the provincial dog of Nova Scotia?
a. The Nova Scotia Terrier
b. The valley bulldog
c. The Nova Scotia duck tolling retriever

3. Nunavut's official symbol is...
a. The polar bear
b. The rock ptarmigan
c. The inukshuk

4. Name Newfoundland and Labrador's provincial flower.
a. The pitcher plant
b. The pink dogwood
c. The wild blueberry

5. Which is the provincial mineral of Prince Edward Island?
a. Atlantic sand
b. Charlottetown soil
c. Glacial gravel

6. Name the provincial mineral of Saskatchewan.
a. Potash
b. Oil
c. Sandstone

7. Which of the following is B.C.'s provincial gemstone?
a. Cubic zirconia
b. Diamond
c. Jade

8. What's Ontario's provincial bird?
a. The common loon
b. The Toronto street pigeon
c. The Canada goose

9. Which of the following is the Yukon Territory's official gemstone?
a. Garnet
b. Lazulite
c. Lavalite

10. Which of the following is the provincial stone of Alberta?
a. Granite
b. VO5 quartz
c. Petrified wood

11. Which New Brunswick provincial symbol is the Holmesville Series?
a. Provincial soil
b. Provincial baseball team
c. Provincial detective

12. The provincial animal of Manitoba is...
a. The great gray owl
b. The bison
c. The aardvark

13. The official mineral of the Northwest Territories is...
a. Gold
b. Silver
c. Bronze

THOMPSON'S NOTEBOOK: POLYGAMY

Surveyor David Thompson traveled through the Canadian interior between 1784 and 1812. Around 1800, he met up with the Piegan tribe, who dominated the plains just east of the Rocky Mountains in what's now Alberta. He observed that "the grown-up population of these people appear to be about three men to every five women." Their solution? Polygamy. Here's what Thompson wrote.

THE WIFE TAKES A WIFE

"The young men seldom marry before they are fully grown, about the age of 22 years or more, and the women about 16 to 18. The older women who are related to them are generally the matchmakers, and the parties come together without any ceremony.

Of the young men, two of them form a tent until they have families, in which also reside the widowed mothers and aunts. Polygamy is allowed, and the wife more frequently than her husband is the cause of it, for when a family comes, a single wife can no longer do the duties and labor required unless she, or her husband, have two widowed relations in their tent. This frequently is not the case; and a second wife is necessary, for they have to cook, take care of the meat, split and dry it; procure all the wood for fuel, dress the skins into soft leather for robes and clothing; which they have also to make and mend, and other duties, which leaves scarce any part of the day to be idle. In moving from place to place, the taking down of the tents and putting them up are all performed by women. Some of the chiefs have from three to six wives, for until a woman is near 50 years of age, she is sure to find a husband.

THE BEST OF INTENTIONS...

"A young Indian with whom I was acquainted often said he would never have more than one wife, since he had a small tent, and one of his aunts to help his wife. Nearly two years afterwards,

Terry Fox went through 9 running shoes during his 1980 Marathon of Hope...

passing by where he was, I entered his tent, and found his first wife, as usual, sitting beside him. On the other side were three fine women in the prime of life, and as many elderly of the same sex, in the back part. When I left the tent, he also came out—and telling me not to laugh at him for what he formerly said of having only one wife—he explained to me how he had been obliged to take three more:

'After I last saw you, a friend of mine, whom I regarded and loved as a brother, would go to war. He got wounded, returned and, shortly after, died. Relying on my friendship, when dying, he requested his parents send his two wives to me, where he was sure they would be kindly treated and become my wives. His parents brought them to me, with the dying request of my friend, what could I do but grant the claim of my friend, and make them my wives. Those are the two that sit next to the door. The other one was the wife of a cousin who was also a friend of mine, he fell sick and died, and bequeathed his wife to my care. The old women at the back of the tent are their relations...'

WIVES IN WAITING

"An old Indian, Sarkamappee, pointed out to me a curious kind of polygamy. Besides his old wives, on the other side of the tent, sat three young women of about 16 or 18 years of age whom about two months before, had been given to him for wives by their parents. I noticed that he treated them as if they were his daughters. He told me that they were placed with him on trust:

> You must know that among us are families far more powerful than other families. Some of the relatives make a bad use of their influence. Two of these young women are sisters and the whole three were betrothed to three young men. They would have been given to them, had not three men of two powerful families, who each already have four or five wives, demanded that these young women be given to them. As their parents are not powerful to prevent this, these three young women have been given to me. In my tent they will remain until this camp separates, and they go some distance, when they will be given to the young men for whom they are intended, and thus each of them will regard me as their father...

Some time after, I met an old warrior whom I had known for a long time. I spoke to him of what Sarkamappee had told me of the three young women in his tent. I had never known such a custom

...Only one was for his prosthetic foot; the others were for his real foot.

among the Indians of the woods, and enquired if it was common among those of the plains. He said, 'It is not common, yet it happens too often.'

'Had one of those men who wanted those young women come to Sarkamappee's tent, and demanded them, what would he have done?' [Thompson asked.]

'If any had been fool enough to have done so, he would have shot him as he would a bear, and as careless of the consequences.'"

* * *

GIVE THAT BACK!

The Order of Canada is the highest honor the government can bestow on Canadians. Past winners include authors, diplomats, prime ministers, physicians, and other important people. But in four cases, the government has inducted recipients into the Order and then removed the honor. Why the about-face?

• In 1989, **Alan Eagleson** (a top lawyer and NHL agent) won the honor for "promoting the sport of ice hockey." Nine years later, though, Eagleson admitted to a bevy of crimes including embezzlement and defrauding players, so the government removed him from the Order, making him the first person ever asked to leave.

• **David Ahenakew** was awarded the Order of Canada in 1978 for his work on behalf of the First People of Saskatchewan. But in 2002, he gave a racist newspaper interview in which he praised Adolph Hitler and claimed that Jews were responsible for the Holocaust. Ahenakew was tried for "inciting hatred" and eventually acquitted, but the government stripped him of the Order.

• In 2001, lawyer **T. Sher Singh** was awarded the honor for his work on improving relations among people of different religions. In 2007, he was convicted of "professional misconduct" (lying, cheating, etc.) and removed from the Order.

• **Steve Fonyo** lost a leg to cancer when he was 12 and, in 1984 and '85, at the age of 19, he ran 8,000 kilometers (4,970 miles) to raise money to fight the disease. He was made a member of the Order in 1985, the youngest person ever admitted. But Fonyo was also a cocaine addict who had trouble with the law. After several convictions for check fraud, impaired driving, and assault, he lost his award in 2009.

THE IRISH ARE COMING! PART II

On page 121, we introduced you to one of the strangest military conflicts in North American history. Here's the rest of the Fenians' story.

REST NOT, WANT NOT
Feeling confident, John O'Neill, the Fenians' unit commander, gave his men another day to rest. Meanwhile, U.S. forces, led by General Ulysses S. Grant, secured the border at Buffalo, preventing 4,000 Fenian reinforcements from crossing the river. The British rallied, and pretty soon, O'Neill's troops found themselves surrounded by 5,000 British soldiers. Lacking reinforcements, O'Neill made the decision to retreat to Buffalo, hoping that his diversionary attack had been sufficient to draw the British army away from Quebec and clear the way for the main invasion.

On their way back, though, O'Neill and his men were overtaken by a U.S. ship and arrested while crossing the Niagara River. President Johnson, having waited for nearly a week to issue a proclamation, finally ordered that the Fenian war-making be suppressed.

ON TO MONTREAL!
The Fenians would not be thwarted, however. In the first week of June, the Irishmen gathered in St. Albans, Vermont, for the attack on Montreal. Residents were not particularly happy about that—two years earlier, while the American Civil War still raged, Confederate raiders had swooped down from Canada, rampaging through town and robbing the local banks of nearly $250,000. Fortunately, by June 6, the Fenians had started marching into Quebec.

They numbered a few thousand—far fewer than the planned 16,000. Still, the invasion went forward in three groupings: one regiment made it 24 kilometers (15 miles) into Canada before being turned back. The second force took a small town called Pigeon Hill. And the main group of 2,000 Fenians marched about 10 kilometers (6 miles) into Canada, taking the town of Frelighsburg (a.k.a., Slab City), and then continued on from there.

Homer Simpson has been declared an honorary citizen of Winnipeg.

REALITY BITES

It was the Fenians' finest hour, but then things started going down-hill fast. First of all, the hoped-for uprising of the Montreal popu-lace was held firmly in check by the presence of British troops, three warships, and the turnout of about 10,000 Canadian militia who had arrived to defend the city from the invaders.

To further complicate things, the Fenians weren't yet aware that they'd been used as a bargaining chip in the reparations issue. While the Irish troops were on the move, the British cut a deal with the U.S. government. President Johnson had accepted $15 million in reparations from them, so he sent troops to neutralize and apprehend any Fenian forces moving toward the Canadian border.

The troops already in Canada were outnumbered and could really only retreat back to the United States. Pursued by the British, they breathed a collective sigh of relief as they approached the border...only to discover that the U.S. commander had given the Brits permission to cross into the United States and continue the battle there. Reports afterward said that the American soldiers stood aside and watched as the British struck down the Fenians with bullets, bayonets, and swords. One Vermont civilian was also killed—a woman named Mrs. Eccles, who was hit by a stray bullet as she watched from her doorway.

A STINGING DEFEAT

As the rest of the Fenians arrived at their base camp in St. Albans, they discovered that it was swarming with U.S. troops who had confiscated their belongings and supplies. The demoral-ized and injured Irish soldiers were disarmed, loaded into waiting trains, and sent back to Boston. And so ended one of the most bizarre moments in North American military history, a brief chain of events that strained relations between the United States and Canada until the alliance of World War II. Although the Fenians were unable to gain independence for their own home country, they inadvertently helped create a different one: the Fenian raids helped Canadians realize that they needed the strength of confederation to forestall future invasions from the south. Instead of being two Canadas—lower and upper—they were headed for a merger.

The Grey Cup was originally awarded to Canada's top amateur rugby team.

I ♥ B.C.

With loads of history and so much natural beauty you could go blind trying to see it all, it's hard to know where to begin…and where to stop. Still, here are a dozen reasons you've just got to love British Columbia.

1. INCREDIBLE WATERFALLS. Canada's tallest waterfalls are in British Columbia, but the province is so used to them that some of the largest don't even have names. Of those that *have* been named and measured, Canada's tallest is Della Falls on Vancouver Island (440 meters/1,443 feet). But seeing it isn't easy: you have to ferry to Vancouver Island, drive to Great Central Lake, boat 20 kilometers (12.4 miles) across to a base camp at Strathcona Provincial Park, and then hike up a 15.5-kilometer (9.6-mile) trail to the base of the falls.

2. TOTEM POLES. They aren't gods, they aren't magical, and they aren't even particularly ancient. Totem poles have been around since about the 1700s, and they used to be small carvings. But their heyday was during the 19th century, when they were used as status symbols to show a family's wealth and prominence. At that time, First Peoples tribes along the British Columbia coast were getting wealthy from the fur trade with Russia, and totems changed from modest indoor carvings to whole-tree extravaganzas of colorful image upon image. The bigger a family's totem, the more money and status they had.

3. THE PIG WAR. Who could hate a war with such a great name, and only one casualty (the pig)? In 1859, an American farmer named Lyman Cutlar was living on San Juan Island, part of an archipelago between Vancouver Island and the mainland. One day in June, Cutlar saw a pig in his garden chomping on his potatoes. Incensed, Cutlar grabbed his rifle and shot the pig. That sparked a land dispute that nearly brought the Americans and the British—who controlled Canada at the time—to war. The pig's owner, Charles Griffin who worked for the Hudson's Bay Company, complained to the British and Canadian authorities, demanding that Culter be arrested for shooting his pig. For his part, Cutlar

complained to the American authorities about the pig being on his land in the first place. And since, at the time, it wasn't clear what country actually owned the island, confusion reigned.

The Americans sent soldiers to San Juan Island to keep the British from landing. The British dispatched warships and pointed their cannons at the Americans. For four months, both sides sent guns, ships, and troops to tiny San Juan Island in an attempt to claim the land and show who was the biggest and the baddest in North America. In the end, diplomacy won out; the two sides split the archipelago: America claimed the San Juan Islands on the south end, and Britain/Canada got the Gulf Islands in the north. They also split San Juan Island for awhile. Eventually, all the troops moved out, and today, San Juan Island is an American national park.

4. CANNABIS. Although beaten out by Quebec as the province with the highest percentage of recreational cannabis smokers, B.C. can claim the nation's high in pot growing, responsible for 40 percent of the total Canadian crop. It also has its own pot party, the British Columbia Marijuana Party, which lobbies for the drug's legalization.

5. SHOW BIZ. Vancouver is often called "Hollywood of the North," but British Columbia has given us more than movies. Consider these contributions to popular culture: actors Raymond Burr, Pamela Anderson, Michael J. Fox, Chief Dan George, Jason Priestly, and Seth Rogan; musicians Joni Mitchell, Sarah McLachlan, Randy Bachman, and Michael Bublé; and writers Douglas Coupland and William Gibson.

6. OGOPOGO, SASQUATCH, ETC. If it weren't for British Columbia's mythical creatures—the Okanagan Lake monster, Ogopogo; the forest-dwelling sasquatch; and cadborosaurus, who supposedly lives in the water near Victoria—Canada would be stuck with just the boring animals like beavers, bears, elk, moose, whales, mountain goats, seals, caribou, salmon, and people.

7. OTHELLO TUNNELS. A number of old railway lines in British Columbia have been turned into hiking/biking trails. The

Othello Tunnels near the town of Hope are especially cool because they take you above the picturesque Coquihalla River Valley and through five long railroad tunnels blasted into the mountains. Signs along the route tell you about the history of the area and the building of the railroad. And if the valley looks familiar, that's probably because it's been in several movies, including a famous scene in *First Blood* in which a helicopter tries to shoot Rambo (Sylvester Stallone) while he hangs from a cliff.

8. CAPILANO SUSPENSION BRIDGE. Okay, maybe you don't feel the same way if you're acrophobic, but we're suckers for swinging bridges over high ravines. When it was first built for the city in 1889, this bridge in North Vancouver was just cedar planks strung together with hemp rope. Since then, it's been completely rebuilt several times and turned into a tourist attraction. The only part that's so sky-high it gives us a nosebleed: the $26.95 admission price.

9. THE PARKS. There are seven—including Mount Revelstoke, the only inland temperate rain forest in the world.

10. MARKETING GONE AWRY. Nowadays, a place with a name like Radium Hot Springs can be difficult to sell when you're trying to entice people for a visit and a soak. But in the late 1800s and early 1900s, it was a big draw. The first European to record a visit to the springs was Sir George Simpson, who worked for the Hudson's Bay Company, in 1841. His report of the healing waters enticed others to trudge through the wilderness to eastern British Columbia and soak for themselves. By 1914, a businessman had bought the hot springs for $160 and set up a resort.

Scientists from McGill University did an analysis and found trace amounts of radon in the water. Radon is created as a by-product when radium decays, and in those days, people believed that radium's radioactivity was healthy; they were even willing to pay money to sit for hours in abandoned radium mines.

11. SPIRAL TUNNELS. Big Hill, a spot with a dangerous grade along the Canadian Pacific Railway's main line through the Kicking Horse Pass, was the site of many fatalities from runaway train crashes. A hurried construction schedule during the late 1800s

First Canadian horse to win the Kentucky Derby: Northern Dancer (1964)

had created a 4.5 percent grade (instead of the 2.2 percent safe maximum) over the Rockies, which often sent trains barreling uncontrollably downhill. The solution? The equivalent of a spiral staircase blasted through the mountains. Finished in 1909, two Big Hill spiral tunnels made the route less steep by allowing the trains to travel through the mountain on more level ground.

12. CLIMATE EXTREMES. There's desert near the town of Osoyoos and so much rain along the coast that the region is often called the wettest in all of Canada.

* * *

CANADA: FROM SPACE

In January 2008, someone logged on to the online encyclopedia known as Wikipedia and edited the page on the NASA spacecraft *Messenger*, which was launched in 2004 to study the planet Mercury. Here's what you could "learn" about *Messenger* and its mission, before someone noticed the crazy entry and fixed it:

> The Canada Surface, Space Environment, Geochemistry and Ranging probe (or MESSENGER for short) is a NASA spacecraft, launched August 3, 2004, to study the characteristics and environment of Canada from orbit. Specifically, the mission is to characterize the chemical composition of Canada's surface, the geologic history, the nature of the magnetic field, the size and state of the core, the volatile inventory at the poles, and the nature of Canada's exosphere and magnetosphere over a nominal orbital mission of one Earth year.
>
> The mission is the first to visit Canada in over 30 years; the only previous probe to visit Canada was *Mariner 10*, which completed its mission in March 1975. MESSENGER has vastly improved scanning capability, with cameras that can resolve surface features down to just 60 feet (18 m) across compared to the 1 mile (1.6 km) resolution of the *Mariner 10*. MESSENGER will also be able to image the entire planet; *Mariner 10* was only able to observe one hemisphere that was lit during its flybys.
>
> In addition to being an acronym, MESSENGER was chosen as the probe's name because Canada was the messenger of the gods in Roman mythology.

Ante up: Canada is home to Poker Lake (ON), Rummy Lake (NWT), and Black Jack Lake (SK

DON'T FORGET THE BARREL, PART II

On page 157, we introduced some of the people who've attempted to go over Niagara Falls...on purpose. Here are a few more.

GEORGE STATHAKIS AND SONNY THE TURTLE
Date: July 5, 1930
Method: Steel and wood
Result: George died, Sonny lived

George Stathakis wasn't just a chef; the 46-year-old was also a great believer in metaphysical experiences, and he wanted to publish books on the subject. But where would he get the money? Like those before him, he thought he'd make a fortune by going over Horseshoe Falls. He enlisted the help of friends in Buffalo, New York, to help him build a sturdy barrel, and they responded with enthusiasm—too much, in retrospect. The barrel was massive—3 meters (9.8 feet) long, 1.5 meters (5 feet) wide, and weighing nearly 900 kilograms (1,980 pounds). Niagara River expert Red Hill Sr. warned Stathakis against using it, but he didn't listen. On July 5, 1930, he packed himself—and his 100-year-old pet turtle, Sonny—into the massive barrel and prepared for the ride of his life.

Stathakis actually survived the fall. He probably felt the initial anticipatory anxiety, the terror of being banged around and suddenly launched downward, and the pain of impact. Afterward, he probably also experienced a profound relief and sense of peace when he realized that both he and Sonny had made it. But then he waited...and waited...and waited. The problem was that the heaviness of his barrel made it fall faster and sink through the waterfall, ending up stuck behind it. Sometime in the night, 14 to 20 hours after the initial descent, the barrel escaped from its watery captivity. Rescuers found it after sunrise, but Stathakis had suffocated long before. His death, however, left enough oxygen for a slow-metabolizing turtle. Sonny emerged from the barrel to continue to live on this side of the misty unknown.

University of Ottawa grad Alex Trebek has a degree in philosophy.

WILLIAM "NATHAN BOYA" FITZGERALD

Date: July 15, 1961
Method: Rubber ball
Result: Survived

As far as Canadian authorities were concerned, the death of William "Red" Hill Jr. was the last straw. They made it illegal to go over Horseshoe Falls without a permit, and made it clear that permits were not going to be easy to come by. For 10 years, nobody tested that law, but then came 30-year-old William Fitzgerald. He'd learned the lesson of Jean Lussier's light rubber ball—in fact, he'd consulted with Lussier when designing his own rubber-ball craft.

On July 15, 1961, at about 11 a.m., Fitzgerald loaded himself into his rubber ball and headed down the river. By lunchtime, he was fished out of the water below the falls by employees of the Maid of the Mist boat tour company...and was promptly arrested. When asked why he'd done it, Fitzgerald answered, "I had to do it, I wanted to do it, and I am glad I did it." After paying a fine of $100 (plus $13 for court costs), he headed home to New York City. Fitzgerald's feat was especially unusual in that he was the first African American to make the trip, and he hadn't done it for fortune and fame. In fact, it wasn't until much later that people even discovered that William Fitzgerald was a maintenance man for IBM and an aspiring novelist with the pen name of "Nathan Boya." Fitzgerald went on to become a doctor of sociology.

KAREL SOUCEK

Date: July 2, 1984
Method: Metal and fiberglass barrel
Result: Survived

The first Canadian to make the plunge, Karel Soucek was a professional stuntman from Hamilton, Ontario. He ended up trapped in rough waters for 45 minutes afterward, so he was probably grateful that he'd equipped his barrel with two tiny windows and a snorkel for breathing. He was eventually fished out, his cuts, bruises, and chipped tooth were put right, and he was fined $500.

Six months later, he was hired to appear at the Houston Astrodome and re-create his Niagara fall. Dropped in a wooden

Canada's heaviest recorded hailstone: 290 grams, fell in Cedoux, SK (1973).

barrel from the same height into a 10-foot-pool of water should've been safer than going over Horseshoe Falls...except the barrel missed the center of the pool and slammed hard against the edge. Soucek was severely injured and died shortly after.

KIRK JONES
Date: October 3, 2003
Method: Clothes on back
Result: Survived

At least 20 people a year accidentally fall or commit suicide by jumping into Niagara Falls. Only three people are known to have survived going over the falls with just the clothes on their backs. One of them was Kirk Jones from Canton, Michigan, who somehow survived an unprotected trip over the falls in 2003. Jones climbed over a barrier and entered the river in street clothes, floating down the rapids on his back until he hit the falls, which he described later as like sliding through "a giant tunnel, going straight down surrounded by water." When Jones hit the water below, which is pretty much like hitting concrete from that height, he incurred no damage besides some sore ribs. Declining a free ride from a tour boat, he swam to the shore.

After the fact, he told stories of believing that he knew a spot where a person could go over without damage, that a drunk friend was supposed to be taking videos but couldn't figure out the camera, and that he had been planning the stunt for years. Others speculated that Jones's fall was really a suicide attempt that failed. Whatever the case, Jones made some decent money giving talks about his experience. Good thing, too, because he had to pay off his $4,500 fine for "mischief" and performing an illegal stunt.

*　　*　　*

TWO GREY CUP FACTS

• The sterling-silver Grey Cup cost $48 in 1909, the first year it was given out. Today it's worth about $75,000.

• The cup weighs more than the NFL's Vince Lombardi trophy, but less than the NHL's Stanley Cup.

A sign outside Biggar, SK, reads: "New York is big, but this is Biggar."

UH…CHIRP, CHIRP?

Canadians are famous for their ability to play sports on ice, but they're also pretty good at sports played on a pitch, specifically a cricket pitch. (Haven't you heard? Cricket is Canada's fastest-growing sport!)

• No one knows for sure when cricket began (maybe the 1300s, maybe the 1500s), but historians think it was developed by English shepherds who set up games in their sheep-grazed fields. One player threw a ball that was either made of wool or wood at the pasture's gate (which, back then, was called a "wicket gate") while another player defended the gate by batting the ball away with a shepherd's staff.

• Today, the basics haven't changed much: basically, one player throws (or "bowls") the ball at a target (still called the "wicket"). Then the defensive players on the opposite team try to bat the ball away from the wicket. There are 11 players on each side.

• The origin of the game's name is also a mystery. It might have come from *cryce*, a Saxon word for "stick," or *criquet*, which means "stick" in French.

• For a long time, cricket was a game only for children; the first recorded cricket game involved students at the Royal Grammar School in Surrey, England, playing something called *kreckett*. Of course, adults know a good thing when they see it, and by the 17th century, they were playing it too. In fact, in 1611, two men in Sussex were arrested for playing cricket when they were supposed to be in church.

• British soldiers brought cricket to Canada during the French and Indian War (1754–63), and people in northern North America really loved it, especially in Ontario: George A. Barber—"the father of Canadian cricket"—founded the country's first cricket club in Toronto in 1827.

• By the 1840s, Canadians had made sports history in the world's first international cricket game. At the grounds of the St. George's Cricket Club in New York, 5,000 spectators watched Canada beat the United States for the very first world title.

Q: What do Errol Flynn, Brendan Fraser, and Henry Fonda have in common?…

MORE FIRST LADIES

Thus continues our celebration of Canadian women who broke through the gender barrier to become first in their fields. (Part I is on page 217.)

MARGUERITE BOURGEOYS (1620–1700), SAINT

Marguerite Bourgeoys was born in France on Good Friday 1620, an auspicious beginning for someone who would become a saint. She was the sixth of 12 children, and her parents died when she was young. At 32, she met a priest who was moving to Montreal to work with poor French and aboriginal children there. He convinced her to follow him, and she opened several schools in the New World. She also led a new order of nuns—the Congregation de Notre-Dame, which is still around today. When Bourgeoys died in 1700, the event was thought to be a miracle: the 80-year-old Bourgeoys prayed that her own life be taken instead of that of a very sick sister; the nun survived and Bourgeoys died.

Bourgeoys was canonized in 1982. She became the patron saint of people who don't want their parents to die, who are poor, who are afraid of becoming impoverished, or who have been rejected by religious orders. She's one of only 10 other Canadian Catholic saints: eight were monks killed in the 1640s by Iroquois when the Jesuits took the Hurons' side in a tribal war (*more about them on page 235*); the other is another woman, Marguerite d'Youville, the first native-born Canadian saint, who founded the Sisters of Charity of Montreal and was canonized in 1990.

KIM CAMPBELL (1947–), PRIME MINISTER

True, she served only 132 days from June 25 to November 4, 1993, but Kim Campbell holds the honor of being the first woman and first baby boomer to serve in Canada's highest office. A former preteen host and reporter on CBC's *Junior Television Club*, Campbell joined Brian Mulroney's cabinet in the late 1980s and took over the office when the hugely unpopular prime minister retired. In November elections, a Liberal landslide swept her Conservatives out of power, leading her to joke, "Gee, I'm glad I didn't sell my car."

ROBERTA BONDAR (1945–), ASTRONAUT

Dr. Roberta Bondar was a neurologist before she got the nerve to become an astronaut. She began astronaut training in 1984, and in 1992 joined a NASA space shuttle flight to spend eight days in the Spacelab. Back on earth, she led a team at NASA that examined astronaut data to better understand the effects of space on the human body. She has since appeared on television, on radio, in an IMAX movie, and in the "Mission: Space" ride at Disney World.

EMILY MURPHY (1868–1933), "PERSON"

In 1916, suffragist and reformer Emily Murphy was appointed as the first female magistrate for Alberta's Women's Court. On her first day, a lawyer challenged her worthiness because women were not considered "persons" under the British North America Act of 1867. The next year, the Alberta Supreme Court ruled that women were indeed persons. Problem solved? Nope. The fight had to start all over again on the national level when Murphy was nominated to the senate. Prime Minister Sir Robert Borden disallowed her nomination, based on a British common law ruling of 1876 that said "women are eligible for pains and penalties, but not rights and privileges."

Incredibly, that interpretation of the law was upheld by the Canadian Supreme Court until October 18, 1929, when England's Privy Council Judicial Committee trumped them and ruled that in fact women are "persons" and can serve in the senate. The pains and penalties of the 13-year quest finally brought rights and privileges, but the ruling came too late for Murphy, who never was appointed to the senate. She died in October 1933.

FROM PILOTS TO PARACHUTISTS

Here are five more Canadian first females:

• **Clara Brett Martin** (1874–1923) of Toronto was not only the first female lawyer in Canada, but many believe she was also the first in the entire British Empire.

• February 29, 1860, saw the arrival of the first female Chinese immigrant to Canadian territory: **Mrs. Kwong Lee** was the first person to disembark when her ship arrived in Victoria that day.

- **Lorna de Blicquy**, an aviation pioneer born in 1931, was the first woman to make a parachute jump from an airplane in 1947. (She was 16.) She was also the first female commercial pilot in the high Arctic and the first to reach the North Pole.

- Non-vinophines have no idea what an honor it is to be voted a Master of Wine by Great Britain's Institute of Masters of Wine, but only 279 people have that "MW" after their name, and only three are from Canada. Vancouver wine steward and educator **Barbara Philip** became the first female Canadian MW in 2007.

IT'S NOT ALWAYS GREAT TO BE FIRST

Some Canadian first ladies are well known for less…ahem… admirable reasons. In 1872, Phoebe Campbell was hanged in Ontario for murdering her husband. She named a farmhand as her lover and accomplice in the crime, but he was acquitted, mainly because the only evidence of his involvement was her less-than-reliable testimony. (At one point, she said the ghost of her dead husband visited her in the night to exonerate both of them.) Technically, this makes Campbell the first woman executed in Canada. (*Yes, yes, on page 56, we told you about Gillette Bonne Bertault, who went to the gallows in 1672, but back then, Canada wasn't officially Canada yet—that was New France.*)

Incidentally, the last woman executed in Canada was Marguerite Pitre, convicted of delivering the bomb that her brother, Joseph Albert Guay, used to commit Canada's largest mass murder. (Guay bombed a passenger airplane in flight in order to murder his wife, who was onboard.) He was hanged in 1951, and Pitre followed him the next year.

* * *

AN OLD (BUT GOOD) JOKE

Q: How did they name Canada?
A: Well, they wanted three letters like the U.S.A., so they put a bunch of letters in a bag. Then the founder of Canada pulled the three out one by one and said, "C, eh…N, eh…D, eh."

Sworn into office a day before his 40th birthday in 1979, Joe Clark was Canada's youngest PM.

CLIFFSNOTES: THE SHORT VERSION

CliffsNotes—the longtime bane of teachers and the salvation of ill-prepared students in more than 70 countries—had its origins in Canada. Here's the story about how an upstart American took a great Canadian idea and ran with it.

THE BOOK EXCHANGE

Jack and Carl Colofsky, sons of a Russian cabinetmaker, had a difficult childhood. Born in Detroit, the brothers spent some time in an orphanage because their parents couldn't always care for them. Eventually, though, their father moved the family to Toronto, hoping to find better work opportunities. He didn't find any. Jack dropped out of high school in 1935, when he was just 15, to get a job to help support his family. Carl turned 22 that same year, and even though it was the height of the Great Depression, the brothers were about to finally have some good luck.

The Depression created a market for cheap entertainment; people didn't have much discretionary income, but what they did have, they liked to use as an escape from their troubles. The brothers figured that books were among the cheapest entertainment around, and they noticed that their Toronto neighborhood lacked a bookstore. So even though neither of them read much, they opened a used bookstore called the Book Exchange. It was a perfect start-up business because buying used books didn't take much money. They were also situated near the University of Toronto, and the brothers sold many used books to students. The Book Exchange became a quick success, allowing Jack and Carl to start selling a few new books as well.

CONSUMER HODGEPODGE

In 1938, the brothers shortened their last name to Cole and renamed the store after themselves at the same time. They opened a second store (also called Cole's) across town just a year later. From there, they opened in other neighborhoods, and then began spreading out their stores across Canada.

Technically, Ontario's Niagara Peninsula is an isthmus.

Neither brother had any deep love for books or the smell of musty little bookstores. Instead, they treated books as a consumer commodity and sold them in bright shops with discounts and advertising gimmicks (for example, they sometimes sold books by the pound). To hedge their bets in the 1950s and 1960s, they also offered sports equipment and toys.

Perhaps because of this irreverence for literature, it made sense that Jack Cole would come up with a way for indifferent students (like he had been) to slide more easily through school. In 1948, he commissioned a series of study guides on a variety of subjects, including chemistry and math. But the first one published was a booklet on the French novella *Colomba* by Prosper Mérimée. When that sold quickly, Shakespeare's *Merchant of Venice* got the treatment next. Pretty soon, Jack Cole realized that the short summaries for students were going to make him a lot of money.

THE AMERICAN ARRIVES

In the mid-1950s, an American book salesman named Cliff Hillegass called on the Coles brothers' headquarters for a sales visit. As he leafed through the study guides, he was intrigued. Figuring that students from his country were probably just as inclined to slack off as Canadians, he negotiated with Jack Cole and leased the American rights to the line.

In August 1958, Hillegass printed up his first 16 study guides, reprints of Cole's Notes synopses of Shakespearean plays. To differentiate the Canadian and American brands, Hillegass called his booklets Cliff's Notes.

In 1965, Jack Cole's heirs revoked Hillegass's rights to reproduce Cole's Notes in the United States. He scrambled to come up with replacement content and hire writers to copy the look and feel of Cole's Notes. It worked. In the years since, Cliff's Notes (which eventually dropped the apostrophe and then the space so that it's now CliffsNotes) became the best-selling study guide series in the world. Cole's Notes are still around too, and it's all thanks to a slacker student from Canada who made it possible for all of us to wind our way through high school carrying summarized versions of literature instead of those big, heavy *books*.

Lucrative loonie: The 1911 Canadian silver dollar is valued at more than $1 million.

THEY ALWAYS GET THEIR MAN

*If the Americans hadn't disrespected Canadian
borders, we might not have the Mounties.*

LAWLESSNESS IN THE WEST

In 1869, with Canada about to take control of its interior from the Hudson's Bay Company, Prime Minister John A. Macdonald outlined his plan for a paramilitary police force to patrol the region. The idea didn't really get going, though, until 1873, after the Cypress Hills Massacre. That year, American wolf trappers in Montana lost a lot of horses to thieves who appeared to be headed for the Canadian border. The trappers followed and lost the trail, but stumbled on a camp of 300 Nakota natives. In a tense standoff full of accusations and alcohol on both sides, the wolf trappers opened fire on the Nakota camp, killing at least 20 people.

The massacre outraged Canadians for a number of reasons, including the fact that Americans were invading their territory with impunity. And it wasn't the first time either. Just a few weeks earlier, whiskey traders had started illegally selling alcohol at Fort Hamilton (nicknamed "Fort Whoop-Up" because of the whiskey trade) near what is now Lethbridge, Alberta, and rumors swirled that the traders had flown the American flag over the fort. They didn't really, but the incident was enough to speed up the formation of Macdonald's police force, which he named the North-West Mounted Police (NWMP), or Mounties. They got guns, horses, and red uniforms, in part to differentiate them from the blue of the American cavalry…just in case the recurring border incursions turned into a full-scale war.

ON THE MARCH…WITH A TRANSFER IN CHICAGO

The first squad of 309 Mounties was assembled in 1874. Scoring an early point for multiculturalism, if not for sensitive language, Macdonald had specified that the new force should be a "mixed one of pure white, and British and French half-breeds." Pay was 75¢ a day, and recruits had to be between 18 and 40 years old,

physically active and able, and literate in either English or French.

On June 6, the Mounties got their first orders to move out. They were headed for the wilds of Manitoba and were to be accompanied by Henri Julien, an illustrator/reporter from the *Canadian Illustrated News.* (Julien had been given an all-expenses-paid invitation to make sure the Mounties' heroic march west received adequate public attention.) The police, dressed in their scarlet best, mounted their horses and prepared for a journey…to the downtown train station. There, they loaded their horses onto train cars—an effort that Julien called "long, tedious, and amusing" in its disorder. At 3:30 p.m., the train whistle blew, and "amid the cheers of a vast crowd, we glided out of Toronto."

They headed across Ontario and straight into the United States. There was no cross-Canada train yet, so this police force, created in no small part to repel American incursions, headed for Chicago, where they transferred to a train that would drop them off in Fargo, North Dakota. After that, they boarded another train that took them to Fort Dufferin, Manitoba, the last outpost of civilization. From there, they marched 800 miles through plains, woods, rivers, and swamps on their way to Fort Whoop-Up in Alberta. Their mission: to clean out the whiskey sellers and horse thieves, keep peace between the Europeans and the people of the First Nations, combat general lawlessness, and enforce a firm border with the United States…by force if necessary.

TAMPING DOWN WHOOP-UP

It took three months for the Mounties to arrive at the fort. By then, the whiskey sellers, having heard the Mounties were coming, had cleared out. There was also no evidence of hostile natives or a gathering storm along the American border. It was an anticlimactic start for the NWMP, but for many, the best sort of anticlimax. Peace was established without a shot, and for their first few years, the Mounties had to deal with few crimes worse than horse theft. Since there was no judicial system set up, the commander at Fort Whoop-Up got himself sworn in as a justice of the peace so that he could judge civil and criminal cases there.

In 1876, the Mounties got their first real taste of combat when they defused a tense situation after 5,000 Sioux, led by Sitting Bull and pursued by the U.S. Army, fled over the Canadian bor-

der. The Americans were seeking revenge for the bloody defeat at the Battle of the Little Big Horn. Mountie commander James Morrow Walsh was assigned to deal with the situation. He organized an ad hoc NWMP headquarters at Wood Mountain, where the Sioux had set up camp, initiated a close friendship with Sitting Bull, and managed to keep the peace.

GOLDEN AGE

Keeping peace in Canada's Wild West continued to be the Mounties' primary mission. In 1895, they headed over the Rockies for the first time to regulate the influx of Americans crossing the Alaskan border during the Klondike gold rush. They collected customs duties, confiscated guns, and required that each miner be equipped with at least a ton of food and survivor gear to prevent mass numbers of needy people overunning Canada. During this time, the Mounties managed to maintain a reasonable amount of order in a chaotic situation, expelling troublemakers while sensibly not making an issue of popular illegalities like prostitution and gambling. Prospectors, not necessarily a law-and-order bunch, were impressed by the Mounties' conduct, and their reputation spread across the world.

Around this same time, though, Canada's government started talking about dissolving the NWMP. Prime Minister Sir Wilfred Laurier thought the Mounties' golden age had passed; they'd done a good job of keeping order on the frontier, but Canada was moving into the 20th century and needed smaller, regional police forces. Despite discussions in Parliament and Laurier's push, the Mounties were popular, especially in the west, and the measure never caught on. Instead, the Mounties became the country's official police force in 1920 and got a name change to the Royal Canadian Mounted Police. They also were becoming the stuff of pop-culture legend.

THEY ALWAYS GET THEIR MAN

Today, the Mounties are one of Canada's best-known symbols, but it wasn't just their crime-fighting ways that made it so. The chief culprit behind the Mounties image in pop culture was a Winnipeg writer named Charles William Gordon, who wrote uplifting frontier adventures under the pen name Ralph Connor. In 1912,

Canada's first Olympic gold medal: men's lacrosse, in 1904.

he wrote a novel called *Corporal Cameron of the North West Mounted Police: A Tale of the MacLeod Trail.* It sold like hotcakes...in Canada and abroad. The book starred an uncorruptible Mountie hero, some satisfying fisticuffs, and the rescue of a pretty girl. It also launched a whole line of Mountie adventures.

Where books went, Hollywood followed. By the 1950s, America's entertainment capital had made a total of 575 films set in Canada, and many of those—including the musical *Rose-Marie,* involved the Mounties. Hollywood's love did not go unrequited; from the early days, the Mounties cheerfully supplied technical advice to filmmakers, and even officers in active service. There were Mounties on the radio—including the popular 1930s show *Challenge of the Yukon*—and when television arrived, heroes like Sgt. Preston made a seamless transition to the new medium (though its snowy outdoor shots were filmed in Colorado and California, not Canada).

These days, the Mounties still appear in entertainment, but they're also a legitimate police force; they act as Canada's federal police as well as the provincial police for everyone except Ontario, Quebec, and Newfoundland and Labrador. (Those have their own provincial forces.) Not bad for a ragtag frontier police department whose first job was cleaning up a little fort called Whoop-Up.

MOUNTIE FACTS

• In popular culture, the Mounties' motto is "They always get their man," but that's actually a Hollywood creation. That phrase comes from an 1877 newspaper story in the *Fort Benton* (Montana) *Record* in which the reporter wrote, "They fetch their man every time." Hollywood producers read the story, jumped on the phrasing, and created the Mounties' "motto."

• The Mounties' distinctive outfit—wide-brimmed hat, red jacket, black riding pants, etc.—is called the Red Serge because the red jackets were originally made from a type of English twill called "serge." The Red Serge is only for special ceremonies and events, like the Musical Ride.

• Women became Mounties for the first time in 1974.

SAUCERS IN THE SKY, PART II

On page 52, we introduced Wilbur Smith and his quest to find evidence that flying saucers had visited Canada. Unfortunately, he died in 1962...just a few years before Canadians started reporting UFO sightings. Here are some of the best stories.

GASSED IN THE AFTERNOON

Where: Falcon Lake, Whiteshell Provincial Park, Manitoba

When: May 20, 1967

What happened: According to Stephen Michalak, he went to the Falcon Lake area in the morning and prospected for silver in a small stream. Looking up at flock of geese at noon, he saw two disk-shaped objects rotating and glowing in the sky. One landed on a nearby rock. Michalak called out to whoever might be inside—in response, a large exhaust pipe blasted him with a hot gas, burning a gridlike pattern through his shirt and onto his chest, leaving Michalak in pain and feeling sick. He waved down a Mountie but wouldn't let the officer get close (for fear of contaminating him with radiation or disease) and declined a ride.

The aftermath: The officer's written report said that Michalak appeared to be drunk, refused to let the Mountie look closely at his shirt and hat, and seemed to have rubbed ash on his chest. No concrete evidence was ever found to support Michalak's claims of a close encounter, save some radiation detected in the rock where he said the craft landed.

Status: Officially, the investigation into the Falcon Lake incident is "unsolved."

E.T., FOAM HOME

Where: Shag Harbour, Nova Scotia

When: October 4, 1967

What happened: In late September and early October of 1967, several residents of southwestern Nova Scotia called authorities,

reporting an object in the sky that had rows of lights on it. Some people described it as looking like a star; others said it looked like a satellite. On the evening of October 4, two groups of Shag Harbour teenagers said they watched the object careen into the harbor. An RCMP constable arrived 20 minutes later and reported seeing an object on the water about 800 meters (½ mile) from shore. It seemed to be sinking. RCMP divers were dispatched to the scene. Fishing boats also joined the search. But all that anyone found was a mysterious yellow foam near the spot where the craft went down.

The aftermath: The coast guard and navy continued to investigate for several days before giving up.

Status: "Unsolved," but some UFO aficionados speculate that the government destroyed reports and squelched the release of information.

SORRY, CHARLIE
Where: Carman, Manitoba
When: May 1975
What happened: In 1975, Carman, Manitoba, became a hotbed of UFO sightings, specifically a red light that looked like a star darting and weaving through the sky before it zoomed away. People who saw it (including an RCMP officer) had been amused by its hide-and-seek movements. Someone dubbed it "Charlie Redstar," and the name stuck. By May, Elaine and Bob Diemert had become accustomed to having near-daily encounters with the playful red star on their farm. One day, they got close enough to see its shape: flat and disklike, with windowed domes on the top and bottom.

The aftermath: Charlie Redstar made appearances over the next year and a half and developed quite a cult following, with people coming from all over to try to catch a glimpse.

Status: Charlie left nothing that could be scientifically substantiated. No official government investigation was launched.

GOING AGAINST THE GRAIN
Where: Many agricultural areas of Canada
When: 1980s to the present
What happened: According to some people, during the 1980s,

aliens began bedeviling earthling farmers by flattening their crops into designs. Exhibiting an assortment of motifs and ability levels, the space travelers largely confined their work to England, for some reason. Finally, though, they got around to practicing their craft in Canada. They've tried wheat, hay grass, corn, sorghum, barley…and have even given peas a chance.

The aftermath: In recent years, a few crop circles have been discovered to be hoaxes meticulously orchestrated by tricksters, but not all of them. On the surface at least, some of the stories behind the crop designs defy explanation. Collections of aerial photos can be found on many Web sites.

QUICK ROUND DOME JUMPS OVER A LITTLE FOX

Where: Little Fox Lake, Yukon

When: March 30, 2000

What happened: Leah Isaac took a morning drive around Little Fox Lake near Whitehorse. As she came around a bend, a large, disk-shaped craft hovered in the air ahead of her—lights shone from two windows in a dome at the top of the craft. The vehicle darted, turned, and zoomed away. Isaac immediately reported the incident to local authorities.

The aftermath: Unfortunately for Isaac, local authorities no longer investigate UFO sightings.

* * *

COUNTERFEIT CANADIAN BANDS

Of Montreal: Apparently being from Athens, Georgia, wasn't cool enough for these guys. (What good music—aside from REM, the B-52s, the Indigo Girls, etc.—ever came from Athens?) Instead, the group has tried to steal some of that French-Canadian cool by choosing a name that implies it came from Old Acadia.

Cross Canadian Ragweed: This band formed in Yukon…*Oklahoma*, which happens to be in *Canadian* County. Furthermore, its singer/ guitarist is named Cody Canada. But despite all these Canada connections, the band's name is actually a fractured amalgam of the three founding members' names: Grady Cross, Cody Canada, and Randy Ragsdale, with a little "weed" thrown in for good luck.

BAD THINGS, GOOD PEOPLE

*If 6,600 strangers got stranded on airplanes at the local airport,
would you just leave them there or would you step in to help?*

NO FUELING THIS TIME
The airport at Gander, Newfoundland, had long been
used as a stop for refueling on international flights. But
on September 11, 2001, it became something else. After suicide
hijackers hit targets in New York and Washington, D.C., and
crashed a plane into a Pennsylvania field, nobody knew if there
were more. An order was sent out to all planes headed to or from
the United States: land now at the nearest airport. Many of those
flights ended up in Canada.

Back in 1936, Gander had been recognized as an excellent spot
for an airport. It was at the northeast tip of North America and
along a reasonably straight line between New York and London.
By 1940, the town's Newfoundland Airport had become one of
the world's largest, sporting four runways to handle a succession
of refueling stops by transatlantic airplanes. When Canada entered
World War II, Gander was identified as the perfect spot for a mili-
tary air base. The Royal Canadian Air Force commandeered it and
quickly turned it into a home to more than 10,000 military per-
sonnel from Canada, the United Kingdom, and the United States.
After the war, the airfield went back to civilian hands with
beefed-up facilities and a new name: the Gander International
Airport (abbreviation YQX).

DAZED AND CONFUSED

On September 11, 2001, YQX's location made it the designated
landing spot for 39 planes. Getting each of them down and onto
the tarmac in quick succession was a challenge, but that was noth-
ing compared to the logistical problem that followed: the 39
planes were filled with 6,600 passengers and crew members,
descending on a town of only about 10,000 people.

Under normal circumstances, that would be hard enough. But

on this day, the passengers were in a state of shock and high emotion. At first, most didn't even know about the terrorist attacks. The passengers—and in some cases, the crew as well—had been kept in the dark during their flights so as to not trigger panic in the sky. They had no idea why they'd landed until they were safely on the ground.

LOCAL CUSTOMS

Meanwhile, the residents of Gander—immersed in their own grief and shock about the unfolding events—were being brought back to issues of the here and now. For example, Murray Osmond was the only Citizenship and Immigration Canada (CIC) official in Gander. He got a call on the morning of September 11: be prepared to process thousands of people, and take special care because nobody knows whether there are still undiscovered terrorists on incoming flights. Osmond had no idea how he would be able to process all the passengers in a timely way, even under the best of circumstances, and heightened security would just make the process more difficult. So he made some calls and located three CIC officers in St. John's who could help out, but because Canadian airspace had also been closed, they'd have to drive...which would take about four hours.

The first plane landed at 10:10 a.m. In the time it took the additional CIC officials to arrive, Osmond had been able to process all the passengers from one plane...but there were 38 more to go. Passengers were going to be waiting a long time; some didn't get to leave their planes until the afternoon of September 12, more than 27 hours later.

GETTING GANDER'S GEESE IN A ROW

There was another big problem: Gander had only 550 hotel rooms, and some of them were already filled with tourists. The airplane crews (who needed to be well rested in case they had to fly at a moment's notice) and the first people off the planes were lucky enough to get a crack at the empty ones. But then what?

Here's where Gander really stepped up. Local people took the passengers into their homes, inviting individuals or entire families to invade their living space; people in outlying communities also reached out to help. Greg King, an air-traffic controller at the

airport, barely had time to call his wife to tell her he was bringing home strangers. But even that wasn't enough. So town manager Jake Turner started calling the local Red Cross and Salvation Army to gather beds and food for the passengers who couldn't be absorbed into households. "We're used to helping people," Gander's mayor Claude Elliott noted later. "I guess our biggest problem was trying to explain to people where they were."

Many of the stranded passengers ended up in school gymnasiums and church recreation rooms that had been jammed with as many cots, air mattresses, and sleeping bags as would fit. Gander's school bus drivers had been on strike for several weeks, but they put down their picket signs and got back behind the wheel in order to shuttle passengers to their new homes. Townspeople raided their cupboards and refrigerators to help the Salvation Army provide enough food; residents of one nearby village made 200 sandwiches and delivered them to Gander. The local telephone company strung temporary lines so that people could have access to phones, Internet, e-mail, and cable TV. As the hours stretched into days, Gander and its neighboring towns offered amusements as well—boat rides, tours, day trips, and movies—to keep people busy and distracted.

The no-fly ban was finally lifted on September 15, and people who had been strangers a few days earlier said good-bye and exchanged small gifts, addresses, and e-mail information, promising to keep in touch. A Catholic church handed each of its departing visitors a slip of paper printed with a reassuring prayer and a small Canadian flag. The Royal Canadian Legion of Gander threw a farewell party for the 141 Aer Lingus passengers it had housed in its hall. And, no doubt, everybody in town and on airplanes flying home breathed a sigh of relief.

FOLLOWED BY FULSOME PRAISE

Since then, the kindness and generosity of the residents of Gander have not been forgotten. On the first anniversary of 9/11, some of the passengers returned to express their thanks. "This town put its life on hold for a whole week to care of us," said one. "That's what's amazing. I can't really imagine that happening anywhere else."

The people of Gander, though, don't consider what they did especially extraordinary. The town's mayor said in 2006, "Most

World's first indoor ice arena: Victoria Skating Rink in Montreal (opened in 1862).

people say: 'I done it. I did it out of the goodness of my heart. I did it to volunteer, to make those people comfortable. I've done my job, they're gone now—that's all. I'm here if you need me again.'" Still, in the Septembers since 2001, the tributes and accolades have poured in. For example…

• People wrote books about the incident, including *The Day the World Came to Town: 9/11 in Gander, Newfoundland.*

• A "Gratitude for Gander" picnic in 2003 fed 4,000 citizens and was organized by caterers Dan and Teresa Seeley of upstate New York…who weren't even on any of the flights.

• A 2008 BBC radio drama detailed Gander's generosity.

• American passenger Shirley Brooks-Jones began a scholarship fund for Gander-area students; by 2004, it totaled $1 million.

• The small, mostly unsung seaside town of Lewisporte, which had housed more than 700 of the passengers, received a single donation that provided enough money to install a new lighting system for its Anglican church.

• Appleton, another small village, built a "peace park" from donations sent by other grateful passengers.

• In late 2009, American newsman Tom Brokaw showed up to tape a tribute, to be shown during the 2010 Winter Olympics.

* * *

GUN SHY

Mitch Helps was getting a prescription filled in an Ottawa pharmacy in 2009 when a man burst through the door, waving a gun. "This is a robbery!" he shouted. "Give me your narcotics." As the robber stuck the gun in Helps's face, the customer noticed something strange about the deadly weapon—it wasn't deadly at all. Helps relaxed, started laughing, and said to the man, "Dude, you're a friggin' idiot. That's a BB gun. What are you *doing?*" Realizing there was no possible way to convince the store to hand over drugs or money, the man ran out the door, was arrested less than two blocks away, and charged with robbery…and a very minor weapons offense.

If Quebec seceded, Canada would drop from 2nd to 5th on the list of world's largest countries.

WORLD'S LARGEST...

*Most Canadians aren't prone to untoward levels of bragging, which makes it
all the more notable when they claim a superlative. Here's one category—
cities and towns that say they have "the world's largest" something or other.*

Gold pan: Burwash Langing, YK

Snowman: Beardmore, ON

Wagon wheel: Fort Assiniboine, AB

Cross-country skis: 100 Mile House, BC

Concrete potato: Maugerville, NB

Fly rod: Houston, BC

Chuck wagon: Dewberry, AB

Tree crusher: Mackenzie, BC

Tractor weather vane: Westlock, AB

Tripod orchard ladder: Summerland, BC

Honeybee: Tisdale, SK

Dragonfly: Wabamun, AB

Sundial: Lloydminster, AB

Blueberry: Oxford, NS

Cookie jar: Deloraine, MB

Hockey stick and puck: Duncan, BC

Curling rock: Arborg, MB

Lamp: Donalda, AB

Putter: Bow Island, AB

Totem pole: Alert Bay, BC

Totem pole from a single tree: Victoria, BC

Piggy bank: Coleman, AB

Illuminated fiddle: Sydney, NS

Badminton racquet: St. Albert, AB

Wooden beaver: Beaverlodge, AB

Softball: Chauvin, AB

Tomahawk: Cut Knife, SK

Mallard duck: Andrew, AB

Western boot: Edmonton, AB

Inukshuk: Schomberg, ON

Painting on an easel: Altona, MB

Fire hydrant: Elm Creek, MB

Bathtub: Nanaimo, BC

Muhammad Ali called Toronto boxer George Chuvalo "the toughest man I ever fought."

CLEVER CANADIANS, PART II

On page 255, we introduced you to some amazing Canadian inventors. Here are a few more.

G-WHIZ

When a body is accelerated at high speeds, the g-force (force of gravity) pressure pushes its blood to the lower extremities, leaving the heart without adequate blood to pump to the brain. Because of this, fighter pilots often fell victim to confusion, blackouts, and sometimes death. Suits to counteract that force had been around since the early 1900s, but none ever worked well enough. Enter Ontario scientist Wilbur Franks and his 1940 invention, the Franks Flying Suit. Water- or air-filled pads in the rubber suit stabilized the bottom half of the body, keeping g-force pressure in check and stopping blood from pooling there…preventing the confusion and blackouts. Today, all anti-gravity suits used by astronauts and fighter pilots are based on the basic design of the Franks Flying Suit.

LEARNING A LOT FROM A DUMMY

The year 1989 saw a breakthrough in CPR (cardio pulmonary resuscitation) training when Dianne Croteau, a graduate of Ottawa's Carleton University, and her partner Richard Brault invented the Actar 911 mannequin. The new design was composed only of the human head and chest, instead of the full-body models used before. This meant the mannequin was less expensive to make and easier to transport. Three years later, Croteau and Brault introduced the Actar 911 Infant, a life-sized, full-body model of a human baby, to help teach CPR for young children. Today, these mannequins are used to train emergency responders around the world.

TAKE OUT THE PAPERS AND THE TRASH…

Every time you put out your garbage, spare a thought for Winnipeg inventor Harry Wasylyk and his Ontario buddy Larry

In March 30, 1848, Niagara Falls ran dry…the only time it did.

Hanson. They created the first lightweight disposable plastic trash bags in 1950 and sold the rights to the Union Carbide Company, where Hanson was employed. In the 1960s, Union Carbide started selling Glad garbage bags.

NO MORE GETTING CAULKY

Most "do-it-yourself" enthusiasts are familiar with the caulking gun, which helps seal glass into windows or cracks in baseboards. This ingenious invention was the brainchild of a handyman named Theodore Witte from Chilliwack, British Columbia. In 1894, Witte was inspired by the plunging action of a cake-decorating kitchen utensil, and wondered if it would work to force caulk into cracks. Before that, most people had to use a blade to smear the caulk into place. Of course, caulk is much thicker than frosting, so Witte developed a ratchet-powered "gun" that used a trigger to provide extra leverage and control.

CAN YOU HEAR ME NOW?

A boat trip in 1927 on Lake Erie fueled nine-year-old Al Gross's fascination with two-way communication after the radio operator let him listen to transmissions on the wireless. Gross spent the next three years experimenting with salvaged radio equipment in his parents' Toronto basement. By the time Gross was in college, he was working on handheld, two-way radios, and in 1938, he patented the first "walkie-talkie," used to aid Allied forces during World War II. Gross then went on to pioneer the CB (citizens band) radio, the telephone pager, and early cordless phones.

SETTING THE PACE

In 1949, National Research Council engineer John Alexander Hopps was in Ottawa trying to find out whether it was possible to use microwaves to pasteurize beer. But he was called away from that important work to travel to Toronto to assist doctors W. G. Bigelow and J. C. Callaghan in their research at the Banting Institute. The two doctors had been experimenting with using hypothermia to slow the heart during heart surgery. Only one problem: there was a fine line between slowing a heart and stopping it. But with Hopps's help, they discovered that they could use jolts of electricity to restart the heart.

An average 15-meter evergreen tree weighs about 4,500 kilograms when glazed by an ice storm.

This accidental discovery turned out to be more significant than their hypothermia work. Hopps went on to produce a pacemaker/defibrillator for human heart patients in 1950. That first model weighed three pounds, was the size of a toaster, and had to be plugged into the wall. But it led to more innovation, and in 1958, a Swedish team created the first fully implantable pacemaker. Hopps himself had a pacemaker implanted in 1984—and he lived for another 15 years.

WHAT DIDN'T THIS GUY INVENT?

After watching injured World War II veterans struggle with manual wheelchairs, Hamilton, Ontario, native George Klein decided to create the first electric wheelchair in 1952. The device allowed users the freedom to move backward and forward using a simple joystick. Klein also made the first microsurgical staple gun, helped to develop the first nuclear reactor outside the United States, and created the gearing system on the Canadarm, the remote-controlled mechanical arm used to capture and repair satellites and move cargo on the U.S. space shuttle. In 1995, Klein was inducted into the Canadian Science and Engineering Hall of Fame.

ASSAULTING AN OLD BATTERY

Lewis Urry from Pontypool, Ontario, was working as an engineer at Union Carbide's National Carbon Company when he was asked to figure out how to make their Eveready common battery last longer. Deciding it would cost too much to significantly improve the old standard, Urry scrapped that model and came up with a whole new battery. In 1959, after much experimentation with a myriad of substances, he created the first alkaline battery—the same kind we use today. In 1980, Eveready became Energizer. Urry's alkaline keeps going and going and going…

*　　*　　*

ABOAT THAT ACCENT…

What's the reason for the stereotypical "Canadian" accent—which sometimes sounds to Americans like it turns "about" into "aboat"? Linguists think it's a result of French speakers and their descendants moving over to English.

The earliest wheat grown in Canada (around 1605) was not on the prairies, but in Nova Scotia

HANS ISLAND

For years, Canada and Denmark have waged a low-key power struggle over a tiny rock island that from the air looks like a flattened cow patty.

LOOK MA, NO HANS!

It's unfit for human habitation and is pretty bare of vegetation and land-dwelling animals. It doesn't have a Starbucks, Internet access, or a cell phone tower. It's sandwiched in the thin, ice-filled passage between Nunavut's Ellesmere Island and the semiautonomous Danish territory of Greenland, and there has been little reason to take note of Hans Island except as a potential navigational hazard. In fact, for most of its history almost nobody has. What is it about this icy rock?

It's possible that indigenous people encountered the island while hunting walrus on the ice. We know it got its present-day name between 1871 and 1873 during American explorer Charles Francis Hall's ill-fated third North Pole expedition (*for more on that, turn to page 152*). Someone decided to name the lump of rock after an Inuit guide the explorers called Hans Hendrik… even though his name was really Suersaq.

Yet, during the 2000s, Hans Island became the center of a bizarre sovereignty dispute between Canada and Denmark. As global warming melts long-frozen ice, opening sea routes that have been impassable for centuries, the ownership of this barely existent island of 1.3 square kilometers (0.5 square mile), could provide benefits in terms of navigation, fishing rights, and natural resources like oil.

Denmark claims that maps point to Hans Island being part of Greenland since 1933. Canada, on the other hand, showed Hans Island as Canadian territory on a map for the first time only in 1967. There have never been any known permanent inhabitants.

KEEP YOUR ILLEGAL DRILLING TO YOURSELF

Canadian oil company Dome Petroleum has been scouting oil on and around Hans Island since the 1980s…without the knowledge of Denmark or the acknowledgment of the Canadian government.

Canada was the third nation (after the U.S. and USSR) to launch a satellite into space.

In fact, it was a chance encounter that uncovered this, gave it international attention, and sparked the struggle over Hans Island. In 1984, Nunavut historian Kenn Harper wrote an article about Hans Island for a tiny newspaper in the palindrome-named town of Qaanaaq, Greenland (population 620). In the article, Harper mentioned meeting a man on the ice near Resolute, Nunavut, who was wearing a hat boldly reading "HANS ISLAND." After striking up a conversation, Harper learned that the man had spent the summer on the island doing research for Dome Petroleum. Harper mentioned this in his story.

The article, published in a tiny, isolated town, made its way to the Danish newspapers, which played it up as an affront to Danish sovereignty. They were half-kidding...but they were also half-serious.

OF COURSE, YOU REALIZE...

The Danish government, though, wasn't messing around. The country's minister for Greenland, Tom Høyem, chartered a helicopter and flew to Hans Island in order to plant a Danish flag, a bottle of cognac, and a message saying, "*Velkommen til den danske ø*" ("Welcome to the Danish island"). That was the beginning of a series of visits by Canadian and Danish officials and fishing crews, both bearing flags and drinking whatever alcohol had been left by the previous group.

Meanwhile, in cyberspace, satirical Web sites waged a battle for the island. One promoted the Hans Island Liberation Front, which claimed that the island's nonexistent inhabitants wanted to cast off the yoke of both Canadian and Danish imperialism. Another "represented" Radio Free Hans Island, a fictional radio station supposedly broadcasting from the frozen wastes. A Swedish radio station even entered the fray, satirically claiming Swedish ownership of the island.

...THIS MEANS WAR!

The governments of Canada and Denmark, though, didn't think the issue was a joke, and tensions boiled again in 2005. In an escalation of the conflict, the Canadian defense minister landed on Hans Island in a helicopter to reassert Canadian claims. That led to outrage in Greenland, where people called the action a foreign

invasion and occupation. This was followed by the visit of a Danish warship to the island. In fact, over the years, both nations have made the effort and taken the expense of sending warships to the area—fortunately, at different times—with no shots fired.

The dispute has quieted down recently. Perhaps both parties are in the process of coming to a mature resolution and a recognition of the fact that the island is probably more trouble than it's worth. As Canada's chief of defense staff, General Walter Natynczyk, noted, "The Arctic is a very harsh environment. If someone were to invade the Canadian Arctic, my first task would be to rescue them."

SPLITTING THE BABY IN HALF

In July 2007, based on satellite imagery, Canadian authorities finally admitted that Hans Island is not completely inside Canadian territory, but that the international border runs roughly through the middle of the island. Although that offers a solution to the Hans Island problem, it also ruins Canada's status as being the largest country with a land border on only one other country. Instead, Canada now can boast of having a 5,061-kilometer-long (3,145-mile) land border with the United States and a 1.3-kilometer-long (0.8-mile) border with Denmark.

* * *

WEIRD CANADA

• In February 2010, Alexander Rodrigue, 23, was arrested in a Regina, Saskatchewan, bakery for sniffing some of the cakes. He was fined $50 for the sniffs and was ordered to make restitution for the cakes. (According to the staff, he had previously been arrested for licking cakes in the store.)

• In December 2009, Sechelt, British Columbia, approved a bylaw making it illegal for licensed dogs to chase squirrels, seagulls, and other wild animals. The bylaw said that dogs could, however, chase squirrels, seagulls, and other wild animals if they were provoked. Asked what might be a provocation, Councillor Ann Kershaw said, "It depends on your interpretation of provocation. A bird fluttering away in front of a dog—that's provocation."

CANADIAN GOURMET

Canadian cuisine hasn't always been as tame as poutine and pancakes. There was a time when "fast food" was something you shot in the woods. If you want classic Canuck cooking at your next dinner party, consider one of these old recipes from the days of fur traders and the frontier.

FLIPPER PIE

Soak a pair of seal flippers in a mixture of water and baking soda for half an hour, then remove the fat. Sauté until browned. Add flippers to a roasting pan along with a mix of onions and root vegetables. Bake for a couple of hours, then drizzle in a simple gravy of flour and water. Cover with pastry crust and bake until brown and bubbly.

JELLIED MOOSE NOSE

Take the upper part of a moose jaw and boil in a large kettle. Let cool, then remove hairs. Place back in kettle with vinegar, onions, and garlic. Bring to a boil, then simmer until tender. Remove and cool overnight. Slice dark and white meat strips off the bone and place in a pan. Boil broth from the day before and pour over meat strips. As it cools, the broth will congeal. Serve jellies cold. (Serve with a good Canadian lager to make the meal complete.)

BOUDIN DU PAYS (BLOOD PUDDING)

Collect the blood from a freshly slaughtered pig. Stir constantly while adding salt. Set the blood aside. Slice up the muscle and organ meat and place in a pot with water, salt, and onions. Simmer for 2–3 hours. Grind the cooked meats in meat grinder and put them back into a pot with spices and onions. Bring to a boil. Drizzle the blood and some flour into the boiling pot. Simmer for another hour to thicken before serving.

SMOTHERED MUSKRAT

To prepare muskrat, skin and defat the carcass, then remove all scent glands, including light-colored tissue inside each leg. Soak in water and salt for 4–8 hours. Chop into pieces and coat the bits

like fried chicken, shaken in a bag of seasoned flour. Sauté in lard until brown. Add in onions, sour cream, or yogurt and simmer for an hour. Add salt and pepper to taste.

FRIED BEAVER TAIL

Skin and wash two beaver tails. Soak in water, vinegar, and salt for 4–8 hours, then rinse. Put tails in pot of water with a bit of baking soda and bring to a boil. Lower heat and simmer for 12 minutes. Cover tails in flour and sauté in lard. Mix in spices of choice, cook for 10 more minutes, and serve.

SAVORY SEAL HEARTS

Soak a big seal heart in water and salt for 4–8 hours. Trim off fat and veins and slice thickly. Place in casserole dish, layering with stuffing (mixture of rice, bread crumbs, and seasoning) and bacon. Drizzle with melted butter and bake for 2–3 hours.

BARBECUED BEAR

Trim fat and cube bear meat. On high heat, sear outside of cubes to seal in juices, then place in casserole dish and set aside. Fry chopped onion in a pan and then add vinegar, Worcestershire, and chili sauce. Bring to a boil and pour over bear meat. Drizzle with ketchup and lemon juice and bake covered for 2 hours.

ROASTED POLAR BEAR

Soak a defatted five-pound polar bear steak in water, vinegar, and salt for 1–2 hours. Roast steak with bacon and onions for a few hours. Add butter and serve hot.

SEAL BRAIN FRITTERS

Thoroughly soak and wash seal brain in salt water to remove the thin film of skin. Boil in water for 15 minutes, adding salt and vinegar as you bring it to a boil. Mash brains and mix with flour, eggs, butter, and milk to make a batter. Salt and pepper to taste. Deep-fry tablespoon-sized balls of batter until golden brown. (Goes great with flipper pie.)

There are about 2 million lakes in Canada.

HEEERE'S JOHNNY!

The United States has Uncle Sam as its national symbol.
Britain has John Bull. And Canada's got Johnny Canuck.

DRAWING ON SYMBOLS

In an anonymous 1870 cartoon, Canada was depicted as a toddler standing unsteadily between Uncle Sam and Mother Britannia. Uncle Sam says, "Let go of him, Granny; if he falls, I'll catch him!" At first glance, it sounds like a benevolent promise…until you see the eager, hungry look on Uncle Sam's face, reflecting Canadian anxiety that the United States—in an expansionist mood and fielding a large army—might just decide to make Canada its newest state.

The Dominion of Canada was only three years old then, and still taking unsteady steps, its east and west eyeing each other with mutual suspicion. The new nation needed to grow up quickly and temper its newfound independence into a sense of national identity. Enter pop culture's contribution to the effort: the political cartoonists' new character, Johnny Canuck.

THE MANY SIDES OF JOHNNY

Unlike Uncle Sam, who sprang already finished from the pen of cartoonist Thomas Nast, nobody quite knows who originated Johnny Canuck sometime in the late 1860s. As a result, there was no definitive idea of what he should look like. Early on, his name was even written as John K. Nuck.

Johnny soon began appearing regularly in Canadian political cartoons. Depending on the desired political message, he might be depicted as a farmer, rancher, lumberjack, politician, or soldier. One theme, however, remained consistent: Johnny stood for Canadian values, independence, and justice. And what about that last name, "Canuck"? First recorded in 1835 as American slang for French Canadians, the term had become a generalized reference to all Canadians by the 1860s.

In 1869, a new weekly magazine from Montreal, the *Canadian Illustrated News*, started running regular sketches of Johnny Canuck standing up to bullies. Sometimes it was John Bull—

England's middle-aged, stout national symbol—but more often the bully was Uncle Sam, typically depicted as a sinister figure with notions contrary to Canada's best interests. For variety, several *Canadian Illustrated News* cartoons also had Johnny confronting an equally menacing "Brother Jonathan," an earlier personification of America dating back to the Revolutionary War days.

DON'T MESS WITH JOHNNY

For most of the remaining 19th century, Johnny Canuck spoke up for Canada in newspapers and magazines across the nation. He often criticized the United States' trade practices or challenged America's claims to fishing rights in Canadian waters. For example, one cartoon called "Johnny's Idea of It" appeared in the July 22, 1871, edition of the *Canadian Illustrated News*. It showed Johnny as a boy fishing at the edge of a pond with a young Brother Jonathan approaching, fishing pole in hand. Says Jonathan: "I say Johnny, your ma says I may fish in your pond, if you like." Responds a defiant, angry Johnny: "Well, I don't like."

Johnny Canuck had a good home in the *Canadian Illustrated News* until the weekly folded in 1883, but by then, he was a fixture of political cartoons in magazines and newspapers across the country. When Canada entered World War I, Johnny saw a resurgence, even becoming the subject of patriotic songs like Gertrude C. Knight's "Good Luck to Johnny Canuck" in 1916. After the war ended, Canada's defender of all things Canadian largely faded from view. But the country hadn't seen the last of him.

JOHNNY TAKES ON THE NAZI MENACE

The 1940s are considered the start of Canada's golden age of comics. An import ban on U.S. comic books caused Canadian publishers to scramble for characters and breathe new life into Johnny Canuck. Like any good superhero, Johnny Canuck re-emerged from obscurity just when his country needed him most— to fight the evils of Nazism. He was a new man. In fact, he was two men. Two different comic publishers sold Johnny Canuck comic books. In both, the hero almost single-handedly defeated the Nazi menace.

• **Johnny #1:** In Maple Leaf Pulps' November 1939 Two-Fisted Tales comics series, Johnny's story picks up deep in the Canadian

backwoods. In the midst of a fierce snowstorm, Johnny, a master woodsman, is nearly killed by a pack of ferocious wolves. A mysterious medicine man saves his life by tapping mystical powers and transforming Johnny into a bulletproof fightin' Canadian with extraordinary strength. Johnny emerges with his newfound powers, wearing a Canadian army uniform and a white shirt emblazoned with a trinity of red maple leaves. His face is covered with a mask like the Lone Ranger's, and in each hand he holds mighty stone gauntlets named "Strong" and "Free." The medicine man instructs Johnny: "A great evil rises like the winter sun. You must fight, white-man, fight for all Canada!" Then Johnny pledges to forever fight against those who would threaten Canada.

• **Johnny #2:** In February 1942, Dime Comics debuted "Johnny Canuck: Canada's Answer to Nazi Oppression," the brainchild of Leo Bachle, a 15-year-old staff artist. This time, Johnny is a full-fledged fighter pilot and soldier called on to battle the threat of Nazism abroad. In the first issue, he single-handedly thwarts a Nazi invasion of a mineral mine in Libya. At one point, the Germans capture him, and Johnny stands before a firing squad. Just as it looks like curtains for the shirtless, muscular hero, he breaks the ropes that bind him and says, "The Germans had better start making stronger rope if they want to hold Canadians captive." As Johnny escapes, he pushes a giant boulder down a hillside, obliterating a legion of German tanks before inviting his readers to tune in next time: "Hey gang!! Don't fail to read my adventures next month, when I meet Hitler—face to face!"

JOHNNY READJUSTS TO CIVILIAN LIFE

After World War II ended, Johnny Canuck—like many old soldiers—again faded away. He didn't reappear until 1965, when he took on a new identity: as a private eye fighting crime in James Moffatt's Blue Line Murder paperback novel series. After that, he had a variety of incarnations:

• In 1975, he got a promotion. Renamed Captain Canuck in an independent comic book series created by Ron Leishman and Richard Comely, Johnny appeared in a tight red-and-white outfit, revealing bulging muscles, with a red maple leaf emblazoned on his forehead. Captain Canuck, the creation of artist Richard Comely, worked for the Canadian International Security Organi-

Watch where you step: Canada is home to about 70 different centipede species.

zation and, not unexpectedly, vanquished many an evil foe.

• In 1995, the Dime Comics incarnation of Johnny Canuck was immortalized on a 45¢ postage stamp as part of Canada Post's celebration of the nation's comic-book superheroes. The classic rendering features Johnny jumping into action, outfitted in his air force flight jacket, goggles, headgear, and high leather boots.

• In its 2008–09 season, the National Hockey League's Vancouver Canucks added jerseys that featured Johnny Canuck's head over a "V." Canada's professional wrestling world even boasts two Johnny Canucks: "Loverboy Johnny Canuck" and "Lumberjack Johnny Canuck."

* * *

YOU STOLE A WHAT?

• In 2004, someone stole a 460-pound pink concrete pig from the front yard of Winnipeg Blue Bombers president Lyle Bauer. The pig was the mascot of the Canadian Football League team. The Bombers are *still* looking for the culprit. Said team official David Asper, "We will never let the terrorists win."

• In 2007, Bert Cooper, 78, was in his back yard on Manitoulin Island, Ontario, when he noticed something strange: someone had stolen the bark off of his birch trees. On closer inspection, he found that about 120 of the trees had about a meter (three feet) of bark missing. "It was so disgusting," he told the CBC. Police said birch-bark thefts were on the rise, adding that the wood was likely being sold for use in arts and crafts.

• Over the course of several years, someone stole ideas for computer technology from Jerry Rose of Nanaimo, British Columbia. The thief stole it directly from his brain, using "invasive brain computer interface technology, research experiments, field studies, and surgery." At least that's what Rose claimed in 2008 when he sued the University of British Columbia, the RCMP, Microsoft, Google, Telus, Wal-Mart, the Great Canadian Casino, and several others, seeking $2 billion in damages. (He lost.)

In 1989, it became illegal to smoke on commercial flights between Canadian cities.

A PRESIDENTIAL WHO-DUNNIT

In 1923, Warren G. Harding became the first U.S. president to visit Canada. A few days later, he doubled over in pain and took to his sickbed. He never recovered, and within a week, he was dead. Some people say it was Canada's fault. (Not us, but some people.)

MR. HARDING GOES TO VANCOUVER

Warren Gamaliel Harding may have been one of the least-qualified men to ever attain the United States presidency. He surrounded himself with crooks who squandered and stole the nation's resources, and his time in office was plagued by the Teapot Dome bribery scandal. Plus, he was—according to another politician of the time—a terrible orator who usually gave speeches that were just "an army of pompous phrases moving across the landscape in search of an idea." And he didn't do a whole lot of work either. Yet at first, he was tremendously popular with the American public. He'd won by a landslide in 1921, promising Americans a "return to normalcy" after the horror of World War I. And they loved him for it.

By 1923, though, the government's investigation into the Teapot Dome scandal—and Harding's involvement with it—was in full force in Washington, D.C., and the president's popularity was dropping. Coincidentally (or on purpose), he decided to get out of town. Harding organized a diplomatic tour called the Voyage of Understanding, in which he and his wife Florence would travel throughout the West to meet ordinary people and explain his policies. After spending some time in Alaska, the tour stopped in Vancouver on July 26, and Harding probably welcomed the chance to spend time with people who didn't much know or care about the scandals roiling the country to the south.

WELCOME TO THE HOTEL VANCOUVER

While in Vancouver, Harding attended a ceremonial lunch at the Hotel Vancouver, hosted by British Columbia premier John

Oliver and the city's mayor, Charles Tisdall. Afterward, 50,000 Vancouverites gathered in Stanley Park to hear Harding give a speech, an event honored today by an ornate memorial erected there by the Kiwanis Club. (Harding was a member.) Afterward, he began a game of golf with a group of local dignitaries.

On the sixth hole, though, Harding started to feel very tired and wanted to quit. Worried about the chaos that might ensue if it got out that the U.S. president wasn't feeling well, the group jumped ahead to the 17th hole and then posed at the 18th for photographers. Immediately after, Harding was hustled off to bed and waiting doctor.

That's when Vancouver got a bum rap that stuck: A few days later, Harding almost collapsed while giving a speech in Seattle, and his aides spread word that the president was suffering from food poisoning, the result of crabs he had eaten in Vancouver. The rest of Harding's public events were canceled, and he was whisked off to the Palace Hotel in San Francisco. On the way, he got very congested and became weaker by the hour. It was clear to almost everyone that the problem was a lot more serious than indigestion.

DEATH OF A PRESIDENT

On August 2, 1923, while Florence Harding read aloud from an article in the *Saturday Evening Post*, Warren Harding literally dropped dead. Doctors in San Francisco concluded that he had congestive heart failure, which caused a fatal heart attack. But his wife refused an autopsy, which led many people to speculate that the president had been poisoned. Who could the perpetrators be? His wife? A group of Americans angry about the Teapot Dome scandal? Rogue Canadians who intentionally fed him rotten crabs?

Probably not. It's unlikely that anyone, especially the chefs at Vancouver's crab and butter luncheon, killed Warren G. Harding. More probable is that his death was the cumulative effect of similar high-fat and cholesterol-laden meals eaten three times a day over his 57 years.

In Nova Scotia, it's illegal to water your lawn while it's raining.

UNSUNG CANADIANS

Let us now sing the praises of two little-known Canadians.

WHO: John H. Dales
WHAT: Invented emissions trading
In 1968, when a professor at the University of Toronto suggested creating a market in the rights to pollute air and water, a lot of people wondered what he'd been smoking. Environmentalists were outraged: what did he mean, the "right" to pollute? Business people were equally dubious: how could you trade pollution permits like soybeans and pork bellies in some sort of mercantile exchange?

After a while, though, the idea almost started to make sense: Set a reasonably acceptable level of total pollution each year and issue a proportion of it in permits to each polluting corporation. If a corporation can figure out how to pollute less than its allowance, it can make a profit by selling the surplus to a company that's polluting more than its allowance. Also, the credits can be bought by anybody—speculators to resell, or even to environmental groups that could retire them unused.

The brilliance of the idea is that it provides a financial incentive for companies to reduce their pollution levels and gives them flexibility on how to achieve those reductions. Those that don't end up paying a premium each year to industries that do.

But would the college professor's plan work? The jury's still out. Today, Dales's idea is being used in worldwide "cap-and-trade" laws that regulate greenhouse gases, but many people (including Dales himself) wonder if the impact will be worthwhile. We'll just have to wait and see.

WHO: Judy Feld Carr
WHAT: Smuggled persecuted Jews out of Syria
Born in Montreal and raised in Sudbury, Ontario, mother and music teacher Judy Feld Carr was galvanized into action in the 1970s when she heard a rabbi talk about the persecution of Jews by the Ba'ath government of Syria. Jews living there were under threat of frequent crackdowns and violence and were not allowed

First Canadian named "Sportsman of the Year" by *Sports Illustrated*: Bobby Orr (1970).

to travel more than three kilometers (1.9 miles) from their homes. From Canada, Carr ran a shadowy organization in which she bribed officials and ransomed captive Jews or, when necessary, arranged for their escape if the bribery failed. Over 28 years, she helped to get nearly all of Syria's Jewish community out of the country…a total of 3,228 people. Most of them relocated to Israel.

To maintain secrecy, Carr and her operatives created a coded language based on alcoholic drinks, obscure Biblical allusions, and Chinese cuisine. Throughout the mission, Carr used the code name "Gin" and often disappeared on missions with little warning even to her family. (Her family later said that they started figuring out she was leaving when she began cooking large quantities of food for them to reheat while she was gone.) Few people knew who she was. Rumors about an operation headed by some unknown, obscure woman in Canada were disregarded as unlikely by the Syrian authorities. Carr said, "I had to live two lives—a life of international intrigue, and then I had to be a mother and do the normal things…The fact that I'm still alive is a miracle." It all lasted until 1995, when her mission was almost over and Israeli prime minister Yitzhak Rabin blew her cover by citing her with a humanitarian award.

Besides people, Carr also helped smuggle out the Jewish community's ancient artifacts and sacred texts, at one point using a hockey bag to transport a Torah scroll. After finishing with the people-smuggling business, Carr—by then a grandmother—retired to Toronto. No longer totally unsung, she received the Order of Canada in 2001.

* * *

CANADA'S OLDEST SUGAR MAPLE

The "Comfort Maple" has stood in Pelham, Ontario, for 500 years. But old age has definitely taken its toll. The trunk—6 meters (20 feet) in diameter—can no longer hold up the nearly 30-meter (100-foot) tree. So some of the larger branches have been reinforced with steel wires, and bricks and mortar were used to heal some old wounds in the trunk. The tree (named after the early 19th-century family, the Comforts) is now part of a historical preservation site.

A grizzly bear can match a horse's speed for 91.4 meters.

LET'S GO TO THE MALL!

*Want to spend an Edmonton winter under a
palm tree on the beach? Head for the mall.*

• The West Edmonton Mall (WEM) encompasses 120 acres—
that's about 20 city blocks.

• It has more than 800 stores, but that's just the beginning.
There's also the Galaxyland amusement park, a water park, an
ice-skating rink, and a miniature golf course. During a visit to the
mall you can skateboard, meet sea lions at an underground aquari-
um, stroll down a crowded street in a simulated Chinatown, or
relax on a sandy beach where the temperature is always 30°C
(86°F).

• There are five statues: one—the bronze *Man Eating Lunch*—sits
at a table in the Gourmet Court.

• The WEM was the idea of the Ghermezian family, who immi-
grated to Canada from Iran in the 1950s. They settled in Edmon-
ton in 1965 and opened the WEM in 1981. The Ghermezians'
inspiration for their megamall came from Iranian bazaars, where
entertainment and shopping have been combined for centuries.

• Sadly, the WEM is no longer the world's biggest mall. In 2004, a
Dubai mall surpassed it.

• But that's okay because, according to *Guinness World Records*,
it's North America's largest enclosed mall. It also holds the
"world's largest indoor" records for its amusement park, miniature
golf course, wave pool, triple-loop roller coaster, lake, and perma-
nent bungee tower. The WEM also has the world's largest parking
lot, with more than 20,000 spaces.

• If you want to stay overnight, you're in luck. Across the street
from the WEM is the Fantasyland Hotel, where you can rent
themed rooms. Themes include Roman (with a hot tub sur-
rounded by marble columns), Igloo (with an igloo-shaped bed),
and Truck (with a bed in the bed of a truck and a stoplight for a
chandelier).

The word "sasquatch" comes from *se'sxac,* an aboriginal word roughly translated as "wild man."

MEASURE BY MEASURE

This quiz is a toughie, and you may need to channel your elementary school geography class. (Answers on page 454.)

1. Which province/territory is closest to the South Pole?
a. New Brunswick
b. Ontario
c. Northwest Territories

2. Which province/territory is closest to the North Pole?
a. Yukon
b. Northwest Territories
c. Nunavut

3. Which province has the longest coastline?
a. British Columbia
b. Saskatchewan
c. Newfoundland & Labrador

4. If you split up Nunavut, giving each resident the same amount of land, about how big a square would each person get?
a. 8 square kilometers (3 square miles)
b. 800 square kilometers (308 square miles)
c. 8,000 square kilometers (3,088 square miles)

5. What if you split up Prince Edward Island equally among its residents—about how much land would each of them get?
a. ¼ of a football field
b. ¼ of a tennis court
c. ¼ of a baseball infield

6. According to official Canadian surveys, which territory contains the North Magnetic Pole?
a. Yukon
b. Nunavut
c. Northwest Territories

Only canine that changes its fur color to suit the seasons: the arctic fox.

7. Based on population, in a tug-of-war with Team Ontario on one side and Teams Quebec and British Columbia on the other, who would probably win?
a. Ontario
b. British Columbia and Quebec

8. Which territory borders the most other provinces and territories?
a. Nunavut
b. Northwest Territories
c. Yukon

9. Which province/territory has 15 of the top 20 highest peaks in Canada?
a. Yukon
b. British Columbia
c. Alberta

10. In recent years, the Northwest Territories was reduced in size by approximately how much?
a. 25 percent
b. 35 percent
c. 60 percent

* * *

MORE LOONY LAWS

• The whole city of Guelph is a "no-pee zone." (It means that public urination isn't tolerated...we think.)

• Purple garage doors are illegal in Kanata, Ontario.

• In Canada, clear-colored sodas cannot contain caffeine.

• No longer enforced, but still on the books in Alberta: Once you're released from prison, the government is required to give you a handgun, bullets, and a horse...so you can get the heck out of town.

The first McDonald's outside of the U.S. opened in 1967 in Richmond, B.C.

HOLIDAY CHEER

If you're one of those Canadians who can't get enough holidays, you're in luck! Somebody in Canada celebrates at least one holiday every month, and now, so can you. (P.S. We've got a great costume—invite us to your next Sir John A. Macdonald Day party.)

JANUARY 11: Sir John A. Macdonald Day
Celebration suggestion: Be like the man himself—put down a rebellion or two. Take bribes. Binge drink, vomit on a podium during a speech, and marry your first cousin.

JANUARY 26: International Customs Day
Celebration suggestion: Rummage through your friends' bags. Volunteer for a strip search.

FEBRUARY 28: Yoga Day Canada
Celebration suggestion: Participating studios often offer free yoga classes, so get twisted and sore in as many meetings as you can during the day. Best bet: take a hot yoga class, and stay warm on someone else's dime.

MARCH 20: Journée internationale de la Francophonie
Celebration suggestion: French fries, French horns, French kisses.

APRIL 9: National Day of Remembrance of the Battle of Vimy Ridge
Celebration suggestion: Round up people from all over Canada and stop them from fighting with each other long enough to capture some farmland in France.

APRIL: Poetry and Records Management Month
Celebration suggestion: Straighten out both your finances and your iambic pentameter. If you think this is a strange pairing, consider that April is also National Oral Health Month and Irritable Bowel Syndrome Awareness Month. (We have no celebration suggestions for those.)

Before it became part of Canada in 1949, Newfoundland had its own anthem.

THE MONDAY BEFORE MAY 25: Victoria Day
Celebration suggestion: Celebrate your own birthday. Since Queen Victoria was born on May 24, there's only one chance in seven that the celebration will actually land on her real birthday anyway. (Still, that's better odds than Queen Elizabeth II. Her birthday is also celebrated on Victoria Day, even though she was born on April 21...and her name is Elizabeth.)

JUNE 21–JULY 1: Celebrate Canada!
Celebration suggestion: What other country has an official holiday with an exclamation point in it? With 11 days of merriment—encompassing Aboriginal Day (June 21), Saint-Jean-Baptiste Day (June 24), Multiculturalism Day (June 27), and Canada Day (July 1)—don't forget to pace yourself and drink plenty of liquids.

AUGUST 15: National Acadian Day
Celebration suggestion: Head down to New Orleans and spend the day with the original Cajuns.

SEPTEMBER 8: International Literacy Day
Celebration suggestion: Offer to help a local literacy program with their outreach efforts and print up a big sign: "If You Can't Read This, Sign Up Here."

OCTOBER 1: International Day of Older Persons
Celebration suggestion: Yell at some kids to get off your lawn.

NOVEMBER 19: Have a Bad Day Day
Celebration suggestion: Screw up at work, burn your dinner, stub your toe.

DECEMBER 31: Make Up Your Mind Day
Celebration suggestion: Make some decisions about how to improve your life...or wait until the next morning and call them "resolutions."

ON TOP OF THE WORLD

Canadians are a brave bunch, and they aren't afraid to go to incredible heights to prove it. Since the first climbers attempted to tackle Mount Everest in 1922, Canadians have had their share of the mountain's triumphs and tragedies…including a bizarre incident when a group got a "hello" from a guy who'd been left for dead.

UP, UP, UP…

In 1852, British colonial surveyors checked and rechecked their figures before concluding that yes, a certain mountain on the border of Tibet and Nepal that they called Peak XV was the tallest in the world. They quickly named it Mount Everest in honor of a retired colleague, Sir George Everest, a former British surveyor-general in India. The mountain already had a name, however—actually several names in the local languages: Sagarmatha (Nepali), Zhumulangma (Chinese), and Qomolangma (Tibetan).

Whatever they called it, there was no way those surveyors were going to the top. In fact, most people back then assumed that Everest's 8,850-meter (29,035-foot) peak was impossible to climb…and that it would be deadly to try. Even now, with the best of equipment and technology, climbers still often don't make it, sometimes joining the 210 people known to have died on the mountain. The remains of some of them are still up there, and a handful—like the body of a man known by climbers as "Green Boots" because his green mountaineering boots are still on his feet—are visible landmarks along popular trails to the top.

And yet people continue to try to reach Everest's summit, and some of them are Canadians. The Canucks who have risked the fate of Green Boots number in the few dozen. These are the stories of some of their attempts, from the tragic to the absurd:

EARL DENMAN
When: 1947
Fate: Failed
In 1947, engineer Earl Denman, the first Canadian to make a serious effort to reach Everest's peak, smuggled himself into Tibet and hired two Sherpas for an illegal climb. (Tibet requires that all

climbs be sanctioned by the government, and Denman's attempt was not.) Nearly arrested by Tibetan patrols, the climbers got as high as 6,700 meters (22,000 feet) before a strong storm pummeled them into giving up. All three returned safely, although not without some suffering. Denman's climbing gear was described as "woefully inadequate" and included boots that disintegrated on the way down, leaving him to walk some of the 500 kilometers (310 miles) back to Darjeeling, India (the nearest large city), in bare feet. Interestingly, one of Denman's Sherpa guides was Tenzing Norgay, who led Sir Edmund Hillary to the top six years later in the first successful climb.

LAURIE SKRESLET AND PAT MORROW
When: 1982
Fate: Success, but at great cost
It would be 29 years after Hillary reached the top before Canadians tried again. The 1982 Canadian Mount Everest Expedition, sponsored by Air Canada, was probably one of the best planned, best financed, best equipped, and largest expeditions to attempt Everest. It included 59 people, days of preparation, and 20 tons of food and supplies.

Unfortunately, it was also one of the most tragic. Four people died, and six of the remaining Canadians threw in the towel, leaving it to Laurie Skreslet to become the first Canadian to reach the summit. He was followed two days later by Pat Morrow.

SHARON WOOD
When: 1986
Fate: First North American woman to climb Mount Everest
Most of us spend a lifetime trying to figure out what we want to do with our lives; Sharon Wood figured it out when her father took her to the top of her first mountain when she was 12. At 20, she joined an all-women expedition to the top of Mount Logan, the tallest mountain in Canada, and a few years later, climbed Alaska's Mount McKinley, North America's tallest. In 1986, her next challenge was Mount Everest.

Climbing with fellow Canadian Dwayne Congdon, Wood became the first North American woman to summit Everest,

and only the sixth woman ever to reach the top. She also had climbed a new route up the mountain—the west ridge to the north face—the first woman to blaze that new trail unassisted by a Sherpa guide.

BYRON SMITH

When: 1998

Fate: Close, but no cigar

Give a climber enough support lines and he might make it safely to the top and back. Unfortunately, the corollary of that statement defined the fate of Canadian Byron Smith, who made it to within 80 meters (262 feet) of Everest's summit, but had to turn back when he literally reached the end of his rope.

SEAN EGAN

When: 2005

Fate: Died

Six years of good luck, in which at least eight more Canadians made it to the top without serious incident, came to an end when 63-year-old professor Sean Egan attempted to become the oldest Canadian to reach the summit. He died of a heart attack before rescuers could get him off the mountain.

ANDREW BRASH

When: 2006

Fate: Abandoned his climb to save a "dead" man

Andrew Brash from Calgary was sure he was going to make it to the top of Mount Everest on his second attempt in 2006. However, after an arduous climb and 200 meters (656 feet) from their goal, his team of four stumbled on a surreal scene: a guy sitting in the snow ahead of them, calmly changing his shirt.

The day before, a different team had made it to the top, but one of its members, an Australian named Lincoln Hall, came down with altitude sickness that caused hallucinations and confusion. Sherpas tried to get him off the mountain, but were ordered by the group's leader to give up—Hall was unconscious and the group leader believed he was dead. Plus, oxygen supplies were running low and snow blindness setting in. So the group abandoned

Last Canadian PM to be knighted: Sir Robert Borden (the guy on the $100 bill).

Hall on the mountaintop and headed back to camp. When they arrived, the group leader issued a statement announcing Hall's tragic death on the mountainside.

Usually that would be the end of it, but the next morning, Brash's team climbed the same route. One of Brash's team members, Myles Osborne, reported in his memoirs what happened next:

> Sitting to our left, about two feet from a 10,000-foot drop, was a man. Not dead, not sleeping, but sitting cross legged, in the process of changing his shirt. He had his down suit unzipped to the waist, his arms out of the sleeves, was wearing no hat, no gloves, no sunglasses, had no oxygen mask, regulator, ice axe, oxygen, no sleeping bag, no mattress, no food nor water bottle. "I imagine you're surprised to see me here," he said. Now, this was a moment of total disbelief to us all. Here was a gentleman, apparently lucid, who had spent the night without oxygen at 8600m, without proper equipment and barely clothed. And ALIVE.

Brash and his group abandoned their upward quest and summoned help, sharing their oxygen and staying with Hall until a rescue team of 15 Sherpas could arrive to get him down the mountain. He recovered fully from mild frostbite and cerebral edema after his ordeal.

A COLD REALITY

The reaction of Brash's team may sound like a commonsense response to someone in mortal danger. After all, observed another of the members afterward, "The summit is still there and we can go back. Lincoln [Hall] only has one life." However, their sacrifice was in stark contrast to the story of another climber, British math teacher David Sharp, who ran into trouble just a few days earlier after reaching the summit.

Climbing solo and without oxygen tanks, Sharp lost consciousness at the same overhang where the body of Green Boots still lies. Over the next nine hours, about 40 other climbers passed where he lay. Some thought he was dead. Others tried to radio for help, but couldn't make contact with anyone. But some climbers actually saw he was still alive…and stepped around him in their hurry up or down the mountain. It took nine hours before a base camp received a call for help—by that time, Sharp was dead.

"THE GREATEST CANADIAN"

Today, Canada has free universal health care. The man who
made it happen: former Saskatchewan premier Tommy Douglas.
Here's his story, another classic from the BRI archives.

LIFE AND DEATH

In 1910, when Tommy Douglas was six years old, he injured his leg and it never healed properly. He developed a life-threatening bone infection, and because his family couldn't afford a specialist to treat it, the doctors wanted to amputate the leg to stop the infection from spreading. Tommy's leg was saved only by chance—a teaching surgeon took an interest in the case and offered to operate on the boy for free, provided that the doctor's students could watch the procedure and learn from it.

Tommy never forgot the experience. A medical crisis could affect anyone—what would happen to people who weren't as lucky as he had been? His situation wasn't at all unusual in the early 20th century. In most countries, there were few options if you were poor and happened to get sick. Hospitals would occasionally admit charity cases, but only rarely. For the most part, if you needed lifesaving medical attention and couldn't pay for it, you died.

HUMAN RIGHTS

After spending his teens at a variety of jobs (printer, actor, whiskey distiller, boxer), Douglas became a Baptist minister and in 1930 took a job as a preacher at Calvary Baptist Church in Weyburn, Saskatchewan. The rural, blue-collar town was devastated by both a drought and the Great Depression. Even if families had money for food, there was none left over for medicine. It reminded Douglas of his own near-tragedy from childhood. He came to believe that medical care was a basic human right and that it should be available to everyone.

In 1934, Douglas realized that he could do more for the poor in politics than he could at a small-town church, and joined the Co-operative Commonwealth Federation. Like Douglas, they advocated

In the 1700s, British soldiers stationed in Canada were entitled to six pints of beer a day.

universal access to health care. (The party also agitated for social reforms to end the Depression, including workers' compensation and unemployment insurance.) Douglas ran on the CCF ticket for the Saskatchewan legislature in 1934...and lost. But in 1935, he won a seat in the national legislature, the House of Commons.

WINS AND LOSSES

Douglas served in the House for nine years but never got the support he needed to institute health care on the national level. The CCF wasn't well regarded in mainstream Canadian politics; their idea of tax-supported, government-run medicine was too reminiscent of the complete state control of the Soviet Union. But Douglas was no communist, and had no interest in totalitarian government. He just wanted universal health care.

Frustrated with the lack of progress at the national level, Douglas resigned from the House in 1944, returned to Saskatchewan, and tried to get his health care plan going on the provincial level. The voters were with him: In the 1944 election, the CCF won 47 of the 52 seats in the Saskatchewan legislature. And since Douglas was the head of the Saskatchewan CCF, the election landslide made him the premier (governor) at age 39. Now he'd have a chance to prove to the rest of Canada that his social welfare programs, especially universal health care, could succeed.

PRESCRIPTION FOR SUCCESS

Douglas's entire plan for governing was built around the idea of universal health care, or "Medicare." Seventy percent of the 1944 budget was allocated to health, welfare, and education. That year, Douglas's government passed 72 social and economic reform laws, most of them directly or indirectly related to health care:

• Douglas ordered the University of Saskatchewan to expand to include a medical school to create and train more doctors.

• Utilities, lumber, fisheries, and other corporations became state-run, generating substantial revenue to pay for health care.

• Douglas and his cabinet took a 28 percent pay cut.

• Retirees were immediately given free medical and dental coverage. Treatment of cancer, tuberculosis, mental illness, and venereal disease were made free to everyone in Saskatchewan.

Canada's first aboriginal senator: James Gladstone (1958).

By 1947, Saskatchewan had one of the strongest economies in Canada. After just three years as premier, Douglas made the province financially stable enough to introduce universal hospitalization for all residents of Saskatchewan for an annual fee of $5.

Access to hospitals and surgery were in place, but drugs and doctors visits were not. There just wasn't enough money. Still, the rest of Canada was beginning to see how well Douglas's program was working and warmed to the idea. When new prime minister John Diefenbaker—a Conservative—was elected in 1957, he offered matching federal funds to any province that started a free hospitalization program. The following year, Saskatchewan had a budget surplus, and in 1959, after 15 years of work, Douglas was finally able to introduce complete universal health care to the province.

JUST THE BEGINNING

Seeing how well Saskatchewan did with health care, legislation began in 1961 to expand it to all of Canada, and by 1966 it was in place, paid for by the provincial and federal governments, each contributing 50 percent. His goal reached, Douglas returned to national politics in the early 1960s. He led the New Democratic Party, a new version of the CCF, and held seats in the House of Commons off and on before retiring from politics in 1979. In 1998, he was elected to the Canadian Medical Hall of Fame. He's one of the few non-doctors honored, but without Douglas's efforts, the Canadian medical—and social—landscape would be far different today.

THREE OTHER TOMMY DOUGLAS FACTS

• In a 2004 poll conducted by the CBC, Canadians were asked to name "the greatest Canadian." Tommy Douglas was voted #1.

• Douglas's daughter, Shirley Douglas, was arrested in 1969 for ties to the Black Panthers—they had helped her organize a free breakfast program for African American children living in poor sections of Los Angeles. Following Shirley's arrest, Tommy Douglas said, "I'm proud that my daughter believes that hungry children should be fed, whether they are Black Panthers or white Republicans."

• Actor Kiefer Sutherland is the grandson of Tommy Douglas. (His mother is Shirley Douglas.) As a boy, Sutherland asked his grandfather what defined a Canadian. Douglas's response: the harsh winters and Medicare.

The suburban inspiration for *Wayne's World*: Scarborough, ON, Mike Myers' hometown.

MISSES AND MISHAPS: WORLD WAR II

Canada's mainland experienced several attacks during World War II. Some of them were serious, but others gave the impression that maybe the enemy really hadn't thought things through. Here are six attacks that made Canadians sit up and take notice.

1. THE LIGHTHOUSE ASSAULT

In December 1941, the Japanese sub *I-26*, commanded by Minoru Hasegawa, was the first to sink an American merchant ship, just moments after Japanese planes attacked Pearl Harbor. Waiting for Japan's surprise attack, Hasegawa had been ordered to stay out of sight until bombs fell on Pearl Harbor. So when the freighter *Cynthia Olson* lumbered down the coast, the *I-26* patiently fell in behind. Finally, at the appointed moment, the *I-26* surfaced and fired a warning shot, allowing the American crew enough time to send an SOS and load into lifeboats before their ship sunk. (Unfortunately, the crew died at sea anyway—a nearby steamer heard the SOS just as the news about Pearl Harbor came in, and the *Cynthia Olson's* transmission was ignored amid the chaos and fear.)

Six months later, on June 20, 1942, Commander Hasegawa directed his crew to a new mission: the submarine surfaced quietly near the Estevan Point Lighthouse off the coast of Vancouver Island as the crew prepared to snuff out the structure and its radio locator.

"Fire!" The first shell screamed away from the sub, but the lighthouse barely shook as trees behind it splintered. The second shell missed, too. So did the third. And the fourth. And the 19th. Finally—after expending about 30 shells and fearing that antisubmarine planes were already on their way—Hasegawa gave up and ordered the *I-26* to slip below the surface.

An embarrassment? Yes. A colossal failure? Well, maybe not, since the sub's "failure" still accomplished its goals: First of all, this first attack on Canada's soil since the War of 1812 evoked terror in the Canadian people. Furthermore, Canadian and U.S. authorities responded by shutting down lighthouses and radio beacons all

Cabbies in Halifax, NS, are required to wear socks.

along the coast in the hopes of confusing the enemy. Instead, the lack of navigational aids confused merchant ships, resulting in disasters and disruption to coastal shipping.

2. GERMAN SUBS IN THE ST. LAWRENCE RIVER

By the end of the war, the Canadian navy had become the third-largest in the world, but they started off badly. At the beginning of World War II, Canada's navy consisted of only a handful of minesweepers and a half-dozen destroyers. The result was that German submarines moved with relative impunity along the coast and into the harbors. The Gulf of St. Lawrence and St. Lawrence River became battle zones, with terrified residents watching as U-boats sank ships in front of their houses, rattled their windows with explosions, and littered the shore with debris and corpses. Eventually, the Canadian government closed the gulf and river to all transcontinental shipping and started attacking the U-boats. By 1944, the Germans had moved on.

3. ENEMY WEATHER STATION SPIES ON LABRADOR

In the fall of 1943, a group of German meteorologists, led by college professor Kurt Sommermeyer, surreptitiously landed at the northern tip of Labrador and set up a weather station. "Weather Station Kurt" lasted three months before its batteries went dead. It stayed dead for the rest of the war after the Allies sunk the submarine that was en route to Labrador with new batteries.

4. GERMAN SPIES

Throughout World War II, the United States was usually the target of the enemy's best spy rings and saboteurs; by comparison, Canada, as always, seemed to get the short shrift. The Germans weren't even trying very hard, sending a few second-rate spies into the eastern provinces. Take, for example, Marius A. Langbein, a secret agent who landed by U-boat near St. Martins, New Brunswick, on a dark night in April 1942. Langbein had been ordered to make his way to Halifax and, using his high-powered short-wave radio, send a stream of reports back to the Fatherland about departing troop ships. Instead, he decided to move to Ottawa, rent an apartment, and spend some time enjoying the country, leaving his handlers overseas wondering what had

400 million years ago, Canada was home to 2.5-meter-long sea scorpions.

become of him. In December, having run through his living expenses, Langbein turned himself in to Canadian authorities.

A little more focused was Werner von Janowski. A U-boat dropped Janowski in Conception Bay, Quebec, and on his first night, he rented a room at the New Carlisle Hotel. Unfortunately for Janowski, the manager got suspicious when he paid for the room with King George V banknotes...five years after George's death had led to a change to Canadian currency. When the Mounties followed Janowski onto a train and arrested him, they discovered spy stuff—including a radio that they convinced Janowski to use to broadcast a stream of misinformation to his bosses. Eventually, he became an official double agent, though many in the government always questioned his loyalty to Canada.

5. FIRE BALLOONS OVER SASKATCHEWAN

In the 1920s, a Japanese meteorologist working with weather balloons first discovered fast-moving wind currents about 9 to 12 kilometers (6 to 7 miles) up. As airplanes became more advanced and pilots started reaching those altitudes, it became clear that aircraft could make amazing time by riding those tailwinds. By the time World War II came around, Japanese military planners had imagined another possible use for the currents. Tracing the route of the jet stream above their country, they figured out that it flew straight across the Pacific Ocean to North America. What if they released hydrogen-filled balloons into those upper-altitude winds to deliver firebombs into Canada and the United States?

It was actually a clever plan on paper, but there were some technical problems. First of all, the balloons had to be pretty big to deliver a bomb that would be worth the trouble. Also, the scientists figured (accurately, it turned out) that only about one in ten bombs would actually fall on the continent, and there was no guarantee they would fall in a place where they would do damage—a populated area or a flammable prairie or forest, for example. So to better their odds, the Japanese decided they needed to send up big balloons by the thousands.

But there was another problem: The balloons couldn't rise too high or sink too low. If they were simply released into the air, the warm sun would force the balloons up; then at night, cool air would make then fall. And anyway, the jet stream is only 1.5 to

4.5 kilometers (0.9 to 2.8 miles) thick: there was no guarantee that the balloons would stay in the stream's main current.

After a great deal of brainstorming, Japanese engineers hit on a solution: an altimeter (a device that measures altitude) with controls to regulate the balloons' height. Additionally, a timer would count off three days from launch. Based on the calculation that the balloon would be somewhere over North America by then, the timer would release its bombs and then spark a fire to incinerate the balloon. With all their problems solved, the Japanese military armed 9,000 balloons with four bombs each, and let them go.

The execution of the plan actually worked well. The balloons went up into the air, and a good number drifted into the jet stream. Fewer stayed there, and fewer still released their bombs at the right time and place. Yet, as predicted, about one in ten was a success, dropping its bombs over the western provinces and states; a few even got as far east as Saskatchewan.

However, the Japanese scientists didn't fully understand how big and spread out North America is. Hundreds of firebombs could drop randomly for weeks and not hit much of anything. Depending on the location and conditions, even a firebomb dropped into a forest or prairie might not start a noticeable fire.

And that's pretty much what happened. More fires were likely caused by lightning during that time than by the firebombs. There were a few tragic exceptions: children picnicking in Bly, Oregon, found one of the unexploded bombs and managed to set it off, killing five kids and one adult. Another bomb might have been the cause of a forest fire in Oregon's Tillamook Forest that killed one firefighter. Still, the U.S. military managed to cover up even those few incidents, no one in North America feared the bomb balloons, and the Japanese shelved the program as ineffective.

6. NEWFOUNDLAND TORPEDOED, DOESN'T SINK
The carnage around the coast of Newfoundland was no laughing matter, with war ships and iron ore freighters being sunk regularly. German U-boats even hit a civilian ferry, killing 136 people, mostly noncombatants. Then, on October 4, 1942, after missing a ship, a torpedo slammed into Bell Island, destroying a dock and making Bell Island the only North American geographic feature to be attacked with a torpedo during World War II.

WEIRD CANADA

Canadians do the darndest things.

DODGE THIS!
Students, faculty, and staff of the University of Alberta decided to take time out from their busy school schedules to break the record for the world's largest dodgeball game. On February 5, 2010, they showed up in the university's sports arena (called the Butterdome) for the battle. More than 1,000 dodgers hurled 400 red balls at each other for an hour, shattering the previous record of 450 people, though *Guinness World Records* has yet to verify the event.

DRINK NOT, DRUNK NOT

Party buses transport people from bar to bar so they won't drive drunk. Usually, it's a smooth process, but in this case, things got out of hand. In January 2010, a passenger (let's call him "Unruly Fellow") on a party bus in Calgary got a bit too rowdy. Unruly Fellow was so drunk and disorderly that the party bus driver made him exit the vehicle at once. He did, but kept pounding on the door and cursing. Then he disappeared. The bus driver, likely relieved to finally be free of Unruly Fellow, started up the bus's engine and pulled away from the curb. Thunk! Unruly Fellow hadn't left after all; he'd slipped on an icy curb, fallen under the bus, and was run over when it started to move. He was rushed to the hospital, treated, and eventually released. In a statement, one owner of a party bus company said, "[This kind of thing is] extremely rare and will get some media coverage so it will be a black mark for sure, but in the bigger picture, party buses do a lot of great things by transporting people who are intoxicated."

CAREFUL WHERE YOU DO IT

When a couple decided to have sex at a 2010 Motley Crue concert in Winnipeg, they likely didn't know the people sitting near them would record the event on a cell phone and post it on YouTube. Other seatmates complained, and the copulating couple was asked to leave. "It's an unfortunate incident," said the arena's spokesman. "I think the people engaged in the activity probably regret their actions." (Plus, they missed the concert.)

Harry Houdini saw his first straight jacket while visiting an insane asylum in Saint John, NB.

THE VANISHED VILLAGES, PART I

The St. Lawrence Seaway was a marvel of engineering that transformed Canada's shipping industry.

A RIVER RUNS THROUGH IT

Historically, the St. Lawrence River was a point of entry to the central region of North America, but it was a barrier, too. Travelers encountered several sets of rapids that required picking up their boats and goods, and trudging across land to get around the rapids. Several canoe-grade canals were dug by 1800, but canoes and flat-bottomed boats weren't enough to transport grain and ore from the heartland to the coast.

By the 1840s, several St. Lawrence canals had opened, smoothing travel for medium-sized boats. It was a big improvement, but it still wasn't enough. These canals and locks were only about four meters (13 feet) deep, meaning that a full-sized ship might run aground if it tried to go through them. These ships had to stop and offload their cargo onto smaller boats to carry it through the canal, then reload it onto another full-sized ship on the other side.

DERAILED BY THE RAILROADS

Businesses first broached the idea of the St. Lawrence Seaway in 1895. The plan was to dam the river at both ends of the rapids, covering them with a huge new lake. Some of the dams would also generate hydropower for the region's burgeoning population, and new canals and locks would allow large vessels to pass through smoothly without offloading and reloading.

The proposal met with overwhelming resistance from residents living along the river and another, more powerful source: railroad executives who didn't want competition from a fancy new waterway. Another hurdle was the United States. Canada had hoped to get the U.S. Congress on board by building a power plant on the American side as well. Unfortunately, America's railroad barons were at least as powerful as Canada's, and the St. Lawrence Seaway initiative stalled and stayed that way for 50 years.

Canada was the only western nation to ban Salman Rushdie's novel, *The Satanic Verses* (1989).

THE FROZEN SEAWAY THAWS

Despite their half-century reprieve, the villagers living on the river didn't exactly breathe easy. Although the rest of the region grew and developed, that narrow stretch of land didn't. The mere possibility of a seaway hung over its head: Who would invest in a new home or business that would eventually end up underwater? Highway 2 continued to bring in plenty of tourists in the summer, but the population of the villages stayed frozen at about 6,500 people, the same number it had been back in 1900.

Finally, after the Great Depression and two World Wars, schemes for the seaway began moving forward again. All the elements started lining up: the railroads' power had been sapped by an upsurge in highways and trucking, government coffers were groaning with new revenue to spend, people were open to "progress" in whatever form it took, and postwar prosperity brought a huge demand for transporting products and raw materials.

IF YOU BUILD IT, THEY WILL COME

Canada was so desperate for the seaway that it was willing to pay for the whole thing and leave the United States out of it. But as it happened, American iron ore was running low just as the nation was demanding steel for its post–World War II building boom. At about that time, iron was discovered in eastern Quebec. Now suddenly, the United States could see the overwhelming logic of streamlining transportation on the St. Lawrence River, and a new power plant would be welcome, too. In 1954, President Eisenhower signed the Seaway Act, and the Canadian Parliament formed the St. Lawrence Seaway Authority to manage the project.

Government officials from the Ontario Hydro power company began showing up at the villages, offering buyouts. But the townsfolk balked at the offers, especially since the impending seaway had depressed land prices for years. So Ontario Hydro came up with an alternative: Instead of a direct buyout, the villagers would be given land in Long Sault or Ingleside, two new villages the government was building nearby. The government would either build the residents new houses or move their present houses there, if feasible. This would allow the displaced river residents to maintain somewhat familiar surroundings and keep their friendships and communities intact. Many accepted the offer, and more than

Good luck: Point one on Wayne Gretzky's 10-point plan to revamp the NHL...abolish fighting.

500 structures were moved, among them the buildings that went to Upper Canada Village Historical Park as a commemoration of what was about to be lost.

MOVING RIGHT ALONG

Ontario Hydro hired a professional moving company from New Jersey that had invented a machine that could lift a house off its foundation and transport it so smoothly that homeowners could leave their belongings in the house during the move. All the moves, which cost between $3,000 and $11,000 per house, were completed without serious incident by December 1957.

Unfortunately, most structures couldn't be moved. Brick houses, factories, and hotels had to be burned or knocked down to their foundations so that they wouldn't be underwater hazards. Trees had to be cut down as well, including apple orchards that had taken years to mature and a beloved 500-year-old elm tree in Moulinette.

BUT WHAT ABOUT GRANDPA?

Cemeteries presented another problem. Villagers were faced with a big decision: either accept Ontario Hydro's offer to let contractors dig up their deceased loved ones and move them to a new cemetery, or leave them where they were. Some families chose the latter. The grave sites of bodies without any known relatives and the graves of those whose families decided to leave them were weighted down with heavy boulders to keep coffins from floating out of the saturated soil and becoming a ghastly navigational hazard.

This was also in the days before the idea of recycling building materials had caught on, so much of the debris was just left behind. But some of the wooden structures were burned with a higher purpose. Scientists from the National Research Council took the opportunity to study how different kinds of buildings burn, with the goal of making them safer. They systematically burned nine buildings to test the safety of different materials and the efficacy of fire alarms. What they discovered changed the fire codes of Canada; among other things, they found out that smoke would usually kill people long before heat triggered a fire alarm, leading to a new emphasis on mandating smoke detectors instead of heat detectors.

The coldest day in Canada, on average: February 2.

CITIES OF RUINS

While some of the workers were dismantling and destroying the villages, others were building dams, powerhouses, and locks. The dams would blot out the rapids by covering them with water and creating Lake St. Lawrence. Billions of tons of earth and steel would go into the seaway's construction. It would stretch 300 kilometers (186 miles) from Montreal to Lake Ontario, and had seven massive locks that lifted and lowered ships between lake level on one end and sea level on the other. The project ultimately cost more than $1 billion and employed 25,000 people.

On Dominion Day—July 1, 1958—60,000 pounds of explosives blew up the temporary watertight construction called a "coffer-dam" that had been holding back the river during construction. Lake St. Lawrence started filling up; it would take three days for the water to cover what remained of the villages. Anything that was still loose floated away. The electrical turbines were powered up for the first time. A year later, the St. Lawrence Seaway officially opened to commercial traffic.

To learn about the towns swallowed up by the seaway's construction, turn to page 393.

* * *

DINO DROPPINGS

Ever wonder what happened to all the droppings left behind by the dinosaurs? Scientists in Alberta have one answer. In the 1990s, paleontologists Wendy Sloboda and Karen Chin discovered a dinosaur coprolite (fossilized animal dung) near the Royal Terrell Museum in Drumheller. The dino turd was 64 centimeters (25 inches) long and 17 centimeters (6 inches) wide, making it the largest dinosaur coprolite ever found.

In 2003, another group of scientists analyzed the fossil and found something even more interesting: Mixed in with the dropping was some well preserved dinosaur tissue, probably from an animal the pooper had eaten. Based on bone fragments left behind, paleontologists believe that the tissue belongs to a *pachycephalosaur*, a small (in dinosaur terms—it actually stood as tall as an average man), lizardlike animal that ran around on its two back legs.

Ontario's first license plates were made of leather.

I ♥ SASKATCHEWAN

Look over there, way in the distance—it's the back of your head! We're kidding. Saskatchewan isn't really that flat, but you still gotta love it. Here are 12 good reasons.

1. ITS OUTLINE IS EASY TO DRAW. Just four straight lines. Saskatchewan is the only province without messy borders meandering along a river, a mountain range, or a coastline.

2. HOCKEY LEGEND GORDIE HOWE, born in Floral.

3. THE TV SHOW CORNER GAS, set and filmed in Saskatchewan. With six seasons and 107 episodes, it's the most successful Canadian sitcom ever. It's also the only one to get its own official provincial holiday. (April 13 is Corner Gas Day.)

4. GREAT TOWN NAMES. They're good for a laugh or a name for your indie band: Saskatoon, Moose Jaw, Buffalo Narrows, Southend Reindeer...

5. THE TUNNELS OF MOOSE JAW. What's not to like about mysterious underground tunnels, built in the early 20th century to connect the heating systems of downtown buildings? Plus, over the years, these tunnels have been frequented by Al Capone's gang, ill-treated Chinese immigrants, neighborhood kids scaring each other, and now tourists.

6. THE ROYAL CANADIAN MOUNTED POLICE, who learn their profession at the RCMP Training Academy in Regina.

7. SASKATOON. It was named by a leader of a Temperance Colonization Society commune...after a berry. In the 1880s, while contemplating what to call his alcohol-free settlement on the east bank of the South Saskatchewan River, John Lake was interrupted by a young disciple offering a handful of locally grown berries. Called *misâskwatômin* by the Cree, the name became "saskatoon" in English.

Toronto's George Dunning directed the animated Beatles film, *Yellow Submarine.*

8. ORNATELY DECORATED CHURCHES, plain on the outside but like Renaissance cathedrals on the inside. They were the life's work of Count Berthold John Von Imhoff, a German nobleman and classically trained artist who moved to Canada in the early 1900s, settled in St. Walburg, and decorated a hundred chapels before his death in 1939. At least five in Saskatchewan are still in good shape, and his St. Walburg studio and gallery are open to the public.

9. GIANT STUFF FOUND ALONG SASKATCHEWAN ROADS. A gargantuan snowman, paper clip, tomahawk, dollar coin, guitar, coffee pot, golf ball...well, you get the idea. (Future archaeologists will probably find these things and conclude that residents of Saskatchewan were at least 30 feet tall.)

10. THE CLOCKS NEVER CHANGE. Unlike the rest of the country, suffering twice a year under the tyranny of Daylight Saving Time, Saskatchewan alone decided, "Thanks, but we already have enough hours in the day."

11. RAWHIDE AND JELLY ROLL, the pet beavers of conservationist Grey Owl. On the shores of Ajawaan Lake in Prince Albert National Park, the two beavers lived with the pioneering naturalist and his Mohawk wife, Anahareo, from 1931 until Grey Owl's death in 1938. Rawhide and Jelly Roll appeared in books Grey Owl wrote and are credited with helping to promote his message of conservation.

12. THE CITY OF ESTEVAN. It's known—by its tourism agency anyway—as "the sunniest place in Canada" because it gets an average of 2,540 hours of direct sunlight a year. (Estevan Tourism also set up a Canadian Crop Circle Research Museum in 2007, but that has since quietly disappeared after being embarrassed when some local circles turned out to be hoaxes.)

* * *

The great bacon debate: American bacon is cured pork fat, usually taken from a pork belly. Canadian bacon is cured pork loin.

A BORDERLINE PERSONALITY

It all came down to bad cartography—or maybe uncertain cartography. Either way, a serious mapping mistake led to the creation of a piece of U.S. land between Manitoba and Ontario known as "the Northwest Angle."

BONUS NOTCHES
All it took was a bad map and a few strokes of the pen. On September 3, 1783, Americans Benjamin Franklin, John Adams, and John Jay met with David Hartley (a representative of Britain's King George III) to sign the Treaty of Paris, thus formally ending the American Revolution.

Within the treaty was a declaration of the boundary between British-controlled Canada and the newly minted United States. Part of this boundary wound its way through islands in the Lake of the Woods, a body of water in Ontario and Manitoba, and then "through the said lake to the most northwesternmost point thereof, and from thence on a due west course to the river Mississippi; thence by a line to be drawn along the middle of the said river Mississippi [southward] until it shall intersect the northernmost part of the thirty-first degree of north latitude."

The plan would have worked out brilliantly if the Mississippi River actually ran through Canada. It didn't, of course; the writers of the treaty had based their knowledge on a faulty map. (The Mississippi begins at Lake Itasca in Minnesota, some 140 miles south of the Lake of the Woods, a fact that would not be established for another 50 years.) So when a joint American/ British survey team arrived in the area to formally map the border in 1819, they were left with a conundrum—where should the border go?

They decided to honor the Treaty of Paris and head south— only they did it directly from the northernmost point of the Lake of the Woods down to the 49th parallel. The result was that a small tip of what had been Manitoba land, and about a third of the Lake of the Woods itself, became the northernmost point in

The name Ottawa comes from the Algonquin word *adawe,* "to trade."

the 48 contiguous United States. And the error still stands today. The area is called the "Northwest Angle"...or just the "Angle" for short.

THE ANGLE'S ANGLERS

American visitors to the Northwest Angle—officially part of Lake of the Woods County, Minnesota—had better bring their passports (or a boat) because the area is accessible by land only if you go through Canada. Most of the 318-square-kilometer (nearly 123-square-mile) land notch is uninhabited but owned by the Red Lake Chippewa tribe. Only 159 people cite the Angle as their permanent residence, and most of them live within a couple miles of the waterfront. The rest live on nearby islands in the Lake of the Woods. There's even a one-room schoolhouse for the kids, the only such school in the state of Minnesota.

Tourism fuels the Angle's economy. About 40 resorts dot the lakefront, where out-of-towners flock each year to catch walleye and muskie. Locals run the resorts, cook meals in nearby restaurants, and act as guides to the best fishing spots.

Living in the Angle isn't always easy since the closest land entrance to the rest of the United States is 57 miles away and requires two border crossings. In fact, there have been calls in the past for the Angle to secede from the United States and become a part of Manitoba. The move would simplify the day-to-day lives of Angle residents, who routinely have to confront the hassle of border crossings (controlled by Manitoba) and the logistics of conflicting maritime and fishing laws (partially controlled by Ontario). No such luck, though—the Red Lake Chippewa tribe is opposed to secession because its leaders prefer to keep the Angle in the United States with the rest of their tribal lands.

BUT THAT'S NOT ALL...

• The border crossing in and out of the Angle is at a spot called Jim's Corner, located on a gravel road that serves as the only land entrance. An unstaffed station the size of a storage shed serves as the customshouse in both directions: incoming travelers must stop and use its videophone to contact U.S. Customs; outgoing travelers use the same booth to contact Canadian Customs.

• There are two *other* disconnected pieces of the United States on the Lake of the Woods. Both are directly west of the Northwest Angle and considerably smaller. One is Elm Point, Minnesota, which measures about 0.5 kilometer (0.2 square mile). West of that is an American-owned triangle, so small it doesn't even have a name, that measures about 311 meters (1,020 feet) wide and protrudes just 120 meters (394 feet) into the water.

• The Northwest Angle is the setting for the 1994 novel *In the Lake of the Woods*, by Tim O'Brien, and the home of Danny Orlis, the teenage hero in a Christian adventure series written by Bernard Palmer between 1954 and 1989.

* * *

THE BIRTH OF BOB AND DOUG

In 1980, after its second season, the sketch series *SCTV* moved to the CBC. Because there were fewer commercials in Canada than in the United States, where the show was also broadcast, the CBC ordered the cast to come up with something "distinctly Canadian" for the extra two minutes that would be seen only by Canadians. Cast members Dave Thomas and Rick Moranis were insulted, complaining that comedy shouldn't be ruled by nationalism. Thomas mockingly asked a producer, "Well, what do you want us to do, put up a map of Canada and sit in front of it wearing toques and parkas and cook back-bacon and 'Talk like dis, eh'?" The producer replied, "Yeah, and if you could have a Mountie in there, that'd be even better."

So begrudgingly, Thomas and Moranis created Bob and Doug McKenzie—two "hosers" who hosted a show called *The Great White North*. They threw in every Canadian stereotype they could think of. Unlike the rest of *SCTV*, the McKenzie brothers sketches were mostly improvised...and ended up becoming the most enduring part of the entire series. The brothers became instantly popular in Canada, but even more so in the United States, when *SCTV* expanded to 90 minutes. The sketch spawned a comedy record album that sold a million copies, a feature film that became a cult classic, and even a cartoon. Said Thomas, "It was done really as a mean-spirited joke."

WHY DOES EVERYBODY HATE TORONTO?

Americans love hating New York, the French love hating Paris, and Canadians love hating Toronto. Maybe that just comes with bigness, or maybe it's something more. Let's take a look at the nation's complicated relationship with its premier city.

LET'S ALL HATE TORONTO

Toronto, Ontario, is consistently rated as one of the world's most livable cities. And why not? Situated on the moderate northwestern shore of Lake Ontario, this culturally diverse global city of 2.5 million offers clean streets, safe communities, and a plethora of entertainment, activities, and dining options. So what's not to like, eh?

Plenty, as far as some Canadians are concerned. In 2006, the movie production company Elevator Films released a documentary called *Let's All Hate Toronto*, which makes a lighthearted attempt to uncover why Canucks hate "Hogtown." The film follows "Mr. Toronto" (actually the film's co-director in an eyepatch) across the country as he waves a "Toronto Appreciation Day" banner and insists that Toronto is "the centre of the universe." Canadians don't buy it; some even spit on his banner. Why? Here are a few reasons:

1. TORONTO'S EDIFICE COMPLEX

Nothing sums up Toronto to some Canadians better than that behemoth structure, the CN Tower. The tower, completed in 1975, boasts the pricey 360 Restaurant that slowly revolves, making one complete turn every 72 minutes—just another indication that the world actually does revolve around Toronto.

2. IT WANTS TO BE NYC, ONTARIO

Toronto is pretty much as close to a United States metropolis— in both proximity and similarity—as a Canadian city can get. Geographically speaking, Canada's biggest city is just 25 miles

north of being part of the State of New York, and it seems to follow in the footsteps of the Big Apple.

Like New York City, Toronto is the most populous city in its country. Historically, it's also served as a welcoming port for immigrants from all over the world, which is a point in its favor; about half of all Torontonians were born outside of Canada, making it the most diverse city in the nation. Toronto even took a stab at constructing its own Times Square of sorts: Yonge-Dundas Square, complete with obnoxiously overblown advertisements.

3. THE MAPLE LEAFS

The only thing more detestable than a rich, winning sports franchise, is a rich, losing sports franchise. The Toronto Maple Leafs are, hands down, the NHL's most expensive team, worth a whopping $470 million according to *Forbes* magazine. Sports fans no doubt know that the Maple Leafs also hold the distinction of being one of the original six National Hockey League teams, dating back to 1917. So they must be capable of great things, right?

Not exactly. The Leafs haven't won a Stanley Cup since 1967 and have failed to make the playoffs for far too many seasons. Yet despite this, in 2009 the Leafs still raised their ticket prices 3.5 percent, making the average cost per ticket about $125, the highest of any NHL team.

The Leafs' owners, Maple Leaf Sports and Entertainment—which also owns the NBA's Toronto Raptors and the Air Canada Centre—claim they are charging what the market will bear. But who can afford to pay more than a hundred bucks to watch a hockey game? Who indeed. That leads us to the next reason some claim to hate Toronto.

4. HOME TO BIG MONEY

The city of Toronto has 10.8 million square meters (116 million square feet) of office space, giving it the largest concentration of businesses in Canada. In fact, most of Canada's corporations are headquartered there. All the banks are there; so is the Toronto Stock Exchange, the seventh largest in the world. In other words, Toronto is where your boss or your boss's boss makes those cold, calculated decisions that can end up costing regular Canadians a pay raise, advancement, or even a job.

Sorry Toronto: Geographically speaking, the center of Canada is Arviat, NU.

Toronto touts a multitude of economic sectors—including aerospace, telecommunications, transportation, media, publishing, software production, medical research, education, and tourism.

5. HARD ON THE HAVE-NOTS

But it's not all glitter and gold in Hogtown. Despite its persistent ranking as one of the most livable places in the world, Toronto has more than its share of problems. In recent years, researchers have identified a disturbing trend that shows the poverty rate in Toronto is growing faster than in other parts of Canada. One report from 2007 revealed that almost 30 percent of Toronto families—some 93,000 households—were living in poverty. That number represented nearly a doubling from 20 years before.

The world financial crisis of 2009 also impacted Toronto. In July of that year, Toronto's unemployment rate hit a whopping 11.5 percent, the highest in Canada, before bouncing back to a more reasonable rate. In the meantime, owning even modest homes continues to be out of reach for much of the city's population.

6. OKAY, SOME ENVY, TOO

But let's face up to it. One of the driving forces behind Canadians' disgust with Toronto may be envy. True, it's a crowded, smoggy city. But woven into that bigness are more than 60 distinct ethnic communities—each offering its own dining, entertainment, and shopping opportunities. The city is home to 5,000 restaurants and a potpourri of theaters, art galleries, dance studios, shops, and markets. It's hard to imagine a more exciting Canadian metropolis.

Kind of makes you want to move there. Okay, maybe just visit.

* * *

YUK, YUK

Q: What do the Toronto Maple Leafs and the *Titanic* have in common.
A: They both look good until they hit the ice.

THOMPSON'S NOTEBOOK: SMALLPOX

In the late 1700s, when white trappers and explorers were regularly traveling west from "Canada" (the eastern seaboard), native tribes suddenly started dying of smallpox.

THE EPIDEMIC

When Europeans began settling Canada during the 1600s, they brought with them all kinds of things the First Nations people had never seen before: guns, metal traps, wool blankets...and new diseases. Measles, cholera, syphilis, smallpox—those diseases were unknown in the New World. They thrive mostly in crowded, urban conditions, and the aboriginals who lived in North America were organized into small, rural, often-nomadic societies that just didn't provide a virile birthplace for communicable disease. Once the diseases were introduced, though, it was a different story. With no immunity, the First Peoples were decimated in droves by sick Europeans who carried the diseases with them to the New World. Over just a couple hundred years, more than 80 percent of the First Nations tribes were wiped out by smallpox and other diseases.

Amateur scientist David Thompson traveled the Canadian interior during the 1790s and documented what he saw in his detailed journals. Here, he describes a smallpox epidemic he encountered during a trip to southern Alberta.

THOMPSON SAYS...

"As usual, we went to York Factory with the furs, and returned with goods for the winter trade; we proceeded about 150 miles up the river to the Eagle Hills, where we saw the first camp and some of the people sitting on the beach to cool themselves. When we came to them, to our surprise they had marks of the small pox, were weak and just recovering...

None of us had the least idea of the desolation this dreadful disease had done, until we went up the bank to the camp and looked into the tents, in many of which they were all dead, and the

stench was horrid. Those that remained had pitched their tents about 200 yards from them and were too weak to move away entirely, which they soon intended to do; they were in such a state of despair and despondence that they could hardly converse with us. A few of them had gained strength to hunt, which kept them alive. From what we could learn, three-fifths had died under this disease. Our Provisions were nearly out and we had expected to find ten times more than we wanted; instead of which they had not enough for themselves.

They informed us, that as far as they knew all the Indians were in the same dreadful state, as themselves, and that we had nothing to expect from them. We proceeded up the river with heavy hearts...

"SOLITARY SILENCE"

"When we arrived at the house, instead of a crowd of Indians to welcome us, all was solitary silence. Our hearts failed us. There was no Indian to hunt for us; before the Indians fell sick, a quantity of dried provisions had been collected for the next summer's voyage, upon which we had to subsist, until at length two Indians with their families came and hunted for us. These informed us that the Indians of the forest had beaver robes in their tents, some of which were spread over the dead bodies, which we might take and replace by a new blanket, and that, by going to the tents, we would render a service to those that were living by furnishing them with tobacco, ammunition, and a few other necessaries.

Thus the former part of the winter was employed. The bodies lately dead, and not destroyed by the wolves and dogs—for both devoured them—we laid logs over to prevent these animals.

From the best information, this disease was caught by the Chipaways (the forest Indians) and the Sieux (of the Plains) about the same time, in the year 1780, by attacking some families of the white people who had it, and wearing their clothes. They had no idea of the disease and its dreadful nature. From the Chipaways it extended over all the Indians of the forest to its northward extremity, and by the Sieux over the Indians of the Plains and crossed the Rocky Mountains.

More men died in proportion than women and children...The countries were in a manner depopulated, the Natives allowed that

far more than one half had died, and from the number of tents which remained, it appeared that about three-fifths had perished. Despair and despondency had to give way to active hunting both for provisions, clothing and all the necessaries of life; for in their sickness, they had offered almost every thing they had to the Good Spirit and to the Bad to preserve their lives, and were in a manner destitute of everything.

A "DREADFUL DISEASE"

"All the wolves and dogs that fed on the bodies lost their hair, especially on the sides and belly. Even for six years after, many wolves were found in this condition and their fur useless. The Dogs were mostly killed.

With the death of the Indians, a circumstance took place which never has, and in all probability never will be, accounted for. Before that dreadful disease appeared among the Indians they were numerous, and the bison, moose, red, and other deer more so in proportion. Provisions of meat, both dried and fresh were in abundance. It was noted by the traders and natives that, at the death of the latter, the numerous herds of bison and deer also disappeared both in the Woods and in the Plains...

"ONE PINE"

"In the following October, six men and myself were fitted out with a small assortment of goods, to find the Peegan [Piegan] Indians and winter with them: to induce them to hunt for furs, and make dried provisions; to get as many as possible to come to the houses to trade, and to trade the furs of those that would not come.

Our road lay through a fine country with slight undulations of ground, too low to be called hills, everywhere clothed with fine short grass and hummocks, or islands of wood, almost wholly of aspen and small, but straight, growth. About the tenth day we came to the 'One Pine.' This had been a fine stately tree of two fathoms girth, growing among a patch of Aspens, and being all alone, without any other pines for more than a hundred miles, had been regarded with superstitious reverence. When the small pox came, a few tents of Peeagans were camping near it. In the distress of this sickness, the master of one of the tents applied his prayers to it, to save the lives of himself and family, burned sweet grass

and offered upon its roots three horses; the next day, the furniture of his horses with his bow and arrows; and the third morning, having nothing more, a bowl of water. The disease was now on himself and he had to lie down.

Of his large family, only himself, one of his wives, and a boy survived. As soon as he acquired strength he took his horses, and all his other offerings from the 'Pine Tree,' then putting his little axe in his belt, he ascended the pine tree to about two thirds of its height, and there cut it off, out of revenge for not having saved his family; when we passed, the branches were withered and the tree going to decay.

For three and twenty days, we marched over fine grounds looking for the Indians without seeing any other animals than a chance bull bison, from the killing of a few we procured our provisions. Our frequent removals led us over a large tract of country, on which we rarely found the bisons to be numerous. Various camps with whom we had intelligence were in the same state. This was confirmed to me by old Scotchmen in the service of the Hudson's Bay Company, and by the Canadians from Canada.

It is justly said that as mankind decrease, the beasts of the earth increase, but in this calamity, the natives saw all decrease but the bears. A strange idea prevails among these natives—and also of all the Indians to the Rocky Mountains, though unknown to each other—that when they were numerous, before they were destroyed by the Small Pox, all the animals of every species were also very numerous. Dried provisions of meat before so abundant that they could not be traded, were now sought as much as furs. The inquiries of intelligent traders into this state of the animals from the natives were to no purpose. They merely answered that the Great Spirit, having brought this calamity on them, had also taken away the animals in the same proportion as they were not wanted, intimating the bisons and deer were made and preserved solely for their use; and if there were no men there would be no animals.

A few years after, I passed over nearly the same grounds and found the Bisons far more numerous."

AN AULD ACQUAINTANCE

Guy Lombardo and His Royal Canadians didn't invent New Year's Eve, but they did provide its soundtrack. Their version of "Auld Lang Syne" remains the gold standard for what to play at the stroke of midnight.

CREATING A CLASSIC

On New Year's, when a saxophone-heavy rendition of "Auld Lang Syne" plays up and down your time zone, tip your hat to Guy Lombardo and His Royal Canadians. Their version of the song made the sentimental Scottish tune an integral part of New Year's Eve traditions throughout North America. The Royal Canadians played it live on radio and television celebrations for 50 years—from 1929 until 1979, two years after Guy Lombardo's death. And the Lombardo recording is still played at the stroke of midnight during New York's Times Square celebration.

The Royal Canadians formed in London, Ontario, in 1917 around Guy and his three brothers. (Carmen Lombardo was the band's lead vocalist, songwriter, sax player, and arranger. He also wrote songs for other stars of the day; Louis Armstrong recorded the Carmen-penned "Sweethearts on Parade" and made it one of the most famous jazz tunes of all time.) The band played on the Canadian side of Lake Erie before crossing over to play in Cleveland for two years. Then they finally headed to New York City, where they spent 30 years as the house band of the Roosevelt Hotel Grill before assuming the same role at the Waldorf-Astoria.

Guy started out as a violinist for the band, but as the orchestra grew, his violin became a prop he held while leading the band with its bow. Finally, he gave up that affectation and just used a conductor's baton.

AW, HOW SWEET

The Royal Canadians were what was called a "sweet" band— heavy on the sentimental ballads and bouncy melodies, in contrast to high-energy, jazz-influenced swing bands. It was a formula that worked—they sold millions of records and racked up many number-one hits between 1929 and 1952.

The polar bear is the only bear categorized as a marine mammal.

ACES OF DIAMONDS

*Diamonds, often characterized as a girl's best friend,
have proven to be one of man's biggest obsessions. In
the 1980s, some of those men turned their attention
north in search of the next big, sparkling prize.*

LOOKING FOR ICE IN THE ARCTIC

Once people discovered that Russia had massive diamond mines in the most northerly parts of Siberia, it didn't take long for the smart guys of the world to start wondering if there might be something similar in other Arctic areas—Canada, for example. The Russian mines opened in 1958, but their operation remained something of a state secret; the government didn't want the backlash that was bound to result from a strict, communist regime making money by selling luxury items to wealthy capitalists. So until the 1990s, when communism collapsed in the Soviet Union, the Russians quietly channeled their diamonds through De Beers, a South African company that since the 1880s had maintained a near-monopoly on the diamond trade.

And the Russians weren't the only ones keeping their diamond dealings quiet. In fact, diamonds have long been a controversial topic, especially recently as the world has become more aware of diamond mining and brokering practices in parts of Africa. In Sierra Leone, for example, a brutal civil war created rebel groups that have maimed and killed large numbers of mine workers, and children have been forced into slave labor in the diamond industry. A whopping $7.5 billion has been generated annually from these gems, now called "blood" or "conflict" diamonds—that's anywhere from 4 to 15 percent of the world's total diamond market. But with the diamond's popularity still on the rise, a total boycott has proven elusive. So what's a diamond buyer with a conscience to do? How about finding newer, more secure diamond sources closer to home? The time was becoming ripe for seeking diamonds in Canada.

A MATCH MADE ON HIGH

British Columbian Stewart Blusson was a surveyor and helicopter pilot for the Geological Survey of Canada, assigned to mapping

projects in the Yukon and British Columbia. In 1969, the introverted Blusson was mightily annoyed by Chuck Fipke—a talkative, clumsy, overly cheerful intern who joined his group for the summer. To get some peace, Blusson assigned Fipke to accompany paleontologist Bill Fritz on a mission to the top of a mountain reachable only by helicopter to search for fossils.

The men spent a few days on the mountain, but when they were supposed to return, the helicopter sent to pick them up crashed. Fipke and Fritz were stranded on the mountain for another week, scrounging for food and water, before Blusson was able to find a second helicopter and could fly the rescue run himself. Both men were fine, and Blusson was impressed by Fipke who, for all his faults, managed to keep his spirits up throughout the ordeal. The two became friends, and at the end of the summer, they promised to keep in touch.

AHH...DIAMONDS

Assigned to a desk job for the winter, Blusson met another talkative intern, who mentioned what he'd done at his previous job: searching for diamonds in eastern Canada for the De Beers cartel. Realizing that he'd said more than he should, the intern shut up again, but it got Blusson thinking about diamonds.

Meanwhile, Chuck Fipke had begun his own geological career searching for copper, but also ended up fixating on diamonds. He spent a lot of time prospecting for diamonds around the world and, by the late 1970s, had turned his attention to Canada. Fipke started studying indicator materials—minerals that were found in places where other, more valuable materials (like diamonds) might be. In 1981, he called Blusson with a proposition: he'd gotten financing to hunt for diamonds—did Blusson want to join him?

MR. RELIABLE AND CAPTAIN CHAOS STRIKE AGAIN

By this time, both men had become well-known geological personalities. Fipke had earned the nickname "Captain Chaos" from, among other things, being absentminded in regards to punctuality and being generally chaotic in nature. Blusson was more centered. But the two became business partners, founding the company Dia Met Minerals to hunt for diamonds in northern Canada. Their first job was to scour the Northwest Territories looking for kimber-

lite, a host rock for diamonds, and indicator minerals like garnets that are found in greater concentrations near diamonds.

But eight years later and with no diamonds to show for their prospecting, their financial backing started to disappear. Their luck finally turned when they stumbled on a secret campsite of De Beers—one among the scores of prospectors quietly on the hunt for diamonds in the region.

A SECRET CAMP GIVES CLUES

Fipke and Blusson surmised from the camp's location that De Beers had found indicator minerals nearby and were using a grid system to search the area, digging up square by square searching for hidden diamonds. However, Fipke and Blusson believed that the De Beers party was way off base. They knew that the camp was in an area of great geological upheaval and gambled that the indicators were creating false assumptions because they'd probably been dragged by a glacier eons earlier from somewhere way outside the De Beers grid. So instead of relying on the indicator minerals, Fipke and Blusson followed the clues of ancient glacial movements and water flow and went "upstream," eventually locating the minerals' source a few hundred miles outside the Arctic Circle near Lac de Gras, Northwest Territories.

With little money left to fund their search, Fipke and Blusson devised a new prospecting strategy: they analyzed a few mineral samples to deduce where to go next, kind of like a geological game of "warmer/colder" combined with a treasure hunt in which one clue leads to the next. In all, they took only about 90 samples—a very different approach from the traditional grid system that had kept De Beers searching in the wrong place for years.

EUREKA!

In 1991, Blusson and Fipke's decade-long diamond hunt ended... with great success. They discovered what became Ekati, Canada's first diamond mine. Ekati opened in 1998 and produces about 3 to 5 million carats a year—6 percent of the world's diamond value. To date, it's produced well over 40 million carats.

Blusson and Fipke weren't the only ones to strike gems, though. There are many other projects in various stages of mining, exploration, and testing in Canada's frozen Northwest Territories. Near

Ekati, a prospector named Grenville Thomas staked a large tract of land that is now the Diavik diamond mine. Also, the De Beers Diamond Company finally found the right prospecting methods and got into the Canadian diamond game by buying the Snap Lake and Victor mines.

From being almost nonexistent in the 1990s, the Canadian diamond industry today is the world's third largest. (Russia and Africa are first and second.) And with certification of Canadian diamonds, buyers can be sure of the country of origin and know there is no association with more controversial "conflict" diamonds from Africa.

AFTER THE DIAMOND RUSH

Chuck Fipke eventually sold the bulk of his ownership in Ekati to investors. Last we checked, he'd moved on to various other diamond-prospecting projects around the world, and had developed a professional passion for racehorses.

Blusson became president of Archon Minerals, a Northwest Territories diamond-prospecting company, and a respected philanthropist. He garnered media attention in 2006 by offering $10 million to the first scientist who could streamline a method for sequencing the human genome.

* * *

CANADA, BY THE SIXES

• The word "Canada" has six letters.

• Canada has six time zones: Newfoundland, Atlantic, Eastern, Central, Mountain, and Pacific.

• Canada has six teams in the National hockey League: the Calgary Flames, Edmonton Oilers, Montréal Canadiens, Toronto Maple Leafs, Vancouver Canucks, and Ottawa Senators.

• Canada has six main geographical regions: the Cordillera (rainy and forested Pacific coastal region); the Interior Plains (the prairies); the Canadian Shield (rocky expanse circling Hudson Bay); the Great Lakes-St. Lawrence Lowlands; the Appalachian Region (far-eastern provinces); and the Arctic Lowlands (mainly an island region in northern Nunavut).

THE NEED TO SPEED BREED

Wealthy Toronto businessman and incessant prankster Charles Vance Millar left a will full of crazy bequests and provisions when he died in 1926. The most famous turned into a great race to procreate.

WHERE THERE'S A WILL

Charles Vance Millar was a well-respected lawyer, financier, and savvy businessman in Toronto in the late 1800s and early 1900s. He was also a prankster known for his outrageous and sometimes curious practical jokes, which he mostly used to highlight the greed he believed was inherent in everyone. One favorite was dropping $1 bills on a sidewalk, hiding, and watching as people walked by and looked around before snatching up the money and rushing away. But Millar's most famous practical joke was probably his final one—his last will and testament, made public after his death on Halloween in 1926.

Being a lawyer, Millar put a lot of thought and effort into making sure his will was airtight and that it followed the letter of the law, especially since it included many unusual bequests. He even acknowledged this in one of the will's clauses: "This Will is necessarily uncommon and capricious because I have no dependents or near relations and no duty rests upon me to leave any property at my death and what I do leave is proof of my folly in gathering and retaining more than I required in my lifetime."

In early December 1926, the will was declared genuine, and it included a number of varied and bizarre bequests...for example:

• Millar left three men who denounced horse racing—W. E. Raney, onetime attorney general of Ontario; Newton Wesley Rowell, member of the board of governors of the University of Toronto; and Ben Spence, head of the Prohibition Union—$25,000 worth of the Ontario Jockey Club stock, on one condition: they had to keep the stock for a period of years and draw dividends. This meant that if the three accepted the stock, they would automatically become members of the horse-racing club they had spoken out against so strongly.

Year the greatest number of people immigrated to Canada: 1913 (400,870 people).

• Several lawyer friends of Millar's, who absolutely detested each other, were each given joint and equal ownership of his vacation home in Jamaica.

But the part of his will that caused the most interest was Clause 9. It took on a life of its own and was quickly dubbed the "Great Stork Derby."

RACE TO THE FINISH

A lifelong bachelor with no children, Millar made history with the derby. It went like this: the woman in Canada who had the most children in the 10 years following his death would receive most of his estate. And if there were a tie, the women would divide his assets between them.

Millar owned stock, land, and property, and had plenty of cash. After all was said and done, that equaled a lot of money, and the women of Toronto were more than happy to throw their hats in the ring. But questions soon arose: What constituted the legal boundaries of Toronto? Did stillborn births or miscarriages count? Would the money be taken away by an as-yet-unaccounted-for relative? And finally, was this even legal?

Indeed, Canada's courts proved itself unpopular when they tried to get the will invalidated over the next 10 years, and some of Millar's (very distant) relatives tried to contest it. Fortunately for the participants, the procreation contest was a long one, allowing plenty of time to resolve all the issues in question. In the meantime, neither questions nor legal wrangling stopped the Great Stork Derby. It started off with a bang, and continued full speed ahead.

HOPING FOR TWINS

Halfway through the derby, the Great Depression hit. Many Canadians were not only out of work but also low on funds, so some citizens took it very seriously. In its September 28, 1936, issue, *Time* magazine recounted how five women were "finalists" to win. The author wrote: "Of these, three would be out of the money if anyone bettered their record of ten children in ten years. A fourth, now pregnant, needs twins before Oct. 31 to win. A fifth, with ten offspring sure and possibly two more off the record, is also expecting to deliver again before the deadline."

The magazine listed the mother's names, ages, and how many

In 1965, Toronto psychoanalist Elliott Jaques coined the term "mid-life crisis."

children they had given birth to in those 10 years. It even listed a dark horse: "Mrs. Grace Bagnato, 43, sturdy Toronto-born Italian court interpreter, who habitually keeps working up to the hour of her confinement. Mother of 23 (14 living), she has already been able to produce nine to qualify for the Millar money. Last week she was due to produce again before time is called, hoped for twins."

AND THE WINNER IS...

The courts eventually lost their attempt to invalidate Millar's will, and the derby ended on October 31, 1936, with four clear winners: Annie Katherine Smith, Kathleen Ellen Nagle, Lucy Alice Timleck, and Isabel Mary Maclean had 10 children each. They were awarded $125,000 apiece (worth more than $1 million today). Two other women ended up receiving a "consolation prize" of $12,500 each. Pauline Clarke had 10 children but admitted that some were by a man not her husband. Lillian Kenney actually had 12 babies, but several had died and she was unable to prove that they were not stillborn. In the end, Millar became a "father" to more than 40 children (if you count the almost winners).

There was even a TV movie made about the contest. The 2002 production followed the travails of Kate Harrington (played by Toronto-born actress Megan Follows), a female reporter who involved herself in the lives of the women competing for the big prize and ultimately cost one woman the win. The movie was nominated for three awards: one Gemini (Best Performance by an Actress in a Leading Role in a Dramatic Program or Mini-Series), and two Golden Reels (for sound editing).

WILL POWER

Just for laughs, here are three more bequests from Millar's will:

• Every minister in several neighboring towns around the Kenilworth Jockey Club in Windsor, Ontario, was left one share each of the club. Most struggled with what to do with the gift: accept it or reject it. (The ministers grappled with the moral implications.) After years of back and forth, it turns out, the shares were worth only a measly half-cent apiece.

• The Orange Lodge is a historical society of died-in-the-wool Protestants. Millar left one share of the O'Keefe Brewery Company to every lodge and to every Protestant minister in the city of

Toronto, forcing them to grapple with their consciences over whether to keep or reject the gift. Why the O'Keefe brewery? It was owned and operated by Catholics. Further (no doubt intentional) embarrassment came when it was discovered Millar had no claim to any shares of the brewery in the first place.

• Millar left a sum of money to a priest he knew, but only for the purpose of saying masses and burning candles for the "soul of a certain prominent citizen," described in the will as someone "who will need [the prayers], wherever he is..." Millar never named the person specifically. Since he was a trickster who liked to stick it to those he considered powerful and greedy, we assume this left a small circle of prominent men in Toronto each wondering if he meant them.

* * *

EVANGELINE OF ACADIE

Who could have guessed that one of America's most famous poets would have found fame with a poem about Canada. In 1840, Henry Wadsworth Longfellow was at a dinner party in Cambridge, Massachusetts, when he heard the story of a young Nova Scotian couple separated on their wedding day by the Acadian expulsion in 1755. Legend said that the woman spent her entire life wandering throughout North America looking for her lost love. Longfellow was inspired, but it would be seven more years before he turned that story into an epic poem, the first of his career. Longfellow extensively researched Acadian culture and the circumstances surrounding the expulsion, and then in 1847, he published *Evangeline: A Tale of Acadie*, which told the story of a woman separated from her Acadian fiancé. She searched all over Canada and the U.S. for him, and finally found him on his deathbed at a Civil War hospital. He died in her arms.

It was an enormous hit. During the first six months of its publication, the poem was reprinted five times. Within 10 years, it had been translated into more than 10 languages. The poem also inspired several movies, including 1913 film that was the first feature-length motion picture ever made in Canada. *Evangeline* also revitalized Acadian history and culture, which had been mostly lost since the deportation, and turned Grand Pré, Nova Scotia, into a tourist attraction.

RAGING RIVER RESCUE

Hundreds of people have gone over Niagara Falls accidentally and left no evidence except a single-paragraph newspaper obituary. But the relic of one near-miss remains a prominent feature just above the falls.

SCOW'S ON 'ER

If you stand upriver from Niagara Falls, you'll likely be impressed by the speed and power of the rapids as they roll, roar, and tumble toward the abyss of the falls. Where the white water starts, about 200 meters (650 feet) offshore from the ruins of the historic Toronto Power Station, a rusting wreck of an old barge is wedged firmly against a rock shoal. It's the famous Niagara Scow, and that barge has an intriguing history.

On August 6, 1918, Gustave F. Lofberg and James Harris were anchored on a scow, working for the Niagara Falls Power Company to dredge sand and rock from the hydroelectric plant's water channels. Once the scow was full of sand and rock, they signaled tugboat captain John Wallace to tow them to the shore.

It was a fairly routine procedure in the slower-moving water above the rapids. Except this time, things didn't go as planned. On the way back to shore, the tugboat's tow cable came loose. Wallace looked on helplessly as the barge floated away from him and down the river toward the rapids that end at Niagara Falls.

DEATH BECOMES THEM

Without a motor or even a rudder, all Lofberg and Harris could do was hang on as the river propelled them into the rapids. Accelerating toward speeds of 34 kilometers (21 miles) per hour, the two men lurched and rolled over stomach-churning waves of white water, staying upright only by virtue of the boat's flat bottom and tons of ballast. Well aware that in about a minute and a half they'd be plunging to certain death, the men screamed, prayed, and hoped for any miracle that might save them.

As if answered by angels, Lofberg and Harris suddenly lurched forward, deafened by an ungodly screech of metal against rock. The heavy scow shuddered, swiveled, and skidded to a stop, sitting dead in the water while the rapids raged around them. Somehow,

Average number of pucks used during a single NHL game: 35.

the boat had gotten firmly lodged on a shoal of sand and gravel just 760 meters (2,500 feet) upstream from the edge of Horseshoe Falls...close enough for the men to see mist rising over the drop-off.

BUT NOW WHAT?

When Lofberg and Harris picked themselves up off the bottom of their boat, they heard only rushing water, but could see people running to the nearby bank, talking, pointing, and gesturing help-lessly. Until somebody figured out what else to do, the two men knew that they needed to make sure the barge didn't get dislodged from the gravel bar where it sat precariously. So they started redis-tributing their cargo of sand and gravel by hand, hoping to keep the scow firmly stuck for as long as necessary.

As the men worked, fire trucks arrived, joining the spectators who lined the shore. Their hope for a quick rescue was fleeting, however, as Lofberg and Harris realized that the trucks' crews did not have a workable plan, either.

GIVE 'EM ENOUGH ROPE

Rescuing the men via boat was impossible—any craft would be swept into the falls that the scow had narrowly escaped. Eventu-ally, though, the fire crew came up with something and waved their arms, pantomiming the plan as best they could.

The local fire department had a small "lifesaving gun"—a cannon that shot a projectile attached to a light rope. They set it up on the roof of the nearby Toronto Power Station and hoped to get the rope to the stranded boatmen. When that happened, the people on the shore could tie their end to a series of progressively heavier ropes until there'd be a strong connection between boat and shoreline. With that firmly in place, they could pull the men back to safety using a breach buoy—a kind of zip line made up of a life preserver with a leg harness attached.

The fire departments of Niagara Falls, Ontario, and Niagara Falls, New York, made several rope-launching attempts, but their projectiles fell well short of the barge. Finally, a rescue crew from the U.S. Coast Guard arrived with a larger gun that had a longer range; it did the trick. Eventually, the two men in the scow had in their tired hands one end of a light rope. Rescuers on the shore

tied their end to a heavy rope and signaled the men to pull it in. As the day headed into twilight, and after hours of labor—during which the rope dragged in the water and threatened to pull the barge off its perch—Lofberg and Harris had their vessel securely fastened to a long rope whose other end was attached to the top of the electrical building.

O, RESTLESS NIGHT

Of course, even though that felt a little more secure, the men were well aware that their situation was still precarious. Even tethered by the rope, their barge could come loose in the dark, swing out in a quarter circle, break the rope, capsize, or be dashed against rocks, dumping them into the water.

Luckily, they were set up in front of an electric plant, so lighting wasn't a problem. Searchlights shone on the men all night. The *New York Times* reported the next day that the power station rigged up a one-word electric sign saying "Rest," so the men would know they had not been abandoned.

BREECH BUOY'S GREATEST HIT

At daylight, work began again in earnest. Up on the power station's roof, the coast guard crew hung a breech buoy on the rope and began guiding it down the rope's incline with thin ropes. At first, its pulley rolled easily down toward the scow. But suddenly, the contraption came to an abrupt halt halfway across. Somehow, the guide ropes had gotten tangled in the pulley and no amount of pulling would get them free.

Then an extraordinary thing happened. A local fellow named William "Red" Hill volunteered to go out there and fix things. Just 30 years old, Hill had been a fixture on that part of the Niagara River for years and had become famous in tales of derring-do and saving people from certain death around the falls and the town. Hill won his first Canadian government lifesaving medal at the age of nine and eventually was awarded four of them—more than anybody before or since. During his lifetime, he rescued 28 people and retrieved the bodies of 177 victims of suicide, accident, or foolhardy stunts from below the falls. (Sadly, his son, "Red" Hill Jr., was killed attempting a feat too daring for even his father: going over Horseshoe Falls in a barrel.)

Q: Which Alfred Hitchcock movie was filmed in Quebec City? A: *I Confess*

Hill hung from the rope and, hand over hand, hoisted himself along until he got to the breech buoy and untangled the guidelines. Close enough to Lofberg and Harris to shout encouragement, he rode the breech buoy back to the roof of the power station and the rescue went forward. By noon, both cold and hungry men had made it back to shore.

AFTERMATH

The barge company, facing a loss of $36,000, contemplated recovering the scow, but decided against it because of the difficulty, cost, and danger. Besides, odds were good that the barge would eventually be dislodged by water fluctuations or the massive ice floes that washed over the river from Lake Erie each year. Nearly a century later, they're still waiting.

For his part, Hill was awarded a Carnegie Medal for heroism. Andrew Carnegie established the award in 1904 for people in the United States and Canada who perform extraordinary acts of heroism. Hill also got a boat.

There's another, lesser-known wreck nearby. It can't be seen except in times of low water, but it's a World War I submarine chaser that got away from a millionaire who bought it to convert to a yacht. One day, it broke free from its mooring and ended up tipped over and stuck on rocks. The millionaire sold the boat "as is" to Red Hill for $1. But Hill gave up on salvaging it, instead leaving it to rust in the white water with the remains of the now-famous Niagara Scow.

* * *

AN AVALANCE OF WISDOM

Appearing in ski jackets all over Canada these days is something called the "Recco Avalance Rescue System." Sewn into the lining of the skier's coat, it's a radar-transmitting device that allows people who are snowbound, trapped, or lost to send a signal (including their coordinates) to authorities for a rescue. It's a great invention, but the jackets do include a disclaimer (in six languages) that says the system "does not prevent avalanches."

OLYMPIC HIGHLIGHTS: CALGARY

Here are some of the highlights, lowlights, and "relights" from Canada's Olympic competitions. On page 87, we told you about the Montreal Summer Games. Now, we head to Calgary.

• Mascots for the Calgary Winter Olympics in 1988 were Hidy and Howdy, twin polar bears. Although they wore cowboy hats and western wear from the waist up, they were bear-bottomed.

• A thousand Canadian kids danced in the opening ceremonies, including 12-year-old Leslie Feist. Who? Nineteen years later, Feist (now a singer) was inspired to copy the ceremonies' costumes and choreography for her award-winning music video "1 2 3 4." (The song became a huge hit after it was used in an iPod Nano commercial.)

• As in 1976, Canada won no gold medals in Calgary, making it the first country to host an Olympics twice but not earn gold medals at either competition.

• Olympic organizers were worried about Calgary's "chinook winds"—unpredictable, warm breezes from the south that can raise the temperature above freezing. Sure enough, the breezes arrived that year, requiring that snow machines run overtime. The worst problem came when some bobsled runs had to be repeated after sand blew onto the track.

• Speaking of warm winds and sand, the Calgary competition was the one in which Jamaica fielded a bobsled team for the first time, as immortalized in the movie *Cool Runnings*. They came in last. However, they did go on to make a stunning advance at the 1994 Olympic Games in Lillehammer, Norway, finishing 14th...ahead of the Russians, French, and Americans.

• Another underdog media favorite was long-shot ski jumper Eddie "the Eagle" Edwards. The sole applicant from Great Britain,

When the Canadian flag flies along with those of the provinces and territories...

Edwards got the public's attention with his unassuming manner, low-budget self-financing, beaklike nose, lack of experience, and extreme nearsightedness, which required thick glasses even when jumping. Because he was 9 kilograms (almost 20 pounds) heavier than the nearest competitor, an Italian paper called him a "ski dropper." But the fact that he came in last in both of his ski jump events seemed to make him even more beloved by the public because he represented the Olympics' original ideal of congenial amateurism.

• Another highlight of the Calgary games: The "Battle of the Brians"—Canadian figure skater Brian Orser versus American Brian Boitano. The two had known each other for years and had also dueled at the 1984 games, where Boitano placed fifth and Orser won a silver medal. The two faced off again in Calgary, but this time, Boitano took the gold and Orser won silver...again.

• The front of the Olympic medals in 1988 featured the year's official emblem (a stylized red snowflake/maple leaf). The back was a little stranger: a First Nations member with a headdress consisting of skis, skates, a luge, a rifle, a bobsled, and hockey sticks.

• Perhaps as a bow to the host country, curling made its second appearance as a demonstration sport in 1988. (It also appeared in 1932.) Curling didn't become an official Olympic sport until 1998.

• Calgary was the first smoke-free Olympics. Cigarettes were banned from all spectator areas, even outdoor venues.

• The closing ceremonies gave Alberta singer k.d. lang her first international exposure.

• Mindful of the uproar when Montreal lost money, Calgary organizers claimed afterward that the games had turned a $90–$150 million profit. However, an audit by the *Toronto Star* disputed that, noting that the organizers had not included government subsidies totaling $461 million.

Turn to page 437 for Vancouver highlights.

...the provincial and territorial flags must fly in the order that they entered Confederation.

DID HE OR DIDN'T HE?

For centuries, the story of Leif Eriksson visiting North America was considered little more than a myth. Then the Americans adopted him, theorizing that he'd landed in New England or even Manhattan. That is, until Canadians shut them up by finding Norse relics in Newfoundland.

A NEW LEIF

Leif Eriksson lived in Greenland until about AD 1000 and then followed a family tradition of escaping west and discovering new lands. Years before, his grandfather had hightailed it from Norway to Iceland after running into trouble over "some killings." And Leif's father, Eric the Red, had to leave Iceland quickly after killing a man with a shovel. He sailed west, discovering and settling in Greenland.

But Leif was a little different from the rest of his clan. For a Viking, he was generally a peaceful guy, and he headed west because he wanted to, looking for a place that had better timber and other luxuries not found in barren Greenland. He consulted with Norse seaman Bjarni Herjolfsson, who reported sighting land west of Greenland. (Technically, this would make Bjarni, not Leif, the first known European to "discover" America, but unadventurous Bjarni never landed and instead sold his ship to Leif.)

WELCOME TO NORSE AMERICA

Leif raised a crew, sailed west, and found not one land but three. First was Helluland, "land of flat stones," perhaps Baffin Island, which he determined to be too much like the place he'd left and, therefore, not worth colonizing. He pushed on and found a place he called Markland ("forestland"), possibly Labrador. This looked a bit better, but Leif still hoped to find something more promising just around the next peninsula. Sure enough, two days later he hit pay dirt. According to his account, his third landfall had streams filled with salmon, green grass year-round, meadows, and grapevines that led Leif to name it Vinland ("wineland").

But there were catches to this heavenly Valhalla that ensured his attempt to found a colony there would end in failure. First of all, Leif and his men had some trouble with the locals, whom they

Pop-punk priestess Avril Lavigne started out in country music.

referred to with the all-purpose term *Skraelings* ("uncivilized foreigners"), the name they'd also given the indigenous people of Greenland. But more important, the Norse settlers who followed Leif to Vinland turned out to be the area's true uncivilized foreigners and spent a lot of time fighting with each other.

After several years of squabbling, things reached a boiling point when Leif's sister Freydis arrived in Vinland with her own group from Iceland. She, too, attacked the local tribes and then turned on the colonists themselves. Freydis followed her family's killing ways and goaded one group of colonists into murdering several others because she believed they had insulted her in a dispute over sailing ships. Shortly after that, the Norse abandoned the settlement altogether and headed back to Iceland.

GOOD-BYE, COLUMBUS

Vinland was all but forgotten, even after Christopher Columbus revived interest in the New World. Into the mid-20th century, Leif Eriksson's voyages remained mired in the hazy realm of doubt and speculation. Italians hinted that the whole thing was a fabrication, made up by Icelanders over a few cups of mead. Others argued that Viking seamen *could* have reached the North American mainland, but there was no evidence they actually *did*. Those naysayers pointed out that the Viking sagas, which included mentions of arriving in North America, were just adventure stories, not sailing directions. Leif's voyages couldn't—and still can't—be replicated with any surety.

From time to time, though, amateur archaeologists and the occasional con men came forward with claims of physical evidence:

• In the late 1800s, a stone carved with Scandinavian runes turned up in Minnesota, purportedly describing a massacre of 10 men on the site in 1362, but most authorities judged it to be a fake.

• In 1930, an iron sword and spearhead were found near Beardmore, Ontario. The Royal Ontario Museum bought them for $500, a huge amount during the Great Depression, and proudly put them on display. Alas, the story of their discovery turned out to be a hoax—the relics, although apparently genuine, had been imported from Scandinavia in the early 1920s. So the museum withdrew them from public view. (They were quietly placed back

The North Pole is not part of Canada—it's not affiliated with any country.

Remaining text.

on exhibit in the 1990s with inscriptions explaining the hoax as a piece of Ontario history.)

• In 1957, a genuine 11th-century Norwegian penny showed up in Maine, but again under suspicious circumstances and without any additional supporting context.

• And in 1958, Yale University in Connecticut fell for an expensive and embarrassing hoax when it published the Vinland Map (worth about $300,000), which supposedly showed Vinland and was drawn a few decades before Columbus. Most experts believe that it's a fake.

THE REAL DEAL

In this context, you can imagine the widespread "yeah, right" reaction in 1960, when a Norwegian husband-and-wife team announced that they'd found an ancient Norse settlement in Newfoundland. Archaeologists Anne Stine Ingstad and Helge Ingstad had made a thorough study of the sagas and old maps. In 1960, they began digging at L'Anse aux Meadow at the northern tip of Newfoundland. There they found traces of an ancient settlement. Over the next eight nears, the pair led an international team from Canada, Iceland, Norway, and the United States in excavating sod houses, cooking pits, a metal forge, and boathouses—the remains of a Norse settlement dating back to the early 1000s. With that discovery, Ingstad and Helge finally proved that the Vikings had in fact reached and briefly settled North America, just as the sagas claimed.

UNSOLVED MYSTERY

But one puzzle remains. Grapes (*vinber* in Old Norse) do not grow wild on Newfoundland, so why did Leif name it Vinland? Some theories:

• Although grapes don't grow there, wild berries do and were suitable for winemaking. He could have meant those.

• The settlement on L'Anse aux Meadows may have been only a base camp, with Vinland being farther south. After all, French explorer Jacques Cartier, who claimed Canada for France, found grapes growing wild south of the St. Lawrence River. And some

reputable Icelandic scholars have claimed that the Vikings traveled down the coast as far south as Manhattan before turning back.

• Another theory holds that the climate was warmer then and perhaps grapes *did* grow wild in northern Newfoundland during the 11th century. Support for this idea is indirect, but thanks to today's global warming, a vineyard was successfully established at Gambo, Newfoundland, in 2002.

• Finally, experts in the Old Norse language recently theorized that we've been misled all along by the name Vinland. According to this theory, the "vin" part may come from a different Old Norse pronunciation that means "meadow." As its modern name suggests, meadows are not at all hard to find around the town of L'Anse aux Meadows.

PANTS ON FIRE?

It's hard to judge among all these theories, but perhaps we don't have to. If none of the above hold true, we at the Bathroom Readers' Institute have our own fallback position that we like to call the "Big Fat Liars Theory." It's based on the fact that Leif Eriksson's family had a history of exaggerating the virtues of property they were pitching. This was a family that knew how to do two things really well: sail west, and promote real estate. Don't forget that Leif's father, Eric the Red, was the guy who called an icy wasteland "Greenland" in order to entice settlers to move there. Is there any reason to believe that his son wouldn't wax eloquent about Newfoundland being a place of green grass, endless salmon, and vines groaning with grapes ready for fermenting?

* * *

OH NO! MY MAPLE SYRUP IS MOLDY!

Don't worry, and don't throw it away. Just skim the mold off the surface, heat the syrup until it starts boiling, and then skim the top again. Rinse the container it was in with hot water, and then refill the container with the hot syrup. It's as good as new.

Q: What do you call a Canadian piggy bank? A: The loonie bin.

ALMOST HEAVEN, EXPO 67

By many standards, Montreal's Expo 67 was the most successful world's fair of the 20th century.

WHAT'S A LITTLE COMPETITION AMONG COUNTRIES?

Expo 67 Canada-style almost didn't happen. Canada's centennial came in 1967, and the country was hoping for a big celebration. A world's fair seemed the perfect fit. But before a country could host a world's fair, there were certain protocols that had to be followed: in particular, any major international exhibition had to be okayed in advance by the Bureau of International Exhibitions (BIE).

That was a major stumbling block. The BIE had been established to regulate the timing and reduce the number of world's fairs. Too many countries had been announcing too many overlapping world exhibitions for the international community's taste, diluting the participation of other countries and reducing attendance. The idea was to keep the occurrence of world's fairs rare enough to be profitable by allowing only one every five years.

The problem was that 1967 was a significant date for more than one country. Sure, the *most* important was the 100th anniversary of the Canadian Confederation, but it was also the 50th anniversary of the Soviet Union's Russian Revolution. And both countries were lobbying hard to get the fair. When the BIE representatives voted, the Soviets won 16 to 14, and that's how Moscow became the site of Expo 67's message of peace, freedom, and futuristic optimism.

NO, WAIT...THAT DIDN'T HAPPEN

Within two years of winning the fair, the Soviet Union gave it back. The reason? The costs would be too high, the government said. But there was speculation that the real reason was that the authoritarian and secretive Soviet government didn't want its people exposed to the affluence and outside influence that a

Prairie farmers harvest enough wheat each year to make 46 billion loaves of bread.

world's fair would bring. Furthermore, the government didn't want to have to deal with opening the country's mostly closed borders to millions of international tourists.

Hearing of the Soviets' turnabout, Canada reapplied, and in November 1962, was awarded the event. But could the country make it happen on such short notice?

COMPUTER SAYS "NON"

Canada had first offered the honor of hosting the fair to Toronto; its mayor said, "Thanks, but no thanks." He didn't want to set his city up for failure. Montreal had no such qualms and snapped it up.

Almost immediately, problems arose. To begin with, people on the organizing committee started resigning. They'd input the steps needed to open the fair into a computerized scheduling program, and the computer returned the verdict: there's not nearly enough time. As a result, many of the committe members quit out of fear.

Fortunately, there were others willing to take their places, and the newly appointed replacements were determined to make it work. They created a core group that called itself *Les Durs*—the Tough Guys. Their mission, should they choose to accept it: to ram the project through whatever barriers appeared, whatever it took.

A TOUGH JOB FOR A TOUGH GUY

One of the Tough Guys, Colonel Edward Churchill, was made director of installations. Churchill was determined to prove the computer wrong. To not waste any of the precious preparation time he had, Churchill relied a new project management tool called the critical path method (CPM). Nowadays, CPM or other programs like it are used in nearly every project large or small, but back then, CPM was something new and only nominally tested.

CPM identifies the steps that need to be done first, and schedules them in tight succession. Then you do multiple things at once, while keeping an eye on that "critical path" (i.e., the big picture) that everything else depends on.

While the Tough Guys worked on the logistics, a group of prominent Canadian thinkers convened to come up with a theme. They decided on one based on a children's book, *Terre des*

Hommes (Man and His World) by Antoine de Saint-Exupéry. It was all about "dreams and hopes for the future," exactly the idea the planning committee wanted to convey for the expo.

THE LITTLE EXPO THAT COULD

After that intellectual heavy lifting was finished, it was time for man and his machines to move earth. The plans called for expanding a small island in the Saint Lawrence River to a much larger size for the fairground, a process that would require about 25 million tons of dirt. That quantity would normally take lots of time, money, and headaches, except for a lucky coincidence: Montreal happened to be digging a subway at that same time and needed a place to put the leftover dirt. One problem solved... 8,432 to go.

Besides the island fairground, builders created a boat pier, a railway to bring in visitors from outlying areas, exhibit halls, and Habitat 67, an entire housing complex. With the exception of Habitat 67—which was billed as a work in progress—all of Expo 67 opened on time in April 1967. Take that, computer!

MINISKIRTS AND MOVIES

According to the fair's guidebook, the event's intention was this: "It will tell the story of man's exploration of the physical world, his drive to discover, understand and produce; of how he assimilates, organizes and uses his knowledge to improve his lot and how, as a social being, he has sought and still seeks to live in peace and harmony with his fellow man." Expo 67 accomplished these lofty goals by displaying hundreds of exhibits and innovations from countries around the world. Here are some of the most popular:

• **The miniskirt.** This daring style had been introduced in England about a year earlier by fashion designer Mary Quant, and the hostesses at the UK pavilion wore uniforms with their scandalously short skirts. The attention they got spurred a legs race, with hostesses at nearly every other pavilion suddenly appearing in short uniforms, spreading the style to expo visitors and across the world.

• **IMAX.** The huge large-screen format first appeared at Expo 67. A product of Canadian film innovators, IMAX also included the

first live-action split screen. Nowadays, it's common to see multiple moving images in live-action collages on a single screen, but before IMAX, the effect was limited by the number of individual projectors you could synchronize in the projection booth.

• **Art.** The rules for a world's fair require that all the participating countries send artists and performing artists to the exhibition. Expo 67 included acts from Italy's La Scala Opera, the New York Philharmonic, and England's National Theatre.

• **Pavilions.** All the participating countries (more than 50 of them) built pavilions to show off their people, industries, and culture. The most popular was the Soviet pavilion, which featured a 25-meter (82-foot) statue of a man and a woman holding a hammer and sickle, an emblem that represented workers and peasants and which has become synonymous with communism.

RECORD BREAKERS

During the fair's six-month run from April to October 1967, 50.3 million people attended. Held by a country with only 20 million residents at the time, Expo 67 set a per-capita attendance record that's never been beaten. It also holds the single-day record of 569,500 visitors on its third day. And Habitat 67, that futuristic housing complex with gardens attached to every unit, is still standing and is now owned by its tenants. The site of the expo is now a city park.

* * *

WEIRD CANADA

• Moira Williams, 67, of Sault Ste. Marie, Ontario, was arrested in March 2010 after she repeatedly called the 911 emergency line in the middle of the night...and demanded that police officers pick her up some cigarettes. She was drunk and was charged with mischief.

• In 2004, authorities in Wasaga Beach, Ontario, closed the beach after a baby's head was found in the sand. The tiny head was sent to a coroner. He determined that it was a plastic doll's head. The beach was reopened.

43% of Canadians believe pets are a good substitute for human companionship.

MORE WIT & WISDOM: DR. LAURENCE J. PETER

Laurence Peter, originator of the "Peter Principle" (which says, "In a hierarchy, every employee tends to rise to his level of incompetence."), had plenty to say about subjects besides business. (His quotes about business appear on page 96.)

"The noblest of all dogs is the hot-dog; it feeds the hand that bites it."

"Going to church doesn't make you any more a Christian than going to the garage makes you a car."

"If two wrongs don't make a right, try three."

"If you don't know where you're going, you will probably end up somewhere else."

"Some problems are so complex that you have to be highly intelligent and well informed just to be undecided about them."

"There are two kinds of egotists: Those who admit it, and the rest of us."

"When in doubt or danger, run in circles, scream, and shout."

"If a cluttered desk is the sign of a cluttered mind, what is the significance of a clean desk?"

"Psychiatry enables us to correct our faults by confessing our parents' shortcomings."

"Originality is the fine art of remembering what you hear but forgetting where you heard it."

"Nobody can be perfect unless he admits his faults, but if he has faults how can he be perfect?"

"Every man serves a useful purpose: A miser, for example, makes a wonderful ancestor."

"Humility is the embarrassment you feel when you tell people how wonderful you are."

JOIN THE CLUB

James Bond and Mad Men *ad executive Don Draper drink
Canadian Club. So did Queen Victoria and Al Capone.
Canada's most famous whiskey has been one of
the country's most effective ambassadors since
its first barrels rolled out in 1858.*

STRIKE UP THE BAN

If it weren't for that puritanical streak that seems to emerge every few decades in the United States, Canadian Club whiskey might have been called "Detroit Club" or "Club USA." Hiram Walker would've been perfectly happy distilling whiskey in the back of his Detroit grocery store. There was only one problem: Prohibition, the first go-round. In 1846, Maine passed a state law restricting the sale of alcohol except for medicinal, manufacturing, scientific, or sacramental purposes. In 1855, Michigan did the same thing.

Walker was prepared. Less than a mile across the Detroit River from his home, he had bought some land outside Windsor, Ontario. He intended to build a distillery on it, not only escaping U.S. laws but also getting the tariff benefits that Canadian companies enjoyed with England. (Because Canada was part of the commonwealth, it didn't have to pay the same import taxes the United States did to sell products in Great Britain.)

In retrospect, all that finagling wasn't really necessary. Walker didn't know it at the time, but Michigan's prohibition laws would be enforced only in conservative areas; the cities refused to limit liquor sales or close down distilleries. Still, playing it safe turned out to be a profitable decision.

WELCOME TO WALKERVILLE

Walker had big plans. He knew that the civil authorities in small towns could have a profound effect on any area businesses (by passing laws, instituting taxes, and so on). So he wanted to build his own town that he could run as he saw fit.

In 1857, Walker commuted daily from his Detroit home to

Summer: Canada is home to Sulky Lake (NWT), Gloomy Creek (AB), and Lac Grouchy (QC).

supervise construction of a distillery, grocery store, and steam-powered gristmill. To make even more money, he bought a herd of cattle that he fattened up on distillery swill (the mash left over after liquor is made), creating what eventually became one of North America's largest dairies. Two years later, to save commuting time, Walker moved his family across the river into his new town—dubbed Walkerville—and set them up in a farmhouse he called the Cottage.

In 1858, the Hiram Walker Company's first whiskey rolled out of the new distillery. It had aged only a few months and wasn't particularly good, but Walker was still able to find a market for it among nondiscerning whiskey drinkers. Walker, however, didn't want to be just a low-end distiller, so he went to work on experimenting and blending new varieties. By 1882, he had 27 different types of whiskey available, with names like Magnolia, Excelsior, and Walker's Old Rye. Many of them sold well, but Walker didn't feel that he'd quite hit the mark yet.

THE MONEY'S IN THE BRAND

Finally, he produced a batch that was really good—Walker called it "Three Star." To drive home the brand, he started actually burning "3 STAR" onto the barrels with a branding iron, something few people did back them. And when Walker discovered that Three Star was popular in the men's clubs that were becoming fashionable among the affluent, he changed the brand to Three Star Club and finally just Club, a name he trademarked in 1882.

Walker's idea was to position Club as a premium liquor at a time when most whiskey was sold unbranded. He played up that his whiskey was aged seven years in wood barrels, when most whiskey barely got one year (and some not even that). Walker also started bottling Club, allowing for more sales and more opportunities to burn the brand into the public consciousness.

Despite his big plans, sales started out slow, and exports to the United States were even slower. In 1884, only 87 cases of 12 bottles each made it across the border. Five years later, exports still hadn't reached a modest 5,000-case level. But 1889 was the turning point, thanks to a small change Walker made to the label—he added CANADIAN to the top to differentiate his whiskey from the heavier, rougher liquors from Scotland, Ireland, and the American

Most popular doughnut in Canada: Boston cream.

South. It was this "Canadian Club" that made Walker's fortune.

Canadian Club, or Canada Club (both names were used pretty much interchangeably in the early years), achieved great success in Canada and the United States. Then, thanks to Queen Victoria's physician, who recommended it to her as a digestive aid, the British upper classes adopted Canadian Club as their own. The Hiram Walker Company became the only North American whiskey maker that was ever an official supplier to the queens and kings of England.

HIRE 'EM INTO WALKERVILLE

Through all the success, Walker hadn't forgotten about his town, and he wanted Walkerville to be "suitable" for his workers (even if it wasn't quite good enough for his children, who returned to Detroit home in the 1880s). From his own pocket, he paid for paved streets, running water, police, firefighters, streetlights, and even state-of-the-art sewage pipes to dump the town's wastes "cleanly and efficiently" into the Detroit River. Ultimately, the town had a population of about 600 people.

But Walkerville was never the workers' town. Walker retained ownership of all properties and insisted that his employees live there. In fact, he wouldn't hire anyone who seemed reluctant to relocate. By having a town populated by people who were dependent on his factories, houses, and good graces, Walker controlled the local government, the stores, and businesses. People could even deposit their paychecks directly into Walker's own private bank. He built a church called St. Mary's in honor of his wife Mary, who died in 1870, and encouraged his workers to attend. And then in 1890, when Walkerville officially incorporated as a town, Walker made sure that his nephew was elected mayor.

AL CAPONE TO THE RESCUE

Hiram Walker died in 1899. His distillery and Walkerville, both now run by his sons, thrived in the first part of the new century. But that ended abruptly when the United States closed its border to all whiskey imports in 1917. And the ban was just the beginning—Canadian Club was in for another disaster: Prohibition.

Ontario passed prohibition laws in 1916 that banned the sale of recreational alcohol. (Prince Edward Island and Alberta had passed

similar laws; Quebec tried, but those were repealed almost immediately due to public outcry.) The United States followed in 1920, and by all expectations, those laws should have been the death-blow for distilleries like the Hiram Walker Company (later called Hiram Walker & Sons). But the company found a loophole big enough to drive a liquor truck through. The Canadian government—eyeing the taxes it would miss out on if the distilleries shut down—said that any liquor made exclusively for export was still legal. Sure, the United States had also made alcohol illegal nationwide, but that wasn't Canada's problem. The government declared that any whiskey transported out of Canada was a legal export.

Enter American gangster Al Capone, who became one of Hiram Walker & Sons' most prolific Prohibition-era distributors. He smuggled thousands of cases of whiskey over the Detroit River in yachts, fishing boats, sailboats, and even rowboats. When that route became too risky, Capone diversified, arranging for shipments to go through remote border checkpoints in Alberta and Saskatchewan and on ships through the Maritime Provinces. Capone's sales kept the distillery afloat through Prohibition, and Ontario finally repealed its antiliquor laws in 1927; the United States also came to its senses in 1933.

THE WALKERS AMBLE AWAY

By then, though, the Walker family was no longer in the liquor business. In 1926, they sold the company to Canadian liquor magnate Harry C. Hatch. Since then, Hiram Walker & Sons has bounced from owner to owner, most recently the French company Pernod Ricard, which also owns Seagram and Absolut Vodka.

And Walkerville? It's now just a small historic spot within a larger city, absorbed and assimilated into Windsor. The Cottage, where the Hiram Walker family lived, is still there. So is St. Mary's Anglican Church and the Hiram Walker plant, which still gives the neighborhood a distinctive smell and still makes Canadian Club on the site where it all began.

*　　*　　*

Did you know? Christopher Plummer (*The Sound of Music*) played many British characters, but he was born in Montreal.

Q: Who is Matthias Boutilier from Cape Breton, NS?...

FROZEN FIELDS

Canadians seem to have a special affinity for sports that can be played on ice. We all know hockey and curling, of course, but what about bunnock, broomball, and ringette?

THE BUNNOCKS ARE CONNECTED TO THE...

If you travel near Macklin, Saskatchewan, keep an eye out for a 10-meter (32-foot) white fiberglass object called "The World's Largest Bunnock." What's a bunnock? It's a horse's anklebone. It's also a game, that uses the aforementioned anklebones. Sometimes called *glockenspiel* or "the game of bones," bunnock was invented by bored Russian horsemen stationed in Siberia in the early 1800s. One attraction of the game was that the equipment came from something the soldiers could get plenty of: dead horses. Another advantage was that bunnock could be played on ice or frozen ground, making it a year-round sport.

The game is played sort of like horseshoes or shuffleboard. Two teams of four members—one of whom must be of "the opposite sex," say the rules—face off from opposite sides of a 10-meter (32-foot) court, trying to knock down 22 bunnocks set at the opposing team's end of the court. To knock down the bunnocks, players throw a *schmeiser*—also a horse's anklebone, painted a different color from the rest. (The term comes from a German word that means "to strike.") Players must knock down the two black-painted bones on either end of the line (the "guards") before knocking down the white ones in the middle. The teams take turns, and the winner is the one that knocks down all the opposing side's bunnocks in the fewest throws. (Nowadays, most bunnock sets are made with plastic bones, which is a good thing because it takes 13 dead horses to make a full bunnock set.)

The game came to Canada in the early 1900s, but it wasn't until the 1960s that it gained mainstream popularity. That's when an Edmonton man named Joseph Gartner (who worked at a horse-meat processing plant) started making and selling bunnock sets. He also created a rule book, and his sets were some of the first to be mass-produced in Canada. Eventually, a few of Gartner's sets made it to the town of Macklin, where residents really fell in love with

...A: The guy who taught Babe Ruth how to play baseball.

the game. It boasts a giant bunnock (9.7 meters/32 feet high) made of fiberglass, steel pipes, and wire mesh, and the town hosts the World Bunnock Championships every year, attracting 320 teams from all over the world.

SWEEPING THE SERIES

Like hockey, broomball originated in Canada. Actually, it's very much like hockey and is even played on a regulation hockey rink. The main differences between the sports are that broomball players wear shoes instead of skates, use a broomlike stick instead of an L-shaped one, and hit a ball instead of a puck.

The origin of broomball is murky, but it's generally recognized as having first been played in Saskatchewan in 1909…though some people say it was invented as far back as the 1890s, and a few contrarians swear it was an 11th-century Icelandic sport. Regardless, broomball has become increasingly popular, with Japan, Italy, and several other countries forming teams. Broomball's spread has even given rise to a governing body—the International Federation of Broomball Associations, which hopes to get the sport into the Winter Olympic Games in coming years.In Canada, broomball is most popular in Manitoba. The town of Saint-Claude calls itself the "Broomball Capital of the World"…adding to its other formidable claims to fame (e.g., home of the world's second-largest smoking pipe and the Manitoba Dairy Museum).

ENGAGEMENT WITH A RING

The problem with a country inventing one good sport is that it's easy to keep inventing it over and over again. How many variations of hockey does the world need, after all? Well, according to Canadians, at least one more. Ringette, another hockey mutation, uses a rubber ring instead of a puck and straight sticks instead of bent ones. It also doesn't allow body contact.

The game was invented in 1963 by Sam Jacks of North Bay, Ontario, for girls and women to play at a time when female athletes were rare and thought to need "easy" sports. These days, it's still most popular with women and girls, but men and boys occasionally play and there are unofficial coed leagues in several cities and towns. It's estimated that, in Canada, there are more than 60,000 ringette players in hundreds of leagues.

The world's largest hockey stick (63 meters high) resides in Duncan, B.C.

I ♥ QUEBEC

*Even Canadian tourists tell us that Quebec is exotic, what
with all that French talk, those Smurf huts, and the
monk's heart. Here are 12 reasons to love Quebec.*

1. SOVEREIGNTY. Okay, yes, the Quebecois have been talking
secession for years and maybe some people call that treason. But
really, it's just regional pride. After all, Quebec is the only French-
speaking province in Canada (about 95 percent of the population
is fluent), and it's the largest by area. They just want some respect.
Fortunately, in 2006, the House of Commons passed a resolution
symbolically recognizing that "Quebecois is a nation within a
united Canada."

2. FILM HISTORY. On June 27, 1896, Frenchman Louis Minier
screened the first movie ever shown in North America at the
Palace Theatre in Montreal.

3. THE KING'S DAUGHTERS. Well, they weren't really
his daughters—they were just called that. In 1663, the French
government became alarmed by the number of English colonists
settling near its New World territories. Concerned that the popu-
lation of New France couldn't keep up because most of the women
there were indentured servants or nuns, the French government
recruited about 800 Frenchwomen of childbearing age (nicknamed
the "king's daughters") to move from Europe to the colony. The
country enticed them with paid passage, a dowry, and an almost
100 percent guarantee of finding a husband. Sure enough, 765 of
the women married, many within weeks of setting foot on land.

4. YELLOW MARGARINE...FINALLY. In 2008, Quebec
became the last province in Canada to repeal its "margarine color"
law. Basically, early Canadian farmers were peeved that a cheap
product like margarine was moving in on their butter market. They
lobbied hard and won: until 1948, it was illegal to sell margarine in
Canada at all. (Though Newfoundland made bootleg margarine
throughout the ban and got away with it. Why? It was still techni-
cally a British colony. But back to Quebec...)

Coldest temperature ever reached in Canada: –63°C in Snag, Yukon (1947).

Then, in 1950, the government washed its hands of the issue, deciding that solving the great margarine debate should be the responsibility of the provinces. To make sure that no one accidentally mistook margarine for butter, the various provinces and territories mandated that margarine be clearly identified, though there was no consensus on how: some said it had to be bright yellow, some said colorless, some even sold margarine in sacks with a tab that released a yellow dye when a consumer opened the package. Quebec chose colorless, but that infuriated margarine makers: why should they be penalized with all the bans and color rules just so dairy farmers could have a corner on the oily breakfast spread market? It took a while, but after decades of trying, the margarine makers won out. You can now buy yellow margarine in Quebec. Whew.

5. TINTIN AND SMURFS. Belgian comics are huge in Quebec...if the province's roadside attractions are to be believed: there's a Tintin rocket in Batiscan and a Smurf hut in Beaupre. And not just any old Belgian comics, but Belgian comics that are drawn by one-named cartoonists. A man calling himself Herge first drew Tintin in 1929; another called Peyo began penning the Smurfs in 1958.

6. THE HEART OF A MONK. St. Joseph's Oratory, a basilica in Montreal, displays the preserved heart of its founder Brother André in a glass jar. André built a shrine at the site in 1904. (He raised the money for it by giving haircuts for 5¢ each.) He also got the reputation of being able to heal the sick. Desperate pilgrims flocked to the basilica, hoping that the monk's touch would work a miracle. André was so beloved that his parishioners just couldn't let him go. When he died in 1937 at the age of 91, the church removed his heart and put it on public display. Every year (except when it was stolen and held for ransom in 1973 and 1974), millions visit the disembodied organ, many of them hoping for some kind of miracle.

7. STONE WALLS. Following the lead of many cities in Europe, Old Quebec was surrounded by defensive walls, the only North American city north of Mexico that still has ramparts. Who were the walls supposed to keep out? First the British, and when that didn't work, the Americans. The walls were built by the French at

the top of a high cliff in the 1700s and then fortified further by Major General Isaac Brock of the British army after American troops tried (unsuccessfully) to take Quebec City during the War of 1812.

8. HOCKEY, FOOTBALL, AND BASKETBALL. Listen up, sports fans, it's time to show a little love to McGill University. Without it, modern college sports would consist of fox hunting, bear-baiting, mumble-de-peg (it involved pocket knives and teeth), and golf. Case in point: McGill and Harvard football players negotiated the rules and played the first game of modern football in 1874. McGill wrote the rules of hockey and replaced the ball with a puck. And former McGill athletic director James Naismith invented basketball on a cold winter's night in a Massachusetts YMCA.

9. THAT GEODESIC DOME. In the 1930s, American architect and futurist R. Buckminster Fuller figured out how to maximize "tensegrity"—basically, how to best find the balance between tension and compression in architecture so that geodesic domes, like Walt Disney World's Epcot Center, don't collapse. His findings set off a dome-building boom that appeared to be the wave of the future. Who wouldn't love a structure that maximized strength and stability while minimizing materials and weight and looking so cool?

When the United States was putting together its pavilion for Expo 67 (Canada's 1967 world's fair), it hired Fuller to design a futuristic dome. Even though the clear acrylic skin turned out to be flammable and burned off during renovations in 1976, the dome still stands; it's now called the Montreal Biosphère and contains an environmental museum.

10. MANON RHÉAUME. Sure, they were only exhibition games, and yes, the Tampa Bay Lightning's general manager, Phil Esposito, later admitted it was mostly a publicity stunt. But Lac Beauport native Manon Rhéaume performed admirably as goalie when she became the first woman to play in the National Hockey League in 1992–93. She went on to be the goaltender for Canada's women's hockey teams in the 1992 and 1994 World Hockey Championships (gold medals) and the 1998 Olympics (silver medal).

World's longest-running sports TV show: *Hockey Night in Canada,* on air since 1952.

11. TRIVIAL PURSUIT. What incredibly popular general-knowledge game was invented by Scott Abbott and Chris Haney, two journalists in Montreal? The 1980s were a time when obnoxious know-it-alls ran free, and no other game better defined the decade than Trivial Pursuit. The game, invented when Abbott and Haney couldn't play Scrabble because some tiles were missing, eventually sold to Hasbro for $80 million US.

12. H_2O. Quebec has more fresh water than any other place in Canada—about 3 percent of the entire world supply. Drink up.

* * *

WIT & WISDOM: ANNE SHIRLEY

Okay, no…she's not real, but the precocious Anne Shirley, the protagonist in L. M. Montgomery's *Anne of Green Gables*, has a lot to say.

"I am very careful to be shallow and conventional where depth and originality are wasted."

"It wouldn't do for us to have all our dreams fulfilled. We would be as good as dead if we had nothing left to dream about."

"Don't you know that it is only the very foolish folk who talk sense all the time?"

"I believe the nicest and sweetest days are not those on which anything very splendid or wonderful or exciting happens, but just those that bring simple little pleasures, following one another softly, like pearls slipping off a string."

"I read in a book once that a rose by any other name would smell as sweet, but I've never been able to believe it. I don't believe a rose would be as nice if it was called a thistle or a skunk cabbage."

"It is ever so much easier to be good if your clothes are fashionable."

"People make fun of me because I use big words. But if you have big ideas, you have to use big words to express them, haven't you?"

"Proverbs are all very fine when there's nothing to worry you, but when you're in real trouble, they're not a bit of help."

During World War I, Berlin, Ontario, was renamed Kitchener.

ONTARIO'S WINGED CAT

Cats with wings? It's a terrifying prospect if you're a bird, a cow…

IT'S A BIRD, IT'S A PLANE, IT'S A…?

On June 24, 1966, Jean-Jacque Revers noticed something strange lurking around his farm outside of Alfred, Ontario. He watched and listened as the unidentified black creature—a bird? a bat?—howled, screeched, and swooped down from the sky, dive-bombing and terrorizing his animals and, according to Revers, making "gliding jumps of 50 to 60 feet" whenever it extended its wings. Revers did what any farmer would do to a varmint threatening his livestock: he shot it. Then he examined the critter, and immediately called authorities to report that he'd just taken out a cat with wings.

A constable arrived to take a look. In his report, he described the creature as having a 35-centimeter (14-inch) wingspan, adding, "Its head resembled a cat's, but a pair of needle-sharp fangs five-eighths of an inch protruded from the mouth. It had a cat's whiskers, tail and ears, and its eyes were dark, greenish, and glassy. I have never seen anything like it in my life."

FEATHERS OR KNOTS?

Police left disposal of the creature to Revers, so he buried it in his garden. A few days later, he had second thoughts—the world needed to know what this unearthly predator… whatever it was. So, he dug up the corpse and mailed it to Ontario's Kemptville Agricultural School. A few weeks later, Revers got the verdict. After careful examination, the school veterinarians determined that the creature *was*, in fact, a cat…but that its "wings" were actually two thick, overgrown tufts of matted hair. The reason for its odd and aggressive behavior: rabies.

But that didn't end the mystery. Even though Revers claimed he saw the cat swooping and gliding, other eyewitnesses said they saw it leap just a meter (three feet) off the ground. To compound the mystery, there was at least one similar sighting in Ontario in 1966. Since then, at least 138 other sightings of "winged cats" have been reported worldwide.

Pierre Trudeau's favorite snack: chocolate chip cookies.

A TRIP TO
THE ISLANDS

*Ever feel like chucking it all and escaping to a remote
exotic island, but don't want to lose the benefits of
living in Canada? Well, consider one of these.*

RATTLESNAKE ISLAND, BRITISH COLUMBIA

Why it's called that: There are lots of rattlesnakes there.
The tall grass that covers the island is a perfect environment for them to hide and hunt.

Getting there: Rattlesnake Island is part of the Okanagan Mountain Provincial Park off of Highway 97 in southern British Columbia. Get ready for some bumpy travel through the park; most roads are gravel. And then you'll have to kayak out to the island.

Population: No people live there (what with all the rattlesnakes), but legend claims that the island and the lake it's in (Lake Okanagan) are home to Ogopogo, a mythical lake monster. For centuries, the Okanagan natives told stories of a beast they called N'*ha-a-itk*, or "snake of the water." And then around 1890, a seaman named Thomas Shorts claimed to have seen a five-meter (16-foot) finned serpent in the water. Sightings have continued since then, but no one has officially confirmed Ogopogo's existence. (He did appear on a postage stamp in 1990, though.)

Amenities: Unless you count pebbled beaches, caves, and pictographs, none.

ENTRY ISLAND (AKA, ÎLE D'ENTRÉE), QUEBEC

Why it's called that: Because it's the first island visible when traveling from the south to the Magdalen archipelago, off the coast of Quebec and Prince Edward Island.

Getting there: The only island in the archipelago without road access, Entry is accessible by sea or air. From May to December, a ferry service offers one-hour trips twice daily to and from the Magdalen main port, Cap-aux-Meules. During the winter, transit is by small plane, weather permitting.

Sixteen of Canada's 22 prime minister's have been lawyers.

Population: About 150, and even though the islands are part of Quebec, their residents are English speakers; their ancestors were English and Scottish immigrants. Some of them, like many of the people in the Magdalen archipelago, are the descendants of people shipwrecked on the island between the 17th and 19th centuries.

Amenities: There are two stores, a restaurant (specialty: the seal fin sandwich), an Anglican church, a three-room school with about 20 students, a historical museum, a post office, and a bed-and-breakfast that operates during the summer. One tourist said there weren't any bars, but there is a local who "sells beer out of his back door."

GEORGES ISLAND, NOVA SCOTIA

Why it's called that: The island was named for Britain's King George II. For more than two centuries, Georges Island was Halifax Harbour's best defense against French invasions of Nova Scotia thanks to Fort Charlotte, which was built by Prince Edward (1767–1820) and named after his mother, Charlotte of Mecklenburg-Strelitz, the queen consort of King George II. Dungeons, hidden tunnels, and mysterious military goings-on have been part of the island's mystique since the early 19th century.

Getting there: Technically, you could probably swim over from Halifax, but you're not really supposed to go there. Georges Island has been declared a National Historic Site, and Canada is working on getting it ready for tourists. In 2009, Parks Canada designated money for a water line from the mainland, sewage system, dock, and visitor facilities, with plans to open the park by 2014. But right now, according to Parks Canada, it's on hiatus "due to the fragile condition of resources."

Population: Historically, most visitors haven't been tourists but unlucky souls held against their will: prisoners, pirates headed for the island's waiting gallows, and sick people under quarantine. Georges Island is also home to an abundance of blueberries and black garter snakes—it has the highest density of snakes per square foot in Nova Scotia.

Amenities: Present-day buildings include an automated lighthouse, a 19th-century fort called a Martello tower (one of only 11 left in North America), and an unmanned radar station.

Las Cañadas is the name of a region in Mexico. (*Cañadas* means "canyons" in Spanish.)

DEVON ISLAND, NUNAVUT

Why it's called that: In the early 19th century, Arctic explorer William Edward Parry named the island after Devon, England.

Getting there: Devon Island is located in Baffin Bay, and you'll need a boat to access it. But beware: icebergs make the bay non-navigable for several months out of the year.

Population: Zero. At 55,247 square kilometers (21,331 square miles), Devon is the world's largest uninhabited island. It's not for lack of trying, though. In the early 1900s, some trappers from the Hudson's Bay Company tried to set up a settlement there, and then in 1934, the government relocated about 53 Inuit from Baffin Island to Devon. But the soil was poor and the weather too cold for anyone to live there for long. By 1936, all the residents had moved away.

Devon Island does sometimes get human visitors, however. The nonprofit Mars Society has used it to research what life might be like for humans on Mars. In 2000, the society established the Flashline Mars Arctic Research Station on Devon, and since then, several crews of scientists and journalists have visited in order to gain insight into what life on Mars would be like. As part of the simulation, they wear spacesuits when they venture outside and communicate by radio.

Amenities: Lots and lots of ice.

* * *

MOST POPULAR TOURIST ATTRACTIONS
1. Niagara Falls (Ontario)
2. Harbourfront Centre (Toronto)
3. Grandville Island (Vancouver)
4. Stanley Park (Vancouver)
5. Vieux Port (Montreal)
6. Exhibition Place (Toronto)
7. The Forks (Winnipeg)
8. Banff National Park (Alberta)
9. Canada's Wonderland (Maple, Ontario)
10. Mont Royal Park (Montreal)

Homosexuality was decriminalized in Canada in 1969.

THE ORIGINAL DRAFT DODGERS

*Promises, promises. At the dawn of World War I, Prime Minister
Robert Borden declared that there would be no draft in Canada.
But as politicians often do, he changed his mind…and fed
a political crisis that haunted Canucks for years.*

SOME THINGS NEVER CHANGE

French-speaking Canadians have been fighting their English counterparts for centuries. (As early as 1624, the French and English battled for control of Lake Champlain.) And as far as the French Canadians were concerned, they never seemed to catch a break. So when World War I broke out in Europe and the prime minister called for a united front, French Canadians were in for yet another round of battles…abroad and at home.

Before World War I, Canada had little to do with what went on in Europe. But when a Bosnian Serb shot and killed Austria's archduke Francis Ferdinand in 1914, it ignited long-standing rivalries among the European nations and set into motion a system of alliances that led to war. England declared war on Germany, and Canada—the largest dominion in the British Empire—found itself drawn into the fight. Prime Minister Robert Borden announced, "When Great Britain is at war, Canada is at war." Most Canadians felt a strong kinship with their brethren across the Atlantic, and more than 30,000 signed up immediately to fight.

Those volunteers were mostly English speakers, though. French Canadians didn't have much loyalty to Great Britain or the English government in Ottawa because they often felt ignored. English representatives in Parliament always outnumbered French ones, and French issues typically took a backseat to other problems. Making things worse, in 1913, Canada's Conservative government passed Regulation 17, a law that banned teaching French in Ontario's schools after Grade 4. French Canadians were incensed. Still stinging from that insult, most of them chose to stay out of the fray when World War I began.

UNCLE BORDEN WANTS YOU!

The early years of the war were tough for Canada; 6,000 of its soldiers were killed or wounded in their first week on the front. And as time passed, things didn't get a lot better: Germany steamrolled into France, coming within 70 kilometers (43 miles) of Paris in just a few weeks. Soldiers choked on poison gas in Belgium, and German submarines attacked ships bringing Allied supplies from overseas. Still, between 1914 and 1916, support for the war remained strong in the English-speaking parts of Canada, with about 30,000 new volunteers enlisting every month.

But as the fighting dragged into 1917, casualties mounted, and Prime Minister Borden realized he wouldn't be able to keep the promise he made early on when he declared that there would be no draft (conscription). The British government now wanted Canada to raise an army of 500,000—about 7 percent of the country's entire population at the time. That would be almost impossible to do just with volunteers.

So in the summer of 1917, Borden proposed and Parliament passed a new law called the Military Service Act, which would allow the prime minister to reinforce Canadian units in Europe by conscripting 100,000 men. More importantly, it would draft them from all over Canada, in English-speaking areas…and in French-speaking ones.

NON THANKS

Most English-speaking Canadians accepted the new law without incident. But in Quebec, angry citizens smashed Montreal store windows, destroyed tram rails, and attacked police officers. In Quebec City, several people were wounded and one was killed during a mass demonstration.

In April 1918, a French Canadian was arrested in Quebec City for defying his conscription order. Residents took to the streets, and soldiers were called in to get things under control. According to one of them, "Rioters had put out the streetlamps; the Lower City was shrouded in mist and darkness…Suddenly, I could make out the fire of several heavy machine guns. It was deafening and gave the impression that a massacre was taking place." By the end of the protest, four people had died, and French Canadians were even more distrustful of the mostly English-speaking government.

The bear-shaped license plates of NWT are the only nonrectangular plates in North America.

WORLD POWER

By the time World War I ended in November 1918, about 66,000 Canadians had been killed and 172,000 wounded. But the conflict also cemented Canada's place as one of the world's major players. During the war, Canada had mobilized troops, raised money, and contributed supplies and weapons. Residents from east to west banded together as "Canadians" instead of "British subjects." And when the war was over, Canada was among the signatories of the Treaty of Versailles. No longer just a dominion of Great Britain, Canada was acting as its own country.

For French Canadians, though, the war just intensified their long-standing conflict with the English-speaking government. Borden's Conservative party lost all support in Quebec in the years after World War I, and French Canada further isolated itself from the goings-on in Ottawa.

"CONSCRIPTION IF NECESSARY"

But that wasn't the end of the story. Tensions flared again during World War II after Canada (now an independent nation) declared war on Germany. Early on, Prime Minister William Mackenzie King recognized that most Canadians were war-weary, so he vowed to keep the country as isolated as possible. Like Borden before him, King pledged, "No...conscription measure will be introduced by the present administration."

That didn't stop the volunteers. At the start of World War II, about 58,000 English-speaking Canadians heeded the call to duty. Another 85,000 signed up the following year. But by 1942, the Canadian army had taken heavy casualties, and King asked the country to let him take back his promise...just in case. He wasn't actually demanding conscription; he was just hedging his bets. King's slogan: "Conscription if necessary, but not necessarily conscription."

ATTACK OF THE ZOMBIES

Again, English-speaking Canadians mostly supported the policy—some 80 percent approved of it—and French Canadians were 73 percent against it. But since French Canadian representatives were outnumbered in Parliament, conscription passed...and angry French Canadians again took to the streets, protesting what they

World's first chiropractor: Toronto-born Daniel David Palmer

believed was government interference without adequate representation. This time, though, most of the protests were nonviolent, probably a result of King's diplomatic skills: he put off actually conscripting soldiers for as long as possible and consistently reassured the public that any draft would be only out of dire necessity.

That came in late 1944, after Canada lost large numbers of soldiers in France and Belgium. In November, King's government started calling up draftees (ridiculed as "zombies" or "the walking dead" at home because they hadn't volunteered to fight). Nearly 100,000 men—both French and English speakers—were sent to boot camps around the country, but fortunately, the war was almost over. By the time Germany and Japan surrendered in 1945, only about 12,000 conscripted Canadians had actually traveled to the front.

Despite the large number of casualties, World War II had many positive effects in Canada: the government passed sweeping laws aimed at aiding veterans, the country's economy boomed, and the important role Canada played in winning the war further solidified its place as a world power. But in French Canada, the people also held firm to their cultural identity and considered the 1917 and 1944 drafts just two more examples of their marginalized role in Canadian government. In the postwar years, Quebec rose economically, and the sovereignty movement gained support. And to this day, many of the people in Canada's French-speaking areas, especially in Quebec, remain "French Canadian" first and foremost.

* * *

NBA VS. NHL

Basketball was invented by a Canadian (Dr. James Naismith), and the NBA's two-time MVP and seven-time all-star Steve Nash grew up in British Columbia. But for the most part, the sport is dominated by Americans and Europeans. In 2009–10, there were just 20 Canadian players in the NBA…about 4 percent.

In the NHL, though, the balance falls the other way. Although just six of the league's 30 teams are based in Canada, about 400 of the 700 active players are Canadian: that's 58 percent.

During filming for Canada's first "talkie," *The Viking*, in 1931…

LORD STANLEY
TOPS THE CHARTS

Legend has it that Lord Frederick Stanley—yes, that Lord Stanley— landed on Canadian shores and, when he wasn't making political or sports history, cut a record. But the story of how and why he did it comes with lots of questions. Here's our investigation into an oft-told tale.

PLAY IT AGAIN, STAN

You probably already know some things about Lord Frederick Stanley, 16th Earl of Derby: he was the governor general of Canada from 1888 to 1893, he created the Stanley Cup, and many things are named after him. But have you heard the story about how he was Canada's first recording star?

Here's how that tale usually goes: On September 11, 1888, after Lord Stanley opened the Toronto Industrial Exhibition (now called the Canadian National Exhibition), he saw Thomas Edison's new cylinder phonograph while touring the exhibits. Impressed, he recorded this message for delivery to the U.S. president:

> Mr. President and gentlemen, the best use that I can make of this wonder of the age, the phonograph, is to bid you on behalf of the citizens of the dominion of Canada, a most hearty welcome, and to assure you that we are, at all times, most happy to meet our friends from the United States in the pursuit of song, of art, and all that may embellish the human life. We bid you a very hearty welcome.

Some say this was the first Canadian voice ever recorded. Others call it Canada's—or the world's—oldest surviving recording. Still others claim it's the world's second-oldest recording ever, topped only by Thomas Edison's ad-libbed recitation of "Mary Had a Little Lamb" in his New Jersey lab.

INSPECTING THE RECORD

But despite the broken-record repetition of this story, it has a lot of holes, so in 2005, Arthur Zimmerman, a writer for the Canadian Antique Phonograph Society (CAPS), decided to look into it. What he discovered answers many of the legends most frequently asked questions.

Was this actually Canada's first recording? No. On May 17, 1878, Edison (whose parents were *mostly* Canadian; his mother moved there in her teens) allowed a demonstration of his first primitive tinfoil cylinder recorder at Rideau Hall in Ottawa. According to an account from Library of Archives Canada, "The Earl of Dufferin [Ireland] and his guests spoke Greek and sang popular songs, and listened as the machine reproduced the sound of their voices." As with all tinfoil recordings, though, the Rideau Hall recordings were only good for a few plays; they didn't survive the over the years.

In addition, a few weeks before the Toronto Industrial Exhibition, a Canadian politician named Erastus Wiman recorded a speech for Edison's representatives to play at the fair.

Is it the oldest surviving recording of a human voice? Nope, it isn't that either. Edison's representatives had been busy in Europe during the summer of 1888, recording music and the voices of Queen Elizabeth, poet Robert Browning, politician William Gladstone, a choir, and others, some of which are still around today. Going further back, a lead-alloy cylinder made for a talking timepiece has been dated to about 1876, revealing the faint voice of inventor Frank Lambert intoning, "one o'clock…two o'clock… three o'clock…"

In 2008, scientists found a way to play sound waves that amateur French inventor Édouard-Léon Scott de Martinville had captured as squiggles on paper in 1860. The result was a 10-second clip of a woman singing "Au Clair de la Lune." However, Lord Stanley's short speech might be classified as "the oldest surviving recording of a Canadian voice."

Was Lord Stanley even at the Toronto Industrial Exhibition on September 11? Yes. He opened the exhibition with a short speech, but he probably didn't make a recording that day. CAPS author Zimmerman looked at contemporary newspaper accounts and Stanley's schedule for the day and concluded that Lord Stanley probably didn't even lay eyes on the phonograph on September 11. Not only was his schedule packed with activities that kept him from taking time to fully see the exhibits, the Edison machine hadn't been set up for exhibition on opening day.

Furthermore, reporters kept a close eye on the newly appointed

Mike Myers made his acting debut at age 12 on the CBC sitcom, *The King of Kensington.*

governor general and reported his activities in great detail. If he had done anything as exciting as recording his voice on a revolutionary new machine, there's no reason it wouldn't have been played up big in all of the Toronto newspapers. Instead, it wasn't mentioned at all.

Does the cylinder's label give any clues? Some clues, but also some red herrings. In 1935, sound technicians from Michigan State University made a re-creation of the actual cylinder Lord Stanley made at the exhibition. It's a good thing they did, because sometime after, the original cylinder disappeared and was never seen again. Luckily, the technicians noted a few details: somebody had written "Lord Stanley, 1888" on the box the cylinder was stored in, and there was a curator's card attached that added a wealth of misinformation: "Lord (Henry M.) Stanley. Greetings from Canada to the United States. 1888? Probably 1890 as it was then that he made his trip to this country."

But Lord Stanley wasn't Henry M. Stanley, the celebrated explorer who found the missing Dr. Livingstone in Africa. That Stanley had no connection to Canada—he was born in Wales and moved to New Orleans when he was a teen. Furthermore, when this recording was compared to known recordings of the explorer's voice, they weren't similar at all.

But the technicians also offered an offhand observation that may have helped crack the mystery: They noted that the recording was "a brown wax cylinder." That may sound like an irrelevant detail...unless you're a phonograph collector. Zimmerman noted that the only recordable cylinders available in 1888 were made of yellow wax—the harder, more durable brown wax didn't appear until March 1889...six months after the supposed recording date.

Was the recording ever presented to the U.S. president? There's no evidence that it was. In fact, there's no evidence that it was supposed to be, despite Lord Stanley's greeting to "Mr. President and gentlemen." After listening to the message again (and again and again), most historians have concluded that it wouldn't make sense for Stanley to bid "welcome" to a world leader who, if he managed to gain access to a phonograph, would be hearing it in his own office far away. You welcome people to your own turf; you don't welcome them to theirs. When that sinks in, consider that

Last time the RCMP used sled dogs: 1969.

in his official capacity, John J. Withrow, president of the Toronto Industrial Exhibition, would also be addressed as "Mr. President." Now, you're on to something...

So if he's talking in Toronto at a Canadian exhibition, why did Lord Stanley address his message to Americans? That mystery might be the one big clue that fixes the recording's time, place, and circumstances. Zimmerman's conclusion: Lord Stanley probably did record this message at the Toronto Industrial Exhibition—but later, near the exhibition's closing instead of at its opening.

Here's what we know: On September 17, 1891, Lord Stanley returned to the exhibition with a free schedule and the intention of seeing things at a leisurely pace. As he wandered the grounds, he was accompanied by Withrow and other dignitaries, and he was described in the next day's newspaper as "one of the most observant of the visitors who attended the exhibition." He stopped, asked questions, touched things, and tried them out. The governor general spent a lot of time in the main building, where Edison's phonograph was drawing crowds. And it just so happened that September 17 was designated "American Visitors' Day" at the exhibition.

Here's what we can reasonably surmise: Given the opportunity to hear his own voice for the first time on a cool new machine, wouldn't anybody jump at the opportunity? Edison was probably testing the new yellow-wax cylinders and invited Stanley to give it a try. But what should Lord Stanley say in his allotted moment? He certainly would assume that the Edison representatives would play his recording to American visitors throughout the day. So he likely began speaking in the manner he'd learned through years of political speeches: greeting the dignitaries in the room ("Mr. President [Withrow] and gentlemen..."), referring to the auspicious occasion with high-flying hyperbole expected by audiences of the day ("this wonder of the age, the phonograph..."), personalizing his message to the audience ("happy to meet our friends from the United States..."), and bidding them "a very hearty welcome" to Canada and its Toronto Industrial Exhibition. And then the recording took on a life (and legend) of its own.

That's probably what happened...or so say most historians nowadays. Do we know that it's absolutely true? Nope, it's just the most logical explanation; we'll probably never know for sure what really happened.

Canadian vaudevillian Thomas P. Kelley created the "pie in the face" comedy routine.

EAU CANADA!

*Eau de toilet, that is. To quench Uncle John's
thirst for information on all things bathroom,
we offer a few factoids of interest.*

• In 2000, a story in *Time* magazine reported on die-hard American water-wasters crossing the border to buy contraband toilets. In 1994, the U.S. passed a law saying that no American-made toilet could use more than six liters (1.6 gallons) of water per flush. But some people don't think those environmentally friendly toilets do the job; they say you have to flush two or three times to get everything to go down. Thank goodness for Canada, the sole high-flow holdout in the civilized world. Canada refused to ban high-flow potties and that has led to a black market in water-hogging 13-liter (3.5-gallon) toilets.

• Canadian filmmaker Ari Grief wondered what life would be like if he didn't have a toilet, so he sat down and thought about it. After years of thinking and research, he did what filmmakers do: in 2006, he released a satirical documentary called *FLUSH! or: How I Learned to Stop Worrying and Love the Toilet.*

• Fact from *FLUSH:* about one-third of the drinkable water used by Canadian families gets flushed down the toilet.

• A 2009 *New York Times* article noted that the American preference for ubersoft toilet paper results in the harvest of old-growth trees in Canada. Americans use an average of 23.6 rolls of soft toilet paper a year per person, the kind that requires long fibers from old trees and can't be found in recycled pulp.

• In 2005, Mr. Floatie—a man named James Skwarok dressed up as a two-meter (six-foot) turd—made the news after he was ruled to be "out of ordure" during a political forum in Victoria. He was there to protest the city's practice of dumping 120 million liters (31.7 million gallons) of raw sewage into the ocean every day. These days, Mr. Floatie continues to push for his cause, and even has his own fan club page on Facebook.

The first province to grant women the right to vote: Manitoba (1916).

I ♥ NUNAVUT

*Large area, small population, and the north magnetic pole—
here are 12 reasons you've just got love Nunavut.*

1. SIZE. Nunavut is huge: 2,093,190 square kilometers (808,185 square miles). If Nunavut were its own country, it would be the 15th largest in the world—just ahead of Mexico.

2. DENSITY. You have to admire a territory that makes Greenland look crowded. In fact, Greenland is about the same size and has twice the population per square kilometer as Nunavut. So how sparse is the territory, really? Each person in Nunavut could have 61 square kilometers (24 square miles) of land…and about 5 square kilometers (1.9 square miles) of water.

3. THE HISTORY. There's evidence that Nunavut's indigenous communities have lived there since 2000 BC. That's about the time that humans began domesticating horses, Egypt was gearing up for another wave of pyramid construction, ancestors of the Latin-speakers were moving into Italy, China entered its Bronze Age, and Britons were finishing Stonehenge.

4. DRY. When you think of Nunavut, you may imagine snowshoes, snowmen, snow mobiles, etc. But in reality, the territory is a polar desert. That means it gets less than 250 millimeters (9.8 inches) of precipitation every year.

5. TRILINGUAL ROAD SIGNS. In Nunavut, signs appear in English and the Inuit languages, Inuktitut, and Inuinnaqtun.

6. LOW TRAFFIC. While the rest of the world has gone car mad, the entire expanse of Nunavut has only about 850 kilometers (528 miles) of roads…a little less than a trip from Ottawa to Toronto and back again. Plus, the only car access to the outside world is an ice highway from the Northwest Territories—it's open for two months each year in February and March.

7. COOL RUNNING. If you're an marathoner who hates stumbling through the dark, a run in 24-hour sunlight might sound like

"Canada is the linchpin of the English-speaking world." —Winston Churchill

a great thing, even if it got pretty cold along the way. In 1978, the Baffin Island community of Arctic Bay (population 500) began staging the annual Nunavut Midnight Sun Marathon at the summer solstice. Running 84 kilometers (52 miles) in temperatures just a little above freezing is a challenge—apparently so much so that the race had a hard time getting competitors; it ceased a few years ago.

8. BASE JUMPING. Baffin Island is one of the world's premier spots for BASE jumping. The acronym stands for "buildings, antennae, spans (bridges), and earth (cliff)." Jumpers put on parachute suits (so they look a little like winged squirrels) and dive off of standing objects. It's like skydiving, but from a lower altitude. Baffin Island has lots of cliffs ranging in size from 900 to 1,200 meters (3,000 to 3,900 feet) high, perfect spots for BASE jumpers from around the world.

9. INUKSHUK. The rock creature pictured on Nunavut's flag is an *inukshuk*, a group of stones piled together to resemble a person. In ancient times, inukshuk served as markers in a land with few natural landmarks; the whimsical-looking rock people marked trails, located significant places, and pointed out good fishing spots.

10. ICE GOLFING. Instead of playing on greens like regular golf, ice golfers play on whites. The Frobisher Bay Golf and Country Club builds its 18-hole ice golf course each winter in the middle of the bay near Nunavut's capital city, Iqaluit. Since golf balls are hard to see on the ice and they freeze rock-hard in extreme cold, ice duffers tee up with brightly colored tennis balls instead.

11. TOONIK TYME. If you get to Iqaluit after the Frobisher Bay ice golf course has started to melt, you can always hit Toonik Tyme, a low-key spring festival that features Inuit sports, music, sled races, crafts, ice carving, and igloo making. Its name comes from the Tunit people, an indigenous group that migrated to Nunavut 1,000 years ago and who are the ancestors of the modern Inuit.

12. ALERT. At the tiptop of Nunavut and recognized as the northernmost permanently inhabited place in the world is the

Canada was the second nation, after Denmark, to pass legislation against slavery.

town of Alert, just 817 kilometers (508 miles) from the North Pole. It's an old Canadian military base set up in the 1950s to monitor the weather, spy on the Russians, reinforce Canada's land claims, and do other mysterious military and intelligence things. The 2006 census listed Alert's population as five, a gross underestimation; the *Canadian Encyclopedia* reports "the military continues to use the base year-round, but does not reveal the number of men or the technology present at the site for reasons of security."

* * *

(DUMB) AMERICANS ON CANADA

"The cool thing about being famous is traveling. I have always wanted to travel across seas, like to Canada and stuff."
—**Britney Spears**

"I want to thank all the Canadians who came out today to wave to me—with all five fingers!"
—**President George W. Bush**

"Congratulations, Canada, on becoming part of North America!"
—**Anonymous American, featured on the 2001 TV show *Talking to Americans***

"Americans know as much about Canada as straight people do about gays. Americans arrive at the border with skis in July."
—**Scott Thompson, comedian**

"When they said Canada, I thought it was up in the mountains somewhere."
—**Marilyn Monroe**

"The Unanimous Voice of the Continent is 'Canada must be ours; Quebec must be taken.'"
—**President John Adams**

"I've been to Canada, and I've always gotten the impression that I could take the country over in about two days."
—**Jon Stewart**

Apollo 11, the first craft to land on the moon, was equipped with Canadian-made landing gear.

THE VANISHED VILLAGES, PART II

On page 327, we told you about the construction of the St. Lawrence Seaway. Before it could be built, though, 10 innocent towns had to die.

GRAND OPENING

On June 26, 1959, cheering crowds lined the shores of the St. Lawrence River, while Queen Elizabeth and U.S. president Dwight Eisenhower waited aboard the royal yacht *Britannia* for an icebreaker to clear away any remains of winter. They were celebrating the official grand opening of the St. Lawrence Seaway. (The unofficial grand opening was on April 25.) Finally, the boat sounded its whistle and a slow-moving parade of yachts and ships ambled upstream, followed by 30 freighters ready to do business.

Despite all the hoopla, there were quite a few people on the Canadian shore who might've had mixed feelings. They were the former residents of the villages swallowed up by the project. In the coming days, as they followed news reports of freighters reaching the locks at Lake St. Lawrence, they may have thought back to their hometowns, which now rested below its waters: the streets, homes, schools, businesses, and even the graves of former residents.

DISPLACED PERSONS

A big event—or sometimes just the march of time—has a way of displacing people. The American Revolution displaced Britain's Loyalists. They fled across the Canadian border toward land that had become available to them by the displacement of the First Nation peoples. After crossing the St. Lawrence River into Canada, most of the Loyalist refugees continued north, but some of them didn't. They decided to put down roots in Quebec and Ontario just a wave and a shout from their old homeland, creating a string of villages next to some powerful rapids. Those towns survived some 175 years before the settlers' descendants were likewise displaced, this time by the needs of international commerce.

Canada's first gas station was in Vancouver (1907).

Even now, more than half a century after the 10 villages were flooded, you can still see traces of the underwater ghost towns. What were once small hills outside the towns are now a string of islands connected by bridges that mimic Highway 2, which once ran between the towns. When the water level falls, campers and boaters report seeing murky sidewalks, roads, and foundations below the surface. Scuba divers get an even closer view. Let's take a look at those towns.

A VISIT TO THE VILLAGES

• The flood displaced 900 inhabitants of **Mille Roches**, the easternmost and busiest of the lost villages. In the early 1830s, it was a thriving mill town, with a marble works and a nearby limestone quarry that may have been the reason for its name, which means "thousand rocks" in French. Mille Roches reached peak prosperity around the beginning of the 20th century, when a nearby canal was enlarged to include a dam and power plant with four turbines. Even though the town lies deepest in the water—some 12 meters (40 feet) below the surface—when the light is just right, its outline can still be seen. Divers who venture down can explore the old turbines and brick arches of the power plant.

• **Moulinette** was just upstream from Mille Roches. Founded in the early 1800s, the town was home to water-powered mills that sawed wood, ground grains, and beat wool into yarn. (In fact, the town's name means "little mill.") In later years, the village had a bustling tourist trade, too: two hotels, a motel, and a group of rental cabins near the railway track. Before the deluge, Moulinette had 311 inhabitants.

• **Wales** was first called Dickinson's Landing Station, after the Grand Trunk Railroad came through in 1856, just 1.6 kilometers (one mile) north of the town of Dickinson's Landing. But on an 1860 visit, the Prince of Wales wondered out loud why such a little town had such a long name, so after he left, the town changed its name to Wales. Before the deluge, it served as an agricultural center with a busy railroad stockyard surrounded by a gristmill, an egg-grading station, and a hatchery. The Connelly Hotel became famous during the 1890s for its annual New Year's ball, which attracted as many as 500 people, some of whom danced all night

"RRC" on the loonie's "tails" side stands for Robert Ralph Carmichael, the coin's designer.

until the last train left at 5:12 a.m. Wales was located pretty far inland, so some of the town stayed above the flood line. The foundation of St. David's Anglican Church can still be seen on Wales Island, which was named to commemorate the vanished community.

• **Dickinson's Landing** was probably the oldest village, settled in the 1600s as a trading post by the French explorer Robert de La Salle. The town was named for Massachusetts-born Barnabus Dickinson, who established a local mail delivery route in the early 1800s. Until the end, the town had a prosperous cheese factory, a distillery, and a popular racetrack. Its lighthouse was saved and relocated to Upper Canada Village Historical Park.

• The hamlets of **Woodlands** and **Santa Cruz** were so small that they shared a one-room schoolhouse until 1957. The industry in Woodlands was mostly agricultural, a few orchards and a large apiary, until the automobile age changed things. From then on, both Woodlands' and Santa Cruz's main industry was enticing tourists to stop over while traveling between Toronto and Montreal.

• **Sheek Island**, sometimes called "Sheik's Island," was named after David Sheek, who leased the land from the Mohawks in 1806. Like the other villages, it was mostly agricultural with some tourism. In 1956, under pressure from the impending flood, University of Toronto archaeologists conducted excavations in Sheek Island and tentatively identified what they believed were remnants of a 3,500-year-old civilization. The university petitioned for a delay in the seaway project so that excavations could be completed, but its plea was ignored, and the project went ahead.

• In its prime, the tiny hamlet of **Maple Grove** consisted of Ernie's Hotel (14 rooms, a men-only bar, and no running water), a flour mill, sawmill, carriage shop, gas station, and the stateliest home in the area: the French-Robertson House, which was moved to Upper Canada Village Historical Park. The 317 remains in Maple Grove's cemetery were moved to a cemetery near Cornwall.

• **Farran's Point** had a population of 300 in the mid-1800s. By the end of the century, the village was home not only to mills of all sorts but also to general stores, taverns, blacksmiths, tinsmiths, livery stables, marble works, and hotels. The town had two churches, and all that remained of the town when it went under

Gabriel Dumont, Louis Riel's right-hand man, once rode in Buffalo Bill's Wild West Show.

were those two churches and a few stores. The water is shallow there, though, and you can still see portions of the old sidewalks when the water level is low during the fall and winter.

• Originally named Charlesville (for reasons unknown), the town was renamed **Aultsville** for the multigenerational family of entrepreneurs and politicians who helped build it from a tiny settlement in the late 1700s to what has been described as the prettiest and most important of the riverside villages. The town's brickworks made crocks, pots, and jugs from riverbank clay—not to mention bricks for houses. Besides those brick homes, the town's population of 400 people left behind a few factories, three churches, two schools, and a poultry farm. Portions of the town remained above the flood line and remnants of sidewalks and foundations can be found near the shore when the water level is low. The underwater area is popular with divers, particularly the spot around the factory's dump, where amateur explorers can unearth all kinds of "valuable" junk.

*　*　*

SMALL CANADA

• Quest University in Squamish, British Columbia, is the smallest university in Canada. It has just 220 students.

• The smallest known dinosaur in North America was found near Red Deer, Alberta. *Albertonykus borealis* was a long-legged, birdlike but flightless dinosaur that lived about 70 million years ago. It was the size of a chicken and weighed just a few kilos.

• The smallest jailhouse in Canada (and in North America) is in the town of Rodney, Ontario. Built in 1890, it measures about 15 by 20 feet, and holds two tiny cells. It serves as a tourist attraction today.

• The smallest city is Greenwood, British Columbia. It's located on Highway #3 in the Kootenay Boundary region (the interior border region with the United States), was incorporated in 1897, and has a population of 625.

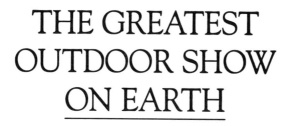

THE GREATEST OUTDOOR SHOW ON EARTH

*Sure, Calgary hosted the Winter Olympics in 1988,
and yes, it led Canada's oil boom in the early 1900s.
But what Calgary's really famous for is its
over-the-top homage to the Wild West.*

PARTY LIKE IT'S 1912

Called the "Greatest Outdoor Show on Earth," the annual Calgary Stampede lasts for 10 days every July. The city's stores and businesses decorate with Western themes. The "put your head in a hat campaign" awards valuable prizes to cowpokes wearing their Stetsons. Hungry visitors line up for a free all-you-can-eat flapjack, sausage, and bacon breakfast served from the back of a chuck wagon. Horse-drawn rigs give free city tours. One visitor even reported looking up at a skyscraper and seeing a horse riding in its glass elevator.

Calgary has been "Stampeding" for nearly a century. Though the festival celebrates all things Western, it was a fast-talking guy from New York who started it all. Born in Rochester in 1885, Guy Weadick left home and headed west when he was a teenager. After working as a cowboy, he got a job as a stunt rider and a trick roper with various Wild West shows in the United States and Europe before he began performing in Alberta.

But Weadick wanted more. So in 1912, he convinced Calgary cattle barons George Lane, Alfred Cross, Archie McLean, and Patrick Burns (known today as the "Big Four") to invest in his big dream: a world-class rodeo that celebrated the Wild West and a way of life that was already nearly gone.

Weadick's backers spared no expense. The first Stampede started with a parade that featured English nobility (the Duke and Duchess of Connaught) as grand marshals and included 2,000 natives on horseback. Prizes for the rodeo events totaled

When John Molson began brewing in 1786, a bottle of his beer cost 5¢.

$16,000, the richest purse ever seen at the time. Nearly 14,000 people showed up on foot, on horseback, or by train to see that first Stampede, and it was such a hit that by 1923 it was an annual event.

ROPE AND RIDE

These days, the Calgary Stampede is still a huge success. The city's merchants call the event "Christmas in July," and millions turn out for it every year. Calgary still holds a Parade Day, just like it did in 1912. Only now, the parade includes marching bands, elaborate floats, and celebrities. Native communities also still attend and perform at the Stampede, and one of the most popular exhibits is the First Nations Village, in which five tribes—the Siksika, Stoney, Blood, T'suu Tina, and Piikani—sing, dance, pose for pictures, and answer questions. It's the largest meeting of the First Nations peoples in all of Canada.

With all that, it might seem that the rodeo itself is neglected. Not so. The Stampede consistently ranks among the world's top rodeos, and since 2006, participation in the professional events comes by invitation only. The prize money is rich—in 2009, the Stampede awarded $2 million in prizes.

In 2006, Calgary introduced a tournament-style rodeo for its six major events: bareback bronc riding, saddled bronc riding, barrel racing, bull riding, tie-down roping, and steer wrestling. Cowboys compete during the week, and the top performers move on to Showdown Sunday, a.k.a. "Rodeo's Richest Afternoon," held on the rodeo's last Sunday. In 2009, the top prize for each event winner on Showdown Sunday was $100,000. How much does that mean to a cowboy? Competitors in the bucking bronc competition, for example, must stay on for eight seconds…which means the winner makes $12,500 a second.

HALF MILE OF HELL

The biggest prize of all, though, is reserved for the centerpiece of the celebration, a chuck wagon race called the Rangeland Derby, another brainchild of Guy Weadick. In the early 1900s, chuck wagons were like mobile restaurants that traveled out to ranches to feed the cowboys. Few people thought of them as fit for speed, but Weadick wanted to race them. He came up with the idea for a

chuck wagon event after watching some actual wagons race each other from a ranch to a saloon—with the losers buying the drinks.

For the 1923 Stampede, Weadick persuaded a group of local ranchers to enter their chuck wagons and compete for a prize of $275. He called the race the Rangeland Derby, and the fast-moving, dust-throwing event immediately became a crowd pleaser. A stagecoach driver from the Yukon won the first race. Today, 36 crews race their chuck wagons to compete for a purse of more than $1 million. The crews consist of a driver, four horses, and four outriders, and the wagons are fully loaded with a stove and other cooking supplies to simulate the weight of real chucks on the range. The course is an 800-meter (half-mile) track with tight curves, obstacles, a figure-eight, and limited space. Although safety measures have been introduced over the years, five men and 22 horses have died since the Rangeland Derby began. And because the race is so dangerous, it's known as "the Half Mile of Hell."

CALGARY CONTROVERSIES
Despite the food, shows, and exciting races, not everyone loves the Calgary Stampede. The most vocal protesters are animal-rights activists who claim that the rodeo is cruel. Since 1986, the Humane Society of Canada has documented more than 40 animal deaths linked directly to Stampede events. In 2009, the organization filed a complaint to stop the government from sponsoring the Stampede's television broadcast. It's against Canada's laws to glamorize cruelty to animals, and Humane Society CEO Michael O'Sullivan said, "Our fascination with the Old West makes these animals pay a terrible price." Still, the event was broadcast on the CBC as planned in 2009.

In addition to the debate over animals, some critics dislike the Stampede's effect on humans. Karen Stewart, founder of a mediation group called Fairway Divorce Solutions, said she sees as much as a 40 percent jump in the number of people filing for divorce in the weeks after the Calgary Stampede. Stewart says that the party atmosphere, the abundance of alcohol, and the fact that people look awfully attractive under a Stetson lead some folks to stray from their vows. She claims too many people follow a Calgary saying that goes, "It's not cheatin'. It's just Stampedin'." Yee-haw!

THE CROSS-DRESSING SPY

A woman disguised as a man disguised as a woman?
It sounds like the plot of a lost Shakespeare play.

OH, BOY…IT'S A GIRL

From the moment that Sarah Emma Edmonds emerged from the womb, she was a disappointment to her parents, especially her father. Born in 1841 in Magaguadavic, New Brunswick, Sarah made the unforgivable mistake of being born a female—just like her four older sisters. Her father had been hoping for a boy to help with the farmwork.

Most fathers who want sons get over their disappointment and soon discover the joys that daughters can bring. But not in this case. According to Sarah's memoir, her father was verbally and physically abusive, and her mother wasn't all that nurturing either.

Not that Sarah didn't try. From an early age, she dressed and acted like a boy, helping her father with heavy labor in the fields. But if they couldn't have a son, what her parents really wanted was a son-in-law—and as soon as possible. They pressured Sarah to marry and, to speed the process along, chose a boy they liked and started the process of organizing a wedding. Fed up, 15-year-old Sarah Edmonds decided to run away from home.

CLOTHES MAKE THE MAN

Packing for her escape suggested a strategy. Edmonds didn't have a lot of petticoats and dresses, anyway, so for comfort and safety on the road, she decided to present herself to the outside world as a boy. Taking the name Franklin Thompson, she traveled through New Brunswick and New England. By 1861, "Frank" was peddling Bibles door-to-door in Flint, Michigan.

In May 1861, Edmonds joined the Second Michigan Infantry of the Union army as Franklin Thompson. By then—it was during the U.S. Civil War—the army was just looking for warm bodies; new recruits didn't even have to take physicals. In August, she

In B.C., it's illegal to kill a sasquatch.

was assigned to mail duty at the Second Battle of Bull Run. On a mail delivery, she and her mule fell into a ditch. Even though she suffered internal injuries, she stayed away from the infirmary, depending on a half-dozen friends to cover her mail duties and nurse her back to health. (Other diaries from the time indicate that at least two men knew her secret, including one who became her wartime lover.)

BEYOND THE CALL OF DUTY

Edmonds served as a "male" nurse through several more major battles until she volunteered to spy for the North to replace a spy who'd been found out by the Confederates and executed. According to Edmonds, she went on 11 missions behind enemy lines in Richmond, Virginia. Historians argue this point: some accept her figure of 11, but others suggest that the true figure might be as few as two or even none. (For lack of evidence to disprove it, and because it's the better story, we'll go with her account.)

She became a master of disguise, which isn't surprising since she'd already had plenty of practice. She walked into the Confederacy camp at various times disguised as a white woman named Bridget O'Shea, a white man, a black woman, and a black man named Cuff. The latter two identities were accomplished by painting her skin with silver nitrate and wearing curly black wigs borrowed from a minstrel show. While working in the camp's kitchen, hospital, or laundry, she kept her eyes and ears open. Once, while disguised as a black laundress, she pocketed some crucial papers that an officer had forgotten to remove from his jacket.

MISSING IN ACTION

In 1863, Edmonds went AWOL. According to her memoir, she had contracted malaria and checked herself into a private hospital to protect her identity as a man. When she tried to return to duty, she saw posters listing Frank Thompson as a deserter. Instead of turning herself in—and risking a date with the firing squad—she fled. The diary she kept at the time, however, tells a different story: her lover was being discharged from the army and she wanted to go with him.

Whatever the case, she ended up in Washington, D.C., as a nurse—female this time—caring for wounded soldiers at a hospital

The West Edmonton Mall covers an area about the size of 104 Canadian football fields.

run by the United States Christian Commission, a government agency affiliated with the YMCA. It was during these years that she also somehow managed to dash off her memoir, *Nurse and Spy in the Union Army.* Rushed into print in 1865, the book sold more than 175,000 copies.

STRANGER THAN FICTION

When the war ended in 1865, Edmonds returned to New Brunswick, where she married a carpenter name Linus Seelye. But she was still upset about being branded an army deserter. So in the mid-1880s, Edmonds wrote to the U.S. War Department and to Congress, telling them her story and explaining the circumstances that caused her to leave her post. She received the following reply from the American government:

> Truth is ofttimes stranger than fiction, and now comes the sequel, Sarah E. Edmonds, now Sarah E. Seelye, alias Franklin Thompson, is now asking this Congress to grant her relief by way of a pension on account of fading health, which she avers [declares] had its incurrence and is the sequence of the days and nights she spent in the swamps of the Chickahominy [River, in Virginia] in the days she spent soldiering.

> That Franklin Thompson and Mrs. Sarah E. E. Seelye are one and the same person is established by abundance of proof and beyond a doubt. She submits a statement…and also the testimony of ten credible witnesses, men of intelligence, holding places of high honor and trust, who positively swear she is the identical Franklin Thompson.

In July 1884, the charges of desertion were dropped, and the vindicated Sarah Edmonds Seelye was awarded a military pension of $12 a month. She moved to LaPorte, Texas, where she died in 1898.

* * *

GOLD MEDAL RATINGS

How big was the 2010 Olympics gold-medal hockey match between Canada and the U.S.? An estimated 26.6 million Canadians (80 percent of the *entire* country) watched at least part of the game in which Sidney Crosby won the gold for Canada during a nail-biter that went into overtime.

Actor Christopher Plummer is the great-grandson of 1890s PM Sir John Abbott.

BIG FEATS

People can do incredible things. Consider these accomplishments.

MAN IN MOTION
Who: Rick Hansen
What: Wheelchaired through 34 countries

The story: After a car accident in 1973 left 15-year-old Rick Hansen paralyzed from the waist down, he adopted the motto "Anything is possible"...and he wasn't kidding. Within a few years of the accident, Hansen became the first person with a physical disability to earn a physical education degree from the University of British Columbia. He also competed in international track events, and won 19 wheelchair marathons between 1979 and 1984.

After winning the Lou Marsh Award in 1983 for Canada's most outstanding athlete—an award he shared with Wayne Gretzky—Hansen decided he needed a new challenge. So in 1985, he headed south out of Vancouver on what would become a two-year, record-setting wheelchair tour. Wheeling more than 120 kilometers (75 miles) per day through all kinds of weather, bad road conditions, illness, and injuries to his arms, shoulders, and wrists, Hansen headed east, crossing the United States, Great Britain, Europe, New Zealand, Australia, Asia, the Far East, and then Canada in the dead of winter. He ended up spanning 34 different countries and traveled enough miles to more than circle the globe. In the process, he raised more than $26 million for spinal cord injury research.

DEEP, VERY DEEP
Who: Mandy-Rae Cruickshank
What: World champion free diver

The story: Ever tried swimming across a pool without taking a breath? Vancouverite Mandy-Rae Cruickshank takes that to an extreme. In 2000, she was introduced to the sport of free diving, in which athletes compete by holding their breath underwater for distance and depth. There are a variety of categories in the sport,

and Cruickshank has set 12 national records and seven world records. Her specialty: the "constant ballast," in which contestants jump into the water wearing weights. The idea is to strap on enough weight to take you deep, but not so much that you can't swim back to the surface before you run out of air. Today, Cruickshank holds the record in the "constant ballast—fins" category (88 meters, 289 feet). You say you can't stay under the surface for at least six minutes at a time, yet hope to beat Cruickshank? All we say is: Don't hold your breath.

GREAT LAKE, GREAT SWIMMER

Who: Marilyn Bell

What: Swam Lake Ontario

The story: Marilyn Bell was only 16 in 1954, but she knew when Canada was being slighted. The Canadian National Exhibition (CNE) was opening in Toronto, and for publicity, it paid an American long-distance swimmer named Florence Chadwick $10,000 to swim the 51.5 kilometers (32 miles) across Lake Ontario. True, Chadwick was probably worth the money; she'd not only swum the English Channel in both directions, but broke the world records each way. Still, Bell—a pretty good swimmer herself—believed a Canadian should've been given a chance to try. So she decided to give the swim a shot herself, for free.

On September 9, 1954, both women entered the water at Youngstown, New York. Chadwick started vomiting and complaining of stomach pains after several hours, and gave up. But the plucky teen underdog continued on, battling cold weather, 5-meter (16-foot) waves, and lamprey eels that sucked on her arms and legs.

The next day, after 21 hours of swimming, Bell reached a breakwater west of the CNE grounds. Newspapers reported that 300,000 people cheered when she reached shore. The CNE, having gotten much more publicity than it ever expected, paid Bell $10,000 and showered her with expensive gifts: a car, a TV, clothing, and furniture. The next year, she became the youngest person to swim the English Channel. Bell retired from swimming in 1956, got married, and moved to New Jersey.

Longest Canadian place name: Pekwachnamaykoskwaskwaypinwanik Lake in Manitoba.

DOWNHILL BATTLE

Who: Lauren Woolstencroft

What: Paralympic gold medalist

The story: Being born without legs below the kneecaps, and without a left arm below her elbow, didn't keep Woolstencroft from hitting the ski slopes at an early age. At 14, she entered her first skiing competition. Six years later, she was representing Canada at the 2002 Paralympic Winter Games, where she brought home two gold medals and a bronze. Woolstencroft went on to win a gold and silver at the 2006 Paralympic Winter Games, earned the Paralympic Sport Awards 2007 Best Female Athlete, and earned a Crystal Globe as the winner of the World Cup overall champion in 2008.

WALKING TALL

Who: Jack Gillis

What: First person to walk across Canada

The story: Jack Gillis began his trek across Canada on a dare. Starting from Nova Scotia on January 31, 1906, Gillis and two buddies intended to walk to San Francisco and back within one year. It didn't quite work out that way. In Montreal, his two friends gave up the quest, but Gillis met a hiker, former lacrosse player Charles Jackman, and they decided to head to Vancouver instead. At midnight on September 24, 1906, the two self-described "transcontinental pedestrians" arrived and were greeted by a cheering crowd as they entered the city.

Gillis's accomplishments didn't end with that long walk, though. He set a national record in the shot put in 1908 and became the Canadian all-around track and field champion, but died of tuberculosis in 1913. In 2006, Jack Gillis was inducted into the British Columbia Sports Hall of Fame.

* * *

LONGEST-SERVING PRIME MINISTERS

21 years: William Lyon McKenzie King (1921–30, 1935–48)

19 years: John A. Macdonald (1867–73, 1878–91)

15.5 years: Pierre Trudeau (1968–79, 1980–84)

15 years: Wilfrid Laurier (1896–1911)

10 years: Jean Chrétien (1993–2003)

The National Film Board of Canada is the world's largest government film agency.

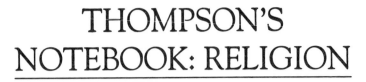

THOMPSON'S NOTEBOOK: RELIGION

*Before Europeans arrived in Canada, the old religions of the native people
thrived. Each had its own myths, and some, as explorer David Thompson
discovered, sounded a lot like the Christian ones he was used to. The
following account comes from Thompson's observations about
the Nahathaway tribe he met while exploring Alberta.*

AN OTTER, A BEAVER, AND A MUSKRAT WALK AWAY FROM A FLOOD...

"They [the Nahathaway] have some tradition of the deluge, as may be seen from the following account related by the old men. After the Great Spirit made mankind and all the animals, he told Weesarkejauk [a spiritual being] to take care of them and teach them how to live, and not to eat of bad roots that would hurt and kill them.

But he did not mind the Great Spirit; became careless and incited them to pleasure, Mankind and the animals did as they pleased, quarreled, and shed much blood. This made the Great Spirit very angry, and he told Weesarkejauk that he would take everything from him and wash the ground clean; but he did not believe until the Rivers and Lakes rose very high and overflowed the ground for it was always raining; and the Keeche Gahme [the Sea] came on the land, and every man and animal were drowned, except one Otter, one Beaver, and one Musk Rat.

Weesarkejauk tried to stop the sea, but it was too strong for him. He sat on the water crying for his loss, and the Otter, the Beaver, and the Musk Rat rested their heads on one of his thighs.

SENDING ANIMALS TO DO A MAN'S JOB

"After musing a long time upon his sad condition, he thought if he could get a bit of the old ground he could make a little island of it, for he has the power of extending, but not creating anything.

All lay buried under the water to an unknown depth. In this sad state, as he sat floating on the water he told the three animals

that they would starve unless he could get a bit of the old ground from under the water, of which he would make a fine Island for them. Addressing himself to the Otter, and praising him for his courage, strength and activity, he persuaded the Otter to dive and bring up a bit of earth.

The Otter came up without having reached the ground: by praises, Weesarkejauk got the Otter to make two more attempts, but without success and so much exhausted he could do no more. Weesarkejauk called him a coward of a weak heart, and said that the Beaver would put him to shame: then, speaking to the Beaver, praised his strength and wisdom and promised to make him a good house for winter. The Beaver made two attempts without success, and came up so tired that Weesarkejauk had to let him repose a long time. Then, promising him a wife if he brought up a bit of earth, told him to try a third time; to obtain a wife, he boldly went down and stayed so long that he came up almost lifeless.

MUSKRAT LOVE

"Weesarkejauk was now very sad, for what the active Otter and strong Beaver could not do, he had little hopes the Musk Rat could do. But this was his only resource: He now praised the Musk Rat and promised him plenty of roots to eat, with rushes and earth to make himself a house; the Otter and the Beaver he said were fools, and lost themselves, and he would find the ground if he went straight down.

Thus encouraged, he dived and came up, but brought nothing; after reposing, he went down a second time, and stayed a long time. On coming up, Weesarkejauk examined his fore paws and found they had the smell of earth, and showing this to the Musk Rat, promised to make him a wife who should give him a great many children and become more numerous than any other animal. Telling him to have a strong heart; and go direct down.

The Musk Rat went down the third time and stayed so long that Weesarkejauk feared he was drowned. At length seeing some bubbles come up, he put down his long arm and brought up the Musk Rat, almost dead, but—to his great joy—with a piece of earth between his fore paws and his breast.

This he seized, and in a short time extended it to a little island, on which they all reposed. Some say Weesarkejauk procured a bit

of wood, from which he made the Trees, and from bones, he made the animals; but the greater number deny this, and say the Great Spirit renovated Mankind, the Animals, and the Trees; in proof of which, the Great Spirit deprived him [Weesarkejauk] of all authority over Mankind and the animals, and he has since had only the power to flatter and deceive."

* * *

NAME THAT PLATE

Quick! Before the Mounties pull you over…identify the province or territory that uses each license plate slogan.

 1. "Canada's Ocean Playground"

 2. "Confederation Bridge"

 3. "Canada's Green Province"

 4. "I Remember"

 5. "Yours to Discover"

 6. "Friendly" (Used to be "100,000 Lakes…")

 7. "Land of Living Skies"

 8. "Wild Rose Country"

 9. "Beautiful…"

 10. "The Klondike"

Bonus!

11. Which two provinces or territories have the same slogan—"Explore Canada's Arctic"—and a license place shaped like a bear?

12. Which province or territory has no license plate slogan?

Answers: 1. Nova Scotia, **2.** Prince Edward Island, **3.** New Brunswick, **4.** Quebec, **5.** Ontario, **6.** Manitoba, **7.** Saskatchewan, **8.** Alberta, **9.** British Columbia, **10.** Yukon, **11.** Northwest Territories and Nunavut, **12.** Newfoundland and Labrador

Neil Young's father, Scott, is in the Hockey Hall of Fame…as a writer.

WEIRD CANADA

Americans are typically the ones who do ridiculous things that make the news. But these Canadians just couldn't help themselves.

HI MOM!

The seven Blair sisters of Hamilton, Ontario, were eating Thanksgiving dinner when they realized something was wrong. Lisa noticed first: there were gray flecks in her mashed potatoes. Then the others saw it too...in the gravy, on the turkey. The sisters initially worried about disease or food poisoning—before they realized what had really happened: Each of them wore a locket containing some of the ashes of their mother, who had died just a few days before. The lockets, which were supposed to have been sealed at the funeral home, were leaking. Said Lisa Blair, "I'm wearing a white sweater, and not only was it in my food, it was all down the front of my white sweater...I just feel like my mum has no dignity." (And on top of that, Thanksgiving was ruined.)

ISN'T IT IRONIC?

Dr. Hulda Clark had some wacky ideas about cancer treatment. After earning a couple of degrees from the University of Saskatchewan in 1949 and 1950, she moved to the United States, where she set up an alternative-medicine practice that urged patients to forego chemotherapy in favor of naturopathic remedies. Her most controversial treatment: a battery-operated "zapper" that supposedly zapped cancer and other diseases from the body and cured patients. Dr. Clark died in 2009...from cancer.

FALSE ADVERTISING

In 2009, Alberta came up with a new provincial motto—"Freedom to Create, Spirit to Achieve"—and the PR materials showed two ruddy-faced, smiling children playing on a pristine beach. Sure, Alberta is landlocked, but it has lakes...right? Not according to Peter Bailey's dad. Bailey moved to Alberta as a kid, and his father sold the family's sailboat because, as he put it, "there's no water in Alberta." Inspired by the seaside scene, Bailey wrote to the provincial government to get the location of that wonderful beach. It turned out that Bailey had quite a journey ahead of him. The

Canadian aboriginals gained the right to vote in 1960.

beach in the photo wasn't in Alberta at all; it was in Northumberland, United Kingdom. The kids weren't Canadian either, leading to outrage among Albertans who thought their land and kids should've been featured in the ad. And what was the government's response to the uproar? Tom Olsen, official Alberta spokesperson, claimed that the British beach and kids showed that "Albertans are a worldly people." Right.

FAUX PAS

In an attempt to foster unity and understanding with the province of Quebec, the Canadian government decreed that all of its soldiers assigned to NORAD—the North American Aerospace Defense Command—should learn French. (In addition to tracking Santa Claus on Christmas Eve, NORAD is responsible for protecting the skies above Canada and the United States.) The catch? Quebec's French schools didn't seem up to the task, so the folks in Ottawa hired an American team to do the teaching. (The Quebecois were insulted.)

TECHNICALLY IT'S AN ALIBI

In August 2009, police in Deer Lake, Newfoundland, arrested three boys for animal cruelty. According to the cops, the boys had beaten a moose until it died. The boys swore they didn't do it, and got some help from one of their fathers. The man said there was absolutely no way the boys could have attacked the moose. Why? They'd been vandalizing a local church when the attack happened.

WHERE ARE WE AGAIN?

Dutch travelers Joannes Rutten and his grandson wanted to visit Sydney, Australia, for their 2009 summer vacation. Yet somehow, when Rutten booked the tickets, he missed the fact that he was ordering them for Sydney, Nova Scotia, instead. Rutten didn't realize his error until after the two had made their connection in Halifax, but when they arrived, Air Canada employees were ready to help. The airline put them up in a hotel free of charge and then flew them back to Holland the next day. But the really weird part is that they weren't the first to make the mistake. Air Canada says that at least two other parties have flown to Nova Scotia when they meant to vacation in Oz.

19th-century Nova Scotian writer Thomas Chandler Haliburton coined the phrases...

MILLION-DOLLAR NAMES, PART III

It makes sense: you build a company and you want to put your name on it. Here are a few more stories of people whose names are familiar, even if they aren't.

EATON'S

At one time, Eaton's department stores were in every major Canadian city. The company also reached into rural homes with its "Family Bible" catalogs. But whatever became of the beloved retail institution that began in 1869 when Timothy Eaton opened a Toronto dry-goods store at 178 Yonge Street?

The first store was on the small side, but it had very large intentions. Measuring just 7.3 x 18.3 meters (about 24 x 60 feet), the store advertised "sound goods, good styles, and good value." By 1883, it had moved to bigger digs down the block, and was the first store in Toronto with an elevator and telephone. (At the time, though, there were so few phones in the city that the store's number was just three digits: 370). Through its catalog, Eaton's offered everything you could possibly need to live a comfortable life—from clothes and appliances to farm equipment and seeds...even prefabricated homes. With all that going for it, the company continued to grow, and by 1911, its employees totaled 17,500.

But unfortunately, simply being born with the Eaton name did not guarantee the business acumen of the original. Timothy and his son John Craig made the Eaton's empire, but by the early 1970s, subsequent relatives had a series of missteps and Eaton's was in trouble. To save money, it discontinued its famous catalog, closed stores, and stopped sponsoring the famous Toronto Santa Claus Parade, which had cemented Eaton's status as Canada's premier retailer since 1905. In the end, the company couldn't adapt fast enough to survive. In 1998, the company went belly-up.

LEON'S FURNITURE

This Canadian superstore chain got its start in 1909 when a Lebanese immigrant named Ablan Leon saved his earnings as a

door-to-door salesman and opened a small dry-goods store in Welland, Ontario. Eventually (and accidentally), though, Leon discovered that furniture had a much better profit potential.

Leon's son was getting married, and Dad decided that the new-lyweds needed a mattress, so he bought one as a wedding gift. Knowing he'd have trouble hiding a mattress at home, Leon had it delivered to his store. He left it leaning against the front window as he went into the back room to make some space to store it. Within minutes, a customer walked back to the storeroom, wanting to buy the mattress. After a brief hesitation, Leon named a price, sold it at a healthy profit, and presumably found a different wedding present for his son. The ball was rolling, though, and Leon's Furniture was born.

When Ablan Leon died in 1942, he left the store to his children. They expanded it, but one store was too small to have that many managers. To reduce sibling squabbling, they spread out, building new stores; today, there are about 50 across southwestern Ontario.

WARNER BROS.

In 1888, a family of Jewish refugees from the pogroms in Poland, crossed the ocean, settled in Ontario, and changed their name to Warner. In 1903, the three oldest Warner brothers bought a movie projector and visited mining towns in Ohio and Pennsylvania, selling tickets to see their single, worn copy of *The Great Train Robbery*. Eventually, it became clear to the brothers that they could make more money by making movies than showing them. So after adding younger brother Jack to the mix, they moved to California and founded what's now the third-oldest American movie studio. (Paramount and Universal are first and second.)

The wily Jack Warner eventually took control of the studio, where he ruled with an iron fist, firing employees and actors with a particular relish. In 1966, Jack Warner sold controlling interest in the studio to fellow Canadians Eliot and Kenneth Hyman.

MACLEAN'S

John Bayne Maclean was born in Crieff, Ontario, in 1862. Beginning as a financial editor for the *Toronto Mail*, he joined with his brother Hugh in publishing specialized trade papers, beginning

with a newspaper called *Canadian Grocer and General Storekeeper* in 1887, and eventually expanding into magazines that had a more general audience. Besides founding the *Financial Post*, *Mayfair*, and *Chatelaine* magazines, he purchased the rights to already-established magazines like *Canadian Homes and Gardens* and something called *Busy Man's Magazine*. Liking its content but not its name, Maclean decided to rename *Busy Man's* with a title he was already fond of: *Maclean's*. By the 1930s, Maclean's publishing company was Canada's leading magazine publisher.

ROBERTSON SCREWS

The good sense of the Robertson screw and screwdriver are not lost on Canadians…and much of the rest of the world. Accounting for 85 percent of all screws used in Canada, the color-coded, square-holed, nonslip design makes you wonder why anybody would use those inferior flat-slot and Phillips screws. (Yet, the Americans continue to do so—the Robertson design accounts for only 10 percent of the U.S. market, and mostly in the manufacture of recreational vehicles.)

You can credit Peter Lymburner Robertson from Milton, Ontario, for the design. According to legend, he gouged his hand when a flat-slot screwdriver slipped and vowed "Never again!" The square hole did the trick: strong, impossible to strip or slip, possible to use one-handed, and unlikely to gouge wood, metal, paint…or hands. Robertson began making his screws and drivers in 1908, and their elegant simplicity caught on quickly—so quickly that he had to struggle against court challengers and patent infringers from the start.

In the end, though, he won out. By 1945, Robertson had a factory with 500 workers, so much money that he could be a generous philanthropist, and six years to enjoy it all before he died.

Parts I and II are on pages 93 and 131.

* * *

"I have a theory of relatives, too. Don't hire 'em."
—**Jack Warner**

Fastest NHL slapshot on record: 169.6 km/h, by Boston captain Zdeno Chara.

THE WILD ONES

These three naturalists found their muse in Canada's wilderness and shared their vision of the country's landscape through art and literature, creating a new appreciation for conservation and the natural world.

ERNEST THOMPSON SETON (1860–1946)

Life and Wilderness: Born in England, Seton arrived with his family in Lindsay, Ontario, when he was six years old; they moved to Toronto when he was 10. He spent his free time exploring the nearby woods, fields, and cedar swamps—and even the local taxidermy shop—to learn about birds and mammals. He liked to pretend he was an aboriginal brave, practicing the lore of the woodlands.

In 1881, he settled on his brother's homestead near Carberry, Manitoba, where, instead of doing farming chores, he could usually be found exploring in the woods. Seton tracked deer and wolves, studied the flora, and kept detailed records of what he found. He also formed friendships with some of Manitoba's First People, learning what he could about their relationship to wildlife and their spiritual heritage. Later, he would call the time he spent in the Manitoba countryside "the golden days, the best years of my life."

Legacy: The Carberry locals thought he was both lazy and crazy, but Seton was actually priming himself for a career as a celebrated naturalist and wildlife artist. In 1885, the Century Company hired him to do 1,000 drawings of mammals for the Century Dictionary, and by 1892 he was made Provincial Naturalist of Manitoba. His illustrated works, *Birds of Manitoba* and *Animals of Manitoba*, became respected reference books. And he wasn't just famous in Canada; his oil paintings hung in Paris, and his work as a naturalist was lauded by another nature lover, U.S. president Theodore Roosevelt. His respect for the wisdom of native peoples led him to found a youth program, the Woodcraft Indians, and later, to co-found the Boy Scouts of America.

Seton described Canada's landscape in *Arctic Prairies*, *The Trail of a Sandhill Stag*, and *Two Savages*. His book on wildlife, *Wild Animals I Have Known*, has never gone out of print and was the inspiration for Rudyard Kipling's *The Jungle Book*. Seton taught his

readers that wild animals were emotional beings who lived fascinating lives, and that they should be protected.

Quote: "Have the wild things no legal rights? What right has man to inflict such long and fearful agony on a fellow-creature, simply because that creature does not speak his language?"

GILEAN DOUGLAS (1900–93)

Life and Wilderness: Born in Toronto, Gilean Douglas was a child of wealth, privilege, and tragedy. Her father was a lawyer who became Queen's Council, and as a child she attended private school and traveled in Europe. But her mother died when she was seven and her father when she was 16. At first, she went to live with relatives, but by 19, she went off on her own.

At a time when women couldn't vote, the teenaged Douglas became a reporter for the *New York Sun* and the *Toronto News*. In her twenties and thirties she lived an adventurous, unsettled life, traveling through Canada, the United States, and Europe, taking on odd jobs and working as a journalist.

At 39, she made a life-changing decision. Following a longing for emotional peace and a desire to be closer to nature, she restored an isolated cabin on the Teal River in B.C.'s Cascade Mountains and lived there alone, without running water or electricity. Wild animals—including lynx and cougars—were her companions. She gardened organically and made studied her surroundings. When a fire destroyed the home in 1946, Douglas bought a small cabin on isolated acreage off the coast of Cortez Island and continued gardening and writing.

Legacy: Douglas lived in areas that were accessible only by boat and or hiking trails, but she traveled and kept in touch with the world through her poems, articles, and books. Her readers marveled at her self-reliance and her knowledge of the wilds of British Columbia. They'd have been even more impressed if they'd known she was a woman, but her publishers thought the public would never believe that a woman knew how to live by herself in the wild. So Douglas's articles and books were written under the pseudonym "Grant Madison." It wasn't until many years later that she "came out" as the true author.

When asked if she'd resented being published as a man, Douglas replied that Grant Madison wasn't such a bad fellow, since he

Canada's last ice age receded 10,000 years ago.

spoke up for unpopular causes of the time—like nature conservation and the rights of women. She continued to write into her nineties and became an inspiration to female naturalists, and a leader in a conservation movement that had caught up with her pioneering ideas.

Quote: "I was led…away from the city, away from the crush of people and out into the quiet and aloneness of the natural world, the world where I am truly at home."

FARLEY MOWAT (1921–)

Life and the Wilderness: Mowat's early years were spent in towns all over Canada: Belleville, Windsor, Saskatoon, Toronto, and Richmond Hill. His father was a librarian, and moved the family from place to place trying to support them through the Great Depression. From early childhood, Mowat had an affinity for animals, and in 1935, he traveled with his great-uncle to the arctic wilderness near Churchill, Manitoba, where he was greatly impressed by *La Foule*, the mass migration of the caribou, and by the snow-covered land he later described as "a soft white nightmare."

Mowat twice went to the Northwest Territories' Keewatin District as a biologist's assistant, but wasn't very good at it—he was too busy gathering material for the books that would make him one of the most famous nature writers in the world.

Legacy: Published in 1952, Mowat's first book, *People of the Deer*, not only gave readers detailed portrayals of Canada's arctic, it revealed the plight of the area's starving Inuit. It eventually brought help to the Inuit and made Mowat an instant celebrity. He went on to write about arctic wolves, the Viking voyages to Canada, and American zoologist Dian Fossey, who studied gorillas in Africa and was murdered in Rwanda in 1985.

Mowat's books have been controversial, but the author has continued to write the truth as he sees it. His books range from passionate defenses of the environment to comic stories from his childhood. Today, he's one of Canada's most widely read and influential authors.

Quote: "We have doomed the wolf not for what it is, but for what we deliberately and mistakenly perceive it to be—the mythologized epitome of a savage ruthless killer—which is, in reality, no more than a reflected image of ourself."

There were more Canadian casualties in World War I than in World War II.

LITERARY LINES

We chose 10 of our favorite Canadian novels and boiled their plots down to a few lines. Can you come up with their titles? (Answers on page 455.)

1. When a young farm couple decides to adopt a boy, they get the surprise of their lives when they receive a plucky young girl instead.

2. Lou, a quiet librarian, has a life-changing experience when he falls in love with a large, furry mammal.

3. In the late 1980s, a trio of very young—and sometimes floundering—adults gets lost in the desert and takes turns telling stories about their modern life experiences.

4. A badly burned soldier meets up with a nurse and other World War II survivors in postwar Italy, where they all slowly reveal their hidden and sometimes shameful pasts.

5. Four people are thrown together during a state of emergency in India, and cross social and economic boundaries and prejudices to form a bond.

6. A love triangle pushes three people to abandon their own self-interests to the surreal dynamic of the group.

7. Daisy Goodwill lays out, in autobiographical form, her family history of loss and discontentedness while struggling to find her own purpose.

8. Moses survives his second—and very difficult—divorce and plunges into a full-blown midlife crisis.

9. A boy survives a shipwreck and ponders life's deeper questions while stranded on a lifeboat with a tiger in the middle of the ocean.

10. A woman deals with subjugation and slavery under a totalitarian regime.

TOWERING OVER TORONTO

The CN Tower is no longer the world's tallest, but it dwarfs anything else in the Western Hemisphere. It can even be seen from another country.

SETTING THE RECORD STRAIGHT

First of all, let's dispel some of the misconceptions about the CN Tower. No, the large round thing at the top doesn't go up and down the base, picking up passengers at the bottom and taking them to the top (although there are elevators inside that do that). Yes, the restaurant inside does rotate slowly, entertaining diners with its sky-high views. No, the CN Tower isn't the world's tallest building, the world's tallest tower, or the world's tallest anything anymore…unless the category is "The World's Tallest Freestanding Tower That Happens to Be in Canada."

Here's what is true: In 1995, 20 years after it was built, the CN Tower was designated one of the modern Seven Wonders of the World by the American Society of Civil Engineers. For 31 years, it was the tallest freestanding land structure in the world before being deposed in 2007 by Dubai's Burj Khalifa skyscraper. It's the only Toronto structure visible from the United States. It's got the highest public observation decks in the World Federation of Great Towers, an association of tall towers and buildings. And it remains a symbol of Canada and a source of pride for Toronto, with more than 2 million visitors gazing out from its observation platform each year.

FROM FLAT TO POINTY

But how did it get started? In the 1960s, the Canadian National Railway had some spare land and was trying to diversify into non-railroad businesses. Its directors had the idea to build and then rent out a communications tower that would be tall enough that any communications tower in Toronto could beam TV, radio, and data waves to and from it.

The CN Tower wasn't originally supposed to be what it turned

out to be. The first designs showed three cylindrical legs with a flat top located where the main level (the large round part) currently sits—and that was pretty much it. But the architects, a consortium of Australians and Canadians, started monkeying with the design to make it more interesting. They came up with the tapered, three-finned base fairly early and the design for the main level shortly afterward. But something was missing.

At that point, one of the structural engineers suggested that they extend the base higher and add a Sky Pod (the glass-enclosed observation area), figuring that wouldn't add significantly to the project cost and insisting that tourists would pay extra to look out from the high observation deck. But the addition made for a bulbous top that didn't look quite right, so someone did some research and realized that if they added a 100-meter (328-foot) spire and antenna above the main level, the design would be about 25 meters (82 feet) taller than Chicago's Sears (now Willis) Tower, which was the tallest building in the world at the time.

FROM ABSTRACT TO CONCRETE

How do you build a tall tower out of concrete? It would be way too heavy to mold it on the ground and then hoist it up. So for the CN Tower, workers created the supporting structure below the main level very slowly in one seamless piece using a "slipform," a moving mold that can raise itself hydraulically.

To simplify, let's say you were making a smokestack. With a slipform, you'd make a doughnut-shaped mold and lay it on top of your foundation. Then you'd pour concrete into it. After a few hours, you'd start slowly raising the mold while still dribbling concrete into it. As the mold crept upward, you'd notice that the once-liquid concrete had turned rock-solid before emerging from the bottom. As you continued dribbling concrete into the mold, it would move slowly skyward as hardened concrete emerged from the bottom. If you pour and lift, pour and lift long enough, your slipform mold will eventually end up at the top of a tall, solid, seamless chimney.

Now think of doing that for something as tall as the CN Tower. It could be done, but would take a lot of concrete, a lot of people, and a long time.

GIVE 'EM THE BIG SLIP

Here's how they did it. They built a huge, adjustable, six-sided slipform mold as big around as the future tower. Then they added hydraulic jacks on all sides, designed to keep the mold creeping upward at a steady rate of 25 centimeters (10 inches) per hour.

At that rate, the crew could increase the tower 5.5 meters (18 feet) every day, and it took a team of 1,532 people working in shifts around the clock to keep the concrete flowing at the right speed. Pouring started in June 1973. By February 22, 1974, the structure had risen 447 meters (1,466 feet) above the ground, making it the tallest structure in Canada.

THE STRAIGHT AND NARROW

Keeping the tower straight during pouring was tough, but workers managed by using massive *plumb-bobs*, a kind of weight that measures whether or not a structure stands straight, hanging from the slipform. As a result, the tower from bottom to top varies from absolute vertical by only 29 millimeters (1 inch).

The main level and Sky Pod were built in place atop the tower's base, using wooden frames as molds for the concrete. Finally, the antenna on the top was added. It was originally meant to be lifted by a giant crane, but the plans changed during construction when the contractor bought a surplus Russian-made Sikorsky S-64 Sky-crane helicopter from the U.S. military. Workers used the helicopter to lift the antenna's 44 pieces to the top. The process took only three and a half weeks instead of the six months that had been expected if done by crane. The tower opened to the public on June 26, 1976.

LOOK OUT BELOW!

The CN Tower now stands 553.33 meters (1,815.4 feet) above Toronto. It's a spectacular sight, but it can be dangerous too. If there's freezing rain, for instance, people below better watch out. A storm in March 2007 painted a thick layer of ice on Toronto buildings, including the CN Tower. Because of its height and overhanging pod, things got tricky when the sun started melting the ice and the wind whirled up to 90 kilometers (56 miles) per hour. Fearing fatalities and smashed cars from falling icicles, police closed the streets around the tower, including a major artery, the Gardiner

Expressway, 310 meters (1,017 feet) away. Even that wasn't a large enough area, though: falling ice smashed into the window of a taxi parked another 180 meters (590 feet) beyond that.

SOME FINAL NOTES

• In 1986, on the 10th anniversary of the tower's opening, expert climber Dan Goodwin scrambled to the top with just his hands and feet. Then he rappelled back to the ground and did it all over again on another side.

• There is at least one record the CN Tower still holds: world's highest wine cellar.

• In its early days, what's now called the "main deck level" was known as "SkyPod," and what's now called the "Sky Pod" was called the "Space Deck."

• On a clear day from the Sky Pod, you can see the city of Rochester, New York (across Lake Ontario).

• Although there's a staircase up the tower (1,776 steps), it's for emergencies only and isn't usually open to the public...except a few times a year for charity stair-climbing events.

• At the top of the tower, there are two reservoirs that hold 113,500 liters (30,000 gallons) of water, which can be routed to fire hoses in case of fire.

• In 1997, the CN Tower's lighting bill was so high—for electricity and constant bulb replacement—that its incandescent lights were removed. Ten years later, they were finally replaced with LED bulbs, which reduced the cost of electricity to a manageable $1,000 a month and offered a spectrum of 16.7 million colors.

• During rain and fog, birds are attracted to light. So during peak bird migration seasons in the spring and fall, the tower's lights are dimmed to reduce the number of avian collisions.

• If you happen to be in Toronto in 2076, go see the CN Tower open its time capsule. Placed inside the walls of the Look Out Level way back in 1976, the capsule includes letters from then prime minister Pierre Trudeau and other politicians, examples of 1976 newspapers and money, and a video about the construction of the tower.

...John Thompson and Charles Tupper, both of Nova Scotia.

THE CARIBOO CAMELS

*One of the last things you might expect to see in the Cariboo
region is a camel. If only you'd been there in 1862...*

ALL THAT GLITTERS

When gold fever hit British Columbia's Cariboo region in
the 1860s, entrepreneur Frank Laumeister was glad that
he had learned two important things from California's gold rush:

1. It wasn't the miners who typically made money from a gold rush,
but the merchants, barkeepers, and prostitutes who sold them
goods and services.

2. Camels were faster and better at carrying a load on narrow, gold
rush trails than any other pack animal.

During the 1850s, the California gold rush set the tone for
what to expect anywhere else gold was discovered. Hundreds of
thousands of hopeful miners flooded the area, panning night and
day for gold nuggets, hoping to lay claim to a major discovery. A
few lucky miners got rich and kept the dream alive for the others,
but the vast majority headed home with an empty pan in hand.
Any spare nuggets of gold they might've stumbled on were quickly
siphoned away by the coolheaded businessmen (and women) who
set up shop in gold country and provided necessities or diversion
at a premium price.

A MAJOR MINER INFLUX

Just as the California fever cooled, gold was discovered in British
Columbia's Fraser River Valley. In 1858, many of the miners who
had been disappointed in California flocked north to see if maybe
this time they could find their fortunes—more than 33,000 miners
descended on the area. By 1861, when the Cariboo region started
yielding big discoveries, many of the Americans had already headed
south to try their luck in the Pike's Peak gold rush in Colorado or
fight in the U.S. Civil War. As a result, Canadians and British
made up the next big wave of gold miners in the Cariboo.

Frank Laumeister was already there and ready for business.
The Canadian businessman had been a pack train operator during
California's gold rush, transporting retail and personal goods, min-

ing equipment, and gold from cities to the fields and back again. Following the migrating California miners, he had ended up in British Columbia with a brilliant idea: camels!

AN AMAZING INVESTMENT OPPORTUNITY

During his time south of the border, Laumeister had seen a few pack camels and noted their ability to carry large amounts of weight over great distances—up to 500 kilograms (1,100 pounds) as far as 50 kilometers (31 miles) per day. They also used less food, pound for pound, than mules, horses, and other pack animals. Laumeister wanted a whole fleet of camels. Importing them would be expensive, but he convinced a Cariboo roadhouse owner named John Calbreath to invest money in a herd of Bactrian camels—the stocky, hardy, two-humped kind from Asia that just happened to be available in San Francisco. With those camels, the two would set up a pack-train service.

Six thousand dollars later (more than twice the cost of the equivalent number of mules), 23 Bactrian camels were loaded onto a steamship in San Francisco and sent up the Pacific coast, arriving in Victoria in May 1862. By June, they were on the narrow, winding Cariboo Trail, laden with packs of supplies for the miners.

Well, 21 of them were, anyway. News of their arrival had traveled far and wide, and large crowds gathered to see them when they stepped off the boat. Reports at the time say one camel—disturbed by the sight and sound of the spectators—sucked up water from a horse trough and blew the load…along with camel bodily fluids…in the face of one of the onlookers before running off into the distance with her calf trailing behind her. This would only be the beginning of Laumeister's problems.

(NOT) PLAYING NICE WITH OTHERS

Things started off well enough in the mountains. As predicted, the camels could haul more weight than other pack animals and for longer periods of time. But as soon as Laumeister's camels encountered other animals, problems arose.

The camels themselves didn't get too worked up. But easily startled horses and mules often broke loose and dashed off into the wilderness at the sight of the furry, hulking camels lumbering toward them. And the smell of the camels was bad enough to

Erik, the brother of actor Leslie Nielsen, was deputy PM under Brian Mulroney.

make even burly drivers balk. But there were also more serious complaints along the trail: the camels were surly and unruly, prone to sitting down and refusing to carry their packs. Reports that the camels snorted, spat, stomped, and bit both man and beast were frequent. Furthermore, the camels were apparently eating everything they could lay their mouths on—not just food, but also soap, utensils, packs, clothing, and other supplies.

ENDANGERED SPECIES

Not only was cargo vanishing, the camels themselves were disappearing at an alarming rate, too. A few ran off into the wild. More than a few fell off the sides of the mountains or broke their legs on the steep, rocky terrain. One, mistaken by a packer for a bear, was shot and killed. And the remaining camels were suffering from wear and tear. Their footpads were so cracked from the sharp, gravel terrain that rawhide booties were made to protect their feet. But even that effort came too late: Laumeister's camel fleet was on its way to extinction.

WHY IT DIDN'T WORK

Logic tells us that there should have been just as many encounters with steep mountain paths, mules, nearsighted men with rifles, and bars of soap in the mountains of California. So why did the camels work so well there, but fail miserably in the Cariboo? One contributing factor was that, by the time camels were introduced to the California mountains, the trails were established, wide, and less rocky. In contrast, the Cariboo trails were still being broken in.

But that doesn't explain everything. So in 2002, Canadian historians Richard Wright and Cathryn Wellner decided to retrace the steps of the Laumeister camels along to Cariboo Trail, accompanied by two camels of their own. What they learned surprised them:

• First, camels are very well equipped for mountainous terrain—even narrow, rocky paths. Although a camel's foot is designed for sand (it expands on impact for traction), if allowed to walk at their own natural pace, their feet are more than capable of gripping hard dirt and rocks and withstanding sharp gravel. That isn't true, however, when they're rushed. Then their pads don't have time to flatten and grip properly, leading to slips, trips, and falls.

• From living with their camels on the trail, Wright and Wellner also discovered that camels have a pretty sweet disposition. They don't tend to get ornery unless they're provoked or under extreme duress.

Both of these realizations led Wright and Wellner to conclude that Laumeister's packers, in an attempt to race large loads up and down the mountain for bigger profit, were probably the primary reason for the camels' bad behavior, debilitating injuries, and deaths.

THE BOTTOM LINE

So, how much did Laumeister lose on his camel venture? In the end, not much. Despite the short-lived scheme, all evidence says that Laumeister was a shrewd businessman who made as much as a 400 percent return on John Calbreath's $6,000 investment.

If the venture was so successful, though, why didn't Laumeister just buy more camels and keep going? It's not completely clear, but there were rumors circulating at the time that the other packing companies were preparing to file lawsuits against him for damages to their businesses. Whatever the reason, Laumeister took his profit and got out of the camel business forever.

BUT WHAT ABOUT THE CAMELS?

No one knows for sure what happened to the few camels that remained of the original 23, but it appears that Laumeister sold some of them to ranchers. The ones that disappeared into the wilderness were never officially seen again, although occasional camel sightings were reported in British Columbia as late as the 1930s.

By 1865, the Cariboo gold rush had all but ended in very much the same way the one in California did: wealthier prospectors laid claim to valuable land and squeezed out the little guy, the merchants took the rest, and the little guy went home with almost nothing to show for his efforts. Laumeister moved on too, no doubt to another business venture, but none so storied as the Cariboo camels.

THE GREAT ESCAPE ARTIST

What do you do when it's the height of World War II and you're stuck inside a German POW camp? RCAF Lieutenant Wally Floody decided to dig three of the most famous tunnels in history and try to get out.

ART IMITATING LIFE
Released in 1963, *The Great Escape* was a World War II action film that became a classic. Appreciated by critics and loved by audiences, the movie is based on the true story of a group of Allied airmen captured by the Nazis and taken to Stalag Luft III, a prison camp that the Germans believed was escape-proof. But as with most other "-proof" things in history (the unsinkable *Titanic*, for one), that prison camp ended up being the site of one of history's greatest escapes.

In the film, Charles Bronson played the part of the "Tunnel King," the prisoner who engineered the escape tunnels. Few people knew that the film's technical advisor was actually the inspiration for Bronson's character. He was former Royal Canadian Air Force (RCAF) pilot Wally Floody.

THE GERMANS ARE GONNA GET YOU

Floody hailed from Chatham, Ontario, and was a teen during the Great Depression. He left school early in the hopes that he could make some money to help his family, but work was hard to come by. Finally, in 1936, he heard that there were jobs in Timmins, Ontario...if you were willing to work in the gold mines as a mucker, the guy who shoveled rock and mud into carts to be hauled up to the surface. It wasn't a job that Floody wanted to make into a career, but he took it—and that training would eventually prove extremely useful in Germany. Floody once complained that he "seemed to spend [his] life down a stinking hole in the ground." But that came later.

In 1940, Canada was at war, and the newly married Floody decided to join up. The next year, he headed off to flight training

in Manitoba and then began an extremely short career with the RCAF. On October 27, 1941, in his first month overseas and on his very first mission, Floody's fighter plane was attacked over France. The Germans shot away his controls, and the 23-year-old pilot bailed out. He was caught by the German military police, who sent him off to his first prison camp, Stalag Luft I in Barth, Germany.

IF AT FIRST YOU DON'T SUCCEED...
At Stalag Luft I, Floody and his fellow POWs wasted no time trying to get out. Between November 1941 and March 1942, they made two tunneling attempts. Both failed. When the Germans discovered that Floody had been among the escape attempts' masterminds, they decided he was trouble and moved him to a more secure camp. That was Stalag Luft III—where the Nazis housed many of their high-risk prisoners.

Located in the forest near what is now Zagan, Poland, Stalag Luft III was a large prison (at its height, it held more than 10,000 men). Surrounded by barbed wire, Stalag Luft III was well guarded, and the Nazis considered its defenses impenetrable. The area's sandy soil made it difficult to create tunnels that didn't collapse, and because the sand was bright yellow, it would also be difficult for prisoners to hide it during the process of digging; the Germans reasoned that the sand was bound to show up on a digger's clothes or shoes. Guards also used sound-detection equipment to listen for the noise of digging underground.

All that was true—Stalag Luft III was an extremely secure prison. But the Germans made a key mistake: they held all the most devious prisoners in that one place, thinking the men would be easier to keep an eye on. But the Nazis underestimated how much the prisoners could accomplish if they worked together. When Floody arrived at Stalag Luft III, he met up with Roger J. Bushell, a squadron leader with Great Britain's Royal Air Force. Bushell already had a plan for a massive breakout.

JUST A BUNCH OF TROUBLEMAKERS
Allied soldiers escaping from prison camps wasn't new, but most POW escapes involved just 12 to 20 men—the smaller the group, the logic went, the more likely the escape would be successful. Bushell wanted to get 250 prisoners out of Stalag Luct III, and he

wanted them equipped with maps, railroad timetables, and papers like fake passports and travel permits. It was an enormous undertaking that would require a lot of time and patience…and probably wouldn't work. But, as Floody said later, he and the other men believed it was their duty to try to escape so as "to cause consternation amongst the enemy."

Among the camp's population, Bushell had already found forgers and mapmakers who could create all the necessary documents. But he needed someone who knew how to engineer and build a reliable tunnel through unreliable terrain. And not just one tunnel, either. Bushell wanted to build three tunnels simultaneously so that even if the Germans discovered one, they would likely concentrate on closing it without realizing that there were two others. That's where Floody came in.

THE TUNNEL KING

Floody drew up plans for three tunnels, code-named Tom, Dick, and Harry. They would go 30 feet deep, where the Germans' microphones couldn't pick up any sounds of digging. Floody also helped to create the tunnels' ventilation and electrical systems, made from scrounged materials found around the camp. The men fastened milk cans together to make ventilation pipes that brought in air to the diggers. They stole electrical wire and secretly tapped into the prison's own electrical board to provide lighting. Bed boards propped up the tunnel shafts, and knapsacks and hockey sticks were used to make air pumps.

To ensure that none of the diggers accidentally gave away the plan by carrying that telltale yellow sand on their clothes, the men changed every time they went into or came out of the tunnels. They also came up with an ingenious idea for what to do with all the loose sand they unearthed: Floody was most often the lead digger, and he spent hours on his stomach deep underground, filling buckets with sand and then passing them back to the diggers behind him. Eventually, it was packed into small bags, hidden in the men's clothes, and reburied outside in places like the prisoners' vegetable garden.

That job earned Floody the nickname "the Tunnel King," but it was also dangerous work, and Floody was nearly killed twice. Once, he was buried under almost half a ton of sandy soil; the second

time, a section of tunnel collapsed on him. Both times, he found an air pocket underground and was able to wait for his friends to pull him out. Still, the work took a toll on Floody's health. For the rest of his life, he suffered from pulmonary problems.

DRAT! THWARTED AGAIN!

In November 1943, the Germans discovered the Tom tunnel. It was more than 198 meters (650 feet) long when the Nazis blew it up. The Dick tunnel had to be abandoned because its exit ended up being in a spot of trees that were being cleared for camp expansion. But Harry was still on track, and Floody used Dick to hold some of the tons of sand taken from the working tunnel. By March 1944, Harry was approaching its final 335 meters (1,100 feet), and the breakout was planned for the first moonless night—March 24.

But just a few days before that moonless night, the Germans smelled trouble. They didn't know what was coming and couldn't figure out what the prisoners were up to, but they decided to err on the side of caution. They transferred 20 of their most suspicious prisoners to another camp that had just been built nearby. One of the men transferred was a bitterly disappointed Wally Floody.

KEEP GOING!

In fact, only a handful of the transferred prisoners were actually involved in the tunnel project, and so, on March 24, under the dark of night, the men of Stalag Luft III started crawling into the Harry tunnel and making their way to the woods. There were problems: Allied airplanes circled the area, triggering an air raid. The Germans turned off the camp's electricity, plunging the men underground into total darkness. By the time the lights came back on, half the night was gone, and Roger Bushell thought that they might be able to get only 100 men out before the sun came up.

In all, 76 prisoners managed to wiggle their way out of the camp; among them were nine Canadians. But being on the free side of the barbed wire was just the beginning. As the guards figured out what was happening and started shooting from their sentry towers, the men scattered into the woods. They headed for towns, train stations, anywhere to find crowds and blend in. But in the end, nearly all of them were caught; just three managed to make it out of Germany and safely back to England. Of the 73

Moose shed their antlers every winter.

who were taken back to Stalag Luft III, 50 were executed. (Hitler wanted to kill them all, as well as the guards who'd been on duty that night, but his right-hand henchman Heinrich Himmler convinced him that that would violate the Geneva Convention.)

Wally Floody spent the rest of the war in POW camps—but alive—and never got over his disappointment at not being part of the escape. Forty-two years later, he told an interviewer, "Every time I tell my wife I might have been one of the prisoners who got away, she reminds me: 'Yes, but you might have been one of the ones they shot.'" Still, Floody was proud of his contribution and the "consternation" he helped create in the enemy. After the escape, Hitler panicked and diverted about 70,000 German soldiers from the fronts to hunt down the 76 prisoners. Floody noted that, even in his new POW camp, the Stalag Luft III escape was big news: "Every fifteen minutes on the [radio], people were warned that the dangerous terror leaguers, as they called us, were loose."

RETURN OF THE KING

After the war, Floody testified about the conditions of German POW camps at the Nuremberg war tribunals, a series of trials that the Allies held to prosecute Nazi war criminals. In 1946, King George VI made him a Member of the Order of the British Empire. Floody also helped found the RCAF Prisoner-of-War Association and attended each of its five-year reunions. His fellow ex-prisoners continued to call him "the Tunnel King," and they weren't surprised when, in the early 1960s, director John Sturges asked him to be a technical adviser for an upcoming film, *The Great Escape*.

On location in Germany, Floody worked 12 hours a day making sure the tunnel sequences were accurate. He told a crewmember that when the filming was on the right track, it brought back memories that gave him nightmares. When the film ended, Floody returned to Toronto. He worked in business, remained happily married, raised two children—and never went back to digging in the mines. He died of pulmonary problems in 1989.

BUT WAIT!

The Great Escape story is the most famous escape during World War II, but it's not the only one with a Canadian connection.

During the early days of World War II, Great Britain was afraid the Germans were going to invade. Besides all the obvious trouble that would cause, the British worried about losing the more than 35,000 German and Italian prisoners being held in POW camps around their country. So they quietly sent many of them to Canada, where the prisoners were dispersed to remote camps across the interior.

One of those was Camp X in Angler, Ontario, which held a few hundred German soldiers. Over three months in early 1941, prisoners at that camp dug a tunnel that stretched nearly 46 meters (150 feet). They planned to escape on April 20, Hitler's birthday, but just before the scheduled date, it started raining...and raining. On April 18, a group of 28 men decided they'd spent enough time waiting. Worried that the tunnel was going to collapse, they made a run for it...well, a slog for it, since the tunnels were filling with water. They made it out of the camp and then took off into the wilderness.

It took about a week, but eventually, all 28 were caught. Some had made it all the way to Montreal, though, and even to Medicine Hat, Alberta, thousands of kilometers away.

* * *

THE DIMES, THEY ARE A'CHANGIN'

In 1968, the Royal Canadian Mint replaced the silver in its dimes, with nickel alloy. But when word got out, Canadians started hoarding the old silver coins instead of spending them, resulting in a dime shortage. The number needed to make up the difference was so huge that Canada contracted with the U.S. Mint to produce half of the necessary dimes at its Philadelphia facility.

The American dimes are almost identical to the ones made in Canada, with one notable difference: the American stamping machines used a slightly different "collar"—the band that fits around the rim of a blank coin so its metal doesn't squish outward when stamped. The collar also creates the "reeding"—the serrated edge on a coin.

So how can you tell if your late-1960s Canadian dime is a Philadelphia interloper? Look at the grooves. The Canadian-made dimes have V-shaped tops and bottoms; the American, flat ones.

THOMPSON'S NOTEBOOK: FLORA & FAUNA, PART II

From 1784 to 1812, David Thompson surveyed and mapped out much of Canada's unknown interior for the North-West Company, a fur trader. Here we've extracted his observations about some of the plants, animals, and First People he encountered. (Part I is on page 189.)

SALMON

"The arrival of the salmon throughout [the Columbia River] is hailed with dances and many ceremonies. Deep attention is paid to what [the First Peoples] believe will keep the salmon about them; for this purpose the beach of the river is kept very clean, no part whatever of the salmon is allowed to touch the river after it is brought on shore, the scales, the bowels & cetera are all cleaned on the land a few yards from the river, for experience has taught them the delicate perceptions of this fish. Even a dog going in the edge of the water, the salmon dash down the current. If any part of one of them is thrown into the water, they do not return until the next day, especially if blood has been washed; in spearing of them, if the fish is loose on the spear and gets away, the fishing is done for that day.

I looked upon a part of the precautions of the Natives as so much superstition, yet I found they were not so; one of my men, after picking the bone of a horse about 10am carelessly threw it into the river. Instantly the salmon near us dashed down the current and did not return until the afternoon; an Indian dived, and in a few minutes brought it up, but the fishery was over for several hours...

It is a firm belief of the Natives of this river, that of the myriads of salmon that annually leave the saltwater ocean and enter freshwater rivers, not one ever returns alive to the sea; they all proceed to their respective spawning places, accomplish this, and soon after (a few weeks) die of exhaustion. It does not appear that they take any nourishment after they leave the sea as their stomachs are always empty, probably from finding in freshwater no nourishment suitable to them.

Canada's oldest dance company: the Royal Winnipeg Ballet.

It is affirmed that no salmon spawns twice. The life and habits of this fish has something curious: some of them are spawned above a thousand miles from the sea, in freshwater, in which they are nourished and continue to be so to the sea; here a change takes place and they now find their support in salt water; until they acquire the power of spawning, when they enter freshwater rivers which now has no food adapted to them, ascend to the very place where they became alive, there deposit their spawn, and die. Whatever the history and the habits of the salmon may be, they form the principal support of all the Natives of this river, from season to season.

BEAVERS

"[According to native tribes,] previous to the discovery of Canada, this continent may be said to have been in the possession of two distinct races of beings, Man and the Beaver. Man was naked and had to procure clothing from the skins of animals; his only arms were a stake, a bow with arrows, a spear, and a club of heavy wood or stone. Man was lord of all the dry land and all that was on it.

The other race was the Beaver. Every river, the banks at the water edge were occupied by their houses. To every small lake and all the ponds they built dams, and enlarged and deepened them to the height of the dams. The dry land with the dominions of Man contracted, everywhere he was hemmed in by water without the power of preventing it: he could not diminish the numbers half so fast as they multiplied, their houses were proof against his pointed stake, and his arrows could seldom pierce their skins. In this state Man and the Beaver had been for many centuries, but the discovery of Canada by the French soon placed the Natives far superior to the Beaver.

Without iron, man is weak, very weak, but armed with iron, he becomes the lord of the earth. For the furs which the Natives traded, they procured from the French axes, chisels, knives, spears and other articles of iron, with which they made good hunts of fur-bearing animals. Thus armed, the houses of the Beavers were pierced through, the dams cut through, and the water of the ponds lowered, or wholly run off, and the houses of the Beaver and their burrows laid dry, by which means they became an easy prey to the hunter.

The second-largest meteorite crater in the world is in Sudbury, ON.

The Beaver is an animal well known; the average weight of a full-grown male is about fifty-five pounds, his meat is agreeable to most although fat and oily; the tail is a delicacy. It is a remark of many, that dams erected by the art of Man are frequently damaged, or wholly carried away by violent freshets, but no power of water has ever carried away a beaver dam. The Indians think the male and female are faithful to each other, they bring up their young for the first year with care and protection until the next spring when the female is about to litter she drives them all away; some of them, before they can be made to stay away, receive severe cuts on the back from the teeth of the old ones. The young Beavers are very playful, and whimper like children.

The Beaver hunter is often at a loss what to do; his shortest and surest way is to stake up the doorway of the house. The doorway being doubly staked, the Indian proceeds to make a hole near the centre of it, to give full range to his ice chisel, and not one escapes, but all are killed with hard labor: Such was the manner of killing the Beaver until the introduction of steel traps, which baited with castoreum [the secretions of the beaver's scent glands] soon brought on the almost total destruction of these numerous and sagacious animals.

MAPLE SYRUP

"In the spring, the natives employ themselves in making sugar from the maple trees, the process of doing which is well known. The old trees give a stronger sap than the young trees; The Canadians also make a great quantity, which, when the sap is boiled to a proper consistence, they run into moulds where it hardens. But the Indians prefer making it like muscovado sugar, this is done simply by stirring it quickly about with a small paddle. The plane tree also makes a good sugar, the sap is abundant, and the sugar whiter, but not so strong. Both sugars have a taste, which soon becomes agreeable, and as fine white loaf sugar can be made from it as from that of the West Indies. The Natives would make far more than they do, it they could find a market.

WOLVERINES

"The Wolverene is an animal unknown to other parts of the world, and we would willingly dispense with his being round here. It is a

strong, well made, powerful animal. Armed with long sharp claws, he climbs trees with ease and nothing is safe that he can get at. By nature a plunderer and mischievous, he is the plague of the country.

A party of six men were sent to square timber for the Factory, and left their heavy axes when they went to the tent for the night. One morning the six axes were not to be found, and as they knew there was no person within many miles of them they were utterly at a loss what to think or do…Fortunately the Indian lad who was tenting with them perceived the footmarks of a Wolverene, and told them who the thief was, which they could not believe. Tracking the Wolverene, he found one of the axes hid under the snow: in like manner three more were found, the others were carried to some distance and took two hours to find because they were all hidden separately. To secure their axes they had to shoulder them every evening to their tent.

His skin is thick, the hair course, of a dark brown color with a value about ten shillings, but to encourage the natives to kill it, it is valued at two beavers, four times its real value.

CARIBOU

"Extending from the most northern part of this continent, bounded on the east by the sea, southward to Labrador and Nova Scotia, on the west by the Great Lakes: this great extent may properly be called the country of the rein deer, an animal too well known to heed description. This region is peculiar to the rein deer, on this continent it is found nowhere else. The Natives have well named it 'Marthee Teek' the 'ugly deer,' and from its migratory habits, the 'Wandering Deer.' Its form and way of life is admirably adapted to the rude countries and severe climates it inhabits, yet when compared with the graceful Antelope, it may be called not handsome. Their sight appears not good, and the eye dull, and has nothing of the brilliancy of the eyes of other deer. When examining anything that appears doubtful, it extends its neck and head in an awkward manner, and cautiously approaches until it is sure what the object is. Its large, broad, hard, hoofs make it very sure footed, and quite safe, and swift on swamps, rocks, or smooth ice…When few in number, and scattered, they are cautious and timid; but when in large herds, quite the reverse and are ready to trample down all before them.

Q: What's the name of the guy on Canadian Tire money? A: Sandy McTire

In the latter end of the month of May 1792, the ice had broken up. Mr Cooke and myself in a canoe proceeded about twenty miles up the river to shoot the rein deer, as they crossed the River; we passed two days, in which time we had killed ten deer. On the third morning the weather cold and uncomfortable, we were sitting by our fire, when we heard a noise as of distant thunder, and somewhat alarmed, put our four guns, and blankets into the canoe, and sat quietly in it; [wondering] what it could be; with surprise we heard the sound increasing and rushing towards us, but we were not long in suspense.

About forty yards below us, a vast herd of rein deer, of about one hundred yards of front, rushing through the woods, headlong descended the steep bank and swam across the river; in the same manner ascended the opposite bank, and continued full speed through the woods; we waited to see this vast herd pass, expecting to see it followed by a number of wolves; but not one appeared, and in this manner the herd continued to pass the whole day to near sunset…The great herd were so closely packed together that not one more, if dropped among them, could find a place.

The next day, a while after sun rise, the same sound and rushing noise was heard, and a deer herd of the same front, with the same headlong haste came down the bank and crossed the river, and continued to about two in the afternoon, attended by small herds on either side, but not with the same speed, and by sunset, finally ceased.

When we returned to the Factory [Thomson's home base] and related what we had seen, they could hardly believe us, and had we not by chance been up the river, nothing would have been known of the passage of this great herd: for the weather, for a long fortnight after the breaking up of the ice is very precarious and uncomfortable. Some time after, conversing with some of the Natives, they said that large herds do sometimes pass in the spring; they had often seen their roads, but had seldom seen the herds.

*　　*　　*

"We are a hopeful people. We have no pessimists in Alberta."
　　　　　　—Alexander Rutherford, Alberta's first premier

The maple leaf was first used as an emblem in Canada in 1834…

OLYMPIC HIGHLIGHTS: VANCOUVER

In the last installment of Canada's Olympics highlights, lowlights, and relights, we present...the 2010 Vancouver Games.

• The 2010 Winter Olympics torch arrived in Victoria from Athens on October 30, 2009...and got to Vancouver 106 days later. Rather than traveling by ferry and arriving in Vancouver later that same day, the torch took a circuitous path of 45,000 kilometers (27,961 miles) all over Canada, making it the longest one-country torch relay ever.

• Celebrity torchbearers included the expected Canadian sports, entertainment, political, and media people, but also one non-Canadian: Arnold Schwarzenegger, governor of California.

• The Olympic Flame looked impressive on TV, but from the ground, it was obscured by a high chain-link fence that kept spectators 100 meters (328 feet) away from it. The visual impact of the elegant cauldron and flame surrounded by a prison-like enclosure led to outraged newspaper editorials and online petitions. The bad press eventually convinced the Olympic Organizing Committee to adopt a solution—they covered the cauldron with a sheet of plexiglass and moved the fence so spectators could get about 30 meters (98 feet) from it.

• During the games, news outlets reported that the supply of 100,000 condoms provided to the Olympic village was running low. (That figure, by the way, averaged to about 14 condoms for each of the athletes, officials, coaches, and trainers.)

• Vancouver was the first Olympics to charge money ($22 to $50) to attend the nightly medals ceremonies. That used to come free at the end of the competitions, and spectators complained. As consolation, each ceremony was capped with a concert by a Canadian celebrity, including Alanis Morissette, Nickelback, Avril Lavigne, Barenaked Ladies, Nelly Furtado, Hedley, and Loverboy.

...by the Société Saint-Jean-Baptiste, who were promoting Quebec nationalism.

• Nearly 30,000 people who went to the snowboard-cross and ski-cross events discovered that their tickets had been canceled at the last minute because rain and warm weather had created "unsafe ground conditions." It wasn't just the ankle-deep mud, but also the fact that the course had been constructed of hay bales and snow imported from Yak Peak, two hours to the east. The fear was that spectators would start falling through the cracks of the exposed hay bales.

• Women's hockey teams from Canada and the United States outscored their nonNorth American opponents by a total of 88–4.

• Three Canadian-made ice-resurfacing machines failed one after another, delaying speed skating until an American-made Zamboni could be flown in from Calgary.

• "Were the Vancouver Olympics Cursed?" asked one Web site before the 2010 Olympics even finished. A lot of things went wrong: A warm winter, light on snow. A tragic death on the luge course. A skater whose mother died on the eve of her performance. An unsuccessful lawsuit about the Olympic committee's decision to exclude women from ski jumping. AntiOlympics protests. A barricade collapse that injured 19 people. A spigot opening during a luge competition and threatening to turn the ice slide into a waterslide. And a technical glitch during the opening ceremonies that left four Canadian athletes waiting for several minutes for cauldron legs to emerge from below the floor, followed by one of the athletes getting short shrift when only three of the four legs came up.

• The closing ceremonies recovered, though, featuring the same defective leg, but this time with a mime "fixing" it with oversized tools. That allowed speed skater Catriona Le May Doan, the slighted athlete from the opening, to finally light the torch.

• Great things happened, too: Canada turned its gold medal drought into a deluge, winning 14 and setting a record for the most ever won by a single country at any Winter Olympics.

For Montreal, turn to page 87. For Calgary, page 356.

WILD, WILD WEST, PART II

*On page 177, we introduced you to two of Canada's most
famous Wild West outlaws. Here are a few more.*

THE McLEAN BOYS

Allan (the oldest of the three, born in 1855), Charley, and Archie were the sons of Don McLean, a Hudson's Bay Company fur trader, explorer, and chief of the company's post at Thompson's River in British Columbia. Their mother was Sophia Grant, a Colville native. Because of their mixed race, the boys were social outcasts from birth, and life was hard for the family after their father died during an 1864 war against the Chilcotin. Sophia received a small pension, but otherwise, the McLeans were pretty much left to fend for themselves. Finally, needing money and hoping for a new start, Sophia sold the family ranch in 1867 and moved to Kamloops, British Columbia.

As the boys grew, they traveled from ranch to ranch, working as horsebreakers and jockeys. Then came the depression of 1877. Jobs were scarce, and the three McLean boys (and a friend, Alex Hare, also of mixed race) began running wild. The four went on a stealing spree—taking horses, ammunition, liquor, food, and clothing. Whatever they wanted or needed, they took.

Thievery run amok: They also got a reputation for violence. When prominent rancher and politician John Andrew Mara allegedly seduced and fathered a child with the McLeans' sister Annie, the boys showered him with threats and raids on his property. However, it wasn't until the outlaws stole a valuable stallion from another rancher named William Palmer in December 1879 that the authorities finally decided to do something about the gang once and for all. The local sheriff issued an arrest warrant and posted rewards, and a small posse formed.

On December 8, the posse surprised the outlaws at a camp near the town of Quilchena, British Columbia. Shots were fired. When the smoke cleared, Allan McLean was wounded, and one of the posse members was dead. The gang then went on the run, stopping at ranches to steal more firearms and murdering another man.

The average Canadian spends about $2.50 per week on condiments.

Back in Kamloops, the residents feared that the whole McLean affair might trigger an aboriginal uprising. So the once-small posse grew to some 70 men, who tracked the outlaws to a lake cabin nearby. There, the criminals surrendered on December 13.

It took two trials (the first ended in a mistrial) before Allan, Charley, and Archie McLean and Alex Hare were sentenced to hang for their crimes. The four met their death side by side on January 31, 1881, in New Westminster. The youngest member of the gang, Archie, who was in his teens, was the youngest person ever hanged in British Columbia.

Redemption: In the years that followed, the surviving McLean family struggled to redeem its reputation. A private in the Canadian army, Allan's son George earned a Distinguished Conduct Medal for single-handedly capturing 19 German prisoners and killing five more during World War I's Battle of Vimy Ridge. Another of Don McLean's descendants, Mel Rothenburger, wrote about his relatives in the book *We've Killed Johnny Ussher!* Rothenburger was elected as mayor of Kamloops in 1999 and worked as editor of Kamloops's newspaper, *The Daily News*.

BILL MINER

Many Canadian outlaws went south to find their fortunes in the United States. In exchange, America sent us Bill Miner, who is credited with being the first to utter the time-honored bandit's directive, "Hands up!" But that wasn't what made him famous. Although a thief and an American, Miner had a reputation for unfailing politeness, earning him the nickname "The Gentleman Bandit."

There were plenty of stories to support the moniker. For example, after robbing a ranch hand of $80 in 1866, Miner returned $10 so the man wouldn't be completely out of money. During an 1871 train robbery, he and two accomplices, Alkali Jim and Charlie Cooper, stole a $5 gold piece, a watch, and the boots from the engineer. Before they escaped, they decided to return the belongings (although they did keep a strongbox full of gold dust and coins worth $2,600). And in a 1904 robbery, Miner was quoted as saying as he rode away, "Good night, boys, sorry to have troubled you."

Robberies on the rails: From 1869 until his death, Miner robbed stagecoaches and trains with several different accomplices.

After his third prison term in the United States, he moved on to Canada where, in 1904, he held up a Canadian Pacific Railway train near Mission Junction, British Columbia. The job netted Miner and his gang about $7,000 worth of gold and bonds. Many sources call this Canada's first train robbery, but a 2006 self-published book by British Columbian Peter Grauer cites an Ontario robbery that occurred 30 years earlier. So Miner's assault may have to settle for the title of being the *second* train robbery in Canada.

On May 8, 1906, the bandits struck the Canadian Pacific Railway again near Kamloops. This time, things didn't go so well. The men barely escaped on foot with $15 and a bottle of liver pills. They were quickly arrested near the town of Douglas Lake, while eating lunch.

You can't hold me! During the trial that followed, Miner became a folk hero for giving the unpopular Mounties a run for their money. When he was sentenced to 25 years, Miner politely warned the judge that there wasn't a jail that could keep him. And it was true. In August 1907, at age 60, he escaped and fled back to the United States. There, Miner continued his cycle of thievery and jail. In 1913, at age 66, the unrepentant criminal died in his sleep at the Georgia State Penitentiary.

Because of Miner's actions, the Canadian Pacific Railway established its own police force and insurance company, and developed a team of special investigators to thwart future bandits. But in 2004, the railway got over its grudge against Miner long enough to stage a 100-year anniversary reenactment of the robbery even though the railroad company claimed to have purged all records of the outlaw out of disgust for his crimes.

* * *

NO OFFENSE...

British writer Rudyard Kipling (*The Jungle Book*, *The Man Who Would Be King*) once called the city of Medicine Hat, Alberta, "the city with all Hell for a basement." Kipling wasn't remarking about the quality of life in the city, though, or the size of its criminal underworld. Instead, he was simply referencing Medicine Hat's large subterranean oil fields.

LONG AND GONE

Let's say you're incredibly tall—so tall that people stop and stare.
You might take some comfort in the idea that after your death
you'd no longer be gawked at. Don't be too sure about that.

OUTGROWING A DREAM

At 2.52 meters (8 feet 3 inches), Édouard Beaupré was Canada's tallest man. He wanted to be a cowboy. Instead, he ended up on display as a freak. When he died, nothing changed: he was still exhibited, but this time without his consent. It would take more than 85 years to find him a final resting place.

Before he got impossibly tall, Édouard Beaupré was a boy living with a poor family in Willow Bunch, Saskatchewan. He was big at birth—some accounts say he weighed 6.4 kilograms (14 pounds)—and he *really* began growing when he hit the age of seven. By the time he was 11, he was taller than his father. Then he kept growing.

Beaupré had practiced his roping, hunting, and horseman skills, and in 1896, at age 15, he quit school to follow his cowboy dreams, getting hired quickly at a ranch. Unfortunately, Beaupré got so tall and heavy so quickly that he lost the job after just two years. To his deep disappointment, even riding a horse became problematic.

Legend has exaggerated this story, claiming that Beaupré had to quit because his feet dragged on the ground—not likely, since a typical saddle horse is 1.5 meters (5 feet) tall at the saddle and Beaupré's legs weren't that long.

At his height and with a weight of 181.8 kilograms (400 pounds), Beaupré's obvious alternative career was show business. He got a manager and toured North America, performing feats that demonstrated his size and strength—too heavy to ride a horse, he had an act in which he carried one on his shoulders instead.

NO ESCAPE FROM FAME

Beaupré's show-business career didn't last long. Exhibiting signs of tuberculosis, he collapsed and died a few days after he began performing with the Barnum and Bailey Circus at the 1904 St.

Someone swears about four times every minute in each episode of *Trailer Park Boys*.

Louis World's Fair. He was only 23. The morgue doctor discovered that Beaupré had a tumor on his pituitary gland that stimulated over production of growth hormones, which explained how he got to be so big.

The circus contacted his family, wanting them to take care of the body, but when Beaupré's father arrived in St. Louis, he was told he'd have to pay double fare to transport his giant son's body…plus another regular fare to accompany it home. The father—with seven other children and the wages of a cheese maker—didn't have the money to do that. So the circus promised to bury Beaupré in St. Louis, and the father went home. But the funeral home's undertaker had incurred significant embalming expenses and wouldn't release it to the circus without payment. At least that was the management's excuse for what they did next: they put the body on display to anyone willing to pay an admission charge.

St. Louis police, reacting to complaints, eventually shut down the exhibit. But the morticians just moved it to another funeral home across the Mississippi River, where the police shut them down again. Next, in 1905, a Canadian businessman bought Beaupré's body and had it shipped to the Eden Museum, a circusy collection of wax figures and curiosities in Montreal. The body attracted large crowds and eventually the authorities. After six months and many complaints, the museum put the body away in a storage warehouse near the city's Bellerive Park.

END IN SIGHT
Soon, the Eden Museum went out of business, and the warehouse and its contents were abandoned. So you can imagine the recurring nightmares incurred by some overly curious children who, while poking around the abandoned building, rediscovered the decaying body of Édouard Beaupré. Eventually, the body ended up in the University of Montréal medical school, but the indignities suffered by Beaupré's remains had not ended yet.

At the university, the body was chemically mummified and put into a glass display case. There it stayed for another 63 years. It would probably still be there now, except for a chance discovery by Beaupré's nephew. In the early 1970s, Ovila Lespérance was a retired farmer and a town councilman for Willow Bunch. One day, the town secretary asked if he knew that his uncle was on display

Canada's first railway (1836) was built by beer baron John Molson.

at the university. (The secretary's son, a doctor, had read about the macabre exhibit in a medical journal.)

LET MY UNCLE GO!

That was how the giant's family finally discovered that he had not been buried in St. Louis after all. Instead, his preserved, naked body was in a glass case and was being featured on university tours.

Without signed donation documents from the individual, you might think it would be easy to get your uncle's body for burial. Not so. Letters and phone calls received no satisfactory response from the university. In 1975, Lespérance and his wife traveled to Montreal to view the body and were shocked to see it displayed in public. They were also saddened to discover that the body had shriveled to 2.2 meters (7 feet 1 inch) and 34.1 kilograms (75 pounds).

Attempts to reclaim the body were rebuffed by the university. They said they were doing it for Beaupré's dignity, because they feared that if his body were buried, it would be stolen and put on display someplace else. That rang a little hollow…seeing that the body was already on display someplace.

Rather than undertake an expensive legal challenge, relatives extracted a promise to at least remove the body from public display. They also continued to request the body's return for nearly two decades.

Finally, in 1989, the impasse was broken. The university agreed to release the body, but only in a cremated state. The family agreed. In front of a life-size statue of Édouard Beaupré on the grounds of the Willow Bunch Museum, the giant's ashes were buried on July 7, 1990. After more than 85 years of post mortem wandering, the local boy was home at last.

TWO TOO-TALL NOVA SCOTIANS

Édouard Beaupré was Canada's tallest man, but he wasn't the country's only giant. Two Nova Scotians also claim the title:

Angus MacAskill: Known in his Cape Breton hometown as the Big Boy, or "Gille Mòr," Angus MacAskill stood 2.4 meters (7 feet 10 inches) tall and weighed 193.2 kilograms (425 pounds). He was born in 1825, and neighbors in his farming and fishing community said he was a helpful young man with "a mild and gentle manner." Good thing, too, because when he did get

annoyed, he didn't mess around: one story tells of his throwing a 136.4 kilogram (300-pound) man over a (3-meter) 10-foot high woodpile after being pestered with a challenge to a wrestling match. Like Beaupré, MacAskill also opted for show business as a career, but he quit while he was ahead. After making his fortune touring, MacAskill operated a general store in a building that was sized to suit his proportions…with doorways 2.7 meters (9 feet) high. When he died in 1863, he was laid to rest in another construction made to order: a Nova Scotian newspaper reported that his coffin as measured "length 8 feet; breadth, 2 feet 6 inches; height, 1 foot 3 inches."

Anna Haining Swan: As with MacAskill, Anna Haining Swan was a Nova Scotian of Scottish ancestry. Born in 1846, one of 13 otherwise normal-size children, she grew to 1.4 meters (4 foot 8 inches) tall at age five, and reached 2.3 meters (7 foot 6) by age 22. At 16, she was exhibited in Barnum's museum in New York. She had the reputation of having refinement, intelligence, and talent in music and theater.

Tragedy almost struck in 1865 when the Barnum Museum caught fire. Swan was too large to escape through a window, so museum employees had to knock out a wall and lower the 159.1-kilogram (350-pound) woman to the ground with a system of pulleys. In 1871, she met, and later married, Martin Van Buren Bates, a 2.2 meter (7 foot 3 inch) man billed as the "Kentucky Giant." The two toured as a married couple and made enough money to retire and settle into quiet farm life in rural Seville, Ohio.

* * *

CURRENT CHAMPION

The tallest man alive in Canada today is Jerry Sokoloski, of Toronto. Born in 1983, he stands 2.3 meters (7 foot, 7 inches). Wearing a size-24 shoe, Sokoloski played high school basketball, but discovered that height isn't everything: he tried to go pro in 2004 but wasn't drafted by an NBA team—they thought he was too slow. He did get engaged in 2009, though. His fiancée is 1.7 meters (5 feet, 5 inches) tall.

Canada's highest town: Banff at 1,383 meters.

I ♥ ONTARIO

*Sure, it's big, crowded, and industrial. True, in summer
it has more bugs than the Temple of Doom. Still,
we found 12 reasons to love Ontario.*

1. ITS PROVINCIAL FLOWER. The white trillium is a simple plant with an interesting reproduction partner: ants. Field ants gather the seeds because the baby ants like to eat parts of them. Fortunately, those are nonessential parts as far as plant reproduction goes. The ants toss what's left into their trash heaps, which are rich in nutrients and make a perfect place for trillium seeds to sprout into new plants.

2. THE "JUMBO THE ELEPHANT" STATUE. For years a central hub of the railway system, St. Thomas was the site of an historic crash. In September 1885, P. T. Barnum's famous giant elephant, Jumbo, was struck by a train and killed there while the circus troupe was touring the area. It reportedly took 150 people to remove the elephant's carcass from the tracks. Today, a giant elephant statue downtown commemorates St. Thomas's deadly connection to the iconic elephant.

3. THE MOSQUITOES...small, large, and larger still. With two-thirds of the province covered with forest and a sixth covered with water, you've got an ideal mosquito habitat. In the town of Upsala, a giant mosquito statue—equipped with a knife and fork and carrying a man with its hind legs—pays tribute to the carnivorous beasts.

4. MULTICULTURAL SQUIRRELS. A population of nonalbino white squirrels in Exeter has spawned a White Squirrel Festival. On the other hand, Toronto is home to a population of rare black squirrels with white tails, also loved and protected by local Ontarians.

5. THE PEOPLE ARE DENSE. Ontario is the most populated province in Canada—well over 13 million and growing. Toronto, meanwhile, is Canada's most populous city, with more than 2.5 million residents.

Rush vocalist and bassist, Geddy Lee's real name: Gary Weinrib.

6. THE GREAT LAKES. Ontario is the only province to border the Great Lakes—well, four of them anyway: Lake Erie, Lake Superior, Lake Huron, and Lake Ontario. (Technically, Lake Michigan is part of the same body of water as Lake Huron and is contained entirely in the United States.) The five lakes make up the largest body of freshwater lakes in the world.

7. CONCRETE PROGRESS. Toronto's segment of King's Highway 401 is the busiest stretch of highway in all of North America.

8. THE WORLD'S LONGEST FRESHWATER BEACH. Sitting on the banks of the Nottawasaga Bay, Wasaga Beach measures about 14 kilometers (about 8.5 miles) in length.

9. OTTAWA, THE UNDERDOG CAPITAL. It began as Bytown in the 1820s, but by 1858, the little wilderness town-that-could had changed its name to Ottawa and was declared capital of the new United Province of Canada. Why Ottawa? That's what bigger, fancier places like Toronto and Montreal wanted to know. But it turned out that Ottawa was situated in just the right spot to win the title: the city was far enough away from the United States (which was always making eyes at Canadian land) and on the border of Quebec and Ontario, Canada's two main regions at the time.

10. THE SKYDOME. Okay, technically it's now called the Rogers Centre, but where's the fun in that? Opened in 1989, the SkyDome is not only home to the Blue Jays and the Argonauts, it's also got the world's largest JumboTron (10 meters x 33.6 meters/ 32.8 feet x 110 feet) and was the first stadium in the world to have a fully retractable roof. Plus, if you lined up all the hot dogs sold at the SkyDome in one year, they would cover the distance between more than 3,000 bases. Ketchup, anyone?

11. FRUITS AND VEGGIES. More agricultural products are produced in Ontario than in any other province or territory in Canada.

12. BIG BRAINS. Ottawa is known as the "most educated city in Canada." More than 50 percent of the city's population has a college degree. And per capita, Ottawa has the highest number of scientists, PhDs, and engineers in the country.

Approximately 100 languages are spoken in Canada.

"THE CREMATION OF SAM McGEE"

On page 82, we introduced Robert W. Service, onetime bank teller and "Bard of the Yukon." Here's another of his famous poems, a funny piece published in 1907. Service modeled the title character after a real Sam McGee, one of his banking customers, and like Sam in the poem, McGee came from the American South and often complained about the cold.

There are strange things done in the midnight sun
By the men who moil for gold;
The Arctic trails have their secret tales
That would make your blood run cold;
The Northern Lights have seen queer sights,
But the queerest they ever did see
Was that night on the marge of Lake Lebarge
I cremated Sam McGee.

Now Sam McGee was from Tennessee, where the cotton blooms and blows.
Why he left his home in the South to roam 'round the Pole, God only knows.
He was always cold, but the land of gold seemed to hold him like a spell;
Though he'd often say in his homely way that he'd "sooner live in hell."

On a Christmas Day we were mushing our way over the Dawson trail.
Talk of your cold! through the parka's fold it stabbed like a driven nail.
If our eyes we'd close, then the lashes froze till sometimes we couldn't see;
It wasn't much fun, but the only one to whimper was Sam McGee.

And that very night, as we lay packed tight in our robes beneath the snow,
And the dogs were fed, and the stars o'erhead were dancing heel and toe,
He turned to me, and "Cap," says he, "I'll cash in this trip, I guess;
And if I do, I'm asking that you won't refuse my last request."

Well, he seemed so low that I couldn't say no; then he says with a sort of moan:
"It's the cursed cold, and it's got right hold till I'm chilled clean through to the bone.
Yet 'tain't being dead—it's my

awful dread of the icy grave
that pains;
So I want you to swear that, foul
or fair, you'll cremate my last
remains."

A pal's last need is a thing to
heed, so I swore I would not
fail;
And we started on at the streak
of dawn; but God! he looked
ghastly pale.
He crouched on the sleigh, and
he raved all day of his home in
Tennessee;
And before nightfall a corpse was
all that was left of Sam McGee.

There wasn't a breath in that
land of death, and I hurried,
horror-driven,
With a corpse half hid that I
couldn't get rid, because of a
promise given;
It was lashed to the sleigh, and it
seemed to say: "You may tax
your brawn and brains,
But you promised true, and it's up
to you to cremate those last
remains."

Now a promise made is a debt
unpaid, and the trail has its
own stern code.
In the days to come, though my
lips were dumb, in my heart
how I cursed that load.
In the long, long night, by the
lone firelight, while the
huskies, round in a ring,
Howled out their woes to the
homeless snows—O God! how

I loathed the thing.
And every day that quiet clay
seemed to heavy and heavier
grow;
And on I went, though the dogs
were spent and the grub was
getting low;
The trail was bad, and I felt half
mad, but I swore I would not
give in;
And I'd often sing to the hateful
thing, and it hearkened with a
grin.

Till I came to the marge of Lake
Lebarge, and a derelict there
lay;
It was jammed in the ice, but I
saw in a trice it was called the
"Alice May."
And I looked at it, and I thought
a bit, and I looked at my frozen
chum;
Then "Here," said I, with a
sudden cry, "is my cre-ma-
tor-eum."

Some planks I tore from the
cabin floor, and I lit the boiler
fire;
Some coal I found that was lying
around, and I heaped the fuel
higher;
The flames just soared, and the
furnace roared—such a blaze
you seldom see;
And I burrowed a hole in the
glowing coal, and I stuffed in
Sam McGee.

Then I made a hike, for I didn't
like to hear him sizzle so;

And the heavens scowled, and
the huskies howled, and the
wind began to blow.
It was icy cold, but the hot sweat
rolled down my cheeks, and I
don't know why;
And the greasy smoke in an inky
cloak went streaking down the
sky.

I do not know how long in the
snow I wrestled with grisly fear;
But the stars came out and they
danced about ere again I
ventured near;
I was sick with dread, but I
bravely said: "I'll just take a
peep inside.
I guess he's cooked, and it's time I
looked";…then the door I
opened wide.

And there sat Sam, looking cool
and calm, in the heart of the
furnace roar;
And he wore a smile you could
see a mile, and he said: "Please
close that door.
It's fine in here, but I greatly fear
you'll let in the cold and
storm—
Since I left Plumtree, down in
Tennessee, it's the first time I've
been warm."

There are strange things done in
the midnight sun
By the men who moil for gold;
The Arctic trails have their secret
tales
That would make your blood run
cold; queer sights,
But the queerest they ever did see
Was that night on the marge of
Lake Lebarge
I cremated Sam McGee.

* * *

THE OTHER NORTHERN LIGHTS

In 1985, the song "We Are the World" was one the biggest musi-
cal events of all time, with a mostly American group of singers and
musicians coming together to record a charity single for African
famine relief. The B-side of the record was another charity single,
"Tears are Not Enough," by Northern Lights, an ensemble of some
Canada's biggest musicians of the era. "We Are the World" went
to number-one in the United States; "Tears are Not Enough" did
the same in Canada. Among the Canadian superstars who sang
solos on the song: Gordon Lightfoot, Burton Cummings of the
Guess Who, Anne Murray, Joni Mitchell, Dan Hill, Neil Young,
Bryan Adams, Corey Hart, Bruce Cockburn, Geddy Lee of Rush,
and Mike Reno of Loverboy.

ANSWER PAGES

WELCOME TO PARKS CANADA (PAGE 7)

1. g. Canada's transcontinental railroad led to the creation of Glacier National Park in 1886, but before the railroad could be completed, engineers had to find a way through the Selkirk Mountains. The solution was Rogers Pass, found in 1881 by Albert Bowman Rogers, an employee of the Canadian Pacific Railroad Company. Laying the tracks through the gap in the mountains was difficult: avalanches plagued the area, average annual winter snow-falls were 12 meters (40 feet), and the gorges the railroad had to pass over were steep. But eventually the railroad workers laid the track through the pass and completed the railroad in 1885. A year later, the Canadian government established Glacier National Park, hoping to bring tourists (and money) to the area.

2. b. In the Cree language, the word *wapusk* means "white bear." It's fitting, then, that the largest known polar bear denning area in the world is Wapusk National Park, which covers an area of 11,475 square kilometers (4,431 square miles).

3. a. About 300 kilometers (185 miles) long, the Cabot Trail is named for Venetian explorer John Cabot, the first European to visit Nova Scotia's Cape Breton Island.

4. f. The only wilderness national park in Ontario (meaning it's a park designated specifically to protect an ecosystem), Pukaskwa contains the least-developed shoreline on the Great Lakes—the northeastern stretch of Lake Superior between Hattie Cove and Michipicoten, Ontario.

5. c. Grasslands National Park protects an area that is one of Canada's last remaining swathes of prairie. The park was estab-lished in 1981 and is home to prairie dogs, lizards, antelope, and many other animals. It also includes the Killdeer Badlands, the site where western Canada's first dinosaur bones were found (in 1874 by scientist George Mercer Dawson), and is the place to which Sitting Bull and approximately 5,000 Sioux warriors fled after George Armstrong Custer's 1876 defeat and death at the Bat-tle of the Little Big Horn.

6. h. Founded in 1914 and encompassing 260 square kilometers

The word "igloo" comes from the Inuit *iglu*, meaning "house."

(100 square miles), Mount Revelstoke contains part of the only inland temperate rain forest in the world.

7. i. Established in 2005, Torngat's name comes from an Inuit word *torngait*, which means "place of spirits."

8. e. Mount Logan in Kluane National Park is not only the highest peak in Canada, it's the second-highest peak in North America. (Alaska's Mount McKinley is first.)

9. j. Point Pelee is still the southernmost tip of Canada's mainland (and is at the same latitude as northern California), but it's lost its sandy point. In March 2006, high winds and storms washed it away. A "no swimming" sign that once stood on the point turned up on a beach in Ohio...about 100 kilometers (62 miles) across Lake Erie.

10. d. One of the most remote parks in Canada's system, Aulavik is most accessible by plane. It's located in the far north of the Northwest Territories on Banks Island. The park is also home to the highest concentration of musk oxen in the world. (Musk oxen are known for their...ahem...musky odor.) More than 68,000 musk oxen live on Banks Island, and about 20 percent of those call Aulavik National Park home.

TEST YOUR HOCKEY IQ (PAGE 91)

1. d. Gordie Howe played from 1946 to 1980. Six decades if you count the one game he played in 1997 for the Detroit Vipers...at age 69.

2. c. It took long enough. Women's teams were common in the early 1900s...their full dresses actually helped with goaltending.

3. b. The brothers often faced each other down at the crease.

4. a. The team's letterman jacket was his big bonus. He ultimately spent 25 seasons with the club.

5. b. Canada won gold in every Olympics from 1920 to 1952, except 1936, when it had to settle for silver behind Great Britain. (The 1940 and 1944 Olympics were canceled because of World War II.)

6. a. He wanted number 9, which belonged to his hero Gordie Howe, but another member of the team already had it. In 2000, Gretzky's jersey number 99 was retired by every team in the league.

The last war fought on Canadian soil: a battle with the U.S. that ended in 1814.

7. c. Before the vulcanized rubber puck became the standard, many early games were played with simple blocks of wood.

8. b. They're frozen to reduce bouncing.

9. c. They did $3,000 worth of damage.

10. c. Plante was mocked by other goalies for being afraid of facial injuries…before they quietly followed his lead.

SYMBOLIC OVERVIEW (PAGE 262)

1. b. Fleur-de-lis is a traditional French symbol of a lily that translates to "lily flower." Both Quebec's and Nova Scotia's flag sport the fleur-de-lis, as do other, more far-flung places in North America that were settled by or named after the French, like Louisville, Detroit, and New Orleans.

2. c. Although the valley bulldog—a bulldog-boxer mix—is also from Nova Scotia, the Nova Scotia duck tolling retriever is the provincial dog.

3. c. Man-made stone figures, called inukshuk, have been used by the First Peoples in the Arctic since ancient times. When Nunavut gained status as a territory in 1999, the government chose the inukshuk as its territorial symbol.

4. a. Pitcher plants thrive in acidic soil around marshy, boggy areas. Newfoundland is loaded with peat bogs, making it a terrific environment for these carnivorous plants.

5. b. Charlottetown soil is a bright red soil found only on Prince Edward Island. The soil's high acidity makes it a great candidate for growing healthy potatoes—P.E.I.'s main crop.

6. a. Potash, or potassium chloride, is mined primarily for use in crop fertilizer. Saskatchewan is the world's largest producer of potash, generating about one-quarter of the world's supply.

7. c. Mostly found in the Cassiar and Lillooet areas, jade has become a solid provincial export, particularly as China's jade mines become depleted.

8. a. The red-eyed, black-and-white common loon summers in many parts of Canada. There are about 65,000 pairs in Ontario during the summer season.

Q: Who coined the term "cyberspace." **A:** Vancouver novelist William Gibson (1982).

9. b. Lazulite is one of the rarest semiprecious stones, and the Yukon is one of the few known sources for this blue-colored mineral.

10. c. Petrified wood is found throughout parts of Canada, including in Alberta's southern badlands.

11. a. Composed of up to 20 percent clay, the Holmesville soil series is a sandy, gravelly, fertile soil found only in New Brunswick and used in agriculture, mainly to grow potatoes.

12. b. This one is tricky; the great gray owl is Manitoba's provincial bird, but the bison is its provincial animal. Thirty semiwild bison live in Manitoba's Riding Mountain National Park, one of the largest free-roaming herds in North America.

13. a. In 1934, when gold was discovered in Yellowknife, Northwest Territories, the town became the area's central hub. Today, Yellowknife is the capital of NWT, and although the mines have closed, there's still a little gold left in them thar hills.

MEASURE BY MEASURE (PAGE 311)

1. b. Ontario's Middle Island in Lake Erie is the southernmost point of Canada. It is roughly 14,849 kilometers (9,226 miles) from the South Pole.

2. c. Murchison Promontory in Nunavut is the northernmost point of Canada, 2,013 kilometers (1,250 miles) away from Santa's purported home.

3. c. Newfoundland and Labrador has the longest coastline with 28,956 kilometers (17,992 miles); British Columbia's is 25,725 kilometers (15,984 miles); and—of course—Saskatchenwan has no coastline.

4. a. With 31,558 people on 1,936,113 square kilometers (747,537 square miles), you've got plenty of room to spread out.

5. b. With just 40 square meters (430 square feet) per person, each gets almost a ¼ of a tennis court. Doubles, anyone?

6. b. The territorial ice mass off Nunavut's Ellesmere Island contains the Magnetic North Pole. But the location shifts with time— some scientists say that the pole might make it to Siberia by 2050.

7. a. It would be close, but Ontario would have about 13 million people pulling on its side; the other team would have only about 12.2 million.

8. b. The Northwest Territories borders five; Nunavut, two; and Yukon, two (plus Alaska).

9. a. The Yukon gets the benefit of having the bulk of the Saint Elias Mountains.

10. c. The Northwest Territories was originally about 3,439,296 square kilometers (1,327,919 square miles). After the eastern part was separated off to create Nunavut in 1999, land area dropped to 1,346,106 square kilometers 519,734 square miles

LITERARY LINES (PAGE 417)

1. *Anne of Green Gables*, by Lucy Maud Montgomery

2. *Bear*, by Marian Engel

3. *Generation X: Tales for an Accelerated Culture*, by Douglas Coupland

4. *The English Patient*, by Michael Ondaatje

5. *A Fine Balance*, by Rohinton Mistry

6. *Beautiful Losers*, by Leonard Cohen

7. *The Stone Diaries*, by Carol Shields

8. *Herzog*, by Saul Bellow

9. *Life of Pi*, by Yann Martel

10. *The Handmaid's Tale*, by Margaret Atwood

* * *

ONE MORE THING...

According to Canoe.ca, Canada's ten sexiest men alive are Ryan Reynolds (actor), Ryan Gosling (actor), Adam Beach (actor), Gabriel Aubrey (model), Kiefer Sutherland (actor), George Canyon (pop singer), Prevail (rapper), Raine Maida (singer for the band Our Lady Peace), Brendan Fehr (actor), and Mike Holmes (TV handyman).

Abe Lincoln's assassin, John Wilkes Booth, had an account at the Bank of Montreal.

THE LAST PAGE

FELLOW BATHROOM READERS:
The fight for good bathroom reading should never be taken loosely—we must do our duty and sit firmly for what we believe in, even while the rest of the world is taking potshots at us.

We'll be brief. Now that we've proven we're not simply a flush-in-the-pan, we invite you to take the plunge: Sit Down and Be Counted! Log on to *www.bathroomreader.com* and earn a permanent spot on the BRI honor roll!

If you like reading our books...
VISIT THE BRI'S WEB SITE!
www.bathroomreader.com

- Visit "The Throne Room"—a great place to read!
 - Receive our irregular newsletters via e-mail.
 - Order additional *Bathroom Readers*.
 - Read our blog.

Go with the Flow...

Well, we're out of space, and when you've gotta go, you've gotta go. Tanks for all your support. Hope to hear from you soon. Meanwhile remember...

Keep on flushin'!